D1267805

THE WORKING CLASS IN AMERICAN HISTORY

Editorial Advisors

David Brody
Alice Kessler-Harris
David Montgomery
Sean Wilentz

A list of books in the series appears at the end of this book.

Down on the Killing Floor

Down on the Killing Floor

Black and White Workers in
Chicago's Packinghouses, 1904–54

Rick Halpern

UNIVERSITY OF ILLINOIS PRESS

URBANA AND CHICAGO

11-8-99

Publication of this book was supported by a grant from the
Illinois Labor History Society.

© 1997 by the Board of Trustees of the University of Illinois
Manufactured in the United States of America
1   2   3   4   5   C   P   5   4   3   2   1

This book is printed on acid-free paper.

Library of Congress Cataloging-in-Publication Data
Halpern, Rick.
Down on the killing floor : Black and white workers in Chicago's
packinghouses, 1904–54 / Rick Halpern.
p.   cm. — (The working class in American history)
Includes bibliographical references and index.
ISBN 0-252-02337-4 (alk. paper). —
ISBN 0-252-06633-2 (pbk. : alk. paper)
1. Afro-American packing-house workers—Illinois—Chicago—History.
2. Trade-unions—Packing-house workers—Illinois—Chicago—History.
3. Packing-houses—Illinois—Chicago—History.
4. Chicago (Ill.)—Race relations.
5. United Packinghouse Workers of America—History.
I. Title. II. Series.
HD8039.P152U538   1997
331.88'L649'00977311—dc21   96-51264
CIP

To the memory of my grandfather,
Joseph Chasin, 1906–73,
who first taught me about the world of work

and

To the memory of my grandmother,
Mary Kaminker Halpern, 1905–92,
who first taught me about justice

Contents

Acknowledgments

This book has been a long time in the making. It began in 1982 as a seminar paper at the University of Wisconsin during my first year in graduate school, expanded in scope and ambition during my wanderings around the Midwest in the mid-1980s gathering oral testimonies from CIO activists, and first took on coherent form as a University of Pennsylvania doctoral thesis at the end of the decade. Since 1989 I have lived and worked in London, and it has been here that the transformation took place from dissertation to book manuscript. Over this fifteen-year period I received assistance from institutions and individuals in at least eight states and on two continents. It is a pleasure to acknowledge their help and encouragement.

My first debt is to my teachers. Walter Licht first sparked my interest in the American working class when, as a sophomore more inclined to literary and folklore studies than history, I wandered into his U.S. survey course. He later supervised my Ph.D. dissertation and, in recent years, has served as a trusted friend and colleague. Likewise Michael Zuckerman, Richard Dunn, and Drew Faust taught me first as an undergraduate and later as a Ph.D. student. Much of who I am as a scholar stems from the rigorous training I received from them, the high standards they set, and the personal examples they provided. In Madison, J. Rogers Hollingsworth, Herbert Hill, and Thomas McCormick provided vital encouragement at an early stage. Not all of them will agree with the arguments I advance here, but I trust that they will recognize their singular contributions. At both Wisconsin and Pennsylvania I was fortunate to find myself in the midst of an unusually talented and supportive group of fellow students: Nancy MacLean, Kathy Brown, Ted Pearson, David Lewis, Alex Lichtenstein, Ed Johanningsmeier, Alan Karras, and Rob Gregg.

Most of the oral history interviews used in this book were made possible by a grant from the National Endowment for the Humanities and by the institutional support of the State Historical Society of Wisconsin. In Chicago, Les Orear, a former packinghouse activist and now the moving force behind the Illinois Labor History Society, facilitated a number of contacts and cheerfully shared his unparalleled knowledge of the packinghouse industry. I owe similar thanks to Richard Saunders, a union founder at Armour, Rachel Helstein, and Rogers Farmer, all of whom made numerous phone calls on my behalf, vouched for my integrity, and patiently put up with endless requests for assistance.

My partner on the UPWA Oral History Project, Roger Horowitz, deserves my most profound thanks. More than any other individual, he has helped me see this project through to completion. Many of the ideas developed in these pages first were formulated in collaboration with Roger. He read virtually every draft, saving me from a multitude of errors and often sharing the fruits of his own research to help me clarify key points. I feel fortunate to have him as a colleague, comrade, coauthor, and friend.

None of this would have been possible without the veteran packinghouse workers who consented to be interviewed for this study. Alas, some have passed away before "their story" appeared in print: Ralph Helstein, Philip Weightman, Svend Godfredson, Jesse Prosten, Harold Nielsen, and Charles Hayes in particular taught me more about the militant democratic unionism of the UPWA than can ever appear in a single volume. I hope I have done them justice in the retelling of their struggles. Several other packinghouse workers deserve special mention: Herbert March, Jesse Vaughn, Sam Parks, Lowell Washington, Marian Simmons, Rowena Moore, Anna Mae Weems, Chuck Pearson, Mary Salinas, and Frank Wallace.

Librarians and archivists at a number of institutions answered my questions and made a host of valuable suggestions. I am indebted to Archie Motley and his staff at the Chicago Historical Society; Harry Miller, Donna Sereda, James Cavanaugh, and James Danky at the State Historical Society of Wisconsin; Bill Creech and Jerry Hess at the National Archives; Jane Boley at the University of Texas at Arlington; and Werner Pflug at the Reuther Library of Labor and Urban Affairs. Alice Hay at the Brooklyn Public Library and Leslie Bugden at the University College London Library handled an endless flurry of interlibrary loan requests with remarkable efficiency and good cheer.

My colleagues at University College London have been unstintingly supportive of this project, even when publication repeatedly was delayed. My head of department, and later dean, Wendy Davies, provided funding for one last crucial round of research. Martin Daunton, Jonathan Morris, Simon Renton, Andy Strouthous, Ruth Dar, and Enrico Dal Lago all helped in a variety of important ways. The members of the fortnightly Comparative Labour and Working Class History seminar deserve thanks as well for responding constructively to several presentations and for providing such a stimulating forum for committed historical inquiry. Peter Alexander and Ron Mendel, in particular, offered vital support at key junctures.

James Barrett, Eric Arnesen, and David Montgomery read this manuscript for the University of Illinois Press. All of them made detailed suggestions that greatly improved the final product. In addition three special colleagues and friends read all or part of the manuscript. Although I did not always follow their advice, Bruce Nelson, Robert Zieger, and Mike Honey helped make this a better book. Of course I take full responsibility for all the faults that remain.

Finally, I thank my family for their support and encouragement along the way. My parents, Ralph and Harriet Halpern, took an active interest in this project from the start and provided material assistance at various points. Unlike many academic spouses, my wife, Beth Landau, did not type the manuscript or subject it to critique. In ways that only she knows, though, she made it possible for me to find the time and peace of mind to think and write. My children—Lydia, Rosa, and Miriam—have lived with this book their entire lives, putting up with my extended absences from home, late hours at the office, and the closed door of my study. I promise it will be easier next time.

Down on the Killing Floor

INTRODUCTION

Race, the Working Class, and U.S. Labor History

"The problem of the twentieth century is the problem of the color-line," W. E. B. Du Bois wrote in 1903.[1] His words proved prophetic. In the United States, most of the major social and economic struggles of the past ninety years have involved the difficult question of the rights of black people and their relationship with the dominant white society. Throughout, the color line has shown itself to be remarkably durable. Its particular form and shape have changed, but the deep fissure of race continues to define and animate life in the United States.

Arguably, the schisms produced by racial doctrines and practices have had their greatest impact upon the working class. Racial self-awareness has shaped the identity of American workers and their families in a myriad of ways. It has influenced their politics and molded their consciousness. It has determined where they reside and under what conditions. It has been a crucial factor in establishing where they work, when they are laid off, and what kinds of opportunities for economic advancement are available to them.

Race has impacted with particular power upon workers' most important institutions—their trade unions. While differences of skill, ethnicity, and gender have proved surmountable, the project of working-class organization has repeatedly foundered upon the shoals of racism. Despite periodic attempts to extend class solidarity across racial lines, until very recently the labor movement generally failed to include blacks in its conception of brotherhood. This failure has had long-term consequences.

It hindered workers' ability to organize in the mass production industries and weakened movements for reform. More decisively than other forms of fragmentation, race has contributed to the failure of organized labor to alter the trajectory of capitalism in the United States.

Labor historians have only recently started to grapple with the thorny question of race and the implications it holds for the study of the American working class. Despite the attention devoted by the "new labor history" to issues of culture and consciousness, it has not produced a body of literature which addresses the interplay of class and race in a sustained manner. The field *does* have what Nell Painter dubbed a "race problem"— that is, it fails to embed race in its analysis, consistently downplays the strength of working-class racism, and shrinks from exploring the ways in which racial consciousness explains the actions of both black and white workers. As David Roediger observes, the assumption remains "that the Black worker enters the story of American labor as an actor in a subplot which can be left on the cutting-room floor, probably without vitiating the main story."[2]

Part of this problem stems from an inadequate conceptualization of race both as an analytical term and as a historical category. Many scholars tend to regard "race" simply as a synonym for "black," and write about the working lives of African Americans as if they were hermetically sealed off from their white counterparts and exerted only minimal influence on the broader dynamics of working-class history.[3] Race, like class, refers to a relationship between groups. John Cell's comments are instructive in this regard. "Only when racially conscious groups collide," he writes, "with the one rationalizing its dominance while the other strives to maintain its identity and integrity, does race become a social and historical factor." Race occupies analytical space on both sides of the color line; employed properly, it is a term that encompasses the interrelated experiences of both blacks and whites.[4]

This book has two principal concerns. On one level, it is a study of the rise of industrial unionism in Chicago's stockyards and packinghouses. As such, it is a contribution to the growing historical literature on the meat industry, the labor movement, and the urban black experience. On another level, this detailed case study is the vehicle for a more wide-ranging discussion of the way in which race has shaped the development of the working class in the United States. A series of fundamental questions guide the investigation throughout: How has the issue of race divided packinghouse workers? How, and under what circumstances, have they overcome this deep cleavage? And, most importantly, what were the limitations of

the interracial workers' movement which forms the subject of this study—
that is, where did white and black workers' interests coincide, where did
they diverge, and how did these boundaries determine what industrial
unionism was able to achieve?

Three distinct time periods are considered. First, 1904–29, when the
initial entry of African Americans into the packinghouses further fragmented a workforce already divided by ethnicity and skill. Second, 1930–46,
when the dominant trend was toward interracial and interethnic unity
under the institutional umbrella of the Congress of Industrial Organizations' (CIO) United Packinghouse Workers of America (UPWA). And finally, the immediate postwar period, when centrifugal forces again asserted
themselves. When we study the packinghouse workforce over such an
extended period, the futility of privileging or assigning dominance to either "race" or "class" becomes abundantly clear. Workers rarely chose one
of these identities over the other, but instead thought and behaved in *both*
class and racial ways.

Chapter 1 provides essential background by detailing the creation of the
modern meatpacking industry and the emergence of a working-class community in Chicago's stockyards district in the late nineteenth and early
twentieth centuries. It devotes considerable attention to the way in which
capital restructured the labor process in such a way as to undermine the
power of skilled butchers and, in so doing, paved the way for an ethnically stratified workforce. Packinghouse workers responded to these changes by organizing, but the obstacles presented by a fragmented workforce
limited the effectiveness of their efforts.

Chapter 2 introduces the black worker and the dynamics of race. While
African Americans began laboring in Chicago's packinghouses at the end
of the nineteenth century, it was not until the World War I era that they
entered the industry in significant numbers. This chapter focuses upon the
organizing campaign which began in 1917 under the auspices of the Stockyards Labor Council, became entangled in the 1919 race riot, and culminated in the disastrous 1921–22 strike. Exceptionally rich primary and secondary sources provide a "window" into the workforce at a crucial
juncture, and highlight the difficulties encountered by union activists en-
deavoring to forge bonds of solidarity across the salient divides of race,
ethnicity, and skill.

Chapter 3 serves as a transition to the next cycle of working-class activity. It examines the experience of Chicago's packinghouse workers in the
1920s, the nadir of unionism, but at the same time anticipates the resurgence
of organizing in the next decade. By concentrating upon the response to the

packers' extensive program of welfare capitalism, this chapter shows how workers pursued "subterranean" shop-floor strategies of resistance and began to negotiate an unprecedented common ground of shared grievances and work experiences. Racial tension ran high in this era, a legacy of the 1921–22 defeat, but by the close of the decade whites grudgingly accepted black workers as a permanent component of the labor force.

Chapters 4 and 5 chart the reemergence of unionism in Chicago's packinghouses by first considering the social basis of the new workers' movement, and then investigating the process through which rank-and-file activists overcame workers' fears and established a degree of trust between the major ethnic and racial groups in the Yards. Black workers stood at the center of the new union movement, participating in an alliance with white leftists and trade union veterans of earlier struggles. The formation of the CIO's Packinghouse Workers Organizing Committee (PWOC) institutionalized this coalition and enabled Chicago unionists to link their struggle with that of packinghouse workers elsewhere in the country.

Chapter 6 tacks back and forth between the national and local levels, exploring crosscurrents and tensions within the packinghouse workers' union. Racial dynamics influenced the evolving institutional structure of the organization, and this chapter emphasizes the overlapping black and Communist "orbits" which flowed westward out of Chicago toward other packing centers and represented rank-and-file interests against bureaucratic needs for centralized policy and organizational discipline. The 1943 creation of the UPWA allowed packinghouse workers to respond to wartime regulation in a unique way and to develop policies and programs that set the union off from the mainstream of the labor movement.

Chapter 7 considers the particular features of this alternative path by examining the packinghouse workers' 1946 and 1948 strikes. It shows how the UPWA contended with forces that threatened to rupture the coalition at its heart, developed a dynamic anti-discrimination program, and adhered to a policy of social unionism in a conservative climate. Although this course resulted in the UPWA's increasing isolation from the CIO as well as in the disaffection of a sizeable segment of its white membership, it produced real gains for its expanding black membership base and allowed the union to play a vital role in the developing civil rights movement.

In addition to using traditional primary and secondary materials, this study draws upon an extensive set of oral history interviews conducted in the mid-1980s for the State Historical Society of Wisconsin.[5] These sources allow the analysis to extend well beyond the leadership level and encompass people who otherwise would remain, historically speaking, "inarticulate." More importantly, the oral histories allow the exploration of the subjective dimension of the packinghouse workers' experience: they provide a glimpse at the outlook and motivations of common people who took part in a movement that succeeded in democratizing an autocratic sector of American society.

Written at a time when the labor movement has reeled from setback to setback and when racial antagonism again threatens to submerge the dream of community, this book shows that ordinary people can unite and bring about change by organizing around their common material interests. As one veteran packinghouse activist put it, "We learned you had to pull together to win the big things because individually you were nothing. Not that we always agreed or always got along, but those problems could be sorted out more easily later on. The main thing, the real important thing, was getting the foot off of our necks."[6]

1

"Hog Butcher for the World":
Chicago's Meatpacking Industry

Industrial labor tends to be performed under unpleasant conditions. But the grease and grime of the automobile assembly line or the cramped confines of the mine shaft pale in comparison to horrors of the packinghouse. Although meat workers quickly grow accustomed to their environment, the screams of terror-stricken animals on their way to slaughter, the gore-covered killing floors, and the nauseating stench of the packinghouse impact powerfully upon outsiders. There is something elemental about death on so grand a scale, a feature captured by meatpacking's most famous commentator, Upton Sinclair, who wrote that one "could not stand and watch very long without becoming philosophical, without beginning to deal in symbols and similes, and to hear the hog-squeal of the universe."[1]

This primal and undisguised ugliness held a perverse fascination for turn-of-the-century observers. In the late nineteenth century, when the mills and factories of industrializing America provoked much comment, Chicago's packinghouses attracted their full share of attention. Incongruous as it may seem, the unpleasant business of slaughtering and dismembering animals readily lent itself to feature articles, news reports, and travelers' accounts.[2] Visitors to the Windy City interested in manufacturing invariably included on their itineraries the steelworks springing up on the South Side, the sprawling Pullman Car Company to the west, and the sooty stockyards complex situated a few miles southwest of the downtown Loop.

Chicago's meatpackers have attracted scholarly attention as well. Business and economic historians have studied the industry's managerial prac-

tices, marketing systems, and distribution networks; historians of technology have commented upon important innovations pioneered by the city's
packing companies such as the moving assembly line and the refrigerated
railroad car. Together they have provided a remarkably detailed portrait
of oligopolistic concentration. But mass production in meatpacking rested
upon more than entrepreneurship and managerial innovation. The packers' greatest accomplishment, and the one that cleared the way for their
better-known business achievements, was the restructuring of the labor
process itself.[3]

Decades before Henry Ford adopted the moving assembly line Chicago's packers pioneered flow production methods, using overhead rails to
move animal carcasses through the killing departments. Initially, this innovation had a modest impact. It speeded production by eliminating bottlenecks caused by the frequent necessity of hauling hogs and cattle from
one work station to the next, but did not significantly alter the manner in
which work was carried out. Yet, this "disassembly line" paved the way
for far-reaching change by allowing the packers to institute an unprecedented division of labor in their plants. This process systematically destroyed
the all-around skills of the butcher, reducing a complicated craft to routin-
ized meatcutting.[4]

The command over the meat industry enjoyed by the large Chicago
packers ultimately sprang from this reorganization of work. It not only led
to dramatic increases in output but also enabled the packers to reduce their
labor costs drastically. Although a small number of highly skilled workers
remained essential to perform the most intricate tasks, the packers were able
to fill most of their manpower requirements by drawing upon a virtually
limitless pool of cheap unskilled labor created by steady streams of central and eastern European immigration.

Chicago's rise to dominance and its role as "hog butcher for the world"
is best understood against the backdrop of meatpacking's early development. The national markets, new products, innovative forms of corporate
organization, and, most crucially, pioneering methods of labor control
which characterized the "mature" industry had their genesis in the slaughterhouses of the mid-nineteenth century.

Until the Civil War, meatpacking was a seasonal business scattered in
small towns across the Midwest. Without mechanical refrigeration, the early
industry was devoted to the processing of cured pork products such as salt
pork, ham, and bacon. Taking advantage of cool weather, operations began in autumn and continued through the spring. This seasonality limited
the size of operations and inhibited specialization. Modest operations, these

rural packing companies rarely employed more than a dozen workers. Essentially merchants in orientation, they regarded trade in pork as a way to attract business from outlying farmers and as a means of paying for goods purchased in the East.[5]

While a majority of packers operated in rural areas, a smaller number of urban slaughterhouses far outstripped their production. Cincinnati reigned as the nation's leading packing center in this era. By 1847 it supported forty separate establishments and processed close to five hundred thousand hogs annually. Dubbed "Porkopolis," the city overshadowed its closest competitors, Louisville and St. Louis, and accounted for 53 percent of the nation's total pork pack. Chicago, by comparison, served more as a way station for livestock en route elsewhere than a major nodal point of the meatpacking trade. During the winter of 1847, its six small slaughterhouses killed twenty thousand hogs—a figure which placed it firmly in the second tier of the industry.[6]

Urban meatpacking firms were not simply larger versions of the rural packers; key differences distinguished them from their country counterparts. More market-oriented, urban packers purchased livestock in large lots from independent drovers and sent their barrels of packed pork downriver for sale in Memphis, Natchez, and New Orleans. The large volumes handled in Cincinnati and other cities required buildings that dwarfed the makeshift structures utilized in rural areas. In addition to holding pens and storage facilities, packing firms needed large indoor areas where upwards of sixty animals could be processed within an hour's time. Similarly, their manpower requirements greatly exceeded those of rural packers.[7]

More important than an enlarged physical plant or expanded workforce, however, was the organization of labor itself. The kind of work carried on within the urban packinghouses was qualitatively different from that performed under the direction of backwoods merchants. As early as the mid-1830s Cincinnati packers had begun to standardize and regularize their operations. Implementing a division of labor, and taking advantage of economies of speed, these firms soon doubled and tripled their output. These innovations mark the first steps toward the development of the highly rationalized disassembly lines found in the houses of Chicago's giant packers in the twentieth century.[8]

Task specialization, time discipline, and the constant flow of animals made it impossible for workers to tarry between chores. When livestock were running, they worked twelve-hour days for weeks on end. With the exception of the few men actually cutting the meat, labor was unskilled. Brawn and a strong stomach counted for more than craft knowledge. Yet, this was a far cry from industrialized mass production. Meatpacking remained a seasonal endeavor. When warm weather arrived, packinghouse workers invariably faced long bouts of idleness. Even the skilled cutters—"butchers," for lack of a better term—sought other employment during the spring and summer. Even the largest firms remained fairly simple operations, achieving no significant degree of vertical integration and involving themselves in neither the procurement and transportation of livestock nor the processing of by-products. The meat they packed was largely undifferentiated; and even though they secured a toehold in various foreign markets, most of their business serviced regional demand. Dependent on water transportation, eastern urban markets remained beyond their reach.[9]

Chicago's Rise to Dominance

The railroad, that great engine of capitalist development, catapulted Chicago past Cincinnati as the country's preeminent meatpacking center. If the river was Cincinnati's life blood, then the steel rails of the Illinois Central formed Chicago's vital artery. The consolidation of a midwestern rail system reaching south to the Gulf of Mexico and linking the prairie with metropolitan areas rapidly transformed the meatpacking industry. With Chicago as its hub, the rail network redrew the paths of commerce. Livestock formerly delivered to the river centers now came north. Taking advantage of the new dynamic, Chicago's meatpackers centralized previously scattered facilities and embarked upon a course of dramatic expansion.

Occurring between 1850 and 1870, this process laid the groundwork for the industrialization that took place during the following decades. It led to the establishment of an infrastructure, the Union Stockyards, and the development of a key technological innovation, the refrigerated railroad car. It also contributed to the expansion of the city of Chicago by attracting a permanent workforce to the area surrounding the stockyards. Known as "Back-of-Yards" (or simply "Packingtown" in the local vernacular), this neighborhood was home to successive waves of immigrants drawn to jobs in the packinghouses. Community dynamics, especially the relationships between various ethnic groups, played a major role in shaping workers' response to the experience of industrialization.

The railroad did not catch Chicago's existing meatpackers unaware. Some of the city's more far-sighted packers contributed to the planning and finance of the first systems radiating outward from the growing metropolis. The railroad greatly increased the supply of livestock available to them. In 1848, twenty-six thousand animals arrived in the city; twelve years later livestock receipts numbered 450,000. In the same period, the number of packinghouses jumped from six to thirty. During the Civil War, the volume of livestock reaching Chicago tripled yet again and the number of packing plants almost doubled. Furthermore, wartime hostilities crippled Chicago's Cincinnati competitors by disrupting their downriver Confederate markets. Early in the war, Chicago eclipsed Cincinnati as the leading packing center; at the time of Lee's surrender, Chicago enjoyed a two-to-one margin over its one-time rival.[10]

An indispensable element in the growth of the packing industry was the 1865 construction of the Union Stockyards, which centralized operations in a single location. Previously, the city's packers relied upon private livestock pens located miles apart alongside the major railroad lines. As the volume of livestock swelled, the problem of intra-urban transport became severe. The new complex eliminated these difficulties and allowed a tenfold increase in capacity. Sprawling across three hundred acres, the yards were the largest such facility in the world. Its two thousand holding pens could accommodate 75,000 hogs, 21,000 cattle, and 22,000 sheep at any given time. With railroad sidings leading directly into the yards, the packers now enjoyed instant access to their raw material.[11]

Five years after opening, the stockyards employed over two thousand persons and had made meatpacking the most profitable sector of the city's economy. The presence of this manufactory rapidly transformed the area. Initially swampland bordered by makeshift shanties constructed by Irish railroad laborers, the neighborhood grew into a permanent settlement of five thousand by 1870. Annexed by the city of Chicago, Packingtown was one of Cook County's fastest growing districts at a time when the whole metropolis was experiencing an unprecedented boom.[12]

Meatpacking thoroughly dominated this neighborhood. The smells and noises of the yards could not be escaped. Large by mid-nineteenth-century standards, the plants towered over the single-story frame houses surrounding them. Most residents drew their livelihoods from the yards and packinghouses. Even though employment continued to be seasonal, these workers formed a permanent labor force. Though they might spend the summer slack season on construction gangs, in the North Side lumber mills, or on Great Lakes vessels, the fall hog rush signaled a return to the packinghouses.[13]

Predominantly Irish, the neighborhood had a mixed ethnic character. A large number of German families settled in Packingtown in the years following the opening of the yards, and by 1880 these two groups enjoyed a virtual monopoly on the more skilled and better paying positions in the

packinghouses. Although the emerging industry had not yet reached the
stage in its development where it depended overwhelmingly upon common labor, hundreds of jobs requiring little more than muscle were available. These were filled by poorer, more recently arrived Irish and, later,
Bohemians and Poles—the first of many eastern European groups to arrive
in the neighborhood.[14]

The plants in which these workers toiled were among the most advanced factories in the world. Their size alone made them remarkable.
Philip Armour's facility, constructed in the late 1870s, consisted of several
multistory structures covering twelve acres and connected by railroad track.
The dimensions of Gustavus Swift's operation, located at the opposite corner of the yards, equaled those of his competitor. Utilizing mechanical
power and taking advantage of new technologies, these plants were beginning to resemble the packinghouses of the twentieth century. The use of
overhead rails, inclined slides, and hoists facilitated the flow of material and
increased the speed at which animals moved through the initial stages of
production.[15]

Hog slaughtering in particular lent itself to mechanization. Steam-pow-
ered "pig hoists" became universal equipment in the 1870s. A rotating
wheel hoisted stunned hogs by their hind legs, attached them to an elevated
rail, and slid them down to a "sticker" who slit their throats with precise
cuts. The animals next moved along to scalding tubs where workers rolled
them down inclines into steaming water. Next, scraping machinery performed the formerly labor intensive task of removing the animals' bristles.
Described by a contemporary as "a grid-iron having a surface of steel
blades," this machine processed one hog every twenty seconds. After toss-
ing about on top of these moving blades "like an india rubber ball," the hog
emerged "snow white" and ready for the butchers. Reattached to the overhead rail, it slid down to the awaiting knives and cleavers.[16]

Hoists and mechanical scrapers resulted in dramatic increases in productivity. One plant that formerly employed twelve men to scrape fifteen
hundred hogs a day installed a machine that handled three thousand hogs
and required only eight men to oversee it. Yet, mechanization progressed
no further than this. Most packinghouse work, especially that requiring
knife skills, resisted replacement by power equipment. If anything, the new
technologies eliminated unskilled labor and, because of the increase in
speed, placed a premium upon the skills of the "knifemen." The adoption
of the scraping machine forced this same plant to hire twice as many stick-
ers, gutters, and trimmers.[17]

The crux of the packers' mechanization problem was the varied and irregular shape of livestock. The pioneer packers quickly discovered that hogs and cattle refused to submit to mechanized blades, revolving cutters, or automatic knives. Inventors flooded the U.S. Patent Office with plans for packinghouse equipment, but few of these devices actually worked. In fact, the only aspect of production that lent itself to mechanization was the transport of meat between work stations. Even here, progress was uneven. Rails and hoists eliminated bottlenecks in hog-killing departments, but had minimal effect on the cattle process, where the animals' bulk stymied efforts to mechanize transport. Actual slaughtering and cutting operations remained dependent on skilled labor performed by hand.[18]

Having reached the limits of technological innovation within their plants, the packers turned their attention to streamlining and improving other aspects of their operations. The problem that received the most study was the tapping of eastern urban markets. The packers had long realized that enormous profits could be made if a way could be found to supply the eastern seaboard with fresh meat. In 1869 a Detroit packer, G. H. Hammond, designed and built a refrigerated railroad car. His prototype met with limited success, and the idea was abandoned. It was picked up again in the 1880s by Gustavus Swift, who hired Andrew Chase, a leading refrigeration engineer, to perfect the design. Chase's technological expertise and Swift's organizational skills proved to be the winning combination that brought full-fledged industrialization to the Chicago stockyards.[19]

Over the next few years Swift's entrepreneurial genius displayed itself. Enlisting support from previously skeptical family members, he constructed a network of branch facilities to store meat and deliver it to retailers. He also moved directly into the manufacture of refrigerated railroad cars, the maintenance of icehouses along rail routes, and the development of "peddler car" delivery service. He thus became the first packer to build an integrated enterprise that coordinated the flow of meat from the purchasing of cattle, through the slaughtering and dressing process, to distribution in distant retail outlets.[20]

Up until this point, nearly all cattle leaving Chicago for the East had done so "on the hoof." Shipped alive in cattle cars, they required feeding and watering along the way. By transporting dressed beef, Swift reduced his costs by avoiding shipping the 60 percent of each steer that was inedible waste. In 1881, he expanded his Chicago plant, building a cattle facility measuring 450 by 150 feet and integrated with a new fertilizer works. The high volume of cattle slaughtered here afforded further savings. Despite the bitter opposition of eastern wholesalers, Swift's high quality and low prices allowed him to muscle into lucrative eastern markets. The writing was on the wall. Noting that the future belonged to dressed beef, a Chicago editor remarked that "the barrel has seen its best days."[21]

"The Greatest Trust in the World": Meatpacking and Monopoly Capitalism

Other packers followed Swift's example, expanding beyond pork into the profitable dressed beef business. One of the first was Philip Armour who, by the end of 1882, had started building a comparable network of branch houses and was competing with Swift for the best locations along the railroad lines. Livestock dealer and pork packer Nelson Morris entered the trade in 1884, with George Hammond close behind. By the end of the decade these packers dominated the industry. Known as the "Big Four," they packed three-quarters of all the cattle slaughtered in Chicago and controlled two-thirds of the national market for dressed beef. Their pork and canning operations kept pace as well, giving the emerging oligopoly a lock on 50 percent of the country's total meat supply.[22]

Yet competition among the Big Four was intense. The high fixed costs inherent in maintaining a national system of branch facilities, the uncertainties of livestock supply, and the limited ability to replace skilled labor with machinery made meatpacking a risk-filled venture. One way in which the packers expanded their slender profit margins was by maintaining high volumes. Keeping their plants running at capacity levels, they were able to keep unit costs down. While their smaller, unintegrated rivals could afford to shut down if livestock supply dwindled or the cost of cattle rose too high, the giants had no choice but to continue operating. "Your expenses go on just the same," explained a Morris executive, "we can't stop doing business even if we wanted to."[23]

Another way in which the packers sought to drive down costs was by utilizing every part of the animals they slaughtered. In addition to rendering their own lard, tanning the hides of their cattle, and grinding bone into meal, Chicago's packers developed new products. Research and development departments discovered ways to utilize materials that previously went to waste. Oleomargarine, fertilizer, and pharmaceuticals quickly became profitable product lines. By the turn of the century, by-products comprised one-fourth of the net value of each steer. Hides alone fetched thirty to sixty dollars apiece.[24]

Canning operations were important as well. Made possible on a large scale by the development of steam-pressured autoclaves in the 1880s, canning provided an outlet for inferior grades of meat and led to contracts with the U.S. military and a number of foreign governments. The export of canned goods gave the packers access to a vast world market. An Armour and Company publication proudly noted that its label was found across the globe, boasting that its cans "mark the desert and Nile routes to Khartoum" as well as "the banks of the Amazon, the Ganges, and the Volga."[25]

In addition to realizing economies of scale and developing new goods, the packers attempted to rationalize production through combination. In 1886, the four leading firms along with Chicago pork packer Samuel Allerton formed the industry's first pool, apportioning the northeastern market among themselves. Devising formulas for uniform profit margins, they used common price lists to bid for livestock and forced recalcitrant retailers to accept their products in lieu of rivals'. In 1893 the Cudahy Packing Company, an offshoot of Armour, was brought into the agreement, which now covered not just the northeast but all southern and border states east of the Mississippi. Each week members of the pool met, exchanged information on shipments and prices, and decided how much each firm could ship to various markets during the next week.[26]

More than marketing agreements joined the large packers together in a corporate oligarchy. They jointly owned hundreds of smaller firms and held controlling interests in the major urban stockyards. They exercised a tight grip on credit and finance as well, owning banks and livestock exchanges in Chicago, Kansas City, and Omaha. The control that the Big Four exerted over the meat industry and its offshoots fueled popular antimonopoly sentiment and gave muckraking writers grist for their busy mills. "Here is something compared with which the Standard Oil Company is puerile," thundered Charles Edward Russell in his exposé, *The Greatest Trust in the World.* Bowing to the trust-busting mood of the times, the Department of Justice ordered the pool disbanded in 1903.[27]

The need to limit internecine competition was a pressing one for the large packers. Even before the government moved against their pool, the packers toyed with the idea of a formal merger. In 1903 they moved into action, merging thirteen independent firms together into a holding company, National Packing. Using National as an umbrella, they regulated their affairs in much the same way as the outlawed pool had done. According to Gustavus Swift, the ultimate goal was to have National absorb the parent firms and thus form a single corporation controlling the entire market. Although a federal antitrust suit forced the liquidation of National in 1912, collusion between the industry's giants continued under cover of the American Meatpackers Association. When the Federal Trade Commission investigated the meat trade in 1916, they discovered that the largest firms had increased their influence over every aspect of the industry, making it practically impossible for independent houses to ship fresh meat out of the locality in which it was produced. The five giants slaughtered over 70 percent of all livestock, owned 91 percent of all refrigerator cars in the country, and exported close to 95 percent of all beef leaving the United States.[28]

Corporate Control of the Labor Process:
From Butchering to Meatcutting

The transformation of Chicago's meatpackers from a group of "pig killing concerns" to corporate giants altered both the manner in which work was carried on within the stockyards and the character of the surrounding community. The most visible change was a staggering increase in size. In 1869, the stockyards provided employment to over two thousand workers and housed thirty-one separate plants. Twenty years later, the largest packers had expanded their facilities and had been joined by thirty-seven other new businesses. In the same period the workforce grew by over 800 percent. By the turn of the century, over twenty-five thousand persons labored in the yards. The largest plants, Armour and Swift, each employed twice as many workers as did Andrew Carnegie at his Homestead Steel Works.[29]

Much of the growth in the labor force took place in departments that handled meat, especially the killing floors and trimming rooms. Slaughtering facilities expanded as the packing companies processed ever higher volumes of livestock. Whereas in 1870 a butcher at Armour or Swift might have toiled alongside two dozen other knifemen, by 1890 his gang included some two hundred skilled members. One source estimates that the packers employed five thousand cattle butchers that year—one-fifth of the total labor force in the yards. The construction of fertilizer works, glue houses, and canning rooms also created as many as eight thousand new jobs.[30]

Most of these positions called for no special skills and the packers filled them with the cheapest labor available. Poles and other Slavic immigrants filled the hide cellars and tank houses, working for as little as a dollar a day. For the first time women entered the yards, staffing the canning and sausage rooms and labeling departments. Most of the growth in female employment occurred after 1890. In that year, there were 990 female packinghouse workers in the nation; by 1904, two thousand women labored in Chicago's packing plants alone. The cheapest labor of all was that performed by children. Circumventing child labor laws, the packers employed at least five hundred young boys in 1900, using them as messengers, door openers, and assistants to older skilled workers.[31]

These statistics only hint at the change that took place in the stockyards; beneath the figures lies a profound transformation of packinghouse work itself. Motivated by the persistence of cut-throat competition, the packers turned their attention to the organization of work inside their plants. They concentrated on the killing floors and cutting departments, critical areas that supplied the entire enterprise with raw material. Having approached the limits of technological innovation, and unable to further mechanize production, the packers instituted a detailed division of labor. By breaking down the butchers' craft into its simplest parts, and linking these components to the already extant "disassembly" line, they freed themselves from their costly dependency on skilled labor.[32]

This restructuring progressed unevenly. Hotly contested by skilled workers whose jobs were at stake, it took hold in piecemeal fashion. Nevertheless, by the turn of the century the all-around butcher capable of performing the multitude of tasks involved in the slaughtering, cutting, and trimming operations had vanished. In his place were dozens of less-skilled men, each performing a single, repetitive task throughout the day. "It would be difficult to imagine another industry where the division of labor has been so ingeniously and microscopically worked out," John R. Commons wrote in 1904. "The animal has been surveyed and laid off like a map . . . skill has become specialized to fit the anatomy." While many jobs continued to require high levels of skill, butchers no longer needed to make judgments regarding the choice of tools, proper positioning, or accurate cuts. "There is no room for individual artistry," *The Packers' Encyclopedia* admonished. "The worker does not decide where or how to make his cut; he does not look at the animal and make an appropriate decision. All cuts are by the book; the instructions are very exact." Emptied of its traditional content and creative dimension, butchering was reduced to meatcutting.[33]

As late as the mid-1880s, a retail butcher would have felt himself on familiar terrain in Chicago's packinghouses. While the beehive of activity differed in intensity from that to which he was accustomed, the work itself—the actual killing and dressing—was essentially the same as that performed in his own shop. By the early twentieth century, the process of death and dismemberment carried out in Swift and Armour's plants bore little resemblance to the butcher's craft with which it shared a common lineage. Karl Lundberg, who grew up on an Iowa farm and later worked in a Dubuque meat market, recalled his first day of work on the beef kill at Swift. Familiar with the methods of home slaughtering and experienced at the "block butcher's" trade, he nonetheless was unprepared for the sight that awaited him. "I had seen blood, and I'd dressed all sorts of animals before, so it wasn't that part of it that gave me a start," he remembered. "It was the way they had the work all divy'd up and the furious pace that things moved along that floor. Nobody even looked up. They couldn't spare so much as two seconds or they'd fall behind." Able to use a knife, Lundberg caught on quickly. Within three years he was working as a rumper, one of the highest paying jobs in the department. But "this wasn't butchering, at least not what I knew to be butchering. This was something else."[34]

As in the past, the hog-killing department proved most susceptible to change. Decades earlier mechanical hoists and scrapers had facilitated the flow of animals through the first stage of the slaughtering process. Now, the second stage of the operation was transformed; workers performed twenty-four separate procedures upon each hog before it reached the cooler. Then, carted manually into cutting and trimming departments, hog carcasses became hams, bellies, shoulders, and scraps used in the manufacture of sausage and other prepared products. Here too previously unified tasks were broken down into their constituent parts. Production remained labor-intensive as the division of skilled jobs into four or five separate tasks actually increased the number of workers in any given department.[35]

Cattle killing underwent a similar transformation. Here, because of the size of the steers, work was performed on the floor. Instead of a line of carcasses moving from one workman to the next, workers moved from carcass to carcass performing their specialized tasks. Cattle killing, however, proved far less adaptable to mechanization than hog slaughtering. The sole technological improvement in this period was the use of a power lift to raise bleeding steers above the ground. However, the animal then was lowered back to the floor, where it was dressed. Because of this constraint, labor was subdivided to an extreme degree. In 1904, a typical cattle gang in one of the large houses numbered around 250 men classified in over thirty specialties and twenty rates of pay. However, only fourteen of them fell into highly skilled categories which paid above 45 cents an hour. Over half of the gang was classified as common labor, earning less than 18 cents for each hour spent on the floor.[36]

From management's perspective this system had the advantage of placing two-thirds of the work into the hands of common laborers as well as increasing the efficiency of time-consuming splitting and skinning tasks. Arthur Cushman, the general superintendent at Armour, explained that while previously butchers were expected to perform almost every task in the packing plant, "few could perform many different jobs with speed and accuracy, so that speed was limited and workmanship irregular." For economic reasons, "it was seen that expert workmanship was essential, and men were encouraged to become proficient in one operation." Packing-house workers viewed the situation quite differently. The specialization that impressed men like Cushman as further advances in rationalization struck workers as an assault upon their craft and an effort to squeeze more labor out of them for less remuneration. "That marvellous speed and dexterity so much admired by visitors," charged Socialist journalist and agitator Algie Simons, "is simply inhuman hard work."[37]

Formerly, skilled butchers determined the speed and intensity with which work was carried out. Paid on either a daily or per head basis, they shared decision making with departmental foremen. Under the new system this power rested solely with capital. Now paid by the hour, butchers and common laborers alike suffered under a general intensification of work. Within a decade, output for splitters—the most skilled members of the cattle-killing gangs—doubled. In 1884, five splitters dispatched an average of eight hundred steers during the course of a ten-hour shift. By 1894, four splitters handled twelve hundred at a lower hourly rate. By 1900, the figure had increased even further. Tallying operational figures in the quiet confines of their offices, management saw only a steady growth in the number of cattle and hogs moving through their plants. On the steamy killing floors, workers concerned themselves with a different set of calculations—one butcher told a reporter in 1904 that "he was now doing precisely twice as much as he was doing fifteen years ago with exactly the same tools."[38]

While the reorganization of the labor process was the most important change to occur in the packinghouses, the introduction of new technologies in the early twentieth century further circumscribed the autonomy of skilled knifemen and further raised production levels. While actual slaughtering and cutting operations still resisted mechanization, the packers now perfected the assembly-line system first pioneered in the late nineteenth century.

By coupling the endless conveyor with the already established detailed division of labor, machines replaced muscle power as the means of moving heavy carcasses from one work station to the next. In 1905 the *National Provisioner* raptly described the workings of the new system in Armour's recently completed plant in St. Joseph, Missouri: "The beef is not moved or lifted a single inch by human force from the time the steer falls on the killing beds . . . until the dressed carcass finally arrives but a few feet in front of the refrigerator car." According to the journal, the volume of meat processed in the newly equipped plant would require ten times as many workers elsewhere.[39]

By 1910, such conveyors were standard equipment in the Chicago hous-

es. Swift even improved on the original idea, building a hog-killing facility containing two parallel disassembly lines. For management, these technological innovations were significant advances which struck a blow
against traditional forms of workers' control over production. Mechanized
conveyors achieved a continuous flow which eliminated a bottleneck that
had plagued the packing companies for decades: no longer could the slow-
est man regulate the speed of the entire work gang. Instead of the men
going to the work, the *Provisioner* observed, "the work comes to them, and
they must keep steadily and accurately at work, for it keeps coming, and
each man must complete his task in an appropriate time or confess himself incompetent for the job." Thus at a single stroke, the packers reduced
the mobility of workers on the shop floor and saved time formerly spent
passing carcasses along the rail. Management rather than labor now controlled the pace of the line. One Swift superintendent bluntly explained, "if
you need to turn out a little more, you speed up the conveyors a little and
the men speed up to keep the pace."[40]

The application of motor power was not limited to the killing floors.
Canning and packaging operations also lent themselves to speed up
through the introduction of conveyors. Here, the work itself continued to
require a modicum of skill—glass jars were still packed by hand, but the
moving line determined the pace of work and undermined workers' efforts
to restrict output. Gertie Kamarczyk, who began working at age thirteen
for Armour in 1916, recalled that "the jars just didn't stop coming, all day
long all you could see was jars, jars, jars. . . . You couldn't leave your place
'cause the empty jars would pile up and the foreman, he'd be on you." The
utilization of motor power in the meatpacking industry increased sixfold
in this era. While the implementation of such technology eliminated much
heavy and dangerous labor, these "savings" did not benefit packinghouse
workers. On the contrary, wherever they were applied, mechanical conveyors and moving rails stripped workers of their ability to control the pace
and intensity of their labor.[41]

Despite the adoption of continuous-flow methods, the packers could
not escape their overwhelming dependence on manual labor. Although
the organization of work had changed dramatically since the pre-industrial era, the actual labor involved in slaughtering and butchering continued to be performed by hand. In joining continuous-flow production
methods with a detailed division of labor, American meatpackers reached
the limits of technological innovation. A government study conducted in
the mid-1920s discovered what the packers long had known: "of all the
large industries in this country, slaughtering and meat packing ranks as

the one which is probably least susceptible to mechanization."[42] Indeed, from 1915 until the mid-1950s, the labor process in the industry remained essentially unchanged.

The Making of a Working Class

Mass production in meatpacking depended as much upon the reorganization of work as it did upon technological and managerial innovation. Low profit margins, the desire to boost speed and output, and the need to bring down labor costs led packing companies to launch an assault upon the power of skilled butchers in their plants. By undermining these craftsmen, the packers gained the upper hand in the struggle for control of the production process. They also changed the character of the packinghouse workforce and the nature of the surrounding community, for their mastery of the shop floor depended upon thousands of unskilled, low-paid immigrants from central and eastern Europe. Moreover, the ways in which these newcomers interacted with one another and with established groups of workers depended in large measure on social dynamics originating in the packinghouses. The growth of Chicago's meatpacking industry entailed not just the emergence of new production techniques and business strategies but the formation of a new working class as well.

The introduction of mass production methods in meatpacking had profound social consequences. The industry's insatiable demand for cheap labor attracted thousands of immigrants to the neighborhood surrounding the stockyards. In the early twentieth century this was a community in flux. Older immigrant groups that provided muscle for the packing industry in its infancy increasingly gave way to newer arrivals. As early as 1900, the outlines of an ethnically stratified geographic unit started to take shape. The Irish and Germans still formed the most cohesive ethnic groupings, together accounting for nearly half of the families in the neighborhood, but Poles and Lithuanians continued to pour into the community during the first decade and a half of the century. By the time World War I arrested European immigration, one out of every two residents was a Pole; and by 1920, three-quarters of Packingtown's dwellers hailed from east of the Danube River.[43]

As the immigrant presence grew, the older, more acculturated families departed. Some Irish and Germans moved out to "better" neighborhoods, following the native Protestants to the new communities springing up on the city's southwestern edge. Others, still tied to the packinghouses, moved several blocks east, leaving the neighborhood more ethnic and more proletarian in character. By 1900, this workers' colony had swelled to over fifty thousand, and had acquired the boundaries which marked it off from the surrounding territory for the next sixty years: Pershing Road and "Bubbly Creek" to the north, Garfield Boulevard on the south, Halsted Avenue on the east, and Western Avenue on the west. Barely exceeding two and a half square miles, this rectangle contained more than seventy-five thousand inhabitants by 1920.[44]

To an outsider, the Back-of-the-Yards neighborhood might have seemed homogeneous—solidly eastern European and decidedly foreign—but this impression belies a reality of social fragmentation. Each immigrant group built its own network of churches, fraternal organizations, and social clubs within which it attempted to re-create the old-world community left behind. Each institution was a declaration of a separate ethnic identity. "We pretty much kept to ourselves," remarked Gertie Kamarczyk, whose parents immigrated from Poland in 1900. She recalled that as a child her budding friendship with a Bohemian girl met with the severe disapproval of her father, a beef lugger at Swift, who "never liked anyone who wasn't from the old country or whose parents weren't." The language, the culture, and even the style of dress set ethnic groups apart from one another. Back-of-the-Yards was not a single community. Rather, it was an industrial neighborhood honeycombed with dozens of ethnic enclaves.[45]

The diversity of Packingtown's population was nowhere more apparent than at the workplace. The labor force in the stockyards was incredibly diverse, certainly more so than that working in the steel mills to the south or the Harvester works to the west. A 1909 survey found over forty distinct nationalities represented in the stockyards, while contemporary accounts rarely failed to remark upon the vast sea of humanity, speaking in different tongues and bidding against one another for jobs at the plant gates. Most departments in the packinghouses must have seemed like the proverbial Tower of Babel, a hodgepodge of peoples and languages furiously working on discrete individual tasks.[46]

Ethnic loyalties and nationalist identities complicated the project of working-class solidarity and provided the packing companies with a powerful weapon against organized labor. In facing the challenge of forging unity amongst a fragmented working class, union activists confronted deep divisions of culture accentuated by differences of skill. One veteran packinghouse worker, an Irish hog butcher who later served as a foreman, captured precisely this dynamic when he noted that his friends from work, the men with whom he regularly stopped at a nearby tavern before heading home, all spoke English, all worshiped at the same church, and all earned "top dollar, not like the rest of the Polacks and what have you workin' away in there."[47]

Ethnic differences accentuated the division between the skilled minority of knifemen and the great mass of common laborers. The former group was comprised of German and Irish workers with small but significant sprinklings of Bohemians and native white Americans; recent immigrants from central and eastern Europe, especially Poland and Lithuania, filled the ranks of the latter group. Over the course of the early twentieth century, though, racial conflict supplemented and then supplanted ethnic tension as the major source of working-class fragmentation in the stockyards. Although black workers accounted for only 3 percent of the total workforce in 1909, they occupied a special and increasingly important position in the packers' calculations. Brought into the packinghouses in 1904 to replace striking workers, their continued presence made it impossible for whites to forget the relative ease with which their employers had bested them and, by extension, the tenuous nature of job security.[48]

Labor Market Segmentation in Meatpacking

Chicago's meatpackers were among the first concerns to take advantage of what scholars recently have termed labor market segmentation.[49] They tapped one market for skilled labor and another, larger one for the remainder of their requirements. A third pool of workers, consisting of African Americans, was held in reserve for use during periods of unrest or labor shortage. Although the three groups might rub shoulders as they labored side by side within the plants, the mechanisms through which they were hired and fired differed greatly, as did the manner in which management treated them. Beyond the world of work, their lives rarely overlapped. They lived in different geographic areas, occupied different social spheres, and pursued different cultural agendas. The maintenance and reproduction of a segmented labor market was crucial to the packers' ability to operate profitably and central to the process of working-class formation.

The packing companies benefited from this arrangement in two major ways. First, they kept their wage bill to a minimum, hiring cheap casual labor as needed and retaining only a small number of highly paid workers with skills essential to production. Second, despite considerable commonality of interest amongst packinghouse workers, divisions of skill and ethnicity remained paramount. The cultivation and utilization of a segmented labor market produced a fragmented workforce unable to challenge the packers' authority effectively. The packers' manipulation of deeply felt ethnic and racial antagonisms fortified their structural control over production by dividing workers from one another.

The packers felt it neither necessary nor prudent to conceal this policy of divide and rule, as John R. Commons discovered in 1904 when he traveled to Chicago to witness conditions in the stockyards and meatpacking industry. Visiting Swift's employment office, he noticed a surprising homogeneity amongst the morning's hirees. Blond-haired, fair-skinned young men sat on benches waiting to be assigned to various departments. "How comes it you are employing only Swedes?" Commons queried. "Well, you see it is only for this week," came the reply. "Last week we employed Slovaks. We change among different nationalities and languages. It prevents them from getting together. We have the thing systematized."[50]

Phillip Armour echoed this statement, candidly explaining to his biographers that eastern European immigrants helped forestall unionism "by displacing experienced and perhaps disillusioned employees . . . who might have been contaminated by contacts with union organizers." Moreover, he admitted pursuing policies intended to "keep the races and nationalities apart after working hours, and to foment suspicion, rivalry, and even enmity among such groups."[51]

Labor market segmentation in meatpacking, and the resulting fragmentation of the workforce, arose from specific policies formulated and implemented by capital. Market forces undoubtedly played a role in this process by facilitating the packers' access to an abundant supply of cheap labor. But deliberate human decisions determined the precise ways in which labor power was recruited and allocated. This important dynamic is the key to understanding the failure of organizing drives in 1894, 1904, and 1917–22. Before turning to examine these campaigns, it is helpful to consider in greater detail the workings of the labor market and the anatomy of the packinghouse workforce.

By conceptualizing the workforce as a horizontally layered pyramid, we can discern a clear pattern—one which joined occupation, skill, and ethnicity in an elaborate hierarchy—amidst what appeared to contemporary observers as tumultuous chaos. A small triangle at the top of the pyramid represents the elite "butcher aristocracy"; and a broad hexagon at the bottom denotes the mass of common laborers. Multiple layers separating these two extremes signify sizeable ranks of semiskilled workers.

The butcher aristocracy formed the most homogenous group of workers in Chicago's packinghouses. In the first years of the twentieth century, Germans and Irishmen made up the bulk of skilled butchers, along with a small number of native whites and a larger sprinkling of recently arrived

Bohemians. English speaking and well assimilated, many of these workers were able to move up into lower level management positions. As late
as the 1930s most foremen were drawn from these two ethnic groups.[52]

The Bohemians arrived later, entering the packing industry in the 1880s,
at a time when the Germans and Irish had consolidated their hold on the
skilled knife jobs. They steadily worked their way up the job ladder and,
by the turn of the century, managed to carve out a small but secure place
for themselves among the butcher elite. While they shared the occupational
status of the Germans and Irish, the Bohemians clearly had more in common with the newer eastern European immigrant groups. Their language
and culture isolated them from the Irish and the Americanized Germans.
They lived in the Back-of-the-Yards neighborhood amongst the rapidly
swelling Polish and Lithuanian populations, and formed their own cultural,
fraternal and religious organizations.[53]

Most of these skilled workers labored on the killing floors. Even though
much of the work was heavy and dirty, this butcher aristocracy enjoyed
relatively high wages and regular work. A floorsman on the cattle kill, for
example, performed the exacting task of removing the steer's hide. For this
he received fifty cents an hour in 1904—the highest rate. In addition to great
strength, this job required considerable skill. Floorsmen had to be ambidex-
trous, and capable of working quickly and cutting accurately for eight to
ten hours at a time. The floorsman's superior position stemmed from the
high cost of a mistake. A slip in one direction marred the valuable hide; an
error in the other direction damaged the meat itself. Cattle splitters, who
wielded heavy cleavers and cleanly separated the carcass into halves, received the same rate of pay. Backers and rumpers, charged with making
precise cuts along the hide, received slightly less.[54]

Skilled workers formed a small minority in their departments. In the large
houses, a typical cattle-killing gang was made up of around two hundred
men, only fourteen of whom were in the top pay brackets. The hog kill had
a similar disparity.[55] In both departments, skilled butchers were surrounded by semiskilled workers and common laborers earning a third or less of
their pay. Before the hog reached the splitter, for example, a gut-snatcher
removed the animal's paunch, stomach, and intestines. The job required a
modicum of skill, and the snatcher received on average ten cents an hour less
than the splitter. Before arriving at the snatcher's station, the carcass passed
the kidney puller, who earned several cents less than the snatcher.[56] Thus,
an elaborate hierarchical job structure existed in each department.

Unlike the bulk of packinghouse workers, who suffered bouts of unemployment and layoff, skilled butchers could count on regular work.

During the summer slack months, for instance, cattle butchers could rely upon at least thirty-two hours of work per week. Stephan Janko recalled wondering as a child why his father, a Bohemian immigrant and floorsman at Armour, had to report for work throughout the slack season when other fathers on his block remained at home. Later, as a teenager, he came to appreciate but still resent the demand for his father's labor: "It helped. It kept us kids in school and out of the yards—at least for a few years. It kept food on the table. But the man worked so hard that we never saw him, never really got to know him."[57]

The wages earned by skilled butchers like Janko's father separated them from other packinghouse workers and placed them on par with some of the better paid craftsmen in the city. Their annual incomes of around $1500 compared favorably with machinists in the nearby Rock Island Railroad car shops and at the McCormick Harvester works. The highest paid knifemen earned considerably more than the male white-collar workers who staffed the packers' offices. But this butcher aristocracy was a small elite. By 1910 it made up no more than 20 percent of the total workforce; and their numbers were shrinking. Because their skills were essential to the process of production and not easily acquired, floorsmen and splitters enjoyed a kind of job security and income wholly foreign to the mass of workers in the stockyards.[58]

While the packing companies could accommodate high turnover rates among semiskilled and common laborers, they found it in their interest to stabilize employment among the butcher elite. This was reflected in paternalistic policies designed to foster loyalty among the skilled workers. Swift led the way, launching a stock purchasing plan in 1906 and establishing an Employees' Benefit Association (EBA) the following year. In 1909, Armour and Morris set up pension systems; and by 1912 most companies had established some form of a guaranteed workweek for their butchers.[59] Of course, not all the packers in the yards experimented with welfare capitalism. Most of the smaller houses could not afford such measures, and many other firms weighed costs against benefits and decided to continue treating labor as a simple commodity.

It is difficult to assess the influence of these programs. Some evidence suggests that workers participated widely. Swift's company union enrolled fourteen thousand employees nationwide within two years of its founding; and two thousand workers took part in the stock purchase scheme. On the other hand, these programs afforded meager benefits. Swift's EBA lacked the power to negotiate wage rates and could effect only symbolic improvements in working conditions. Workers could acquire no more than a few shares in the company, and certainly no one became wealthy as a result of their stock ownership. Likewise, pension plans had stringent service requirements which made it all but impossible for workers to retire. Stephan Janko recalled that each time his father verged on accumulating enough time to qualify for a pension, his foreman laid him off for a day or two, thus breaking his service.[60] Welfare capitalism in this era was aimed at a small, highly valued segment of the workforce. Most production workers were not offered the option of participation. These policies thus enhanced the skilled butchers' sense of exclusiveness and further accentuated the gulf between them and the unskilled.

Standing between the butcher aristocracy and the thousands of common laborers was a group of semiskilled workers who performed a wide array of jobs. The feature they shared was the use of a knife. Some of these jobs required considerable training and paid hourly rates just a few cents below that of the butchers. Others, however, could be picked up quickly and consisted of simple repetitive motions. These jobs were closer in pay to the common labor rate. In the pork-trimming department, ham boners and rib pullers exemplify the first type of job. Both required accuracy, speed, and judgment. In the same department, other workers lifted the hog's tail and removed it with a knife—a job requiring only that the worker keep pace with the line.[61]

This group of semiskilled workers was ethnically heterogeneous. It contained significant numbers of old stock immigrants but was dominated by newcomers, most notably Poles, who by 1905 comprised the largest foreign-born group in the packinghouse workforce. The Slovaks and Lithuanians who followed after the turn of the century had a more difficult time adjusting to the industrial setting, in part due to their smaller numbers and, consequently, greater isolation. Unattached and unsettled, isolated by the formidable language barrier, these ethnic groups occupied the lowest space on the social ladder.[62]

Not surprisingly, semiskilled workers drawn from the earlier immigrant groups held most of the better jobs in this category, even though the situation was more fluid than that prevailing among the butchers. In large part this fluidity was due to the detailed division of labor and the seemingly arbitrary distinctions in pay between essentially similar jobs. Having acquired rudimentary knife skills, workers could move easily from one specialized task to another. When Stephan Janko entered the Armour plant in 1915, he already knew how to hone and steel a knife and was familiar with the basic work routine. Before long, he was working as a utility man on the pork trim, spelling tired workers and filling in for absentees. He quickly learned to perform almost all the jobs in the department. He was one of five Bohemians in a department of 120 men under an Irish foreman. About fifty of the other workers were Poles, and the rest Slovaks, Lithuanians, Greeks, and Russians.[63]

Most of the newer immigrants worked not in semiskilled slots but as common laborers, earning between sixteen and eighteen cents an hour. By 1910, common labor accounted for two-thirds of the workforce, but even within these vast ranks a hierarchy existed.[64] At the upper end of the scale were "regular" employees—workers who returned daily to the same departments and jobs. Most of these involved the application of brute muscle power—hauling, carting, trucking, or hoisting. Others called for some kind of decision making, but little skill or judgment. Gertie Kamarczyk's brother, who worked at Swift grading pork, serves as a good example. He secured the job, his first, in 1916 and with only short interruptions held it until leaving the industry in 1934. Sorting ribs by size and quality, he received a few cents above the base rate, although he occasionally earned more for filling in on other jobs. On good terms with his foreman, he rarely suffered prolonged layoffs, and managed to accumulate a small amount of savings, which he used to establish himself in business.[65]

Kamarczyk's brother was lucky. His escape from the Swift plant to the world of commerce was an exception to the norm: most packinghouse workers remained in the plants until they were too old to continue. "They just used you till they got everything out of you and then they dumped you when they didn't need you anymore," remarked social worker Evelyn Ostrowski. In fact, many workers died on the job. "There was no such thing as retirement, no pensions or anything so a lot of folks worked till they dropped. They had no choice. . . . On those hot summer days, when it would be well over 100 degrees up on those killing floors, we all worried about the older guys," recalled Pat Balskus, who worked at Armour, Swift, and some of the smaller houses.[66]

Common laborers constantly worried about job security. Whereas knifemen could count on employment throughout the fall and winter rush and were likely to see at least some work during the rest of the year, common laborers led a precarious economic existence. During slack periods, management preferred to keep part of a gang working full-time rather than employ the entire gang on reduced hours. When reduced livestock supply necessitated layoffs, those on the lower rungs of the job ladder were thrown out of work.[67] Uncertainty was a constant part of life. "You never knew when the layoff would hit," Pat Balskus explained, "so we were always trying to save, to put something away to see us through. And when you're bringing home peanuts for pay that's not too easy." Packinghouse workers devised a number of strategies to maintain the solvency of their households. Most families counted more than one wage earner among their members, since even a child's small paycheck could spell the difference between hard times and ruin. Up until World War I, most families lodged at least one boarder; and in addition to presiding over this system, women took in washing, sold preserves, and served as midwives. Children scavenged for food and salvageable materials in the garbage dumps below Thirty-ninth Street; and men often traveled considerable distances in search of work when laid off. The boxcar journey of Jurgis, the fictional hero of Sinclair's *Jungle,* was one traveled in real life by countless Packingtown residents desperate for work.[68]

At the bottom of the pyramidal job structure stood thousands of casual workers hired on a temporary basis. Between 20 and 30 percent of those laboring in the stockyards during the 1910s and 1920s were employed by the day, or even by the hour.[69] Many of these workers were Packingtown residents; most probably lived in the Chicago area. Others were part of a transient population of laborers constantly on the move throughout the margins of the industrial economy. Because it served as the hub of the nation's railroad network, Chicago attracted a large number of casual workers. Employment agencies and flop houses dotted the streets and alleys in the vicinity around Union Station a few miles northeast of the stockyards. The surplus of casual labor in the city was more severe than elsewhere and kept wages at an absolute minimum.[70]

The institution which serviced the packers' fluctuating labor needs was the morning "shape-up." Starting before dawn, hundreds of workers gathered outside the doors of the packinghouses hoping to secure employment. Foremen surveyed the assembled crowd and chose the dozen or so extra laborers required to round out their gangs. At other plants, operating on a more rationalized basis, employment officers received requests from the various departments and then hired those needed.[71]

Job security was nonexistent for these laborers. "A man never knows if he is hired for an hour or for a week," an industry expert informed a congressional committee. While some workers succeeded in parlaying a day of work into regular employment, most soon found themselves on the other side of the gate. Unfettered by any constraint, management treated labor as a simple commodity. This was an essential component in the packers' system of labor recruitment, allocation, and control. Since the supply of labor outstripped demand, the casual market helped the packers' keep a ceiling on their wage bill.[72]

The psychological impact of casual labor was profound. The crowds massing in search of work each morning loomed in the minds of packinghouse workers. With the exception of the skilled elite, workers were acutely aware of how easily they could be replaced. Stephan Janko explained, "You'd complain . . . and the boss, he'd look at you and point outside. 'Get your time and get out of here,' he'd holler. 'There are plenty of Bohunks I can get to do your job and keep their mouths shut while they're doing it.'" Supply and demand operated in such a way that even during the fall and winter livestock rush, when the gangs were full and work plentiful, men gathered at the gates hoping for employment. In such a setting, no packinghouse worker felt secure.[73]

Of equal, if not greater, psychological importance was the presence of a small number of black workers in the stockyards. Even though they had worked in the industry since the 1880s, black workers were confined to the most menial positions and were concentrated in the most disagreeable departments. Unlike the Bohemians and Poles, who entered the stockyards at about the same time, black workers made negligible gains in promotion and advancement. Accounting for no more than 2 or 3 percent of the workforce, they nonetheless exerted an influence disproportionate to their minuscule numbers, serving as a visible, daily reminder of the inexhaustible supply of reserve labor to which the packers could turn if confronted with labor unrest. They introduced a powerful element of fear and mistrust into a situation already tense with ethnic frictions.[74]

In responding to their African American co-workers, both on a daily basis and in times of strife, white packinghouse workers drew upon an historical legacy dating back to the initial entry of blacks into the industry as strikebreakers. A particularly vicious pattern of race relations was established as early as 1894, when the packing companies first used black labor to undermine a strike called by white workers. This pattern was given powerful reinforcement a decade later when the packers recruited thousands of southern blacks to put down the Amalgamated Meat Cutters. Rooted in a distinct set of historical circumstances, white hostility toward blacks came to form the most formidable obstacle to workers' solidarity in the stockyards.

Early Unionism and the Origins of Racial Conflict

Before 1894 the few blacks working in the stockyards attracted little notice. Alma Herbst suggests that there was little friction between these men and their white co-workers. "To stand beside a black man was an unfamiliar experience which at first created an element of curiosity and interest rather than conflict." In a rapidly changing industry that was starting to absorb immigrants from the far reaches of the globe, it appeared that blacks might not be treated differently from the other ethnic groups drawn to the yards in search of work.[75]

This promise was never realized. In the summer of 1894, striking workers at the Pullman car works appealed for help. Several thousand butchers walked out of the packinghouses in sympathy with the rapidly spreading strike. Although unskilled workers joined the walkout, when the knifemen met to formulate a set of demands they made no effort to encompass the grievances of the common laborers. When they dispatched representatives to spread the strike to other midwestern packing centers, they instructed them to direct their appeals to skilled butchers rather than to the workforce as a whole. This strategy proved to be their undoing.[76]

The Chicago packers responded swiftly and decisively. Brushing aside their employees' demands, they began recruiting replacement workers. With foremen and superintendents performing the skilled work, the packers utilized hundreds of Polish and black strikebreakers to maintain production. After several weeks desperation set in and violence erupted. Even though a far greater number of white immigrants crossed the butchers' lines, most of the strikers' hostility was directed against the black scabs. Crowds mercilessly harassed strikebreakers as they made their way to and from work, but a special animus was reserved for blacks. Effigies with the words "Nigger Scab" scrawled upon them hung from lampposts around the stockyards; and numerous attacks and assaults were recorded.[77]

While the butchers remained solid, many other departments refused to take part in the strike. Once the larger Pullman conflict died down, hundreds of packinghouse workers trickled back to their jobs. When rail traffic resumed, the packers augmented their loyal core of butchers with skilled men from Kansas City, Omaha, and other packing centers. After nine weeks the effort was abandoned, a failure that had sown formidable seeds of discord.[78]

Defeat underscored the obsolescence of craft unionism in meatpacking. The extreme division of labor prevailing inside the plants not only undermined the bargaining power of the few highly skilled butchers but made them vulnerable to replacement by less-skilled knifemen whose own jobs could then be performed by workers farther down the job ladder. Nonetheless, skilled butchers tenaciously clung to the craft model, declining to reach out to the growing mass of unskilled workers, thus ensuring their ineffectiveness in the face of the packers' superior power.

Part of the butchers' reluctance to include the other workers in their unions stemmed from the considerable cultural distance between them and the new immigrants. Early union leaders and activists tended overwhelmingly to be Irishmen. Their organizations were part of a cohesive Irish-American working-class subculture that drew upon a republican tradition which the Slavs found alien and unintelligible. Even the names of these organizations reflect a strong nationalist orientation—the Blackthorne Club and the Maude Gonne Club, for example. Finally, nativist sentiment among the Americanized Irish was an additional factor sustaining the butchers' aloofness from the unskilled.[79]

Shortly before the turn of the century, packinghouse workers formed their first national organization—the Amalgamated Meat Cutters and Butcher Workmen (AMC). The initial impulse came from the retail trade, but the union's founders soon realized that control of the packinghouses was essential to success. Organization proceeded slowly until Michael Donnelly, a sheep butcher from Omaha, assumed leadership of the fledgling union. Due largely to his oratorical talents and indefatigable energy, the AMC enrolled over four thousand members in the smaller packing centers before setting its sights on Chicago's Union Stockyards, where more than a third of the industry's total labor force lay.[80]

Arriving in Chicago in the spring of 1900, Donnelly first determined to wear down the legacy of bitterness and fear lingering in the wake of the 1894 debacle. He succeeded in forming several clandestine locals built around veterans of earlier struggles. For over a year, organization followed the old pattern: the new locals did not extend beyond the narrow strata of skilled butchers; immigrant laborers, isolated by the formidable barriers of language and skill, were left to fend for themselves. Soon after the AMC came out in the open in mid-1901, union leaders recognized the folly of this course and sought ways to bring the unskilled into the fold. One solution, federal locals affiliated directly with the AFL, was tried and found wanting when the AMC discovered it had difficulty influencing these bodies. The only alternative was department-based units, in which all workers in a given department, regardless of skill, joined the same local. Many rank-and-file butchers balked at this suggestion, and Donnelly found it necessary to campaign tirelessly in order to win them over.[81]

Recruiting interpreters from the major foreign language groups, the Amalgamated began to spread its organization down the job ladder, first reaching those workers whose jobs placed them in contact with the killing gangs, and then moving down another step to the cutting and trimming departments. Despite some reluctance on the part of the skilled elite, the

AMC strove to integrate the immigrants into the union. Meetings and rallies featured the translation of speeches into seven or eight languages; and a number of locals elected eastern European officers. On the shop floor, stewards from each ethnic group represented workers and handled disputes. By the time the Amalgamated's strength and influence peaked in 1904, the union arguably was one of the more important institutions in Packingtown. Contemporary observers, such as social worker Mary McDowell, depicted the AMC as a major stabilizing influence in the community, one which introduced immigrants to the workings of the political system in the United States while breaking down "clannish" attachments to the ethnic enclave.[82]

Despite these efforts to unite across lines of skill and ethnicity, the Amalgamated remained deeply divided. An inclusive membership policy hardly turned it into an industrial union. With locals organized on a departmental rather than plant basis, workers identified more with their specific occupations than with the broader movement. Moreover, the AMC did not attempt to include the hundreds of carpenters, coopers, steamfitters, and other auxiliary craftsmen working in the yards, for this would have infringed upon the jealously guarded jurisdictional claims of other unions.[83]

Still, the world of work provided unionists with common ground, and the Amalgamated built upon this shared experience. Floorsmen and splitters labored directly alongside unskilled men who shared the same boss and suffered under the same system, even if they spoke in a foreign tongue and held brooms or squeegees instead of knives. Yet, one must not overdraw the unifying effect wrought by the AMC. Outside of the plants, life continued to revolve around national identity. Poles lived amongst other Poles; Lithuanians resided in clusters with their countrymen. Despite their shared Catholicism, ethnic groups formed their own churches and worshiped separately. Few opportunities for crossethnic fraternization existed. Culturally and socially the community remained fragmented.[84]

Although in the minority, skilled knifemen formed the functional core of the Amalgamated, filling most of the official positions and directing the union's shop-floor activity. A department-based steward system orchestrated slowdowns, stoppages, and other forms of job actions aimed at regaining a modicum of control over the labor process. "House committees" comprised of representatives from each "trade" coordinated the activity occurring throughout each plant and presented demands to management.[85]

The power of these house committees ultimately stemmed from the ability to disrupt production on the killing floors, for here the elaborate division of labor rebounded against the packers. Stoppages on the part of a few skilled men brought the entire department to a halt and, if unresolved, soon idled adjacent cutting and trimming rooms. With livestock awaiting slaughter and perishable meat left hanging on the rails, these kinds of actions demanded management's immediate response. The continuous flow of material through the packinghouses created other strategic points where workers could exert leverage. Not all of these were dependent upon skilled labor. If work ceased on the loading docks, for instance, where burly "luggers" loaded railroad cars, untold havoc was unleashed in dozens of other departments. Yet, the killing floors were the key to workers' power because the peculiarities of the labor process protected skilled knifemen. Faced with a job action on the loading dock, foremen could easily replace luggers with new hirees—and at times entire gangs were discharged. A competent floorsman or qualified hog splitter, on the other hand, was exceedingly difficult to find.[86]

Job actions revolved around the regulation of hours, wages, and output. They represented an effort to impose "workers' rationalization" upon an industry that looked to the balance sheet as the arbiter of all questions. This decentralized, informal system operated at a remove from the official union apparatus. Indeed, rank-and-file activists often found themselves in conflict with the Amalgamated's leadership. With the exception of Donnelly, these men came out of the retail trade and advocated a businesslike approach to industrial relations. Anxious to achieve stability, they regarded the militant house committees with unease. Believing that union gains resulted from responsibility and conservatism, they viewed the committees' growing propensity to strike with alarm. Although more sympathetic to rank-and-file activity than other officers, Donnelly devoted much time to containing shop-floor militancy, counseling restraint, and defusing situations in which job actions threatened to escalate into full-blown strikes.[87]

Ironically, these efforts to keep a lid on rank-and-file militancy further eroded the authority of union leaders. Part of the problem stemmed from the disparity between the gains registered as a result of shop-floor pressure and the rather meager advances won through negotiations. Shop-floor action was aimed not at boosting wages but restricting output and slowing the debilitating pace of labor. Where workers' organization was strongest, on the killing floors, the speed of the line was reduced between 25 and 50 percent. In many departments, workers addressed the problem of seasonality, forcing the retention of the entire gang during slack periods; in others, workers regulated the pace of labor by forcing the addition of extra gang members. Elsewhere, stoppages led to promotion and layoff based upon seniority rather than favoritism. As early as 1902, shop-floor pressure had forced the packers to concede a ten-hour day, with overtime being paid beyond that limit. By contrast, the national contracts secured by the AMC codified only a small range of issues and covered only skilled knife workers. Moreover, they carried provisions stipulating that union officials handle all disputes, thus effectively "outlawing" the job actions which led to such impressive improvements in conditions.[88]

Undoubtedly, the packing companies' desire to stabilize conditions contributed to their decision to sign agreements with the AMC. However, the contracts did little to curb the activities of the house committees. If anything, they encouraged them to step up the struggle for control. The frequency of strikes rose, with many spreading beyond single departments and becoming plantwide walkouts. In at least one instance, house committees orchestrated a nationwide stoppage in the Swift chain after a Chicago foreman laid off part of a beef-killing gang in spite of an earlier agreement to retain all members. In late 1903 the *National Provisioner* complained that Chicago was "in a state of siege" as a result of unauthorized stoppages. Even sympathetic observers commented on the "defiant" manner of rank-and-file leaders who "acted as though they had more authority than the superintendents."[89]

By mid-1904, it was apparent that the union's leadership had lost control of the organization. At the AMC's convention delegates rejected Donnelly's plea for caution and instead demanded across-the-board wage increases. While the packers considered raising the skilled rate, they drew the line at boosting the pay of common laborers. "Their wages naturally are regulated by *supply and demand*," explained a spokesman, "and ought not to be regulated arbitrarily by a joint trade agreement." The continued availability of cheap labor was vital to the packers' profitability; and earlier agreements with the union had excluded the unskilled men. With rank-and-file pressure mounting, Amalgamated officials could not back down. The lines were drawn for a major confrontation.[90]

While important, the wage issue served primarily as a catalyst. The true sticking point was control of the shop floor. The packers soon spelled this out, declaring that the domination of the packing plants by the union had become unbearable. "The proprietor of an establishment had forty stewards to deal with and nothing that failed to suit them could be done. . . . the packer could not run his own plant. It was run by the stewards." For three years, a battle had raged inside the packinghouses, during which time the union gained the upper hand. But this "domination" owed little to the Amalgamated's orderly approach to collective bargaining; it sprang from the house committees' willingness to engage in direct action. In the summer of 1904, the employers decided that conditions favored an offensive. The fall livestock rush had not yet begun, and high unemployment in the city meant that replacement workers could be found with ease. Further, the packers believed that the craft divisions which proved debilitating to labor in the past again would undermine the union. "It is doubtful if a union of unskilled workers can be maintained," they predicted. "There is nothing to hold the men together."[91]

When the strike began in July, the packers must have reconsidered this assessment. Workers walked out in a disciplined way, and for the first time skilled and unskilled stood together in solidarity. Negotiations soon resumed, and an agreement seemed close at hand with the employers willing to submit the original questions to binding arbitration. Although neither side could claim a clear victory, the Amalgamated triumphantly ordered its members back to work. However, when workers in Chicago reported at the plant gates the following morning, the agreement began to unravel. Foremen barred union leaders from the packinghouses; and many of those rehired were subject to insults and abuse. Seizing the initiative, local leaders declared the strike back on. By the time Donnelly arrived on the scene, the renewed strike was widespread, with resentment directed against his leadership. Confronted with mass pressure from below, he reluctantly granted his sanction and telegraphed the other packing centers to resume the walkout.[92]

The second round proved disastrous for the union. Whether the packing companies' violation of the first agreement resulted from cynical calculation or a simple misunderstanding cannot be determined. Their swift reaction to the resumption of the conflict suggests that they planned from the start to discredit the Amalgamated and then move against the strikers. They immediately began recruiting strikebreakers from other areas of the city, and within a week had brought in skilled workers from small rural plants. Trainloads of immigrants arrived directly from Ellis Island, and railroad cars filled with southern blacks pulled into the stockyards and up alongside the packinghouses.[93]

The pattern of 1894 repeated itself as white workers confronted the estimated ten thousand blacks whom the packing companies recruited. This time, violence against the scabs was more pronounced, with blacks singled out for severe treatment. An angry mob mauled a black laborer and his ten-year-old son; another black lost both eyes when caught by a crowd of enraged whites. At least one black worker was stabbed to death; and others were reported to have been drowned in the fetid waters of "Bubbly Creek"

north of the yards. At times, the violence assumed a generalized character, as whites attacked any black unlucky enough to be found in the vicinity of the plants.[94]

Of course, not all blacks were strikebreakers. Many of those who had been
in the packinghouses prior to the strike took their place beside their white
co-workers. To its credit, the Amalgamated made a sincere effort to include
blacks, and had enrolled at least five hundred black members. Still, the packing companies had little difficulty persuading other black laborers to enter
the yards, and were more deliberate in their actions than during the Pullman
conflict. Labor agents plied the streets of the emerging ghetto, enticing men
into the packinghouses and receiving a dollar a head for their efforts. Other
agents recruited black workers in the South, boarded them on special trains,
and shipped them to the stockyards where they were lodged under police
protection. As many as fourteen hundred of these black southerners arrived
in a single day. While it is true that other groups served as strikebreakers,
blacks formed the largest single component. "Without the colored men and
women now employed in the plants," said a union organizer, "the companies would not be able to operate." In desperation, the Amalgamated appealed to Booker T. Washington, requesting that he intervene and halt the
influx of southern blacks. Washington declined to help.[95]

Flush with replacement workers, the packers operated their plants at
substantial levels throughout the strike. Especially damaging to the union
was the ambivalence of workers in other packing centers who either ignored the second strike call or drifted back to work after a few days. When
the Illinois Board of Arbitration attempted to bring the two sides together,
the packers, sensing victory, declined the offer. Similar efforts by city officials and the U.S. Bureau of Commerce met with the same response.[96]

The strike dragged on into August, with the community presenting a
solid front to the employers and to the rest of the nation, which followed the
conflict in the press. The union organized daily mass pickets at the gates to
the yards and held regular parades and rallies. The Chicago Federation of
Labor threw its considerable resources into the struggle. Care was taken to
avoid violence, but fighting between crowds and strikebreakers inevitably
occurred. Frequently, local magistrates sympathized with those arraigned
before them, often dismissing dozens of cases each day until the bitter protests of the packers and the police forced a change of venue to nearby middle-class Hyde Park. Packingtown's churches lent the strike their support;
and the business community formed a "Stock Yards Aid Society" which set
out to raise $100,000. Chicago's Socialist Party lent strong assistance, hold-
ing rallies and distributing literature in various languages.[97]

The community's resistance was bold but ineffectual. In early August the packers reported having twenty-nine thousand men at work in the yards, including over eighty-five hundred at Armour and Swift. On 29 August, the packers rebuffed Donnelly's request for an audience. A settlement was secured the following week only when Mary McDowell and Jane Addams intervened: the Amalgamated called off its strike and the packing companies agreed to take back workers "as fast as needed." Wages for skilled knifemen returned to their old levels, and common labor rates, not even mentioned in the settlement, were left to the vagaries of supply and demand.[98]

The Experience of Defeat

The 1904 strike defeat carried with it long-term consequences for Chicago's packinghouse workers. In its aftermath, the Amalgamated retreated entirely from the packinghouses, preferring to concentrate its efforts within the secure confines of the retail meat trade. This, in turn, allowed the packers to complete their project of restructuring the labor process unimpeded by union challenge. Accordingly, the demand for unskilled labor increased dramatically over the next decade, accelerating the movement of Poles, Slovaks, Lithuanians, and other eastern Europeans into the stockyards. Most importantly, the 1904 strike marked the arrival of the black worker as a permanent component in the packinghouse labor force. Henceforth, successful organization needed to transcend not only the considerable divisions of skill and ethnicity but the more problematic cleavage of race.

Ironically, the black presence in the packinghouses shrank in the period immediately following the 1904 strike. While strikebreaking had financial rewards, few replacement workers secured permanent positions. Most were discharged as defeated whites straggled back to the plants. The trains which brought the strikebreakers north now carried them back below the Mason-Dixon line. Those northern blacks who stuck with the union suffered in the strike's aftermath. One black veteran of the conflict bitterly remarked, "we got the worst of everything. Skilled Negro butchers were put at the commonest work and at the lowest wage." The enmity of returning whites was severe. They tormented the scabs whenever the foreman's back was turned; at least one man was killed in a knife fight. No doubt this rancorous atmosphere led other blacks to quit. By 1910, only a small nucleus of 319 African Americans continued to labor in the stockyards.[99]

While the numbers of black workers shrank, the memory of 1904 did not. As William Tuttle has observed, after the strike the words "Negro" and "scab" were synonymous in the minds of white packinghouse workers. Shortly after the defeat, South Carolina's Senator Ben Tillman met with a group of stockyard workers in Chicago. "It was the niggers that whipped you in line," he told them. "They were the club with which your brains were beaten out." To many workers Tillman's crude words rang true. Subsequent events seemed to bear out the demagogue's logic. In May 1905, Chicago merchants brought in trainloads of blacks to break a strike called by the powerful Teamsters union. The appearance of these drivers on the streets spurred violence which dwarfed that displayed during the packinghouse conflict. Reports of shootings, knifings, and beatings filled the daily papers. According to one account, "the hostility of the striking whites toward strikebreaking blacks had been generalized into hatred for the black race as a whole; any black man was a potential target." Another source noted that the teamsters strike "brought Chicago to the brink of a race riot."[100]

In this manner economic conflict shaped racial prejudice. The role played by black strikebreakers in these labor struggles produced an image of them as a "scab race." Racist politicians and union leaders helped mold this perception, as witnessed by Tillman's remarks and by AFL official John Roach, who described the black scabs as "huge strapping fellows, ignorant and vicious, whose predominating trait was animalism." Conversely, the exclusionist policies of most craft unions in this era discouraged the trust of black workers. "The Negro workman is not at all sure of the sincerity of the unions," wrote the NAACP's Walter White in 1919. "He feels that he has been given promises too long already." In many instances, strikebreaking was the only means through which African Americans could secure industrial employment. Although many southern blacks were wholly ignorant about unionism, northern black laborers cannot be faulted for regarding the "white man's union" with suspicion and mistrust.[101]

Of course it was more than the workings of the free market that threw white and black labor in competition with each other. The appearance of black strikebreakers in 1904 resulted from deliberate policies pursued by capital. After 1894, the packing companies were well aware of the volatile response the black scabs would arouse. The contribution of black strikebreakers went well beyond their labor power—they aggravated divisions among the workers and added conflict to a situation in which it was already rife. Again on this score Armour's biographers felt no need for circumspection, speaking freely of Armour's making "real henchmen of black and brown men in the yards" during his "labor wars."[102]

The wounds of 1904 continued to fester long after the strike ended because of the day-to-day relationship between white and black workers. Whites had little interaction with blacks, most of whom labored in the most menial jobs and the most unpleasant departments such as those that handled offal or processed animal by-products—the hide cellars, glue works, hair houses, and fertilizer rooms. Even when they worked together, black and white workers kept to themselves as much as possible. On the killing floors, they worked side by side, but rarely spoke to one another. One white worker, an Irishman, who occasionally fraternized with blacks during breaks found himself ostracized by the Poles who dominated the gang. Similarly, the saloons that lined Ashland Avenue directly across from the yards drew a clear color line. Even those that welcomed black patronage maintained a segregated interior. The opportunities for interracial contact were few and far between.[103]

Moreover, Chicago was a strictly segregated city in the early twentieth century. Practically its entire black population was crammed into a narrow finger of land wedged between Bridgeport and Wabash Avenue. Thus, outside of the workplace, whites and blacks had virtually no occasion for social intercourse. One Polish worker recalled, "we only saw the colored when we were at work or coming home. They'd all live over past the Halsted side . . . and off they'd go that way and we would go this way." Geography and a kind of social and cultural apartheid kept black and white workers apart and prevented them from exploring any common ground.[104]

The Amalgamated Meat Cutters never fully recovered from the beating it absorbed in the summer of 1904. Commenting on the magnitude of the defeat, David Brody notes that the union paid "not in concessions on wages or hours, but with its very existence" in the packinghouses. In the months following the strike, packinghouse workers deserted the Amalgamated en masse. Union membership in Chicago plummeted from 34,400 to 6,200 before the year was out. While most members simply drifted away from their defunct locals, many resigned in embitterment. The Sausage Makers quit the International as a body; and the Sheep and Cattle Butchers threatened to split off and form their own craft organization. Charges and countercharges flew back and forth between local leaders and union officials, creating a discouraging atmosphere that further eroded the faith of rank-and-file workers. Of the twenty-six local unions in the Chicago stockyards at the time of the strike, only six remained a year later—and these were comprised almost exclusively of skilled workers.[105]

The response of the Amalgamated's leadership did little to inspire confidence. Meeting in September, the executive board chose to adopt a "waiting policy" rather than mount any effort at reorganization. Meanwhile, the union journal berated packinghouse workers for their timidity, claiming that half the membership was "lying down whining like a whipped school-boy and imagining that all is lost."[106]

But all was lost—at least as far as the fortunes of the Meat Cutters were concerned. The Amalgamated's presence in the yards continued to shrivel. By 1908, five more locals had expired, leaving only Cattle Butchers No. 87 to carry the union standard.[107] Over the course of the next decade, the AMC occasionally considered the possibility of a packinghouse campaign, but such deliberations usually resulted from outside pressure. In 1912, for example, when Mary McDowell urged Amalgamated officials to take up the packinghouse problem, the union sidestepped the issue by telling AFL president Gompers "to plan his own campaign, manage it in his own manner, and organize anyone in the Stock Yards into any craft or calling he saw fit, paying no attention to the Amalgamated." When the Chicago Federation of Labor launched an abortive stockyards organizing campaign in October 1912, it did so without even bothering to enlist the support of the once-powerful Meat Cutters.[108]

Those workers fortunate enough to retain their jobs returned to the packinghouses without a union, much less any hope of the continuation of collective bargaining. Common laborers found their pay reduced to fifteen cents an hour (where it remained for close to ten years). Skilled workers suffered proportional cuts in their wage rates and lost some of the privileges they had earned during the previous decade. Working conditions, which had steadily improved during the Amalgamated's heyday, deteriorated markedly as the packing companies reaped the fruits of their victory.[109]

Management's consolidation of its command over production took several forms, three of which in particular merit attention: expansion of the foreman's power, technological innovation, and the cultivation of a segmented and hierarchical labor market. For all but a handful of workers, "management" was an abstract concept, one that assumed concrete form only in the person of the foreman—the man who hired and fired, distributed job assignments, settled grievances, gave raises and promotions, and often was called upon to settle arguments and break up fights.

The critical link between management and workers, foremen were indispensable to the "drive" system of authority relations upon which the packers' control over production relied. Attempting to realize further gains in efficiency by increasing output, the packers tried to inspire workers with awe and fear.[110] Under pressure themselves from plant superintendents, and acutely aware of the importance of labor costs, packinghouse foremen squeezed more production out of the work gangs wherever possible. In many plants, management established a competitive system under which foremen strove to get out the most work at the least possible cost. One foreman explained, "if I could save ⅟₂₅ of a cent on the expense of killing each beef I knew that I would be preferred over other foremen. I was constantly trying to cut down wages in every possible way by driving bargains with separate men." This drive system led to abuse in a myriad of ways. The foreman's power was absolute, and the shop floor was his empire.[111]

One of the most significant accomplishments of the house committees in the period prior to the strike had been the curbing of the foreman's power. Where they were strong, the committees succeeded in regulating hours of employment, instituting a seniority system, regularizing wages, restricting output, and countering disciplinary measures. Without the countervailing power of these structures, foremen moved to regain their lost authority, discarding seniority in favor of the old system based on favoritism and individual bargains. No longer subject to negotiation, foremen unilaterally established production standards. Hiring and promotion as often as not depended on kinship or outright bribery. In some instances, the absolute power wielded by the foreman reached extremes that seem to belong to an earlier stage of capitalist development. When Arthur Kampfert began working at Sulzberger and Sons in 1914, he was shocked to see his fellow workers, recent immigrants from Poland and Lithuania, doff their caps and kiss the hands of the foremen and superintendent each morning "as if they were their master."[112]

In virtually all departments, the pace and intensity of work increased as packinghouse workers labored without union protection. The human toll exacted by this speedup is revealed in the skyrocketing injury rate. Packinghouses, which had always been dangerous places, came to rival coal mines as the nation's most perilous worksites. Swift reported thirty-five hundred injuries for the first six months of 1910 alone; in 1917, the Armour plant functioned with a 50 percent injury rate, averaging twenty-three accidents per day.[113]

Packinghouse workers were not, of course, completely powerless during this era. Even without benefit of formal organization, workers asserted themselves on the shop floor. Machinery mysteriously "broke" when the pace of work exceeded a certain level. Work gangs learned to disguise slowdowns in order to limit production. Butchers made repeated trips to the whetstone when their gang was shorthanded, the weather too hot, or the pressure too intense. Workers constantly devised new methods to cut their workload and restrict their output. Even the messenger boys employed in the front offices learned to pace themselves. Rather than deliver each piece of mail as it arrived, the boys waited until a pile had collected. Then one boy made the rounds, allowing the others to continue their card or dice games.[114]

No one was more keenly aware of the potency of these kinds of "guerrilla" tactics than packinghouse foremen, who quickly learned to reestablish tacit understandings with their underlings lest they fail to make the quotas imposed upon them by their superiors. Tommy Megan, a foreman at G. H. Hammond, explained that accommodation with the gang was much preferred to confrontation which inevitably led to conflict with the superintendent. "They knew I needed to get those hogs moving down the line and I knew they weren't gonna let me go above a certain speed. I mean this was understood, all around." From the workers' perspective, the foreman represented authority and was to be outwitted or outmaneuvered whenever possible. "It was a constant tug of war," recalled John Wrublewski. "He'd always be pushing us and we had our ways of pushing back."[115]

Still, this kind of unorganized, sporadic guerrilla warfare was no substitute for unionism. The packers realized this and consistently refused to bargain collectively on any level. This intransigence, and something of the attitude behind it, is revealed in a favorite anecdote of William Z. Foster. In 1915 Foster secured a job in the stockyards, working in Swift's railroad car repair shop. Always willing to lend a hand in building unions, he found himself accompanying a delegation of workers seeking to discuss a steamfitter's grievance with an Armour vice-president. The workers succeeded in gaining a hearing but quickly grew frustrated. Each time one of their number raised a substantive issue, the executive responded by commenting on the weather. Tensions mounted. Finally, the vice-president shouted at the representatives to "go back to your trade union friends and tell them Organized Labor will never get anything from this company that it hasn't the power to take."[116]

2

The Stockyards Labor Council

The period between 1917 and 1921 was a crucial one in the history of packinghouse unionism. These years witnessed the emergence of a working-class movement in the stockyards which sought to overcome the barriers imposed by a hierarchical job structure and reinforced by divisions of ethnicity and race. Initiated and led by activists within the Chicago Federation of Labor, the movement took the form of an alliance between different segments of the industry's polyglot workforce. Its strongest base of support lay with the Polish and Slavic workers who filled most of the industry's semiskilled jobs. By incorporating the remnants of the Amalgamated Meat Cutters, the movement also secured the allegiance of the predominantly Irish and German "butcher aristocracy." Most important, given the racial antagonism produced by the 1904 strike defeat, the movement established ties with the black workers who streamed into the packing industry in record numbers during this era.

The movement drew its strength from several sources. The support of the Chicago Federation of Labor threw the resources of a dynamic local movement behind the campaign, endowing it with a degree of autonomy from the craft-dominated Amalgamated and encouraging the emergence of new, inclusive forms of organization that anticipated the industrial unionism of the 1930s. The existence of powerful shop-floor organizations, especially on the critical killing floors, further augmented the movement's power. Finally, the intervention of the federal government, in the form of imposed binding arbitration, led to dramatic improvements in wages and working conditions which helped the movement consolidate its position in the stockyards.

Ultimately, these gains were undone and the movement destroyed, torn apart from within by internal factionalism and racial strife, and countered from without by the superior power of the packing companies. This outcome, however, does not mean that the steps taken in the direction of interracial and interethnic solidarity were insignificant. In its insurgent phase, the union campaign transformed racial and class experiences in the stockyards. The packinghouse workers who sought to unite behind common economic interests grappled with a series of questions that remained open and unresolved for the next forty years. Questions concerning the rights and relationships of white and black workers, the ways in which racial and class consciousness become intertwined, and the impact of unionization upon race relations molded workers' self-perceptions and defined the future course of packinghouse unionism.

The Wartime Context

The balance of power in the stockyards shifted considerably with the outbreak of World War I. The packers still held the upper hand, but hostilities in Europe set forces in motion that redefined the context of industrial relations. First, the war shut off immigration from Europe, depriving the packing companies of their cheap labor pool. Between 1914 and 1918, immigration to the United States dropped by 80 percent.[1] This decline, coupled later with domestic conscription and enlistment, produced severe labor shortages throughout the industrial economy.

In meatpacking, the situation was especially acute as many workers seized upon the opportunity to secure jobs in more attractive settings. Turnover rates in Chicago's packinghouses rose to dizzying heights. The Department of Labor calculated that between 1917 and 1918, annual labor turnover in the industry stood at 334 percent.[2] Employment on the assembly line at Western Electric or at the McCormick Harvester Works might not yield more pay than meatpacking, but the work itself certainly was cleaner and often lighter.

For the packing companies, the labor shortage was particularly vexing since it cramped their operations just when the allure of enormous profits beckoned. Well before the United States entered the conflict, the packers were wrestling with large war shipments. As early as 1914, European demand for meat products had canning departments in Chicago humming with activity. That year American meatpackers exported 30 million tons of canned beef, 31 million tons of fresh beef, and 183 million tons of bacon to the Allies and neutrals abroad.[3] To capitalize on increased foreign demand, the packers needed to keep their plants operating at full capacity. They did this by tapping an important new source of labor: the stream of black migrants arriving in Chicago in record numbers from the Deep South.

A crisis in the South's cotton culture set off the northward movement of African Americans known as the "Great Migration." The spread of the boll weevil, a series of disastrous floods, and plummeting agricultural prices combined to force countless sharecroppers and tenants off the land. Pulled north by the availability of industrial jobs, half a million blacks left the South between 1916 and 1920. Approximately fifty thousand of these migrants found their way to Chicago. The packing companies played an active role in directing the migratory stream, especially in its early stages. Using labor agents, they offered transportation and the promise of jobs to laborers agreeing to travel north. They also took out advertisements in the widely circulated *Chicago Defender* and transferred blacks to Chicago from their southern branch houses.[4]

More important than labor agents or want ads were the letters migrants sent to their friends and families. One man in Chicago wrote a friend in Alabama, "it is true that the (col.) men are making good. Never pay less than $3.00 per day for (10) hours." Another recent arrival wrote, "I am well and thankful to say I am doing well. I work in Swifts packing Co., in the sausage department. . . . We get $1.50 a day. . . . Tell your husband work is plentiful here and he wont have to loaf if he want to work."[5] In this manner, the migration generated its own momentum. The names Armour and Swift were already familiar to many southerners since the packers supported branch houses throughout the region. Now that their friends and relatives were employed by these same companies, northern meatpacking figured prominently in their imaginations. "The packinghouses in Chicago for awhile seemed to be everything. You could not rest in your bed at night for Chicago," recalled one migrant who had come to Chicago from Hattiesburg, Mississippi.[6]

Poor education and lack of skill were no barrier to employment in an industry so heavily dependent on common labor. The transition from rural agricultural work to an urban industrial setting could be difficult to negotiate, but monetary rewards eased the way. The contrast between wages in Chicago and those in the South was enormous. To a former sharecropper or tenant farmer unaccustomed to currency and knowing only an ever-increasing burden of debt, the prospect of a regular weekly paycheck of twelve dollars or more must have seemed too good to be true. Even experienced industrial laborers from the South often realized a dramatic increase in income. Joe Hodges, for example, had worked as a patternmaker's assistant on the Southern Pacific Railroad, earning twenty cents an hour. Soon after arriving in Chicago from Texas, Hodges was working on the beef kill at Wilson and Company at an hourly rate of forty-five and a half cents.[7]

In the short run, reliance upon black labor allowed the packing companies to increase production and reap record profits. In 1916, the packers sent 70 million tons of canned beef, 262 million tons of fresh beef, and more than half a billion pounds of bacon abroad. That year Armour and Swift registered profits in excess of twenty million dollars apiece, up from six and nine million respectively prior to the start of the war.[8] In the long run, the turn to black labor affected far more than the packers' balance sheets. It led to a dramatic recomposition of the workforce and decisively shaped the form and character of organized labor's response to the wartime context.

The most pronounced change in the labor force was its sheer increase in size. During the war years, employment in Chicago's packinghouses almost doubled. In 1914, thirty-seven establishments utilized 26,408 workers. In 1919, before demobilization had taken its toll, 45,695 packinghouse workers earned a living in Chicago's forty-six plants. Beneath this expansion lay a demographic shift, the most important contour of which was a climb in the proportion of blacks from 3 to 25 percent of the labor force. In some of the larger plants African Americans accounted for more than 30 percent of the total figure. Indeed, the meatpacking industry was the single most important source of employment for blacks in Chicago. By the end of the decade one out of every two black men who held jobs in manufacturing was employed in the stockyards.[9]

If the war offered the packers the chance to fill their coffers with profits, it also provided labor with a fresh opportunity to organize workers in the stockyards. The labor shortage and the employers' need for full production created the most favorable climate in over a decade. Unrest flared as workers tested their newly enhanced power. Mary McDowell, always attentive to developments in the yards, noted that "when the workers, mostly Poles, Slovaks, and Lithuanians, became conscious of the undersupply of labor they grew restless. In separate departments there were constantly sporadic, unorganized strikes."[10]

Arthur Kampfert's account of his activities during this period reveal something of the spontaneous nature of these job actions. In the spring of 1916, Kampfert led a stoppage in the Sulzberger and Sons pork-trimming department aimed at securing a five-cent-an-hour increase. The strike quickly spread to adjacent offal and casing departments. Workers met hurriedly and elected a bargaining committee which successfully negotiated a four-cent raise. Management, however, tempered the victory by discharging three of the leaders, including Kampfert. With labor in high demand, though, he soon found employment at one of the smaller plants, Western Provision. Less than a month later, he was at the center of another work stoppage. This one spread to the killing floor and effectively shut down the entire plant. After three hours, management gave in and announced a general five-cent wage hike. Word of the victory spread, unleashing a wave of strikes throughout the stockyards.[11]

Conducted without benefit of formal union leadership, these sorts of stoppages occurred at a frenzied pace throughout 1916 and 1917. Although they pushed up wage rates and secured minor improvements in working conditions, the absence of any overall coordination limited their effectiveness. Confined to one or two departments, these job actions aimed at narrow goals and depended upon the initiatives of a few militants such as Kampfert rather than mass organization of workers. Nevertheless, their frequency and the way in which they tended to spread and involve other workers demonstrated the existence of considerable pro-union sentiment in the packinghouses.

Clearly, the stockyards were ripe for organization. The Amalgamated, however, was slow in responding to the challenge. Hobbled by internal factionalism and uncertain about the desirability of reentering the packinghouses, the Amalgamated stalled by requesting that the AFL shoulder the burden of organization. In Chicago and elsewhere, packinghouse workers refused to wait. The stoppages continued unabated. Business, complained one industry executive, "cannot be conducted in an orderly manner . . . in this age of unrest." In the summer of 1916, major strikes idled thousands of workers in Sioux City and East St. Louis, but the AMC continued to equivocate.[12]

The Stockyards Labor Council

While the AMC ignored the ferment occurring in the packinghouses, other elements within the local labor movement moved into action. The stoppages led by men like Kampfert attracted the attention of a small but influential group of labor radicals who, in the summer of 1917, persuaded the Chicago Federation of Labor (CFL) to sponsor a campaign in the stockyards.

The idea of a formal organizing drive originated with William Z. Foster, working at the time as a railroad car inspector in the yards. Foster had built a base of support within the Chicago District Council of Railway Carmen, and used this body to advance his organizing plan. In July 1917, he and a committee of carmen approached a nearly defunct local of the Butcher Workmen and gained its reluctant endorsement of a resolution calling for a conference of all unions with jurisdiction over workers in the stockyards for the purpose of launching and carrying on a united and vigorous organizing campaign. A few days later the federation's delegates passed the resolution unanimously. On 23 July 1917, the CFL formed the Stockyards Labor Council (SLC). Martin Murphy, a hog butcher, was elected president, while Foster was chosen to serve as secretary.[13]

The Stockyards Labor Council bore the unmistakable imprint of the syndicalists who had been working with Foster within the CFL since the early 1910s. Choosing to "bore from within" existing AFL unions, these radicals had established a visible presence within Chicago's labor movement. The defining characteristic of their activities was an effort to promote "proto-industrial" forms of organization: wherever possible they experimented with organizations that crossed the narrow lines of craft jurisdiction, skill, and union bureaucracy. Their greatest success came in the early 1910s when they formed a Chicago Railroad District Council made up of locals of all rail unions. Despite bitter opposition from the established railroad craft unions, the council idea spread throughout the country.[14]

In many regards, the SLC was modeled after the railroad council. Over a dozen unions with jurisdiction in the yards were represented. Firmly locked together under a single executive board, the component unions hoped to form a solid front. With a set of organizers affiliated directly with the council, problems of internecine rivalries and competing jurisdictional claims could be bypassed. "We infused our whole movement with the spirit of industrial unionism," Foster wrote; and indeed, the SLC represents a halting step away from the craft structure of the AFL.[15]

Working alone, Foster and his comrades could never have made the SLC a reality. Although many rank-and-file workers respected their leadership, and despite their circumspect approach to politics, the radicals did not enjoy warm relations with the city's craft unions. Only by enlisting the active support of the Chicago Federation of Labor was the creation of the SLC made possible.

The CFL in 1917 was unlike any other labor council in the country. Led by John Fitzpatrick, the CFL advanced a militant, class-conscious style of unionism that, in the words of one historian, allowed Chicago to "challenge London for the title of trade union capital of the world."[16] In addition to overseeing mass organizing drives in meatpacking and steel during the 1917–19 era, the CFL launched a Labor Party, supported the effort to unionize female teachers and clerical workers, and played a leading role in the movement to free imprisoned labor activist Tom Mooney. Fitzpatrick welcomed progressives of various stripes into the CFL, putting their organizational talents to use in local campaigns. Edward Nockels, the CFL's secretary, headed a group of mainstream activists that included Margaret Haley and Lillian Herstein of the teachers' union and socialist carpenters Tom Slater and Anton Johannsen. The most cohesive grouping of radicals, however, were the syndicalists associated with Foster. Committed to industrial unionism, Fitzpatrick was able to work comfortably with these activists.[17]

The CFL's endorsement was instrumental in securing the support of the constituent unions which made up the Stockyards Labor Council. Federation sponsorship also allowed radicals such as Foster and Jack Johnstone to play leading roles in the day-to-day formulation of strategy and tactics. Their presence acted as an important counterweight against the conservative tendencies of the craft unionists. This became especially clear over the course of the next two years in two areas of vital importance: the movement's relationship to black workers and the SLC's response to government arbitration.

The SLC's drive began slowly. The first mass meeting attracted ten thousand workers, but the results were meager. Although the crowd received the speakers warmly, only a handful of individuals came forward and actually joined. Packinghouse workers were anxious for action, but an awareness of spies and fear of company reprisals compelled them to remain aloof. The fact that Amalgamated officials shared the platform did not help inspire confidence. Workers remembered the 1904 debacle and, in Foster's words, the "long years of AFL betrayal and incompetence" in the meatpacking industry.[18]

By November, however, the drive had gathered momentum. The submission of a list of specific demands, including substantial wage increases, equal pay for women, and an eight-hour day, generated enthusiasm and sparked an influx of workers into the union. "The effect upon the discontented mass was electrical," Foster recalled. "At last they saw the action they wanted." Especially encouraging was the response among the foreign born. In the space of a single month, more than ten thousand Poles and Lithuanians poured into Laborers' Local 554. Native skilled workers proved more difficult to organize, but by the year's end they began to come around. The SLC still faced an uphill battle, but it had gained a solid foothold in the stockyards.[19]

While the packing companies mulled over the SLC's demands and formulated a response, organizing continued. The greatest challenge was reaching out to the twelve thousand blacks laboring in the stockyards. While close
to 90 percent of the white workforce had entered the union fold, most blacks
kept their distance.[20] Organization of these workers was imperative if the SLC
hoped to stand up to the packing companies; yet several formidable obstacles had to be cleared away before this could be accomplished.

The most immediate problem was where to place black workers once
they were organized. Most of the craft unions in the SLC barred blacks from
membership by constitutional decree. The Machinists, for instance, limited membership to "white, free born male citizens of some civilized country," and Foster's own Railway Carmen specified that only "a white person, male or female, of good moral character" could join the organization.
The real issue, of course, was much larger than these legalisms. How far
did the institutional racism of the unions extend? Were they willing to
abandon Jim Crow in order to demonstrate goodwill toward black workers? Opinion was divided. In a quandary, SLC leaders secured permission
to enroll blacks excluded from the craft unions into separate "federal" locals affiliated directly with the AFL.[21]

This compromise was a poor solution. Federal locals segregated blacks
from whites and hindered the building of solidarity. This was made clear
by the pressing problem of where to place the much larger mass of black
packinghouse workers. Initially, leaders planned to enroll these workers
directly into the Amalgamated Meat Cutters, which drew no color line and
had accepted blacks into its ranks in the past. Within a short time, however, blacks began to protest their minority status in these locals. Whether
these complaints originated with black leaders influenced by the packing
companies, as Foster later suggested, or whether they were bona fide concerns raised by workers is unknown. In response, the SLC established two
all-black locals, no. 651 for men and no. 213 for women. This move exposed
the SLC to accusations of fostering segregation. "Almost overnight," Foster recalled, "the cry of 'Jim Crow' went along State Street with devastating effect."[22]

Anxious to counter this criticism, SLC leaders worked out an agreement
whereby the mass Amalgamated locals composed of laborers would be
established on a neighborhood basis, with membership interchangeable
among them. However, it is doubtful that any black workers attempted to
transfer into Local 554, based in the Back-of-the-Yards, and even more
unlikely that any white ventured over to Local 651, headquartered in the
the Black Belt. The decision to create community-based locals had the ef-

fect of furthering de facto segregation, deflecting rather than resolving the racial dilemma. Alma Herbst accurately terms this move a "sincere, albeit calculating gesture from organized labor. Necessity demanded that recognition be given to the strength of the Negro group; expediency dictated the membership policy."[23]

The SLC's tortured maneuverings around the race issue raised black suspicions. The hiring of additional black organizers and the election of A. K. Foote, a black hog butcher, as vice-president of the labor council only partially allayed the fear that the "white man's union" was up to its old tricks. At the end of 1917, efforts to organize black workers had yielded meager results. While a majority of northern-born blacks responded to the union's appeal, the SLC made little progress among the thousands of southern migrants in the stockyards. "If we were dealing with what we call the northern negro, we should not have very much difficulty," Fitzpatrick lamented in December. "They understand the necessity of organization, and they are organized . . . but the southern negro is different. We figure that his slavery days ended at about the time that he came up here to work in the Packing houses."[24]

Part of the difficulty in recruiting blacks lay in the fact that most southerners only dimly understood the concept of unionism. Irene Goins, a black female organizer, reported that her work had proceeded slowly because "my people know so little about organized labor that they have had a great fear of it." Others echoed her remarks. Simple ignorance, the paternalism of the packers, and the dramatic contrast between conditions in Chicago and those in the South frustrated the efforts of organizers to win black support. Mary McDowell illustrated the point with a story about a black man approached on the job by a union delegation. After listening to their appeal he asked, "It all sounds pretty good to me, but what does Mr. Armour think about it?"[25]

Moreover, many black workers who were familiar with unions had a negative view of them. "Unions ain't no good for a colored man. I've seen too much of what they don't do for him," remarked one worker. The labor movement's history of racial exclusion haunted the SLC's efforts to forge a new path. Lowell Washington, who moved to Chicago in 1915 from Mississippi, refused to have anything to do with the Stockyards Labor Council. Soon after arriving he sought work bricklaying, a trade he had mastered in Vicksburg. White unionists not only denied him credentials but assaulted him for his "uppityness." Resigned and bitter, he took a job in the yards, earning money to bring his family north. When union organizers approached him at the beginning of the campaign, he "turned his back on them, just wouldn't have nothing to do with them, wouldn't listen to those white men and wouldn't talk to them neither." Countless other blacks experienced similar rebuffs. The perception that unions operated to benefit whites at blacks' expense was widespread and not easily shaken.[26]

Thus, despite SLC efforts to forge ties with the black community, sentiment there toward the union campaign was ambivalent at best, and unremittingly hostile at worst. The most important institution, the black church, actively opposed the union cause. Archibald Carey, an AME bishop, expressed the dominant view of the religious establishment when he declared, "the interests of my people lies with the wealth of the nation and the class of white people who control it." A number of black churches, including the influential Trinity AME, received generous contributions from the packing companies and were reluctant to endanger this support by giving sanction to a union drive which had yet to prove its integrity and intentions. Still, the church did not close ranks on the issue. Reverend Lacey Kirk Williams of the large and influential Olivet Baptist Church and a few other ministers offered limited support, even while warning against unspecified radical elements. Hoping to sway some of the more religious black workers, the SLC secured a representative from the Baptist Ministers' Alliance to address meetings, and even hired a preacher, G. W. Reed, as a part-time organizer.[27]

Winning the approval of the black press was no easy task; even its qualified support was difficult to gain. The community's leading newspaper, the *Chicago Defender,* vacillated throughout the campaign. It ignored the start of the drive and, when it did take notice, counseled its readers to exercise utmost caution in dealing with the union. Aware of the importance of packinghouse employment to blacks, the *Defender* at times seemed to side with the packing companies. For instance, in a 1918 article it proclaimed: "The name of Armour has always been a sign of justice, so far as our Race is concerned." Yet at other moments the paper supported the union effort— as when publisher Robert Abbott agreed to address workers on behalf of the SLC.[28] The second largest paper, the *Broad Axe,* disregarded the union entirely, while the *Advocate* consistently opposed it at every turn. Only the small circulation *Chicago Whip* backed the drive and encouraged its readers to do the same. Although the *Whip*'s enthusiasm later waned, it featured a regular column by John Riley, one of the black organizers at work in the stockyards.[29]

No one was more keenly aware of the resistance of blacks to unionism than the packing companies. Heavily dependent upon black labor when the SLC drive began, the packers now increased their numbers in the workforce even further. The Department of Labor calculated that during 1917–18, the black labor force in Chicago's packinghouses jumped three to five times.[30] This was a deliberate response to the successful organization of white laborers. Even while the SLC was in its formative stages, Swift directed its plants to begin quietly discharging activists and replacing them with "colored help." Such policies could not be kept covert for long. Soon the packers were openly moving against the union and sowing seeds of racial discord. When a group of conveyance truckers struck at Armour, for instance, management promptly replaced them with blacks. In some departments, especially all-white ones, foremen threatened that if "we had anything to do with the union guys, then we'd find ourselves cleaning casings [a particularly disagreeable task] while the colored girls would be on our jobs." Such threats were common occurrences, prompting the CFL to accuse the packers of fomenting racial friction and antagonism.[31]

In late 1917 the brewing conflict boiled over when Libby, McNeil and Libby—a Swift subsidiary—fired sixty union members. By this time the movement had spread to other midwestern packing centers; SLC militants began to believe that momentum was on their side. Led by Foster, they seized upon this provocation and pressured the Amalgamated into taking a national strike vote. On Thanksgiving eve, packinghouse workers voted overwhelmingly to empower the leadership to call a nationwide walkout. At this juncture, however, the union leadership divided into opposing camps. Amalgamated officials, feeling bound to the wartime no-strike pledge and afraid of sharing authority with the Chicago radicals, opposed taking action. In their view, the vote simply served to strengthen their hand. Fitzpatrick, too, felt that a premature walkout might jeopardize their gains. On the other hand, Foster and Johnstone wanted to press forward with the strike, believing it the only way to induce the packing companies to sign an agreement with the union.[32]

This was the first open manifestation of the internal tensions within the SLC. Amalgamated officials distrusted Foster's group, even though its initiative had revived the AMC's sagging fortunes. They complained about the power exercised by Foster's comrades who, in their view, had injected themselves into a movement to which they had only a tenuous connection. In addition, AMC leaders resented the way in which the SLC dominated negotiations and the formulation of overall policy. These were matters best left to the constituent unions; the heavy-handed roles of Foster and Johnstone caused them to chafe. For their part, the radicals felt the Amalgamated remained too firmly wedded to an outmoded conception of organization and lacked sufficient backbone to face down the packing companies. In one of his many autobiographies, Foster accused "reactionary" Amalgamated officials of reneging on promises of financial support and opposing the "militant line" favored by both SLC leaders and rank-and-file organizers.[33]

Whether a strike could have been won in the winter of 1917 soon became a moot question. Before the internal conflict could play itself out, the federal government intervened in the stockyards dispute. Fearing that a strike would disrupt essential production, Secretary of War Newton Baker ordered the President's Mediation Commission to defuse the situation. After several weeks of wrangling, an accord was reached. On Christmas Day, the packers and the unions signed an agreement prohibiting strikes and lockouts in the eleven major packing centers for the duration of the war. A government administrator would impose binding arbitration where negotiation failed to settle grievances.[34]

While the AFL unions embraced arbitration, Fitzpatrick, Foster, and Johnstone harbored deep reservations. To start with, the agreement did not call for union recognition. It was no substitute for a contract, and the radicals feared it would demobilize the organizing campaign. Moreover, other attempts at arbitration had failed when intransigent employers refused to accede to elementary union requests. In such cases, Foster argued, "workers naturally conclude that if the Government can do nothing with their autocratic employers it is useless for them to keep up the fight."[35] If government intervention had prevented a strike, it failed to resolve the conflict between labor and capital. When arbitration expired at the war's end, the struggle would resume. Similarly, if the entry of the government precluded an open split within the union ranks, it did little to reduce the tensions between radicals guiding the SLC and more cautious trade unionists.

In all likelihood, the presence of the radical faction within the SLC facilitated federal intervention. From the start of the campaign, Foster, Johnstone, and other militants sought to develop the threat of a strike, fully intending to use that weapon if the packing companies continued to refuse to redress workers' grievances. This aggressive posture not only signaled to the mediation commission the seriousness of the situation in Chicago, it helped more conservative union leaders convince the packers to submit to arbitration. The existence of both syndicalist-oriented radicals and moderate unionists within the SLC improved labor's position in its confrontation with state power. The relationship between the two groups was not entirely antagonistic either; in many ways it was mutually beneficial. The established trade unions profited from the agitation of the radicals, rebuilding their own organizations and enhancing their own stature and power. Likewise, syndicalists profited from the cover of legitimacy provided by their affiliation with the CFL and their links with the AFL unions.

Despite their reservations, both Foster and Johnstone played active roles in the first round of arbitration. Throughout February 1918, Judge Samuel Alschuler listened to testimony offered by packinghouse workers and their families. Social workers and economists testified as well, but the spotlight remained fixed upon ordinary workers. "It was as if the characters in *The Jungle,* quickened into life, had come to tell their story from the witness chair," Foster wrote. Frank Walsh, the former director of the U.S. Commission on Industrial Relations, represented the union. In a brilliant performance, he established the justice of the union's demands and demonstrated the packers' ability to meet the increased costs. The hearings received considerable media attention. One typical headline screamed "LIFE'S HARDSHIPS TOLD BY WOMEN OF STOCKYARDS: One Lived in Chicago Six Years, Never Saw Movie, Park, Nor Lake Michigan." Attorneys for the packing companies attempted to defend their labor practices, but the evidence overwhelmed their arguments and mocked their efforts to paint a picture of corporate benevolence.[36]

Three weeks after the hearings closed, Alschuler announced his decision. Hailed by Arthur Kampfert as "the Magna Carta for packinghouse workers," the award granted an eight-hour day, a forty-eight hour week, time and a quarter for overtime, the full dollar-a-week raise demanded by the union, a proportional increase for all piece-rate workers, and equal pay for men and women.[37] The reaction in Packingtown was celebratory. A large crowd assembled for a union-sponsored rally in Davis Park, directly across from the packing plants. "It's a new day," Fitzpatrick proclaimed to the interracial gathering. "Out in God's sunshine, you men and you women, black and white, have not only an eight hour day but you are on an equality."[38]

The arbitration decision boosted the union cause. Throughout the spring holdouts poured into the locals. Ida Glatt, an officer of the Women's Trade Union League, anticipated 100 percent organization in the near future. The union's secretaries, she reported, "do nothing but take in applications from morning to midnight." In a ten-month period the Amalgamated reported a doubling of its national membership. Even the normally pessimistic Foster sounded a bright note, writing to Walsh, "We are doing well here in the Yards. The organizations maintain themselves very good, in spite of the croakers who said they would fall to pieces as soon as the excitement died out. I think the foundations of unionism have been laid in the packinghouses for a long time to come." Beneath this confident surface, however, there were signs of trouble.[39]

The union hoped that federal mediation would lead to a contract with the packers. The employers, however, consistently blocked efforts at direct negotiations, refusing to meet with union representatives or even to sign arbitration agreements on the same piece of paper. Moreover, not all of Judge Alschuler's subsequent decisions were as favorable to the workers as his first. Additional wage increases were small and failed to keep pace with soaring inflation. Alschuler also rejected union demands for recognition, a shorter workweek, and double pay for overtime. Especially disheartening was his response to testimony detailing racial prejudice inside the plants. Having secured a weak commitment from the packers in the first round of hearings not to discriminate, the judge declined to rectify specific instances of inequity in hiring and promotion.[40]

The loyalty of black workers remained indispensable to the ultimate success of the organizing drive. The labor council went out of its way to demonstrate its willingness to defend blacks as equals. Union officials estimated that a disproportionate 40 percent of the grievances taken up by the SLC came from black workers. Blacks served alongside whites as stewards and committeemen in most major departments, and on a number of occasions white rank and filers took action to support their black co-workers. In one instance, a strike forced the removal of a foreman who had abused a black worker. There were some unprecedented steps toward social equality. At a union-sponsored ball, two thousand black and white workers and their partners mingled freely, although there were no mixed couples on the floor. Interracial picnics and social affairs similarly flouted the established racial mores.[41]

Very little is known about black union supporters in this period. As indicated above, most of the black workers who enrolled in the union were northerners who had been in the packinghouses for several years. Local 651 served as a focal point of activity for these unionists. It played an active role in the organizing drive, established a grocery cooperative, and helped launch the Colored Club of the Cook County Labor Party in early 1919. Still, the local was unstable, at least in comparison to its white counterparts. Monthly membership fluctuated wildly, peaking at three thousand but averaging below one thousand, suggesting that beyond a committed core most members were ambivalent about the union.[42]

On the killing floors and other departments where blacks were concentrated, rank-and-file leaders emerged. Yet, the shop-floor presence of black stewards must be treated carefully. In some of the larger plants white-dominated gangs elected blacks to lead them. On the beef kill at Wilson and Company, for instance, black unionists Frank Custer and Robert Bedford shared the stewards' responsibilities with two whites. Any one of the four men was empowered to represent the gang. But in other cases, rather than signifying interracial solidarity, black stewards represented an accommodation to Jim Crow. On the killing floor at G. H. Hammond, black stewards dealt only with black workers and their grievances. Walter Gorniak, the Polish steward, admitted, "I don't have anything to do with the colored men."[43]

Among their own race, black unionists were a minority. Their efforts often met with scorn and ridicule. "You are nothing but a lot of white folks' niggers, or you wouldn't be wearing that button," taunted one holdout. While white laborers returned from work each day to a community that was supportive of their cause and lived amongst fellow unionists, residential segregation meant that black workers were surrounded by people who shared neither their values nor their commitment to unionism as a vehicle for advancement. Their efforts to promote a class solidarity that crossed racial lines were often rejected outright or misunderstood as toadying up to whites. Journeying to work, black unionists encountered verbal harassment on the streetcars, and once in the plant had to contend with threats and intimidation. Foremen and straw bosses openly discriminated against black unionists, passing them up for promotion or refusing to let them work if they were late in reporting. Opposed by their own race, never fully accepted by white unionists, and targeted for reprisal by their employers, black unionists occupied a precarious and uncomfortable position.[44]

Conflicting loyalties to race and class pulled black packinghouse workers in different directions. Shared work experience and common grievances pushed them in the direction of an alliance with their white co-workers. On the other hand, the persistence of racial discrimination and the social dynamics of ghetto life produced a race consciousness that militated against making common cause with whites. The situation was markedly different for the white workers living Back-of-the-Yards. For them, ethnic and class loyalties were overlapping and easily reconciled. Religious and civic leaders tended to support the union drive, as did fraternal orders and recreational clubs. Part of a broad community mobilization, the union drive was embedded in the culture of Packingtown. Rather than weakening the bonds of class loyalty, ethnic identity reinforced it.[45]

Sharp differences between the proletarianization experience of blacks and whites help explain the black migrants' ambiguous response to unionization. In contrast to the experience of many of their white co-workers, the emergence of a black proletariat did not entail a fundamental loss of autonomy or de-skilling. Compared to sharecropping or domestic and personal service jobs in southern cities the movement of blacks into northern industries represented an upward thrust in economic status. The migrant's focal point for comparison was the world they left behind. The marked contrast between conditions in Chicago and those in the South blunted the appeal of unionism: if packinghouse jobs were dangerous, dirty, and exploitative, they nonetheless offered both respectable wages and the possibility of advancement.[46]

Aware of the union's strength among whites, the packers regarded the black workforce as the weak link in the union's armor. When the war ended and the buffer of arbitration was removed, whichever side commanded the loyalty of the black workforce would enjoy an incalculable advantage. Accordingly, the packing companies moved to draw blacks into their orbit. Possessing financial resources that dwarfed those of the union, they solidified their ties to the black community. Especially important in this regard were their links to two major ghetto institutions—the Urban League and the Wabash Avenue branch of the YMCA.

Founded in 1915, the Chicago branch of the National Urban League quickly became one of the more active chapters of the national organization. Responding to the black migrants flooding into the city, the league worked to smooth their transition from the rural South into an urban, industrial environment. It helped secure housing for the newcomers, as well as providing them with social workers and welfare counselors. Its primary function, however, was economic. Seizing upon the opportunity for racial advancement created by the severe labor shortage, the league tirelessly and successfully worked to convince area industrialists to hire blacks. It placed over twenty thousand black men and women in jobs between 1917 and the summer of 1919, when it took over the operation of the U.S. Employment Service's Black Belt office—in itself a measure of the league's importance to both the black community and Chicago industry.[47]

Although the league valued its independence and sought to remain on friendly terms with labor while assisting capital, its function as a recruiting agency and its financial dependence upon large corporations placed it firmly on the side of the employers. The league's social workers sought to cultivate model workers by instilling in them values associated with a capitalist work ethic—efficiency, punctuality, regularity, and thrift. Since the league's reputation depended upon the successful assimilation of black workers into the plants, its Industrial Bureau took great care in recommending for employment only workers that "fit the job" and who were not likely to cause trouble.[48]

The Urban League enjoyed a particularly close relationship with the packing companies. Contributions from Armour and Swift helped the league establish itself, and by 1919 a full 20 percent of the annual budget came from the Stockyards Community Clearing House—the welfare agency set up by the packers. Although some of the league's staff, including president T. Arnold Hill, privately sanctioned the campaign in the stockyards, the need to please benefactors prevented them from publicly expressing support. Other staff members, most notably Industrial Secretary William Evans, were implacable foes of unionism. Although one should bear in mind James Barrett's caveat against the assumption that league policies were determined solely by its relationship to the packers, it is difficult to escape his conclusion that "the packers clearly saw the organization as a way of undermining the unions."[49]

The South Side branch of the YMCA served the packers in a more blatant manner. Established in 1911 as the Jim Crow counterpart to the uptown YMCA, the Wabash Avenue building became one of the Black Belt's most important social and cultural institutions. Like the Urban League, the "Y" was heavily financed by Chicago area industrialists. After 1916, this support returned handsome dividends, as the YMCA turned increasingly toward industrial work. While its job placement service was more modest than the league's, it found employment for between fifty and one hundred men each month. Far more important, however, were the joint programs the YMCA sponsored with the packers for their employees.[50]

Many of these programs were recreational, such as the glee club organized through the Morris and Company plant in 1917. The immensely popular singing group drew crowds of four hundred and more to its performances. The YMCA also sponsored a baseball league in which teams like the "Armour Premiums," "Libby, McNeil Giants," and "Swift Star Lambs" competed. In an era when the major leagues were lily-white, these contests had enormous appeal in the black community. In 1919, the league played a full fifty-six game schedule which attracted over ten thousand fans. In addition to providing an outlet for pent-up energy, these kinds of activities fostered a sense of loyalty and identification with the employer. For these reasons, the packers boosted the Y among their employees, even allowing a representative of the organization access to the plants in order to sign up members. At Armour, as a way of encouraging participation, blacks received free membership in the Y after their first year of service.[51]

The centerpiece of the packers' efforts to use the YMCA as a weapon against the union was the Efficiency Club Program. The brainchild of the Y's executive secretary, A. L. Jackson, the clubs were organized at the same time as the formation of the SLC. They sponsored a series of educational forums dealing with such topics as "Electricity in the Yards" and "The Progress of the Negro in the Packing Industry." For a time workers received actual training in knife and butchering skills. Club meetings were well attended, with upwards of 250 workers present at each session. Foremen urged workers to participate and in some cases, an individual's work rating would be upgraded if he did so. The packers claimed the purpose of the clubs was to instill a sense of responsibility among members, but SLC officials charged that they were stridently anti-union. In testimony before Judge Alschuler, Jack Johnstone bluntly stated that workers attending club meetings were "taught the thing they have to do is keep out of organized labor." Others complained that the clubs were a kind of company union and were actively engaged in spying.[52]

The Wabash Avenue YMCA also promoted the American Unity Labor Union (AULU), a creation of Richard Parker, a Black Belt publisher, entrepreneur, and politico. Advertising himself as "the man who was always with his race right or wrong," Parker attempted to woo black packinghouse workers away from the SLC and into the AULU by appealing to their sense of racial pride. "GET A SQUARE DEAL WITH YOUR OWN RACE," one of his advertisements proclaimed. "Get together and stick together is the call of the Negro. Like all other races, make your own way; the other races have made unions for themselves. They are not going to give it to you just because you join his union. Make a union of your own race." Yet Parker's motives and the legitimacy of the AULU were suspect. His activities in 1916 on behalf of the packing companies and steel firms betrayed his motives. Traveling south as a labor agent, he boasted he had "imported more negroes than any man in Chicago." The AULU's ties with the YMCA raise further doubts about the union's legitimacy, as does the fact that AULU agents were allowed to recruit inside the packinghouses. Even if it offered no real competition with the SLC, its presence in the yards confused many workers. "BEWARE THE STOCKYARDS UNION," warned a handbill distributed by Parker, "DO NOT JOIN ANY WHITE MAN'S UNION." Intentionally or not, these kinds of activities played into the hands of the packers.[53]

The economic demobilization which followed the end of the war intensified the contest for the loyalty of black workers. The signing of the armistice placed the continuation of federal arbitration in doubt. No specific expiration date had been set, but both union leaders and the packers now anticipated the opening of a new stage in the struggle for power.

Peace in Europe rewrote the rules governing black employment in Chicago. The labor shortage that had opened job opportunities for black men and women became a labor surplus. Foreign orders for meat products fell off and repeated rounds of layoffs swept the packinghouses. Other areas of potential employment dried up as well. By January 1919, the situation had become desperate. Production remained sluggish, and returning servicemen augmented the continued flow of migrants into the labor pool. In a grim report to his superiors, one U.S. Employment Service official wrote, "for the past few days, there has not been a single vacant job in Chicago for a colored man." In early May, over ten thousand black laborers were searching for work, a figure representing 20 percent of the city's unskilled unemployed. In the short run, this situation worked in the packers' favor. Keenly aware that their color rendered them the most expendable group of workers, many blacks did not want to jeopardize their already precarious position by unionizing.[54]

Unemployment and uncertainty led to a heightening of racial friction, palpable throughout the city, especially in and around workplaces where blacks and whites competed for increasingly scarce jobs. "The relationship between the two races in certain industries where a large number of Negroes are employed such as the packing houses for instance is becoming increasingly delicate," noted a worried Department of Labor official in a letter to Fitzpatrick.[55] Fistfights broke out regularly in the charged atmosphere of the stockyards, and frequently these altercations escalated into brawls involving bricks, knives, and even guns. In May and June, already frayed nerves were set on edge with the well-reported news of race riots in Texas, South Carolina, and Washington, D.C.[56]

The SLC's decision to push forward with an aggressive campaign for 100 percent union membership in June 1919 did little to cool tempers. In fact, it had the opposite effect. A deal struck between the Amalgamated and the packing companies the previous month, however, left the council's leaders with few other options. Aware of considerable sentiment within the SLC for a showdown, the packers approached Secretary of Labor William Wilson and requested a one-year extension of federal arbitration and with it the no-strike agreement. Bypassing the SLC, which had resolved to conduct a referendum on the question of renewal, Wilson drew the Amalgamated into negotiations. Without referring the matter to its rank and file, and without consulting the other unions, the Amalgamated signed the accord. Predictably, SLC militants were furious and accused the meat cutters of selling them out. Foster termed the episode "one of the most shameful stories of betrayal in American labor history."[57]

Relations between AMC leaders and the SLC deteriorated rapidly. Given this bitter factionalism, it is remarkable that the union was able to consolidate its position and make further gains in the early summer of 1919. The key to its growing strength was the power exercised by informal groupings of workers within the packinghouses. While their leaders fought amongst themselves, shop-floor committees independent of the official apparatus repeatedly engaged in job actions designed to force the remaining holdouts into the union.

Typically, these actions began on the killing floors, where the perishable nature of the product gave workers additional leverage, and then spread to adjoining departments. Workers were precise in their demands, usually warning management in advance of their actions. At G. H. Hammond, for instance, the hog kill steward repeatedly demanded that the foreman either discharge the nonunion workers or require them to join. When he refused to intercede, the gang stopped work, leaving one hundred carcasses hanging from the rail. The stoppage quickly spread to other pork operations, idling nine hundred workers. On the Wilson beef kill, stewards posted a message on payday instructing everyone to wear a union button the following morning or be denied work. When nonunion workers assumed their places on the line, the gang began killing and dressing cattle, waiting until the chain was full before downing their tools.[58]

The committees orchestrating these actions were autonomous bodies. Work gangs elected and recalled their stewards directly. Although some of the more radical union leaders may have helped coordinate activity among different plants, most officials were only dimly aware of the existence of the shop-floor organizations. Bound by the arbitration agreement, they could not openly sanction the stoppages. For their part, many rank-and-file workers believed that the arbitration agreement was void. John Maldek, a floorsman at Wilson, curtly told Judge Alschuler that "the war is over, we can do as we please." Stewards who admitted to understanding that the agreement had been extended, defended the stoppages by referring to the democratic workings of the committees. Joseph Sobyro, a steward on Wilson's loading dock, explained that his power was limited to carrying out group decisions. His gang approached him with their demands and told him to communicate them to the foreman. When Alschuler asked Sobyro why he had not ordered the gang to return to work, he replied, "they all have got as much to say as I have."[59]

Since most of the holdouts against whom the stoppages were aimed were black, the 100 percent campaign further polarized the races. The packing companies manipulated this situation in order to exacerbate divisions among the workers. Management at Wilson, for example, responded to one stoppage by selecting nonunion blacks to take the places of the strikers. The company also brought a number of black workers to Chicago from its southern plants and directed them to agitate against the union.[60]

One of these workers, Austin "Heavy" Williams, served as a straw boss on the beef kill and a leader of the Wilson Efficiency Club. According to the department steward, Williams rarely worked. "He stands around and his principle [sic] job is when new men are hired to button-hole them and tell them to keep out of the union. His job is going downstairs to the employment office and bringing up men and he brings up all non-union men and keeps the non-union men from joining the union." Williams enjoyed considerable authority. As straw boss, he made job assignments and allowed workers relief for rest breaks. Co-workers charged that in return for small payments, he arranged for afternoons off and other favors. A talented speaker, Williams constantly preached against the union and frequently backed up his beliefs with his powerful fists. He did not act alone. Because of his size and stature, he was the most visible member of a group of about fifteen southern black workers who agitated on the killing floor against the union.[61]

In the spring and summer of 1919 several strikes attempted to neutralize "agitators" like Williams. Unionists complained that these men received preferential treatment and often employed violence in their anti-union campaign. One steward reported that his members were "afraid to work when they had their back turned toward [the nonunion men], for fear of getting a knife jabbed into them." One man was accused of throwing bricks at a group of Polish workers distributing union literature at the plant gate. Another worker, arrested for maiming a black unionist with an iron bar, received legal counsel from Wilson and Company's attorney. These activities added fuel to an increasingly volatile situation.[62]

As shop-floor tensions rose, union strategists faced a difficult dilemma. On the one hand, they considered the 100 percent campaign an essential measure. Given the uncertainties of continued arbitration, a strong organization seemed the best way to safeguard hard-won gains. Yet on the other hand, the campaign pitted white and black workers against each other, allowing the employers to exploit the resulting animosities. With no clear-cut solution, SLC leaders pressed forward while redoubling their efforts to promote racial harmony and understanding.

The high point of this program came in early July 1919. In an effort to bring black and white workers in contact with one another, the SLC planned a "giant stockyards celebration" to commence with an interracial parade winding its way through the Back-of-the-Yards, into the Black Belt, and on to the Beutner Playground at Thirty-third and LaSalle. The thought of such a public display of solidarity worried the packers, who succeeded in having the march banned on the grounds that it would provoke racial violence. Undaunted, the SLC held two separate parades, with black and white marchers joining together at the playground.[63]

Despite the interference, the mood of the marchers was upbeat. The packers' effort to quash the affair sharpened the issues and afforded an opportunity for rebuttal. One placard declared: "The bosses think that because we are of different color and different nationalities that we should fight each other. We are going to fool them and fight for a common cause— a square deal for all." Addressing the crowd, which the CFL estimated at thirty thousand, Jack Johnstone reiterated this theme. "It does me good to see such a checkerboard crowd," he told the assembly. "The workers here are not standing apart in groups, one race huddled in one bunch, one nationality in another. You are all standing shoulder to shoulder as men, regardless of whether your face is white or black." The speakers who followed returned to this point time and again. Speaking in Polish, John Kilkulski urged racial cooperation and respect. A black organizer, Charles Ford, pointedly remarked, "You notice there ain't no Jim Crow cars here today," and went on to outline his hope for a future democracy that drew no color line.[64]

In light of the racial status quo, this assembly of thousands of black and white workers was remarkable. Union leaders were jubilant, believing a major barrier had been surmounted. "If the colored packinghouse worker doesn't come into the union, it isn't the fault of the Stock Yards Labor Council," editorialized the *New Majority*. Subsequent events seemed to bear out this confidence, as the buoyant mood generated by the celebration translated into concrete organizational gains among the previously aloof black workforce. When the packing companies responded to these advances by directing their special police to break up crowds in the yards and harass organizers, a strike of ten thousand workers forced the withdrawal of the "Cossack Patrol." For a brief moment, it appeared that Chicago's packinghouse workers were ushering in a new era of interracial unionism.[65]

The Chicago Race Riot

As it turned out, this optimism was misplaced. Under normal circumstances, the racial attitudes and prejudices of the past might have been overcome. But Chicago in the summer of 1919 was one of those places in time when "history came off its leash."[66] The race riot that broke out on 27 July extinguished any hope that black and white workers might close ranks behind a common purpose. The orgy of violence and its tragic aftermath not only sealed the fate of the SLC's organizing drive but also drove a wedge between the races that remained firmly in place until the mid-1930s.

The spark that ignited the riot occurred on the lakefront when a group of blacks attempted to gain access to a beach traditionally reserved for whites. A fight ensued, during which a young black boy, Eugene Williams, drowned after being struck by a rock thrown from the shore. As distorted rumors of the drowning and brawl spread through the city, a full-scale race war erupted. Five days later, twenty-three blacks and fifteen whites lay dead. Over five hundred other persons suffered serious injuries, and hundreds of homes were burned to the ground.[67]

Although the riot began several miles from the stockyards, much of the violence and bloodshed played itself out in the vicinity of the packing plants. This was largely due to the role played by Irish street gangs who saw the disorder as an opportunity to attack blacks with impunity. The official investigation of the riot concluded that without the gangs' wanton assaults, "it is doubtful if the riot would have gone beyond the first clash." Many of these gangs were based in Bridgeport, just east of the stockyards, and seem to have been associated with Ragen's Colts—an "athletic club" sponsored by Democratic alderman Frank Ragen. As black workers left the yards on the evening of 27 July, they were only vaguely aware of the disturbances raging in the city. Heading east toward their homes, many of these workers became the riot's first casualties. Enjoying a certain immunity because of their political connections, gang members boldly roamed the streets of the South Side, pulling blacks from streetcars and making occasional forays into the Black Belt itself. A fresh cycle of violence was initiated the following morning when black workers attempted to make their way to the yards.[68]

Unlike Bridgeport, Back-of-the-Yards remained relatively calm during the riot's initial stages. Most of the attacks that occurred here took place at the yard gates, and were committed by Irish gangs from the east. The immigrant community did not play a role in the violence; in a number of instances, Back-of-the-Yards residents interceded to protect blacks from pursuing mobs. This response can be attributed, at least in part, to the impact of unionization on the community. Since the start of the organizing campaign, SLC leaders had stressed the need for interracial solidarity. Judged by the response of the neighborhood to the riot, this principle appears to have taken hold.[69]

In dramatic contrast to the inflammatory rhetoric that filled the English-language press, the major Polish newspapers remained sober during the riot, consistently counseling restraint and caution. *Dziennik Zwiazkowy* even ran an article on African American history which concluded by asking rhetorically, "Is it not right they should hate whites?" *Glose Rabotnica,* a labor paper published by John Kilkulski, reminded its readers to keep their sights fixed on their true enemy, the packers, and hinted darkly that the employers had a hand in provoking the unrest. At a public meeting, Father Louis Grudzinski, a respected parish priest, termed the riot "the black pogrom" and appealed for calm. The Polish National Alliance and settlement house workers likewise labored to forestall bloodshed in the streets of Packingtown.[70]

The most important force working to preserve order during the riot was the Stockyards Labor Council, whose leaders recognized just how much was at stake. In a plea entitled "For White Men to Read," the *New Majority* implored union members to use their influence in the community to shield blacks from the frenzy of race prejudice. Portraying the riot as their movement's "acid test," the article explained that a critical juncture had been reached: "Right now it is going to be decided whether the colored workers are to continue to come into the labor movement or whether they are going to feel that they have been abandoned by it and lose confidence in it." That crucial question remained unresolved during the troubled days of early August. Anxious to preserve their strained ties with the black workforce, the SLC took the bold step of holding mass interracial meetings. Later, when it became impossible for blacks to reach the yards safely, the council organized relief for them and other victimized families.[71]

These efforts proved insufficient. A week after the start of the riot, a new crisis arose which widened the gulf between black and white packinghouse workers. Early in the morning of 2 August, arsonists torched forty-nine homes in a Lithuanian enclave located on the western edge of Back-of-the-Yards. Although the postriot investigation fixed the blame upon Irish gangs, rumors that vengeful blacks had committed the deed gained quick currency. Despite the improbability of blacks sneaking undetected into the area, the moderation that had prevailed in the neighborhood evaporated and was replaced with hatred and malice.[72]

Significantly, a new round of racial violence did not take place at this point. Still, the fire soured relations between white and black packinghouse workers. Something of the bitterness that swept the community appeared in a column printed in the conservative *Narod Polski,* the official Polish organ of the Catholic church. Comparing the race riot to anti-Semitic pogroms in Europe, the article implicitly sanctioned violent action against Jews and blacks, arguing that both groups were under Communist control. While extreme, this example nonetheless testifies to the change in mood and spirit occurring in the aftermath of the fire. Observing the growing rancor in the community, John Fitzpatrick lamented that the breach between the races had grown "so broad that it is almost impossible now to cement or bridge over."[73]

Up to this point, the packing companies had maintained a low profile. However, amidst the turmoil following the fire, the packers saw an opportunity to administer a mortal blow to the union movement. Declining to involve either Judge Alschuler or union representatives, they met secretly with city officials and proposed a plan whereby armed troops would escort black workers into the stockyards. Notified of this scheme just before its implementation, union leaders reacted in horror. "You must be insane to attempt such a thing," a delegation charged. "These men will be on the killing floor of the packing plants. They will have cleavers and knives. They know how to use them."[74]

Unmoved, the packers rejected an SLC alternative which would have established a closed shop and charged the union with responsibility for the conduct of its members. Anxious to avoid a bloodbath, the SLC reluctantly took a step away from interracial solidarity and called its members out on strike. On 8 August, black workers returned to the yards guarded by machine guns and fixed bayonets. A majority of whites stayed home, heeding the strike call and thereby forestalling what surely would have been an ugly coda to the recent riot. "We have worked day and night to keep this situation in hand," Fitzpatrick reminded the authorities, "not your police, not your soldiers . . . but the union men and women of the stockyards" have preserved the peace. This was to be the SLC's last hurrah. Its organizing campaign ground to an abrupt and permanent halt. To add final insult, six hundred strikers, including some blacks who remained loyal to the union, were discharged. Judge Alschuler upheld the firings on the ground that the workers had violated the no-strike clause in the agreement with the packers.[75]

The union movement unraveled during the following weeks. Despite some bold public displays of interracial goodwill in the yards, members began to slip away. Particularly hard hit was Local 651 which, decimated by defections, was kept alive only by the determined efforts of a handful of black activists. Prior to the riot, their task had been a difficult one; now it became virtually impossible to convince black workers to make common cause with whites. "If a thing can't help you when you need help, why have it?" one man reasoned, giving voice to the sentiments of hundreds of others. Many of the community institutions that previously offered lukewarm support now came out against organized labor. Others that had attempted to remain neutral now discarded their careful balancing act.[76]

Hastening the demise of the movement was the Amalgamated's decision to pull out of the Stockyards Labor Council and set up a rival body. Ordered to sever their connections with the SLC, the skilled butchers' locals complied while the mass units of common laborers remained committed to the council. This split arrayed skilled Irish and German butchers against unskilled Poles and Slavs. The ethnic cleavages of the past reappeared once again.[77]

Rising nativism within the Amalgamated helped provoke this split. The American officers of the AMC felt isolated from the foreign-born workers. Secretary Dennis Lane complained that he "could speak but one language—the American language—and [had] no chance whatever to be heard." Moreover, the system of proportional representation within the SLC insured the dominance of the unskilled, a fact which rankled many Irish and German butchers. The new body established by the Amalgamated, District Council 9, dispensed with this system, giving the craft elements control even though they comprised a numerical minority. The AMC capitulated to nativism in other ways, abandoning foreign-language columns in the *Butcher Workman*, adopting a "100% American" campaign, and amending its constitution to require all officers to hold U.S. citizenship. Further, while the hallmark of the SLC's campaign had been its appeal for interracial solidarity, the Amalgamated was more ambivalent on this crucial issue. Without pressure from the SLC, the AMC quickly backpedaled on its commitment to equality.[78]

The Amalgamated's action undermined the Stockyards Labor Council. For a short period, the two groups competed with each other while the CFL attempted to work out a compromise which would preserve some semblance of unity. This was a confusing period for workers in the yards who only dimly understood the issues underlying the factional fighting. Eventually, the Amalgamated prevailed over its rival—but only after it expelled over thirty thousand workers who refused to abandon the SLC, and then enlisted the support of the AFL's national office, which threatened to revoke the CFL's charter for failing to respect jurisdictional claims. By then the damage had been done.[79]

The Amalgamated paid dearly for its triumph. Having destroyed the SLC and, in the process, alienated itself from the CFL, the union now faced the daunting task of carrying on the stockyards campaign in isolation from the Chicago labor movement. The goal of 100 percent organization, within grasp a few months earlier, was now an impossibility. Membership tumbled while the union's treasury emptied at an even faster rate, suggesting a loss of confidence among dues-paying members. Disgusted with the Amalgamated, as many as four thousand die-hard unionists defected to the IWW's Food Workers. More ominous was the Amalgamated's total inability to organize black workers. An attempt to strengthen Local 651 resulted in a flurry of "hectic impotent activity" but no real gains. By 1921, the local—still the key to workers' power in the yards—contained only forty-nine paid-up members.[80]

As the Amalgamated disintegrated, the packers went on the offensive. They consolidated their ties to key institutions in the black community, took advantage of an economic recession in 1920–21 by selectively laying off shop-floor leaders, and instituted a system of employee representation designed to woo workers away from the union. This latter measure was part of a broader program of welfare capitalism which remained in place through the 1920s. All of the major packers established company unions in the period following the destruction of the SLC. Given various names— the Joint Representation Committee at Wilson, Employees' Representation Plan at Armour, and Employees' Benefit Association at Swift—these organizations marked a turn away from repression as a method of control and toward a more sophisticated ideological struggle. Through employee representation and other welfare measures, the packers sought to demonstrate not only that harmonious relations were possible but that workers' interests were linked with those of their employer.[81]

For two more years, the packing companies and the Amalgamated continued to submit disputes to arbitration. Judge Alschuler continued to adjudicate these matters impartially, frequently ruling in favor of the union. While this system helped the Amalgamated retain some influence in the packinghouses, it favored the employers in the long run by diluting the union's strength. This was made clear when the packers withdrew from the arbitration agreement in 1921, leaving the AMC without any shop-floor organization to which they could turn.

The final chapter came late in 1921, when the Amalgamated called its members out on strike in response to wage cuts imposed by the packers and ratified by the company unions. Lacking a firm base of support in the plants, and unable to count on the loyalty of the black workforce, the Amalgamated was hardly operating from a position of strength. Despite Dennis Lane's confident claim on the eve of the walkout that "tomorrow morning will see the packing establishments closed tight," the strike was ineffective. Less than a third of the workers heeded the initial strike call. Of the large packers, only Wilson was shut down.[82]

In the days that followed, the ranks of the strikers grew. Key departments in Armour and Swift joined the protest, and the Back-of-the-Yards community closed ranks behind the strikers. Donations rolled in, while religious and fraternal organizations voiced their support. Battles fought between crowds estimated at one hundred thousand and the police resulted in national headlines and the threat of federal troops. Nevertheless, the strike was doomed. Particularly damaging was the decision of the Teamsters and Elevated Engineers to cross the AMC's picket lines. Sweeping court injunctions further hindered the action.[83]

Ultimately, it was the ease with which the packers secured replacement workers that crippled the strike. Unemployment in Chicago had reached a five-year high in December of 1921, resulting in an ample supply of reserve labor. "Scouts" and "runners" for the packers positioned themselves at railroad stations, elevated platforms, saloons, and pool halls, sending hundreds of recruits to the yards each day. That at least half of these strikebreakers were black was not an accident but conscious design. As soon as the union issued its strike call, the packers set up an employment office in the heart of the Black Belt and arranged for transportation to and from the stockyards. As in 1904, this local pool was augmented by several thousand black southerners, brought to Chicago aboard special trains and carried through the gauntlet of angry strikers into the yards.[84]

While some black packinghouse workers stuck with the union, the great majority elected to remain at work during the strike. This decision was a pragmatic one, based on a careful weighing of options. Given the events of 1919, the jobs offered by the packers were more important than any potential benefits the union hoped to provide. For many other black workers with no previous experience in the packing industry, the strike was an opportunity for economic advancement. Even after the wage cuts, packinghouse employment paid far more than other jobs available to black laborers. Moreover, the community's leading institutions lined up with the packers. "Self-preservation is the first law of nature," declared the *Defender*, a theme echoed by the Urban League, which enthusiastically carried on its placement work during the strike. The black churches actively opposed the "white man's union" as well. On the Sunday before the strike, union representatives attended the fifteen most influential black churches. In all but one of these, ministers read a communication from the packers urging workers to disregard the strike. Several days later, when a black AMC organizer attempted to present an appeal to these same pastors, he was told they were attending a meeting called by Armour and Company.[85]

By Christmas, the mood in Packingtown was one of grim desperation.

The smoke billowing from the plants testified to the strike's waning strength. The Amalgamated began putting out peace feelers, sensing the futility of prolonging the conflict. When the packers stonewalled, the only remaining possibility for a settlement lay in federal mediation. In January, however, representatives of the Department of Labor advised the union to no longer hold out any hope for intervention. By the time the AMC's executive board met and conceded defeat, the strike had been dead for weeks and the packing plants were operating as open shops.[86]

In many ways, the true moment of defeat had occurred some two years earlier, when the race riot alienated the majority of black workers and the destruction of the Stockyards Labor Council fragmented the white labor movement. Rather than representing the climax to the organizing drive that began in 1917, the 1921 strike is best regarded as its epilogue. This is not to deny the historical importance of the strike. Rather, it is to suggest that its significance lies not with the events that preceded it but with those that followed on its heels. The memory of the 1921 debacle remained indelibly etched in the minds of Chicago's packinghouse workers for years to come. The experience of defeat was the critical reference point in forming subsequent responses to their employers, to workers of other races, and to future union appeals.

3

Chicago's Packinghouse Workers in the 1920s

Long after the Amalgamated Meat Cutters called off its strike in February of 1922, the memory of defeat remained vivid in the minds of packinghouse workers who struggled through that long, desperate winter. Stephan Janko remembered reporting for work at Armour and Company after it became clear that the cause was lost. "When we went back inside of that plant it wasn't like men. It was more like a bunch of poor dogs that had been whipped for forgettin' who the master was." A skilled butcher, Janko found himself at the mercy of a vengeful foreman who forced him to cart scraps at unskilled wages while a scab performed his job. "I never wanted to hear the word 'union' again in my life," he recalled, "and I never wanted to stick my neck out for nothing. Just wanted to work and take home my pay."[1]

In the same plant, Gertie Kamarczyk and her friends in the canning department returned to find scabs "on all the best jobs." Subject to relentless verbal abuse and powerless to stop the foreman's sexual harassment, she contemplated quitting. The needs of her fatherless family kept her on the job, but a deep-seated bitterness welled up within her. "I hated that job. I would wake up and start crying because I had to go into Armours." Kamarczyk did not hold black workers responsible for the collapse of the strike. Yet, neither did she believe that the racial unity which characterized the SLC was possible any longer. "We didn't understand why they went to work when we were out, and I guess they just couldn't trust the white people. . . . We lost the union because of that and I didn't think we was ever going to have one again, not with so many coloreds in there. I just thought I'd be slaving away at Armours till I died."[2]

Philip Weightman's experience differed markedly from that of Janko and Kamarczyk. A black hog butcher from St. Louis, Weightman enthusiastically embraced the union when organizing first began. A respected rank-and-file leader at a Swift subsidiary plant, he directed several work stoppages and earned a reputation for militancy. Yet during the 1921–22 strike, Weightman crossed the Amalgamated's picket line and remained on the job, his initial enthusiasm for the organization destroyed by the Jim Crow treatment he received at the hands of white members. The episode, he recalled, "destroyed my desire for unionism. I didn't want to see unionism coming or going. And somebody talk to me about a union, I'd almost call him a bastard or something." Soured on the prospect of making common cause with his fellow workers, Weightman sought security and protection by demonstrating an unswerving loyalty to his employer. He became active in the Swift company union, where his considerable organizational talents and boundless energy found an outlet in the departmental baseball teams that competed in the YMCA's Industrial League. "I was a company man in every sense of the word," he affirmed.[3]

Thousands of other packinghouse workers shared the frustration and disillusionment felt by these three individuals. The 1920s were lean years in Packingtown; and like Stephan Janko, many workers wanted only to put in their time, to make it through another day in the plant. Like Gertie Kamarczyk, countless workers clung to jobs they despised, having abandoned hope of obtaining any material improvement in conditions or wages. And like Phil Weightman, many workers decided that devotion to the company was more likely to lead to security than fidelity to a union.

Economic security, however, proved elusive. While the packing companies profited from a series of banner years, packinghouse workers contended with chronic insecurity and hardship. For them, the 1920s were hardly a prosperity decade. At a time when large sections of the working class in the United States supposedly enjoyed "unparalleled plenty," packinghouse workers saw their real wages decline and their working conditions deteriorate.[4]

The wage reductions that precipitated the 1921–22 strike were followed by successive rounds of smaller cuts, while the introduction of piecework in many departments further reduced workers' earnings. In 1929, average wage rates in the industry were actually 10 to 20 percent lower than at the start of the decade. Moreover, seasonal layoffs increased in both frequency and duration, affecting all but a few privileged workers. Decreased earnings and reduced employment obliterated the meager savings of many families and brought about an overriding concern with holding on to one's job at all costs.[5]

Discussing the periodic abeyance of working-class struggle, Richard Oestreicher reminds us that "what seems possible always limits a sense of what is just." In the stockyards during the twenties, the sense of possibility was very narrow indeed, forcing would-be activists to exercise cautious and pragmatic self-restraint. Except for a brief attempt in 1923–24 to revive the Stockyards Labor Council, unionism remained dormant in the stockyards.[6]

The packers believed that they had secured for themselves "a millennium of labor peace."[7] They could point to their employee representation plans and claim that their workers had repudiated adversarial unions in favor of a more cooperative approach. At the same time, they could hold up their new foremen-training programs or management-schooling courses and pronounce that labor relations had been placed upon an enlightened "scientific" footing. More darkly, they could candidly explain that the thousands of blacks working in the plants gave them a kind of "strike insurance" that made a repetition of past conflict unlikely. And still more ominously, they could quietly call attention to their private police forces, well-stocked arsenals, and network of informers and confidently assert that the balance of forces operated in their favor.

Yet, despite their intentions and efforts, the packing companies did not succeed in buying themselves more than a decade of labor peace, much less a millennium. Unionism resurfaced in the stockyards in the 1930s, at first haltingly in response to the encouragement afforded by the New Deal and later, when the CIO targeted the industry, with an unprecedented force and fury.

Despite their earlier protestations, Stephan Janko, Gertie Kamarczyk, and Philip Weightman all became involved in the CIO's Packinghouse Workers Organizing Committee (PWOC). Janko, who had vowed never again to stick his neck out, repeatedly risked his job in numerous confrontations with management as a steward in the Armour pork trim. Kamarczyk was more cautious. Like many white women, she joined the union at a relatively late date, having waited until it demonstrated its ability to protect members from management reprisal. Given his pronounced antipathy to unionism, Weightman's conversion was the most dramatic. Remaining a "company man" well after initial organizing activity began in the Swift plant, Weightman reevaluated his position after the company arbitrarily fired the man who had worked by his side for years. Shortly afterwards he approached suspicious union leaders, paid his dues, and requested six buttons. At a time when workers dared not make an open display of their union membership, Weightman reported for work with all six buttons affixed to his cap. No longer loyal to the company, he became, in his own words, "a belligerent, evil, cantankerous employee." He soon organized the rest of the hog kill, later emerged as a leader of the Swift local, and eventually rose to the position of vice-president of the United Packinghouse Workers of America.[8]

The roots of the working-class movement that culminated in the formation of the PWOC in the 1930s are located in the 1920s. The legacy of fear and racial hatred that originated with the collapse of the 1921 strike can be comprehended best by examining the way in which it affected workers in the years immediately following the defeat. In the 1920s new forces arose that contributed to the further fragmentation of the working class, notably the recomposition of the labor force and management's attempt to reform industrial relations through welfare capitalism. These developments influenced both the structure and character of the CIO movement in the stockyards. In the 1920s Chicago's packinghouse workers were more isolated from one another than ever before. However, their traditions of solidarity and militancy were not completely extinguished but persisted on a subterranean level, receiving nourishment from unexpected quarters.

Sources of Working-Class Fragmentation

The calamitous events of 1921–22 seemed to prove the packers' omnipotence. The defeat they inflicted upon the Amalgamated was so devastating that the union dared not venture into the stockyards for close to twenty years. Blamed for the destruction of the Stockyards Labor Council, denounced for calling an ill-timed and poorly conceived strike, and reviled for abandoning the strikers and their families in the depths of winter, the AMC had exhausted its credibility among packinghouse workers. "They considered that Denny Lane had sold them out," explained one veteran, "that had been a very bitter blow." A legacy of distrust had been created, and it proved tenacious and long-lived. A sociologist conducting fieldwork among Swift employees in the early 1950s found that when he mentioned the Amalgamated to the old-timers still laboring in the plant they invariably frowned and muttered, "No good, no good!" Had the Amalgamated attempted to recoup its losses and preserve a remnant of its shattered organization in 1922, it would not have fared well. As it was, the union retreated entirely from the packinghouses, as it had done in 1904, and clung to the more secure ground of the retail trade.[9]

Throughout the 1920s the packinghouses remained open-shop citadels. More than just the lingering memory of the strike and the lack of a credible organizational vehicle prevented a resurgence of unionism. Like other large employers throughout the country, the packing companies took steps to insure that nothing like the postwar labor upsurge occurred again. In a characteristic combination of consent and coercion, they attempted to win the allegiance of their employees through company unions and welfare benefits while they instilled fear through the blacklist and the stool pigeon.

Repression followed quickly after the 1922 defeat. Wholesale and indiscriminate firings of union activists occurred. "They cleaned out and fired anybody they could lay their hands to," recalled Jane March, "They just cleaned out every militant they knew." Cases of mistaken identity resulted in the blacklisting of innocent people. Stephan Janko lost several weeks of work when Armour discharged him for allegedly assaulting a foreman; he protested and eventually was reinstated. Few of the accused were so fortunate. Although some of those discharged by the large packers secured employment in the labor-hungry independent houses, most never again worked in the industry.[10]

These kinds of reprisals produced an atmosphere of intimidation that was augmented by the packers' private police force and the extensive system of spies operating within the plants. In addition to their regular watchmen, Armour employed more than three dozen special policemen. These officers developed a reputation for cruelty and capricious harassment. They operated out of a station located in the company's main building which they kept visibly stocked with tear gas, rifles, and sawed-off shotguns. At Wilson, workers remembered security personnel following them into the toilets and locker rooms to prevent clandestine meetings. Many of the taverns that surrounded the yards were known to be cased by company spies. Fear militated against collective action. Pat Balskus remembered that workers in her department would not speak to one another lest their private conversation raise suspicions. "People were scared," she said. "They were beaten down and weren't going to risk what little they had left. Armours and Swifts and Wilson, they just seemed too strong for the little people to stand up to."[11]

Perhaps the most important force contributing to working-class fragmentation in the 1920s was the continued influx of new workers into the meatpacking industry. Although total employment dropped by almost 25 percent during the decade, the labor force underwent a significant recomposition. Restrictive quotas prevented the renewal of eastern European immigration cut off by the war. Always in need of cheap labor, the pack-

ers continued to look to Chicago's expanding African American community for recruits, knowing that the wages they offered compared favorably
with other employment opportunities available to blacks. They also turned
to two other groups of workers—Mexican laborers and white women. The
work experience of each of these three groups differed significantly; their
impact on labor relations, however, was the same. In the short run, their
presence in the industry complicated the project of working-class unity and
exacerbated the tensions inherited from the earlier period of struggle.[12]

Chicago's black community continued to grow during the twenties. Although the migration of southerners into the city did not approach the levels of the late teens, neither did it abate. Between 1920 and 1930, the city's
black population more than doubled, approaching the three hundred thousand mark by the end of the decade. Most of this increase was due to the
continued migration of southerners to the city whose name had become virtually synonymous with freedom and opportunity. For black laborers, one
of the more sought after opportunities remained a job in the stockyards.[13]

Many Chicago employers refused to hire blacks; other industrial firms
employed them only as custodians or janitors. The packers, in contrast, welcomed black workers. The wages they paid more than offset the unpleasant
conditions prevailing in the plants. While employment in the steel mills or
on the railroads offered comparable remuneration, only the packinghouses
offered the chance for occupational advancement. Lowell Washington, whose
father was a butcher at Swift and who later worked as a ham-boner himself,
poignantly remembered that "my dad worked hard but because of it we were
pretty well off . . . to be a top man at Swifts or Armours meant that you could
pay your bills, feed your family, have your kids in clothes and shoes, and
have more than a little bit of respect from your neighbors." He explained that
a black workingman could aspire to be a Pullman porter "but the next best
thing was to earn top dollar over in a packinghouse." Faced with persistent
and widespread occupational discrimination, blacks depended on the packing industry. Significant numbers of college-educated blacks, unable to secure professional-track jobs, turned to the stockyards for employment. There,
the "color of your skin didn't matter. Mattered just about everywhere else
but not in the packinghouses."[14]

The opportunities available to black workers in the stockyards were
real. While their numbers in the industry remained constant throughout the
decade, they made substantial gains in employment, moving into skilled
jobs previously beyond their reach. Whereas in 1920 fewer than one out of
four skilled workers was an African American, in 1930 more than a third
of the semiskilled and skilled segment of the labor force was black.[15]

These gains owed little to the packers' sense of equity and justice. They indicate instead the companies' continued commitment to the policy of divide and conquer that had served them so well in the past. Even if no longer manipulating racial tensions in an overt manner, the packers continued to exploit and benefit from the ill-will that existed between white and black workers in the yards. When Alma Herbst examined employment practices in the industry at the end of the decade, officials at a number of establishments candidly explained that they regarded blacks as a form of "strike insurance" which would "see them through" times of unrest. "We took the Negroes on as strikebreakers in 1921," one executive stated, "and have kept them in ever since in order to be prepared for any kind of outbreak."[16]

The promotion of black workers into positions previously reserved for whites was both an attempt to diffuse ethnic solidarity among skilled workers and a conscious effort to sow seeds of racial discord. Black occupational advancement occurred within a context of resentment and prejudice, especially on the killing floors, where large numbers of former strikebreakers labored.

In 1924 Jesse Vaughn went to work at Roberts and Oake. "At that time, them Poles wouldn't let you use no knife, not no blacks at that time," he recalled. Yet within a few years, Vaughn was trimming fat-backs, having been taught the essential knife skills by his foreman during lunch breaks. By the early thirties, he had advanced to the highly paid position of hamboner. Whites resented both him and the foreman but were powerless to interfere. Elsewhere, the promotion of blacks occasioned outbursts of anger which accentuated the cleavage between the races. At times these flare-ups became violent. Elmer Thomas, who began working on the Swift sheep kill in 1927, remembered that when foremen moved to upgrade black workers, "white men on the floor didn't like to see it. They'd do almost anything to keep them from learning, throw anything they could lay hands on at them, knives, sheep-fat, cups, punches—that's tools we work with—anything." Crawford Love, an Armour worker, recalled that management intentionally fueled this kind of opposition. Whites "had been told by the company that if we were allowed to become skilled they would lose their jobs to us."[17]

In addition to physical abuse, aspiring black butchers had to contend with isolation and ostracism. Robert Jenkins, who had come to Chicago from Texas shortly before the 1921 strike, displayed a dogged determination to master the knife. One of three black butchers in the gang, he endured all sorts of mistreatment from the whites around him. "They wouldn't talk to him, they wouldn't look at him, they would try to make his job as hard

as they could. Dull his knives, refuse to spell him . . . but he kept at it."
White workers who assisted blacks were subject to the same sort of cold
shoulder. John Wrublewski made the mistake of helping an older black
worker with a particularly heavy assignment soon after he began his employment. "Well, next thing I know, the rest of the guys aren't talking to
me or nothing. Seems he scabbed during their big strike or something. Now
how was I to know any of that, just coming on and from another city? . . .
Finally, someone took me aside and explained and that was that. I mean
that's how things were at that time."[18]

Black workers did not enjoy limitless opportunity in Chicago's packinghouses. While they moved up the job ladder on the killing floors, other
departments remained lily-white. This was especially true of the cleaner,
lighter, and hence more desirable jobs. Scaling and checking, which in many
ways had more in common with white-collar office labor than production
work, remained beyond the reach of blacks. The female-dominated sliced-
bacon and oleomargarine rooms, for example, were strictly off limits. "They
wouldn't take a Negro girl if she was a college graduate," explained Mary
Hammond, "that's too good to give a colored girl." The packers may have
been bowing to prevailing racial attitudes here. The sliced-bacon department was a regular stop on visitor's tours; and the packers believed that
guests might take offense at the sight of blacks handling food that whites
later would eat. In some areas, the color bar was completely arbitrary; in
others employment followed lines of caste—the company hired light-
skinned blacks but turned away darker ones.[19]

Racial discrimination assumed other forms as well. When fluctuations
in livestock supply necessitated layoffs, black workers were the first to be
let go. Black stars marked their time cards so that foremen could easily and
quickly identify them when the call came to reduce the size of the gang.
On some jobs, blacks received less pay than whites in identical positions;
and taken as a group blacks lagged well behind whites in earnings. Although significant numbers of black men became floorsmen, splitters, and
ham-boners, none advanced into supervisory positions. Blacks dressed in
segregated locker rooms, often at a distance from their work departments,
which were inferior to the facilities used by white workers. Often they were
unheated in winter, lacked running water, and were infested with rats and
cockroaches. These practices divided workers from one another and reinforced mutual antagonisms.[20]

In comparison, Mexican workers had far fewer opportunities to advance up the job ladder. The most recent arrivals, they occupied the bottom rungs. Their language isolated them from both blacks and whites, and

the small Mexican community proved largely unable to provide the institutions that helped sustain earlier immigrant groups when they first settled in the shadow of the stockyards. The majority of Mexicans were single men who had made their way to Chicago as contract laborers on the railroads or as migrant harvest hands. Most had been in the United States for less than five years. Their initial break into heavy industry came during the 1919 steel strike, and the South Side mills continued to provide their single most important source of employment well into the 1940s. The packing companies first turned to Mexican labor during the 1921 strike, but the number of Mexican strikebreakers was negligible.[21]

Unlike the unskilled laborers whom the packers recruited from previous immigrant groups, many Mexicans who reached Chicago in the twenties had experience in the packinghouses of Omaha and Kansas City. This fact, coupled with the location of their community immediately to the south and west of the packinghouses, helps explain the steady growth of Mexican employment in the industry. By the middle of the decade, Mexicans comprised 5 percent of the workforce at Swift and Armour and 3 percent at Wilson. With few exceptions they held the least desirable jobs, working in the hide cellars, freezers, glue houses, and fertilizer departments. They received few promotions and the wages they earned were among the lowest in the yards. Like black workers, Mexicans felt the effects of white prejudice and discrimination. They suffered at the hands of racist foremen, many of whom felt that their dark complexions made them "Spanish niggers." Jesse Perez, a beef lugger at Swift, told a WPA interviewer, "The bosses in the yards never treat Mexican worker same as rest." Yet, because as a group Mexicans did not figure into the packers' divide-and-conquer labor policy, they were not encouraged to advance into skilled knife jobs. Arguably, they formed the most exploited segment of the packinghouse workforce.[22]

Much of the hostility that white workers directed at the Mexicans arose not as a result of job competition or past strikebreaking but out of tensions within the community. The Mexican enclave, centered around Forty-fifth and Ashland, grew steadily until it numbered around three thousand persons at the end of the decade. This expansion brought Mexicans in conflict with their neighbors as they sought access to housing, commercial space, and community services. Rather than ameliorate tensions, shared Catholicism actually exacerbated conflict. Many churches refused to admit Mexicans; and parishes were uninterested in establishing facilities for the Mexicans, whose style of worship they disdained. "Prejudice against them was quite, quite bitter," admitted Father Vito Mikolaitis of the Lithuanian Holy Cross Church.[23]

The Mexicans' appearance and language set them apart from other immigrant groups and made them easy targets for bigotry. Violent clashes between Mexicans and Polish youths occurred regularly. "Practically every Saturday, if you didn't kill one or two Mexicans, you sent them to the hospital," recalled one Packingtown resident with only slight exaggeration. Encarnacion Chico, one of the first Mexicans to settle in the area in the 1920s, remembered learning to avoid the alleys and dimly lit streets where whites waited in ambush for "spics" and "greasers." Compounding the problem was the indifference of the largely Irish police force to the Mexicans' plight.[24]

Mexicans responded to adversity by turning inward and drawing upon their own networks and resources. Many men secured employment in the yards through the intercession of relatives already working there. A modified *padrone* system functioned in which groups of Mexicans, headed by a gang leader, approached the packers and sought employment. Unlike the European immigrants, large numbers of Mexicans periodically returned home. Thus a common response to a foreman's abuse, long layoff, or disagreeable work assignment was simply to pack up and leave.[25]

Although their alien status shut them out of politics and the protection offered by patronage and the Democratic machine, Mexicans tended to be more left-leaning and politicized than other workers. Many of the older men experienced the Mexican revolution and had been influenced by the radically democratic campaigns of Zapata and Villa. Organizationally, a high proportion of Mexican workers were active in the Chicago affiliate of the Confederación de Trabajadores—a fact that seems to have escaped the careful surveillance of the packers; and a strong egalitarian, anticlerical tradition flourished in the community. These traditions helped sustain the Mexican colony in Packingtown while nourishing the legacy of labor militancy and struggle.[26]

The entry of large numbers of women into the packinghouse workforce in the 1920s largely resulted from new immigration laws which curtailed the flow of Europeans into the United States. By drastically reducing the number of single immigrant men, restrictive legislation led to the collapse of the boarding system, formerly the most important way in which women contributed to the household economy. In order to compensate for this loss of income, many families released wives and daughters to wage labor in the packinghouses. Other women, particularly first-generation Americans, entered the yards in order to gain a measure of financial independence and freedom from the restrictive ethnic household. Still others turned to the packing plants in order to help their families survive some hardship or financial calamity. When Lottie Kamarczyk's father was injured on the job, she left school and went into Armour's smoked meat department. Initially, she thought her career as a packinghouse worker would be temporary. As it turned out, she remained a wage laborer for thirty-two years.[27]

For many female workers, packinghouse employment was a last resort—something to fall back on when no other opportunities panned out. It carried with it a certain stigma, especially for married women whose husbands' income failed to support the family. "You were kind of ashamed of working in the yards," remembered Estelle Zabritski. Both she and Mary Hammond observed that many women lied about where they worked, even to other packinghouse employees. "But you always know they're lying," Zabritski pointed out, "because their fingernails are cracked and broken." However, the situation was markedly different for the small number of black women in the yards at this time. Although confined to departments like casings—"the nastiest, most evil, kind of work you could imagine"— black women entered the workforce with very different expectations than whites. As with black men, packinghouse work was prized employment, and black women tended to remain in the plants for much longer periods than whites.[28]

Mechanization and the continued subdivision of labor opened many jobs to women. On the killing floors, for instance, women worked scraping lard, tying intestines, washing and shrouding carcasses, and exposing organs for government inspection. This was unskilled labor; and women received several cents an hour less than men on the same jobs. In the trimming departments, the work available to women required more skill and paid better wages—although the gender differential was just as great. Most women, however, worked in departments where the only men were supervisors or occasional laborers. In the sausage department, for example, women prepared the casing, stuffed the sausage, linked the individual pieces, and packaged the finished product. Men carted meat scraps into the sausage room, filled the hopper of the chopping machine, and trucked away the wrapped packages. Likewise, men operated the machinery in the sliced bacon department, but women packaged, weighed, and wrapped the product.[29]

Generally paid for piecework, women in these female departments earned more than those working alongside men on the killing floors. Although a very few took home paychecks that almost equaled those of highly skilled males, most women did not earn enough to support their families. A 1928 survey found that nearly half of the women in the industry belonged to families with two or more wage earners in meatpacking. More-

over, a full three-quarters of these families had all their wage earners toil-
ing in the packinghouses. Although work itself was relatively light in female departments, the speed and intensity with which it was carried out
created considerable stress. Anna Novak remarked how older women
"would be so gray in the face after a day's work, almost dead-looking. They
have to sit down there on the floor and rest for half an hour after work
before they have the strength to get up and go home." When the foreman's
back was turned, younger women relieved their faltering elders but the
practice was a risky one and often resulted in punishment.[30]

Women were more insecure in their jobs than men. They suffered disproportionately from seasonal layoffs—80 percent of those included in the
1928 study had lost some time during the previous year; and almost a third
of those surveyed had been laid off for twenty-seven weeks or more. "All
the time, I mean all the time you just lived in fear that the boss was going
to decide that it was your turn," recalled one worker. "I don't think there
was a day that I didn't go into there thinking 'I hope there's no layoff, I hope
it's not me that gets it.'" Little protection was available. In some departments, women attempted to rationalize employment. "We take turns stay-
ing home a couple of days," a worker explained. "We've got a pretty good
gang and we hate to see anyone get laid off, so the bosses and us fix it up
by ourselves." Most women had little choice other than to accept employment fluctuations as "just part of the job," and hope for a recall notice.
Pregnancy compounded the problem of job security for women. Most of
the packing companies routinely discharged pregnant women. With no
provisions for maternity leave, many women attempted to disguise their
pregnancy as long as possible, often leading to medical complications,
miscarriages, and even death. Another policy instituted in the 1920s imposed an age limit of thirty on new female employees. Although this was
unevenly enforced, it served as a rationale for the companies' refusal to
recall middle-aged women from layoff.[31]

The packing companies' turn to female and Mexican labor further fragmented a workforce already deeply divided by race. Since women tended
to be grouped together in certain departments, they were isolated from contact with other kinds of workers; they faced special problems and pressures
which further distinguished them from males. Although Mexicans labored
alongside white ethnics and blacks, their language and culture isolated them
from the rest of the workforce. Hostility stemming from their relations to the
Back-of-the-Yards community created another formidable obstacle to their
integration. Yet, both of these new groups developed collective means of

coping with the burdens imposed by wage labor. In their own ways, they resisted exploitation and developed strategies for survival.

Reform from Above: Welfare Capitalism in the 1920s

The large packing firms joined the most progressive segment of American business in advancing a new variety of welfare capitalism in the 1920s.[32] As discussed previously, the packers first experimented with pension plans, stock ownership, and recreational activities earlier in the century. Initially, these programs were designed to win the loyalty of a narrow segment of the workforce—the elite butcher aristocracy whose skills remained essential to production, or the black workers whose reserve labor figured critically into the packers' calculations. In the twenties, a more ambitious program was put in place. It encompassed all hourly workers and, unlike the earlier effort, aimed to increase efficiency and productivity as well as inculcate a sense of allegiance to the employer. Far more complex than the modest programs that preceded it, welfare capitalism in the twenties had a contradictory impact upon labor relations.

Swift, the most paternalistic of the large packers, led the way, hiring industrial relations expert John Calder to design and implement programs for all of the company's eighteen plants. Armour and Wilson followed this lead, modeling their respective plans on Swift's. The creation of a joint Committee on Industrial Relations under the auspices of the Institute of American Meatpackers lent a certain degree of coordination to these efforts. Although the brands of welfare capitalism practiced by the large packers were not identical, they shared the same basic features: employee representation through company unions, a restructuring of work relations through wage incentive schemes and foreman training, and an expanded range of benefits and recreational activities designed to reduce turnover. Each of these areas merits investigation, for in each case reality differed significantly from capital's original intent.

In each plant, the company union functioned as the centerpiece of welfare capitalism. The packers hoped this institution would resolve shop-floor conflict, provide employees with a voice in management, and counter more threatening forms of workers' organization. In each department workers elected delegates who met regularly with an equal number of appointed management representatives in a "joint conference" or "assembly." The assembly oversaw company-sponsored recreational activities, attended to its own procedures and elections, and, most importantly, considered griev-ances brought to its attention by disgruntled workers.[33]

Most of these cases concerned wage adjustments, disputes with fore-men, and working conditions. Hearing between five hundred and eight hundred cases a year, the conference decided in favor of the employee in three-quarters of the disputes.[34] This surprising figure prompts one to ques-tion both the nature of grievances which found their way from the shop floor to the conference board as well as the kinds of workers elected to serve as representatives. At least half of the cases heard by the board involved relatively trivial matters. Wage adjustments often referred to instances in which a workers' paycheck was short a few cents, a frequent occurrence for those performing piecework in which complex calculations were re-quired. The far more important question of wage rates was outside the board's jurisdiction.[35]

Other cases concerning safety, recreation, and food service posed little threat to power relations in the plant and could safely be decided in favor of the employee. "I could have asked for a new towel, or for some new soap in the wash basin," one worker recalled, but "if I would have asked for a raise would I have gotten that?" Moreover, at both Armour and Swift, plant superintendents exercised veto power over the board's rulings, making it unlikely that matters of substance would be decided as a result of the griev-ance process. At Wilson, the grievance mechanism was a transparent sham. Soon after going to work in the plant, John Wrublewski appealed a two-day suspension received for "sassing" his foreman. Nothing was done. When he pressed the matter, his representative shrugged, saying "we can't have workers bossing the bosses now can we?"[36]

At the other end of the spectrum were those cases in which the griev-ance system upheld management's authority. Here the involvement of workers' representatives often helped legitimate unpopular policies and diffuse resentment. When women in Armour's canning department asked for rubber mats upon which to stand, their representative reported back that "the company couldn't afford mats but they would consider putting out some rags and old papers." Workers realized that this pecuniary ratio-nale was preposterous, but in the weeks that had elapsed "the matter just kind of died." By handling grievances on an individual rather than a col-lective basis, the system served to isolate workers from one another. Plainly the company union never served as any kind of bargaining agent, even if it could act within the joint council as a workers' advocate.

How individual representatives in the company unions voted in these matters is not known, but workers who served in this capacity tended to be older, male, skilled employees with a demonstrated loyalty to the company. A majority of the representatives were native-born; and those who immigrated hailed from Ireland, Canada, or Germany. Numerous restrictions on eligibility—including U.S. citizenship and fluency in English—ensured that few Poles or Slavs served as delegates. Other workers, whose loyalty was suspect, were prevented from serving by bureaucratic subterfuge or outright prohibition. Describing these delegates, one Armour manager stated that the company "picked out and selected people throughout the plant who were . . . respected." Workers elected their representatives, "but they had to be agreed upon by management," thus ensuring that "hotheads" and troublemakers remained out of positions of authority. Moreover, the packers coached delegates about the limits of their responsibilities. Swift warned representatives that although workers looked to them for protection, "be careful not to embarrass both the Assembly and management by exceeding your authority or by creating false expectations in the minds of employes."[37]

Black workers were especially active in company unions. They, too, tended to be older men who wielded considerable influence in their community. "Big" Mitchell, the representative from the Armour pork trim, was a respected churchman who had worked for the company since 1916. Sometimes the company cultivated these black delegates. Lowell Washington, who remained at work during the 1921–22 strike and made no effort to disguise his aversion to "the white man's union," was repeatedly badgered by his foreman to run for office. Other blacks participated not so much out of loyalty to their employers but because, as one delegate explained, there was considerable "prejudy" against colored men in the unions while this was largely absent within company-sponsored representation schemes.[38]

The preponderance of "company men" involved in the employee representation plans turned many workers away from participation. C. H. Talley, the treasurer of Armour's Joint Conference Board, also held a position in the company's credit union where he reviewed workers' applications for loans. Since he was intensely disliked, his very presence on the board discredited it. Les Orear recalled that workers had no real links with their divisional representatives and regarded the Armour setup as a joke. "These guys were just like professional employee representatives. They never worked. They had nominal jobs but they wandered the plant in their white coats." Many workers refused to have anything to do with the company unions, even when subject to punishment or fines for refusing to vote in elections. Although the companies claimed that over 80 percent of their employees were active members, many workers participated under duress.

The weekly ten-cent dues payment was "like a bribe," recalled Milt Norman, and often was extracted under threat of layoff.[39]

Although the employers heralded the company unions as "new institutions of freedom" which would render obsolete the "old aristocracy of unionism," most packinghouse workers placed little stock in them.[40] While on the surface their structure appeared democratic, in reality they were not very representative and possessed a limited ability to meet workers' needs. However, employee representation was not inconsequential. Although lacking independent power or authority, company unions exerted an important influence upon workers' lives. Beyond their limited ability to secure on-the-job improvements, they gave many future CIO activists their first organizational experience, providing them with practical training in parliamentary procedure, grievance writing, and bargaining. Organized on an industrial rather than craft basis, these bodies had the unintended consequence of bringing workers together across the salient divisions of occupation, skill, ethnicity, and race. In the short run, such unions may have contributed to the maintenance of capital's hegemony; in the long term they functioned as foils for bona fide unionism and as "schools" for workers.

The second element of the packing companies' welfare capitalism, the restructuring of work relations, had greater impact upon workers' lives. Here the rise of personnel departments and the introduction of wage incentives changed the nature of labor in many departments. Again, the actual results of these reforms were vastly different from those anticipated by the packers. Centralized hiring offices and training programs might have reduced the power of foremen, but they continued to dominate the shop floor. "Fitting the worker to the job" sounded good in the companies' annual reports, but meant little when most jobs were interchangeable and when fluctuating production levels necessitated frequent layoffs. Bonus plans might have enticed some workers to labor more diligently, but they allowed very few of them to take home larger paychecks. Instead of creating a community of interest, they produced confusion, discord, and resentment.

These attempts to rationalize labor policy resulted from management's realization that past unrest stemmed largely from workers' resentment over the treatment they received at the hands of immediate superiors. By standardizing jobs and wages and by investing control of hiring and firing in centralized personnel departments, the packers hoped to improve the way in which workers experienced company authority. While the near total autonomy exercised by foremen was necessary during the earlier struggle to deprive skilled craftsmen of control over production, it now jeopardized the company's hold over its employees. Accordingly, special training programs designed to sensitize supervisors to the "human factor" when handling workers and to familiarize them with the "executive viewpoint" were instituted. At the same time, trained engineers armed with stopwatches and slide rules began making many of the production decisions previously determined by departmental foremen.[41]

Yet the policies formulated by the "I-R" specialists rarely translated into rational, scientific practice in the rough-and-tumble world of the shop floor. Despite the training programs and development courses, foremanship largely remained a matter of brawn. The selection of straw bosses and foremen "wasn't really what you call a corporate operation," recalled one worker. "It was just who was the toughest guy down there." Tommy Megan, a kill floor foreman at a Swift subsidiary plant, thought that the pamphlets and guidelines that the company gave him were "a load of crap. . . . You knew how to get the job done because you'd been out there yourself, you'd come up through the ranks, not because some book said to do it one way and not the other." Many foremen resented the intrusions of college-educated time-study engineers and ignored the "eggheads" who "knew how to make numbers dance but couldn't tell a steer from a sow."[42]

The "foreman's empire" did not collapse in the face of reform. In the key areas of hiring, firing, and promotion, departmental foremen continued to wield significant power. As far as hiring was concerned, two parallel processes emerged. The centralized employment office managed the daily "shape up," selecting common labor from the morning crowd of job seekers and assigning the hirees to departments in need of additional hands. Although the packing companies devoted considerable lip service to the use of employment specialists and the need to distribute proper "types" of workers in the labor force, the hiring of casual labor remained a simple matter of physically sizing up the potential recruits. Typically, the employment manager tapped an applicant's chest, felt his muscles, and even checked his teeth. "You'd think he was buying a horse," one worker recalled.[43]

Since foremen were more likely to reside Back-of-the-Yards than white-collar specialists, they continued to play the major role in hiring. Their personal contacts among packinghouse workers were a far more valuable resource than the files of the employment manager. This was especially true for skilled labor. When Tommy Megan's gang was short, he would send a runner to the homes of neighbors and relatives whom he knew would appreciate the opportunity to fill in. Moreover, many workers hired through the personnel office gained entry there by waving a recommendation from a foreman or by referring to him by name.[44]

Job security and promotion were equally dependent upon the goodwill of the foreman, even though company policy supposedly dictated such matters. Favoritism did not decline in the 1920s; foremen continued to reward those workers they liked and to penalize those whom they did not. Armour workers commonly referred to "half-pint" seniority, "On all the holidays, Christmas, Easter, Holy Week, Good Friday, you'd see the men coming to work with their pockets bulging and taking the foremen off in corners, handing over their half pints. Your job wasn't worth much if you didn't observe the holiday custom." At other times of the year a cigar, a cash bribe, or other gift often meant the difference between work and layoff.[45]

Women contended with another kind of pressure; their accounts are filled with stories about unwanted sexual advances and the threats which followed their rejection. "You could get along swell if you let the boss slap you on the behind and feel you up," grumbled Anna Novak. Married women were not immune from this kind of harassment. "They'd tell you you was going out with them, *tell you*," remembered Gertie Kamarczyk. "And if you didn't, they'd make it rough . . . they'd put you on a tough job, or they wouldn't let you leave to go to the john, or they would fool with your pay. . . . What could you do? They was the boss, the union was gone, we were scared and needed those jobs so bad."[46]

An important change in packinghouse work that occurred in the 1920s was the introduction of wage incentive schemes in almost all of the Chicago plants. Each of the large houses and several of the independents replaced straight time and piecework remuneration with some kind of bonus system. At first a number of methods were employed—"Manchester Piecework," "the Halsey Premium," "Taylor Differential Piecework," "the Task-and-Bonus Plan"—each of which involved the calculation, using time motion studies, of an hourly standard for each job. Workers who exceeded the standard received a weekly cash bonus tied to their individual production. By the end of the decade, however, the system devised by French industrial engineer Charles Bedaux had been universally adopted.[47]

The Bedaux system reduced each job to a unit termed a "B"—the amount of work performed in one minute by a normally skilled operator working under normal conditions at his normal rate of speed. A B value then was assigned to each job, with sixty B's established as the normal amount of work per hour. While workers continued to earn their base hourly wage, they received a premium if their production during eight hours exceeded 480 B's. At the end of the week, each employee received two paychecks—one for straight time and another which reflected 75 percent of the bonus. The other 25 percent went to the company, which, in turn, shared its gain with the worker's foreman.[48]

Within each plant, the Bedaux system was applied in different ways. Swift, the first packer to implement the system, was the most committed to it. All production workers stood to earn bonuses if they exceeded established rates. Armour initially followed Swift's example, but soon retreated, applying incentives only to those tasks originally performed on a piecework basis. Wilson did the same, although there the system was abandoned in 1929 on all but a few select jobs. The packers hoped that the incentive plans would simultaneously boost productivity and provide workers with a sense of investment in the company. They also expected that the lure of bonuses would break down group solidarity, discourage restriction of output, and isolate individual workers from one another. "When each worker is paid according to his record there is not the same community of interest," one executive frankly stated.[49]

To a certain extent, incentive systems encouraged competition between employees and pushed workers to increase their productivity. But such systems did not improve workers' self-image about their status as wage earners. Part of the problem stemmed from workers' difficulty in earning sizeable bonus payments. As production rates increased, management revised the standards downward. One study found that over 20 percent of workers in positions to earn premiums failed to do so, while 85 percent took home less than five dollars a week in bonus pay. Another study revealed that in many departments, net pay actually decreased after the introduction of the bonus system.[50]

Even when workers benefited from wage incentives, they rarely evinced an understanding of the complex calculations that determined the size of their payment. "I never could understand how it worked," admitted Porter Jackson, "I dunno how they actually figger it, those bonus hours. Because I know some men get a higher bonus 'n another 'n for doin' the same job." Some employers tried to explain how they arrived at the incentive, but the complex calculations were beyond the limited mathematical abilities of most workers. Thus, instead of recognizing a correlation between exertion and remuneration, workers regarded bonus pay as a fickle and unpredictable occurrence which "seems to rain upon them as a gift from the gods." Bill Voorhis put it this way: "the bonus is like playing the horses. You work hard an' you expect him. You get nothing. You work easy. You get a lot." Another mystified worker concluded simply, "you get just what the bosses want you to have."[51]

Like piecework, wage incentive plans could have a deleterious effect upon group solidarity. Complaints about cutthroat competitiveness abound in workers' testimony. Marian Simmons, who experienced the incentive system in a Kansas City packinghouse, recounted that women in the casings department remained at their stations when their menstrual periods arrived, working in feverish pursuit of the bonus while blood ran down their legs. Philip Weightman recalled that workers trimming pork scraps at Swift often skirmished amongst themselves over choice pieces of meat. "One would reach over here for a big piece of meat that had a lot of lean on it, and another one would walk over and start fighting with the hook to get it." On numerous occasions, Weightman was called upon to break up these physical altercations.[52]

Yet not all workers became unabashed individualists. Instead they found collective ways to protect themselves from the system's excesses. In Swift's sliced bacon department, workers agreed not to exceed the limit of 144 packages per hour, even though larger bonuses beckoned. "A new girl would come in and the oldtimers would train her. They would help her out so that gradually by the end of a certain period of time she was doing the 144. But they would never let anyone go beyond the 144 packages," remembered Vicky Starr. When one "smart-aleck" newcomer attempted to break the limit, co-workers sabotaged her efforts by sending unusable scrap bacon to her station. "We took a loss just to show her," Starr recalled. Another Swift employee, Marie Dalton, held a favorable opinion of the Bedaux system but bowed to the pressure exerted by her fellow workers. "I don't want nobody mad at me," she explained. "I would rather have friendship than all the money."[53]

Every job had certain tricks and shortcuts which workers passed along to one another. When the time-study man entered the department, the shortcuts were left aside and extra, unnecessary motions added to the routine. On certain jobs, the calculation of the bonus involved weighing workers' buckets of trimmed meat. Here, cheating was widespread and often engaged in collectively—workers buried bones or gristle in the bottom of their pails "to make it come out on the heavy side." In some gangs, workers cooperated, storing extra meat that was used to stretch the output of slower workers so that everyone received the same pay. This kind of informal organization stemmed from workers' intimate knowledge of the production process. It was a defensive measure that did not subvert the system, or even challenge it. It did yield a sense of control and power, however circumscribed, that helped workers survive from day to day.[54]

The final element of the packing companies' welfare capitalism consisted of the various benefits and amenities provided to workers. Some of these were, in theory, available to all who desired them—medical care for work-place injuries, company credit unions, and an expanded range of recreational activities. Other benefits, such as vacations and pensions, were available only after certain service qualifications were met. Obviously these programs did not directly affect worker productivity. Whether inspired by a sense of noblesse oblige or a more calculating desire to woo workers away from their own institutions, they were designed to promote a feeling of loyalty to the company. In some cases this undoubtedly occurred, but as the packers soon discovered, allegiance to the company could coexist with allegiance to a host of other sources—family, church, ethnic community, or class. Many workers took advantage of company-sponsored benefits but at the same time continued their membership in fraternal orders, kept up their insurance policies, and retained their subscriptions to labor periodicals. Sensing the unreliability of their employers' programs, they hedged their bets, demonstrating a certain savvy while looking out for their families' welfare.[55]

The provision of health care provides a good example of the limited nature of benefits which encouraged workers to take a jaundiced view of welfare capitalism. Packinghouse work has always been among the most dangerous kinds of industrial labor, and injuries occurred daily in Chicago's packinghouses. Before the reforms of the 1920s, injured workers simply were sent home. Early in the decade, the large plants opened infirmaries and hired physicians and nurses to staff them. In addition to treating the cuts, bruises, and broken bones that resulted from on-the-job accidents, medical staff provided lunch hour talks on hygiene and diet, oversaw safety campaigns, and even made house calls.[56]

However, workers soon came to suspect and resent the ministrations of the company doctor. Lectures on health and nutrition often were tinged with nativist condescension toward ethnic cultures and foodways. While some distrust was borne out of old-world suspicion of modern science, many workers had good reason to avoid the company doctor. A negative health report, a slight heart murmur, or even the suspicion of tuberculosis could mean discharge.

Moreover, the quality of the care itself frequently left much to be desired. Armour workers nicknamed the plant infirmary the "butcher shop," and bemoaned the treatment provided there. "The doctors are lousy in that place," Jean Solter declared. "They don't give a hang about you. The girls always joke about the 'treatments' they give you. Got a headache? Here you are. White pill. Dizzy spell? Take a pink pill. Cold? Take an aspirin. Sore throat? Take an aspirin." More serious ailments rarely received adequate attention. Pulmonary and dermatological diseases were rampant in the yards and resulted from working conditions themselves. The dusty wool houses and fertilizer departments produced a kind of infectious brown lung; and hundreds of workers suffered from "pickle hands" and "hog itch," debilitating eczema-like conditions caused by constant contact with brine or entrails. Since they were unwilling to take preventive measures, the medical care the packers provided was inadequate. Workers recognized the hypocrisy involved. "If they really cared about us, they would have cleaned up some of the filthy hell holes in that plant. What good was a band-aid or an aspirin when I was standing up to my ankles in cold water, freezing half to death?" reasoned Laura Rutkowski.[57]

Of course, poor medical attention was better than none. Some workers benefited from the company infirmary, such as the man whose life was saved when a doctor revived him after a freak electrocution or (in a somewhat different vein) the woman who pilfered medicine for her sick child. Other programs had a similar effect. Loans from the company credit union helped some workers purchase homes or see their families through hard times, even as the burden of debt tied them more firmly to their employers. Likewise, company baseball teams gave some workers, especially African Americans, special recreational opportunity and the chance to wear "real uniforms that matched," even if that meant ceding leisure time to the employer and having his name emblazoned on their jerseys. Sometimes the trade-off was a minor one; at other times it involved greater compromise.[58]

By and large workers were cognizant of their employers' intention to "attach strings" to them through welfare programs. When they applied for a loan or bought into a pension plan, they did so in a calculating way. If welfare capitalism complicated the relationship between capital and labor, it also had unintended consequences. By instituting paid vacations and pensions for long-service employees, the packers planted in workers' minds the belief that they had a right to such benefits. This became especially clear in 1929 and afterwards when, responding to fiscal crisis, the companies abandoned many of the welfare programs they had proudly instituted and in so doing sharpened the edge of workers' bitterness.[59]

In her study of Chicago's mass production workers Lizabeth Cohen notes that welfare capitalism gave workers new reasons and methods for communicating with one another. Employer-sponsored activities engendered more than the "family feeling" that management intended. Such events could just as easily intensify collective identity as diffuse it. In meatpacking, where working-class fragmentation reached a level exceeding other industries, welfare capitalism ironically provided vehicles that could point in the direction of unity. Company-sponsored glee clubs, sports teams and social clubs provided packinghouse workers with a bit of common ground upon which they could come together across lines of ethnicity and race.[60]

The very existence of company unions, ineffectual as they were, prompted workers to think about the shape that bona fide unionism might assume. Later, in imagining the form their own collective institutions might take, workers discovered that the major lesson to emerge from the 1921–22 defeat was the overriding need for interracial solidarity. Regardless of their racial attitudes or inherited prejudices, they realized that a divided movement stood little chance of success against the packers. Gertie Kamarczyk explained there was a "kind of feeling that we just had to work together . . . or the bosses were just gonna let us have it in the neck again." Joe Zabritski, who worked at Reliable Packing in the early 1930s, recalled that the old-timers, including many blacklisted veterans of past struggles, resigned themselves to including blacks in the new campaign. "They didn't come in and hug 'em and kiss 'em," he quickly admitted. "But they knew they had to be together, period. Even though some of them were anti-negro, they still knew you had to be together to form a union and to win some of their demands." Thus, while the defeat of the AMC resulted in a legacy of fear and distrust, it also spelled the end of exclusionary, craft-based unionism in the stockyards.[61]

The packing companies' policy of placing black workers in strategic departments and advancing them into skilled positions rebounded against them. Unlike the black migrants who were newcomers to the yards in the 1917–22 period, the blacks who labored alongside whites at the close of the decade were seasoned packinghouse veterans. The grievances they shared with other workers provided the most important common ground for the movement that emerged in the 1930s. Especially on the killing floors, where the pace of work was most intense, blacks and whites cooperated in order to survive. When the cattle pens were full, foremen, feeling pressure from their own superiors, pushed these workers to the limits of their endurance. Job actions in these departments continued unabated throughout the 1920s without benefit of formal organization. Here, and in other areas of the packinghouses, the relations of production sustained a tradition of militancy and promoted solidarity among workers. During the twenties, this tradition remained submerged. It required the shock of the Depression and a shift of class forces as a result of the New Deal to bring it to the surface.

4

"Negro and White, Unite and Fight!": The Rise of the Chicago PWOC

I. H. Bratton waited a long time for the CIO. A black coal miner active in the labor movement for nearly sixty years, Bratton cut his teeth in the Knights of Labor, rose to a leading position in the United Mine Workers, and was employed as an organizer by the Amalgamated Meat Cutters during the fateful 1917–22 period. Repeatedly during his long career, he saw his hopes for a powerful interracial labor movement dashed. Retiring in the early 1930s, Bratton must have concluded that his life's work had been in vain—the labor movement lay moribund while a cruel depression drove workers' living and working conditions downward, with black workers and their families suffering disproportionately. Moreover, it must have seemed painfully apparent that the organizing of the World War I era represented the end rather than the beginning of the AFL's experiment with industrial unionism.

Yet, by the close of the decade Bratton had reason for a more sanguine assessment of labor's prospects. The CIO's dramatic emergence suddenly brought the elusive goal of organizing mass production workers within reach. Living on Chicago's South Side, Bratton closely monitored the growth of the new unionism in steel and then meatpacking. Somehow the presence of this veteran activist made itself known to leaders of the fledgling packinghouse union, who seized the opportunity to reinforce their call for interracial solidarity by publicly honoring him. Awarded a life membership in the vanguard Armour local, Bratton noted that the packers' traditional tactic of encouraging racial antagonism had lost its effect and linked the efforts of the CIO pioneers with those of an earlier generation. "A new type of union is in the field. It is one which I have seen coming all my years," he remarked, adding that for his entire career "I've fought for full equality for the Negro worker. Today, I've found those things in the CIO."[1]

The term "CIO" signifies many things. Institutionally it refers to both the Committee on Industrial Organization formed within the AFL in 1935 and the independent Congress of Industrial Organizations, established in 1938 but arguably institutionally autonomous for two years before that. In a broader sense, the CIO was a social movement, rooted in the working class and primarily concerned with economic issues, that strained at and overstepped institutional boundaries. Explanation of the origins and initial development of the CIO in Chicago's packinghouses must tack back and forth between institutional and social levels of analysis while remaining firmly focused upon the day-to-day activities of packinghouse workers, especially the ways in which they organized and learned to exercise power at the point of production.

This perspective allows a social history of an institution, the Chicago Packinghouse Workers Organizing Committee, to emerge. The central feature of this social history is the unification of a workforce fragmented by skill and ethnicity and divided by race, a process that occurred in two separate but continuous stages. First, in the mid-1930s, a core alliance of union militants took shape. This nucleus was comprised of three major groups: Communists who were relatively new to the industry, skilled veterans of earlier organizing campaigns, and black activists who had been in the plants since the late 1910s and early 1920s. Second, in the latter part of the decade, this coalition won the support of the majority of workers in the packinghouses. It did so not by supplanting bonds of ethnicity and or dissolving ties to specific community institutions but by forging a "culture of unity" that linked material well-being with solidarity and empowerment at the workplace.[2]

The "CIO as social movement" was well advanced before the formal 1937 entry into meatpacking of the "CIO as institution." The genesis of the workers' movement in the stockyards owed relatively little to the institutional labor movement and, in fact, defined itself largely in opposition to it.[3] More than chronology is at issue here. The nature of the early union movement and its relationship with the CIO had important future consequences. Even after the chartering of the PWOC, tensions between defiantly autonomous rank-and-file packinghouse workers and their CIO-appointed leaders continued to manifest themselves. Opposing efforts of appointed PWOC leaders to impose centralized control over the new union, packinghouse activists ensured that effective power continued to reside closer to the PWOC's mass base than its national office.

A set of key questions guide this investigation as it moves from community to workplace, from shop floor to local union, from the stockyards and their environs to regional and national developments. What changes occurred in the plants and in the community that allowed Chicago's packinghouse workers to overcome the debilitating legacy of racial distrust engendered by earlier defeats? How did the various component parts of the interracial coalition that lay at the heart of the PWOC interact? How, exactly, did the "sparkplug" unionists who built the new union—black and white, radical and conservative—spread their organization beyond a core group of committed activists to the mass of packinghouse workers?

The Depression Back-of-the-Yards

The Great Depression hit Chicago earlier and harder than other industrial cities. Already serious by mid-1930, unemployment and homelessness reached crisis proportions over the next two years. In 1931 over 40 percent of the workforce was jobless, and those fortunate to have work found their hours drastically reduced. In the summer of that year, over two hundred families faced eviction each week, while thousands lived in the makeshift "Hoovervilles" that had sprung up at the foot of Randolph Street and in Grant Park. The hub of the nation's transportation system, Chicago attracted an estimated ten thousand transients in the first two years of the depression alone, further straining its limited capacity to adjust to the crisis.[4]

Insolvent even before the crash, the city was wholly unprepared to cope with the situation. Failing to meet its own payroll, it turned to the state and local charities to handle relief. Private sector welfare agencies struggled along, doling out five dollars a week to those few families lucky enough to qualify for assistance. A wave of bank failures in 1932, however, swallowed up the funds that allowed these charities to function. With nearly one out of two wage earners out of work, Mayor Anton Cermak turned to the federal government, suggesting that it might be better for Washington to send $150 million to Chicago now rather than to send troops later.[5]

Chicago's citizens did not equally share the misery inflicted by the depression. The working class bore the brunt of economic and social dislocation. Institutions upon which working people depended weakened or collapsed entirely. Mutual benefit associations failed to meet their obligations; fraternal insurance societies declared their insolvency. Ethnic building and loan organizations and community banks failed by the dozens. The resources of the church proved inadequate to meet the burgeoning demands placed upon them; and employers abandoned their welfare schemes. "Everything nailed down is comin' loose," the Angel Gabriel observed in Marc Connelly's depression-era drama, *Green Pastures*. And so it must have appeared to Chicago's working class as virtually every familiar reference point gave way under the strain.[6]

While the depression erased the status quo, it also created new possibilities. By presenting workers with a set of common problems, and by loosening the bonds of dependency which had tied them to traditional institutions and community leaders, the depression opened new opportunities for working people to engage in collective struggle. Ethnic antagonism and racial enmity softened as new, more inclusive movements and organizations arose in response to shared economic distress. For packinghouse workers, the early 1930s marked a sharp break with the past. Forces that had contributed to class fragmentation were arrested and temporarily overcome by ones leading to unity. First in the unemployed movement, then in the workplace organizations which emerged in response to the New Deal, and finally in the fight to build an industrial union, packinghouse workers expanded the common ground available to them.

The depression had a different impact upon white ethnics residing Back-of-the-Yards and black packinghouse workers living in the city's Black Belt. These two neighborhoods formed the crucibles within which workers' received attitudes were transformed as well as the settings within which organized activity first took place.

The stock market crash of October 1929 occurred in the midst of the meatpacking industry's fall livestock rush. The stockyards were filled to capacity, and employment in the packinghouses had hit its annual peak. Few paid more than passing attention to the economic calamity. The following months gave little cause for undue alarm—employment dipped slightly, but the decline was relatively mild when compared to other industries. Employment in steel and agricultural equipment, for example, dropped precipitously as the market for capital goods fell. On the other hand, consumer demand for meat products remained steady, and coupled with plummeting livestock prices allowed the packing companies to operate profitably through the early 1930s. Indeed, meatpacking retained a greater number of workers than any other industry.[7]

Packinghouse workers were hardly immune from the economic catastrophe, but its impact on Packingtown was gradual rather than sudden. By 1931, the community was reeling. Although employment was off by only

16 percent, *underemployment* had become widespread. Layoffs stretched from weeks into months. Adopting "share-the-work" plans, the packers uniformly reduced hours. Workers dubbed the plans "share-the-misery," and their impact was devastating. Dempsey Travis's father and uncle, both accustomed to working six ten-hour days a week, now put in three eight-hour days. Successive rounds of wage reductions further eroded families' abilities to contend with hardship. The women who worked in Armour's canning department, for example, saw their wages fall from $20 a week in the 1920s to $13 a week in 1933. Laboring nearby in the dried beef department, Sophie Kosciolowski watched her hourly pay fall from 32 cents to 22 cents. Still, she considered herself lucky to have a regular job. Many of the smaller houses suspended operations for weeks at a time. Tommy Megan reported for work at G. H. Hammond one day only to find the doors closed. "No notice, nothing, just tough luck fellows. That's the way it was and it happened more than once. Two weeks, three weeks, sometimes only three days, but you never knew when and for how long."[8]

Early in 1932 the four largest Back-of-the-Yards banks failed, setting off a chain reaction through the business community. By the end of the year, half of all the Lithuanian businesses had gone under. Small stores that had survived by extending credit to customers exhausted their funds and closed. Families that had managed to scrimp by now became desperate. "The whole world came tumbling down," recalled Jacinta Grbac, whose family had immigrated from Croatia in 1921. "We had worked so hard and we lost everything." John Wrublewski, although still employed at Wilson, found his meager earnings inadequate. "By the time we turned over the rent, and paid off just enough of our debts to get some more coal and some more food there wasn't a penny left." Vicky Starr, who arrived in Chicago from a farm in Michigan, was shocked by the hunger and deprivation she saw in the city. A number of women she knew turned to prostitution in order to survive.[9]

The neighborhood's needs overwhelmed local charities. A soup kitchen at St. John of God Church attempted to feed the hungry and the University of Chicago Settlement House assisted the neediest families. These efforts hardly sufficed. After more than tripling its budget, the Catholic archdiocese confessed that "charity cannot and should not be expected to meet the terrific strain. . . . It was never meant to aid the majority." Swift and Armour collected charitable contributions from workers and dispensed small sums to loyal employees who had fallen on particularly hard times. At the same time, however, the packers discarded other welfare measures; and already financially strapped workers resented the weekly solicitations. Democratic Party ward heelers did what they could for their constituents, but prior to the coming of the New Deal the machine in which they were cogs delivered precious little relief.[10]

One organization that seemed to offer destitute workers a faint glimmer of hope was the local Unemployed Council. Launched by the Communist Party in the winter of 1929–30, the council had eighty neighborhood branches throughout the city two years later. Headquartered in the Ukrainian Hall at Forty-eighth and Ashland, the Yards' branch attracted several thousand members through its direct action tactics. Gathering old bread from bakeries and food from area stores, the council fed upwards of five hundred people each day, occasionally supplementing this fare with meat stolen from one of the packinghouses. It also took up the cases of families denied relief, holding demonstrations at city offices and social work agencies to demand immediate redress.[11]

The Unemployed Council's most visible activity concerned rent evictions. In hundreds of instances in the early depression, council members moved the possessions of evicted families back into their dwellings. Sometimes these actions were planned in advance. At other times they were spontaneous. "Someone would run into the Hall . . . and announce that Mrs. So-and-So was being thrown out into the street, and that would start the whole thing rolling. A bunch of guys would run off on that direction and by the time they got there it would be a huge crowd," remembered Joe Zabritski. Such actions attracted new recruits and enhanced the reputation of the Communists. "They were the only ones out there trying to *do* anything, trying to do something about all this misery. That's what attracted me, I think, not any kind of ideology—that came later—but the fact that they were taking action," explained Pat Balskus.[12]

The Back-of-the-Yards council periodically coordinated its efforts with branches elsewhere in the city. In March 1930, the Communist-led councils cooperated with the Socialists in staging a massive march on city hall. Thousands of demonstrators converged on State Street, paraded to city hall, and presented Mayor William Thompson with a petition bearing five hundred thousand signatures demanding $75 million for relief, a moratorium on evictions, free food and fuel for the jobless, and hot school lunches for children of the unemployed. In January 1932, simultaneous demonstrations were held at all the relief stations in Chicago. In April, the Unemployed Council organized a march on the stockyards to demand jobs. Over two thousand people took part, including a large contingent from the Black Belt. The most impressive display of numbers occurred later in the year when relief funds were cut in half. Rallying twenty-five thousand of the unemployed in freezing rain, the council staged a march through the downtown

Loop. Authorities promptly secured a loan from the Reconstruction Finance Corporation and rescinded the cut.[13]

Such activity in Packingtown brought together workers who otherwise might never come in contact with one another. "Polish, Lithuanian, Catholic, Protestant, or whatever, it didn't matter who you were, just that you needed help," recalled Joe Zabritski. "Sure some of the old suspicions were there, but they fell away once people saw what they could do together." Mexicans were especially active in the Back-of-the-Yards unemployed movement, and their participation helped break down one of the more formidable barriers in the community. Two highly visible leaders of the Unemployed Council, Refugio Martinez and Jose Rodriguez, were Mexicans. Both men later became CIO packinghouse activists, Rodriguez in the Swift plant and Martinez on the PWOC's staff. Dozens of other Mexicans participated in demonstrations and eviction protests, risking deportation if arrested. When Yards' residents participated in citywide unemployed mobilizations, they acted in concert with black demonstrators. "Here was something new," observed Horace Cayton and St. Clair Drake, "Negroes and whites *together* rioting against the forces of law and order." In this way, the Unemployed Council helped pave the way for the interracial organizing that took place later in the decade.[14]

Most of those active in the unemployed movement had no specific political orientation; they gravitated to the council out of desperation or because it had intervened to secure a relief payment, provide a meal, or stop an eviction. Yet the unemployed provided the Communist Party with a fertile recruiting ground. Many persons received their first real political education in the unemployed movement; a small but significant number then became active in the Back-of-the-Yards CP unit.

Jacinta Grbac was one such individual. Trudging home after a fruitless day of job seeking in 1931, she passed an unemployed demonstration in an empty lot. Attracted by the commotion, she joined the protest, "not knowing very much what it was all about." From there she went on to play a major role in the local council, and soon was recruited into the Young Communist League (YCL), where she was one of a core group of fifteen activists. Her political development and organizational commitment flowed from conditions in the neighborhood. "It was so easy," she commented. Pat Balskus, who also became involved in the YCL, expressed similar sentiment. "It was the right thing to do and it made perfect sense at the time. In addition to protesting and trying to organize, I wanted to know why this [depression] had happened and they had an analysis that seemed to explain it. No one else did."[15]

Leadership of the unemployed movement also gave the Communists their first mass following. They learned to cast their appeal in concrete terms and to address the existing concerns of the unemployed. Sectarian issues and revolutionary sloganeering took a back seat to showing workers how the Communists could help them solve their immediate bread-and-butter problems. Steve Nelson, secretary of the Chicago Unemployed Council, recalled that "we spent the first few weeks agitating against capitalism and talking about the need for socialism. But . . . the day to day work of the earliest councils focused on the practical grievances brought to them by the people in the communities." These issues, rather than abstractions about the contradictions of capitalism, brought the Communists into the mainstream of working-class life. "It was from the involvement in daily struggles that we learned to shift away from a narrow dogmatic approach to what might be called a grievance approach to organizing," Nelson observed. This was an important lesson, one that served Party activists well in their later involvement in the industrial union movement.[16]

Although small, the Back-of-the-Yards CP section was a spirited group that made its presence felt in the neighborhood. In addition to supporting the Unemployed Council, it concentrated its activities in two areas: forging ties with community residents and laying the groundwork for organization in the packinghouses. Working through the University of Chicago Settlement House, the Communists were able to reach and influence a number of Mexicans and Poles. Settlement House social workers welcomed Jacinta Grbac because of her fluency in Spanish. She befriended women who attended meetings of the Mothers Club, helping them secure food and clothing for their families. She drew upon her experience in the unemployed movement—leading a group of women to Goldblatt's department store, for instance, to obtain winter clothing for children. Put off by its Protestantism, few Poles took advantage of the Settlement House. Many of those that did were alienated from the Catholic church, and their anticlericalism meshed readily with the Communists' appeal. Grbac and Vicky Starr convinced the Settlement House to sponsor a Sunday afternoon Women's Club. At first meetings were purely social, but gradually politics assumed a place on the agenda. Always gathering names and addresses—"my pockets were full of scraps of paper with scribbled writing"—Starr made contacts that proved useful when the union organizing drive took off a few years later.[17]

Whereas the CP's organizing efforts in the community met with a favorable response, they met greater resistance in the stockyards. Workers who remained employed in the depths of the depression tended to be older and more cautious. Family obligations weighed heavily on these men and women, who often remained the household's sole wage earner. This situation changed when employment picked up in response to the NRA, allowing many activists to secure jobs inside the plants. Until then, the CP "was on the outside looking in," to use the words of Pat Balskus. "I think we might have had two or three people actually working in the yards. It was frustrating."[18]

Despite this unfavorable climate, Communist activists persevered. With the help of sympathetic students from the University of Chicago, the group printed and distributed a newspaper, *The Yards Worker*. A mimeographed sheet, the paper promoted the idea of industrial unionism, contained articles on working conditions in the plants, and ran columns on the history of the labor movement. Workers were generally unreceptive. Most refused to take the paper. Others crumpled it up as soon after it was thrust into their hands. "You have to understand the fear at that time," explained Balskus, "to be caught with one of those or even to be seen taking it or talking to those handing it out could mean your job." Still, numerous copies found their way into the plant, smuggled in under workers' clothes. "I would come in real busty. Then I'd go into the washroom and leave the papers around," commented Starr, who began working at Swift in 1933.[19]

Other efforts to "start something rolling" in the yards met with the same degree of success. Zabritski and Starr recalled attending meetings where industrial unionism was discussed. Often old-timers who had worked with Foster and Jack Johnstone in the SLC were present, but "we just couldn't get anything moving at that time. The sentiment was there, but there wasn't any hope, any indication that we had a chance of making it, so people held back." Estelle Zabritski and Pat Balskus succeeded in forming a club for women workers that met regularly at a YWCA branch, located at Forty-eighth and Ashland. Later, this group helped advance the union drive into resistant female departments, but in the early thirties it "was just a place to go and gab, maybe gripe about work, but not to do anything 'subversive.'" Generally stymied in their attempt to build an organization in the packinghouses, the CP nonetheless began preparing the ground for the movement that soon emerged. "It was no real organizing drive," admitted Grbac, "but we certainly had ideas."[20]

The CP's activities Back-of-the-Yards were only part of the general response to the depression and touched only a small portion of the neighborhood's residents. Many others turned to the church for solace and strength; some relied on family networks to survive. A number fell under the sway of right-wing demagogues such as Father Charles Coughlin.[21] Yet in the absence of other communitywide mobilizations, the organized Left virtually alone assumed a leadership role in the fight for relief. Similarly, the Communists began agitating in the stockyards at a time when the labor movement had written off the packinghouses as a lost cause. Eventually, these endeavors produced results that exceeded the activists' most optimistic expectations. In mid-1933, however, in the depths of the depression, the future seemed quite dark.

The Depression in the Black Belt

A few miles away, in Chicago's Black Belt, the depression's impact was more severe and the situation appeared even bleaker. Black banking institutions, the weakest link in the financial system, were the first to collapse. Jesse Binga's bank, the pride of the middle class, closed its doors in 1930. In the following twelve months, the community's second largest bank and most of the local insurance companies expired. Since black workers tended to be the first let go in a business downturn, unemployment in the community surpassed that of white neighborhoods. The Urban League estimated general unemployment at 45 percent in 1931; and certain sections of the first and second wards reported a staggering jobless rate of 85 percent. Although the black population comprised only 7.7 percent of the population, black families accounted for over 30 percent of those on relief.[22]

While white packinghouse workers remained on the job in greater numbers than workers in other industries, blacks were not as fortunate. As early as 1929, the industrial secretary of the Urban League reported with alarm that "every week we receive information regarding the discharge of additional Race workers who are being replaced by workers of other races." In the stockyards, the large firms seem to have pursued such a policy. Elmer Thomas bitterly recalled that "they were hiring young white boys, sixteen and eighteen years old, raw kids, didn't know a thing, but there were plenty of colored boys waiting for the same chance who never got it." Arthur Kampfert suggests that the packers practiced a form of triage, trying to direct scarce employment opportunities toward whites who now proved willing to take disagreeable jobs they previously shunned. Black packinghouse workers were not shielded by their occupation; they shared the ordeal of the general community.[23]

As the depression rolled back the employment gains achieved by black workers in the 1920s, traditional leadership institutions such as the Urban League and NAACP were thrown into a quandary. The old policy of reliance upon capital's goodwill for racial advancement was clearly inadequate in the face of the current economic reality. Yet attempts to formulate new programs failed miserably. Elitist in their orientation and accustomed to working behind the scenes, both institutions eschewed mass involvement. As a result, the Urban League and the NAACP became increasingly marginal forces in the Black Belt and ceded effective leadership to new organizations willing to employ mass mobilizations and confrontational tactics.

Although aware of the magnitude of the crisis, the Urban League at first operated as if the depression had not occurred. As late as 1932, it concentrated its efforts in job placement, even though the results were dismal. Dependent upon white philanthropy for its funds, the league was forced to enact staff cuts and curtail operations when the purse strings contracted. The national office temporarily prodded the Chicago branch out of its lethargy in 1933, encouraging the establishment of an Emergency Advisory Council which monitored the state of black employment and the effect of government relief programs. The council gathered important data but did little to assist the working class. The old uplift theory of racial advance lay at the heart of the council's efforts. One official explained that "the less intelligent and more dependent and disadvantaged members of our group must look to those of us who occupy a point of vantage for some measure of relief." Avoiding direct contact with the mass of unemployed, the league was largely invisible in the black community.[24]

The Chicago branch of the NAACP enjoyed a higher public profile than the Urban League, but its reputation among the working class was not entirely positive. Many workers perceived the NAACP as an exclusive club—"a silk-stocking tea-sipping organization," in the words of Todd Tate, an unemployed packinghouse worker. One historian concluded that the organization entered the depression decade "without having registered any notable accomplishments in either the racial or economic spheres." Membership drives in the early 1930s produced embarrassing results. Slightly over a thousand persons joined the association in 1933. The following year saw no campaign, and in 1935 only 750 signed up. By the end of the decade, the association contemplated closing the Chicago branch—the 1939 annual drive was a miserable failure, producing only a handful of new members and a paltry $600. "Something is radically wrong here," the national office field coordinator remarked. "Any city of over 260,000 Negroes that has as much difficulty as Chicago in trying to sell the NAACP has something fundamentally wrong."[25]

The Republican Party, traditionally a major source of patronage in the Black Belt, also failed to provide much in the way of relief. Mayor William

Thompson's tenure in office was due in large measure to black votes, but his corrupt regime had led the city into bankruptcy even before the depression struck. Forced to lay off teachers, policemen, and fire officials, the machine had little to spare for relief. Moreover, black loyalty had begun to shift away from the GOP. In 1928 nearly a quarter of the Black Belt's residents voted for Al Smith, and in 1931 a small but significant proportion of black voters helped defeat Thompson by electing Democrat Anton Cermak. This trend toward the Democrats, while slower in Chicago than in other cities, accelerated in subsequent years as blacks voted "for bread and butter instead of the memory of Abraham Lincoln." Democrat Arthur Mitchell's 1934 upset victory over longtime black GOP boss Oscar DePriest in a congressional race signaled the arrival of a new era in local politics, one cemented the following year when Mayor Edward Kelly polled over 80 percent in Black Belt wards that previously formed the core of Republican support. By the close of the decade, astute black Republicans such as William Dawson switched parties and became partners in the emerging Democratic machine while the mass of black voters "turned the portrait of Lincoln to the wall." This shift in electoral loyalty removed a serious point of contention that had long divided black and white workers.[26]

The timidity displayed by the Urban League and the NAACP isolated them from the bulk of the community, while the influence of the GOP waned as its ability to provide services and relief diminished. The failure of these organizations to address economic problems directly created a vacuum in black Chicago and encouraged a flurry of activity among the black working class. A revived Garvey movement and other nationalist organizations such as the African Legion and the Black Cross moved to fill the void, as did Communist, Socialist, and Trotskyist groups.[27] Characteristic of all these movements was their reliance on mass mobilization, their utilization of direct action tactics not sanctioned by traditional institutions, and their direction by non-elites.

One of the first mass movements to sweep the Black Belt in the early 1930s was the "Don't Spend Your Money Where You Can't Work" campaign spearheaded by the *Chicago Whip*. Targeting national chains with franchises in the black community, the campaign went beyond an economic boycott and included daily picketing and mass meetings. Its crowning moment arrived in October 1930 when, after seventeen weeks of picketing, Woolworth's capitulated and agreed to employ over twenty blacks at its new Fifty-first Street store. Dependent upon large-scale mobilization and a high level of racial consciousness, the campaign marked "the advent of direct action in the twentieth century into the lives of black Chicagoans." At its peak, it involved most community institutions, even dragging the Urban League belatedly into the fray.[28]

The campaign had a lasting impact. It spawned a permanent organization, the Negro Employees Improvement Association, which carried the struggle for jobs into other areas and demonstrated the efficacy of mass pressure tactics. It also introduced large numbers of people to the politics of protest. Lowell Washington recalled being "caught up in the excitement. People were moving, agitating, if we was gonna starve at least we'd put up a fight. . . . It really opened my eyes to the power that's available if only people will use it." Participating in numerous other protests, Washington eventually fell in with "a group of Reds" who were trying to establish an organization for WPA workers. "Those guys really threw me," he remembered. "I mean here were these white fellas who were helping us out, really meaning it. I'd never seen anything like it." Although he never joined the Communist Party, Washington was influenced by its philosophy. Especially important in this regard was what Steve Nelson termed "a grievance approach to organizing." Washington explained: "They took up the things that really mattered—jobs, food, places to live—can't get more basic than that, and they fought for those things. You might not agree with them all the time, but you had to stand with 'em when they was fightin' for you."[29]

The Communists had been organizing in the Black Belt since the mid-1920s, trying to attract a following through agitation around housing and civil rights. Aside from the short-lived Negro Tenant's Protective League and a semisuccessful campaign protesting the showing of D. W. Griffith's *Birth of a Nation,* the Party encountered little success enrolling African Americans into its ranks. In 1929, it had fewer than two hundred black members in Chicago. Nor did there seem to be much support among sympathizing "fellow travelers." When Communist Gordon Owen ran for Congress in 1924, he received thirty-two out of sixty thousand votes in his district; four years later when the Party fielded a candidate against controversial GOP boss Oscar DePriest, he garnered a mere one hundred votes.[30]

Over the next few years, however, the Party's fortunes changed dramatically. The turning point came in 1931 when the CP's defense of the Scottsboro Boys, nine Alabama teenagers charged with raping two white women aboard a railroad boxcar, brought it to the attention of thousands of blacks. The national campaign, which ultimately saved the lives of the accused, boosted the Party's work in black communities across the country. Membership in the Communists' previously moribund League of Struggle for Negro Rights took off, and the ILD (International Labor Defense) became a household word. Chicago Communist leader Harry Haywood recalled that Scottsboro greatly lessened blacks' suspicions of white radicals. "White comrades doing work among the unemployed told us that the case was really an entree into the community. Once people knew they were communists, they were accepted because communists were always associated with Scottsboro." When the CP ran a black man, James Ford, as its vice-presidential candidate the following year, the Party's credibility in the Black Belt rose a few more notches.[31]

The Communists' practice of demanding equality within their ranks and their willingness to combat racist attitudes among white members further enhanced the Party's standing among blacks. The *Chicago Bee,* a respectable black paper, recognized the CP's advanced stand: "On the race issue the Communists went the whole length in recognizing the demands of the Negro. 'Complete equality' in all matters, economic and social, was the slogan of the Communists." The *Chicago Defender* even went a step further. When the Party expelled a white member for segregating black guests at a social function, editor Robert Abbott ran a column entitled "Why We Can't Hate Reds." Reviewing the events leading up to the expulsion he asked, "How, under such circumstances, can we go to war with the Communist Party? Is there any other political, religious, or civic organization in the country that would go to such lengths to prove itself not unfriendly to us?" Noting he did not approve the CP's entire program, Abbott ended by stating "there is one item with which we do agree wholeheartedly, and that is the zealousness with which it guards the rights of the Race." A few months later, the *Defender* criticized police attacks upon CP activists organizing black garment workers. So what if the organizers were radicals, Abbott asked. "Take some of these same policemen off of the pay roll for six months and they will be Communists too." At a time when the white press screamed about "shock troops" from Moscow and worried about the growing "Red Menace" in Chicago, this kind of acclamation coming from black middle-class organs indicated a growing respect for Communist activists at work in the black community.[32]

It was the Communists' guidance of the unemployed movement, above all else, that gave them the greatest visibility in the Black Belt. Several locals of the Unemployed Council were active on the South Side, and their militant tactics won them a sizeable following. They were responsible for some of the largest demonstrations held in Chicago during the 1930s, including the notorious 1931 "eviction riot." Throughout the summer of that year, groups of unemployed gained celebrity throughout the community by restoring evicted families and their belongings to their residences. These actions dwarfed similar protests occurring Back-of-the-Yards. Dubbed the

"Black Bugs" by the black press, these groups engaged in increasingly bold confrontations with bailiffs and police as the summer wore on. In July, they attracted a crowd of over twenty-five hundred on South Wabash Street that forced the police to withdraw. A month later, a larger assembly estimated at five thousand gathered to restore a seventy-two-year-old widow to her dwelling at Fiftieth and Dearborn. Evidently prepared for violence, the police opened fire on the crowd, killing four blacks. Hundreds of others, including several police officers, were injured in the street fighting that followed.[33]

The community's response revealed the Left's growing popularity in the Black Belt. Twenty-five thousand persons lined up to pay homage at the Oddfellow's Hall where the bodies of the slain activists lay in state, and a week later a crowd of thirty thousand marched in an interracial funeral parade down State Street. A local Party leader who participated described the march as the greatest demonstration of black and white solidarity she had ever witnessed. "The crowd just took over State Street—there wasn't a cop in sight," Haywood later wrote. "As people walked, they carried open sheets with them; the crowds watching on the sidewalk threw money into the sheets, to help defray the families' expenses." Summoned back from vacation, Mayor Cermak met with leaders of the unemployed and the revived Garvey movement (significantly, NAACP and Urban League officials were not present) and declared a temporary moratorium on evictions. In subsequent months, the unemployed movement grew in leaps and bounds and with it the Communists' reputation. An anecdote related by Horace Cayton conveys their growing prestige: "When eviction notices arrived, it was not unusual for a mother to shout to her children, 'Run quick and find the Reds!'"[34]

In contrast to the CP's activities Back-of-the-Yards, the Party's actions in the Black Belt were distinguished by their marked interracial character. Otis Hyde, who arrived in Chicago from Texas in 1930, recalled that it was in the unemployed movement that he first learned to trust and work with whites. Lowell Washington felt much the same, "I'd never really even talked to a white man before, and I certainly hadn't said more than two words to a white lady, and here I was being treated with respect and speakin' my mind and not having to worry about saying something that might rile 'em up. . . . Let me tell you it changed the way I thought about things." The willingness of the white leadership to share power and authority with blacks also impressed Washington. "You'd be at some gathering and up stage wouldn't be all white fellows, it would be two three black guys and one or two white. Now that meant something to me." In general, white deferral to blacks was genuine and not patronizing. Especially important in this regard was the autonomy the Party allowed its Black Belt organizations, encouraging them to expand their activities to encompass neighborhood concerns tangential to the Communists' program but of high importance to local residents.[35]

One of the major focal points of interracial radical activity in Chicago was Washington Park, located near the Black Belt and a mile and a half east of Packingtown. Large crowds of the unemployed gathered daily here, whiling away time while listening to an endless succession of street speakers. Known popularly as the "Bugs Club Forum," this regular gathering was Chicago's equivalent of Speakers' Corner in London's Hyde Park. Not all who spoke were radicals. "Just about anyone could get up on a box and gather a crowd around him," recalled one frequent visitor. Horace Cayton described the park as a place where "jack-leg preachers joust with curbstone atheists, and Black Zionists break a lance with sundry varieties of Reds." On occasion, professors from nearby University of Chicago appeared to debate the soapboxers. Yet, it was the Left that furnished the most popular speakers. David Poindexter, an old Garveyite who had made the transition to the CP, always drew a sizeable throng with his colorful speeches; and Justin DeLemos, who had been a labor organizer in the Canal Zone, could be relied upon to gather a few hundred around him.[36]

A public expanse, Washington Park formed a neutral space between three neighborhoods—the Black Belt, Packingtown, and Hyde Park. It attracted whites, blacks, and left-wing students who normally would not cross each others' paths. More important than the oratory heard there was the park's role as a staging ground for eviction protests and other actions. On an almost daily basis, crowds left the park en masse and headed to an unemployed rally or to take part in some direct action. One of the more infamous episodes occurred in September 1930, when William Soders led several hundred unemployed men from the park to a construction site at Fifty-second and South Park where, demanding jobs, they seized tools out of the hands of a gang of Italian laborers. Only the intervention of city officials prevented a violent clash with police. As a result, several black men were added to the white gang. Similar marches to other building sites took place in the weeks that followed, meeting with varied success.[37]

A number of future black packinghouse unionists took part in these demonstrations, and for many they were critical formative experiences. In the radical interracial milieu of Washington Park, they learned to work with white allies, acquired specific organizational skills, and gained a respect for the Left's leadership. Todd Tate, a burly 6'6" giant of a man who later served as a steward in the Armour plant, joined many "flying squadrons" mobilized from the crowd to rush to the scene of evictions. It was in the park that Tate first met Richard Saunders, a union founder at the Armour Soap Works, and Leon Beverly, later president of his own local. Saunders recalled that Communist speakers provided him with the "method and know-how" that allowed him to organize on the job. "Some of the things they would preach I could pick up on, and go back in my plant and institute." While never a Party member, Saunders felt an attraction to the Communists. "I didn't care about nobody joining the Communist Party. . . . The thing was issues, the issues that were important to people. And some of these guys, Communists or no Communists, they dealt with issues." This outspokenness, especially with regard to black equality, led Saunders to join the CP-sponsored John Brown Society and to participate in numerous protests.[38]

The Communists were not the only organization to fight for the unemployed and to struggle for black equality, but they were the most effective group to do so in the early 1930s. More than any other organization, the CP was responsible for the adoption of direct action tactics, the inclusion of blacks and other marginalized groups in the broader working-class movement, and the breakdown of racist attitudes among workers. The search for collective solutions to shared problems expanded the common ground available to white and black workers. The rise of interracial activity on an unprecedented scale, led by the organized Left, paved the way for the industrial union movement that emerged later in the decade.

First Stirrings

The flurry of working-class activity that occurred in Packingtown and the Black Belt in the early 1930s was not immediately mirrored in the stockyards themselves. With friends, neighbors, and relatives out of work, those with jobs felt it imperative to hold on to them. "Miserable as a job might be, it was better than no job at all and there was tremendous fear," remembered one worker. Karl Lundberg, whose work at Swift "wasn't what you'd call steady but regular enough," had his wife's parents to support as well as an infant daughter. When Gertie Kamarczyk was laid off for seventeen weeks in 1932, her husband's position at Wilson became all the more important to the family. John Wrublewski, whose brother-in-law lost his job at U.S. Steel's South Works, also felt an added burden on his shoulders. "I wasn't going to start raising hell, not with that many to feed."[39]

The passage of the National Industrial Recovery Act (NIRA) in 1933 helped provide an opening for union-minded activists in the stockyards.

The labor provision of the act, section 7(a), raised workers' hopes and fostered the belief that federal protection for organizers was forthcoming. In truth, expectations of government intervention were illusory; the Labor Board established by the legislation lacked enforcement powers. "It had no teeth . . . no effectiveness," observed Herbert March. Nevertheless, he added, "while the workers had no rights, the *illusion* that they had rights had its impetus on their moving and fighting and stirring, and that was the important thing." The NIRA affected the yards in a second important way. It carried with it a temporary blanket code for industry, known as the President's Reemployment Agreement, which reduced working hours and boosted employment in the packinghouses. Among the new hires were hundreds of young men and women with experience in the unemployed movement, as well as a core of Communist organizers.[40]

First to capitalize on the ferment was a group of older skilled workers, veterans of the 1917–22 drive, who had been blacklisted by the large packers and now labored in the small independent plants. Shortly after Congress rushed through the NIRA, they met and reconstituted the Stock Yards Labor Council, even installing the SLC's old leader Martin Murphy as president. Calling for across-the-board wage increases, equal pay for women, and the establishment of a guaranteed thirty-hour week, the new SLC made considerable headway in the plants of the "Little Six" packers (Roberts and Oake, P. D. Brennan, Illinois Meat, Miller and Hart, Reliable Packing, and Agar) as well as G. H. Hammond, a Swift subsidiary. Work relations in these small plants were more intimate than those prevailing in the larger houses, and butchers retained more of the "all-around" knife skills eliminated elsewhere. Consequently, skilled labor was more powerful in these packinghouses, giving the SLC leverage it might not have enjoyed at Armour or Wilson. In early 1934, the union claimed to have enrolled five thousand workers, but organization remained restricted to the independents.[41]

In addition to the SLC, two other groups opened campaigns in the stockyards in 1933–34: a Communist-led TUUL affiliate, the Packinghouse Workers Industrial Union (PHWIU), and the Amalgamated Meat Cutters. Operating independently, each of the three groups met with limited success, and each represented a different strata of the workforce. The SLC's major base of support came from skilled, ethnic whites in the small plants. The PHWIU cultivated a small but loyal following among black workers in the Armour and Wilson plants supplemented by white leftists, while the Amalgamated's active membership was restricted to the Irish livestock handlers working in the livestock pens.

The Packinghouse Workers Industrial Union owed its existence to the dynamism supplied by Herbert March, a brilliant young activist who had come to Chicago from Kansas City, where he had directed the activities of the Young Communist League. Born in the Brownsville section of Brooklyn in 1913, he grew up in a socialist milieu and joined the YCL at age sixteen. Active in local labor struggles, March came to the attention of Party officials during a 1929 silk strike in nearby Paterson, New Jersey. In 1930 he accepted appointment as the YCL's southwestern organizer at a salary of $5 a week. Involved in antilynching and unemployed activity in Kansas, Missouri, Nebraska, and Oklahoma, he moved to Chicago after marrying Jacinta Grbac, whom he had met at a Party function.[42]

After Herbert arrived in the spring of 1933, the couple moved in with the Grbac family and turned their attention to the task of local organizing. March's boundless energy and enthusiasm revitalized the Yards CP unit, and his strong commitment to racial equality pushed the group to forge ties with black workers in the Yards. March himself secured a job in Armour's boiled ham department in the fall of 1933, and other members of his group began to "colonize" in other plants. Progress was slow and membership never rose above five hundred, most of which was concentrated on Armour's heavily black hog and sheep kills. Yet this modest figure belies the PHWIU's influence. Colonizers at Swift and Wilson established important contacts among skilled maintenance workers, while those in Little Six plants pursued a policy of supporting the SLC. Moreover the nucleus of white radicals and blacks at Armour prefigured the alliance that later sustained the PWOC.[43]

The growth of the SLC and the PHWIU occurred without assistance from the labor movement. Before launching the SLC, Murphy and his colleagues asked the Chicago Federation of Labor for help, hoping to revive the old 1917 arrangement, but that body denied their request. The Communists, pursuing a policy of revolutionary dual unionism, defined themselves as opponents of the "reactionary" AFL and neither sought nor received backing from the CFL. The appearance on the scene of the Amalgamated thus represented the "official" labor movement's attempt to translate working-class unrest in the packing industry into concrete organizational gains. After a hiatus of more than a decade, however, the AMC was ill equipped to meet this challenge. Although it assigned full-time organizers to the yards and absolved incoming members from dues payments, results were disappointing. A union official later griped that although the Amalgamated "made a real earnest effort to help the packing house workers . . . they did not take advantage of what we were doing."[44]

Much of the Amalgamated's difficulties stemmed from its unfavorable reputation. "People weren't about to hop into bed with Denny Lane again. Most would have joined up with the Salvation Army before they signed on with the AF of L," commented one veteran worker. Another problem arose from the Amalgamated's insistence on organizing on a craft basis— an approach that outraged those working to build inclusive industrial unions. Blacks in particular felt alienated from and distrusted the AMC. Speaking for many, one worker explained that he opposed the Amalgamated "because they would separate us—put the whites in one local and the coloreds in another." Finally, the AMC's stubborn refusal to cooperate with the two other unions in the yards compounded its troubles. While the SLC and the PHWIU settled into a supportive relationship, the Amalgamated threw obstacles in their path, even employing local hoodlums to disrupt meetings. Attacking the SLC as an "IWW organization subsidized by the packers," and assailing the PHWIU as a "band of Bolshevists," Amalgamated officials irked potential allies by claiming sole bargaining rights for the industry.[45]

Nevertheless, the Meat Cutters did appeal to a certain narrow group of workers. The union's commitment to craft organization, and its old-immigrant (especially Irish) leadership attracted more exclusionary-minded tradesmen. Its status as an AFL affiliate endowed it with a degree of respectability that further heightened its allure to more conservative elements. Thus the AMC competed with the SLC for the allegiance of butchers in the smaller plants. It also recruited the Irish-dominated livestock handlers working for the Union Stockyards and Transit Company. Proud of their reputation as the "aristocrats of the yards," the handlers were an unusually homogeneous, tightly knit group. Politically conservative, they were nonetheless quite militant around work-related issues. In November 1933, acting on their own initiative, they walked off the job, demanding a return to 1929 wage scales. The two-day strike paralyzed the yards and brought a halt to operations in the surrounding packinghouses. It also caught AMC officials by surprise. Hoping that the NRA would force the packers to recognize their organization, President Lane and Secretary Patrick Gorman had portrayed the Amalgamated as a stabilizing force in the industry. The stockyards strike revealed the lack of control they exercised over their locals, while the union's inability to use the action to recruit new members pointed up its isolation from the bulk of packinghouse workers.[46]

The strike, which ended with an agreement to increase wages by 10 percent, electrified the stockyards. Especially encouraging was the way in which the action spontaneously spread to many of the Little Six plants. The SLC offered to pull out its members in support of the handlers; and the

PHWIU reported that unorganized workers at Armour and Wilson were prepared to down their tools as well. The handlers' quick victory—attributable to their strategic position in the production process, for without their labor no livestock reached any of the plants—was a forceful display of workers' power. A sense of insurgency was building, and reports from other packing centers contributed to a feeling that workers everywhere were on the march. News of a strike at Armour's St. Paul plant led by a PHWIU local rocked the yards, as did word of a plant occupation at the George Hormel Company in Austin, Minnesota. These developments emboldened activists who had been organizing secretly and prompted other workers who had been holding back to come forward.[47]

The Hormel strike had a special impact in Chicago because a number of skilled butchers regularly traveled to Austin and knew union leaders there. Stephan Janko recalled that the Austin situation "was the talk of the town . . . and we started thinking, well if they can go ahead and pull something like that, well maybe we should stick our necks out a bit and stir things up." At G. H. Hammond, killing-floor workers openly displayed union buttons for the first time the day after learning about the Austin strike. Led by Arthur Kampfert, workers there pressed forward, enrolling over half the company's fifteen hundred workers into the SLC. By mid-December, although management refused to consider a contract, union representatives in the plant were adjusting grievances with departmental foremen.[48]

This advance was only the most dramatic of those registered in the fall of 1933. The PHWIU succeeded in organizing the largely black workforce at Illinois Meat into their union, and using contacts supplied by Jack Johnstone carried Reliable Packing into the SLC. This small slaughterhouse was a refuge for Polish and Russian butchers blacklisted in 1921. Militant and able to draw on their previous union experience, these veterans soon controlled the killing floors and cutting departments. "That packinghouse was theirs," commented a younger union organizer. Evidently these gains alarmed the packers. For the first time since the early 1920s, the *National Provisioner* commented on labor unrest, dismissing the disturbances as the result of agitation on the part of an "IWW element" and carefully noting the absence of "regular union" participation.[49]

In late December the packers mounted a counteroffensive against the nascent union movement. The first blow was directed at the Hammond plant, where Kampfert and other organizers were preparing to petition the Labor Board for an election. The day after Christmas, management fired two hundred employees, including forty leading activists. The episode weakened the union. Grievance committees ceased functioning, and workers no longer displayed their buttons. When the SLC appealed the discharges to the Chicago Regional Labor Board, they discovered the tentative and limited nature of the government's power. Due to company intimidation, witnesses failed to appear for the first two hearings and the board seemed disinclined to intervene. Persistent, the union brought supporters from other plants to protest, and eventually prevailed upon a number of workers to testify. The board recommended reinstatement, but lacking powers of enforcement was unable to secure Hammond's compliance.[50]

Firings of union activists occurred in other plants where the SLC was strong. At Agar and Company, nearly all of the plant's five hundred employees supported the union. Leadership here was shared by an older group of Polish workers and a younger cohort of blacks who had only recently entered the plant. Management attempted to divide the two groups, spreading rumors that key activists had accepted bribes. When this dodge failed to produce the desired effect, they summarily discharged "the dozen or so ringleaders." Roberts and Oake took more drastic action. When organizing came out in the open, the company temporarily closed the plant and laid off the entire workforce, effectively squashing the drive.[51]

The packers also turned to more subtle methods of combating the unions. They tried race-baiting, suggesting to whites that blacks dominated the SLC and would use it to steal their jobs. And in some cases they succeeded in buying off unscrupulous leaders with promotions and cash payments. They also revived company unions in the larger plants, and established new ones in some of the independents. This proved irksome, for it provided the packing companies with a semilegal rationale for spurning requests from the Amalgamated and the SLC for direct negotiations. When confronted with such entreaties, they responded that collective bargaining already was in effect. In plants where company unions competed for members with independent organizations, representatives of the latter group were at a distinct disadvantage. They could not openly solicit on the job, nor could they claim any ongoing bargaining relationship with management. By contrast, company union delegates roamed the plant at will, received encouragement from many departmental foremen, and frequently employed thinly veiled threats to persuade workers to join or to pay dues. On several occasions, company unions took credit for grievances settled by SLC representatives; and when the large packers instituted a pay hike in October 1934, they attempted to boost the standing of the company unions by attributing the increase to their efforts. It is difficult to gauge workers' response to this situation. Certainly more active unionists saw through the ploy. One Wilson worker derisively noted that delegates to the Joint Representation Committee "are called for a meeting not knowing what its [sic] all about and click, click, the magic trick is over. They sit there with their mouths open, then when they come to they start congratulating themselves." Other workers, however, must have been confused by the existence of two or more unions operating in their plants.[52]

Equally perplexing to many workers was the apparent ease with which the packing companies circumvented the provisions of the NRA and the inability of government authorities to do anything about it. Not only had the Labor Board proved impotent when taking up cases of workers discharged for union activity, but working conditions in many plants continued to deteriorate. Meeting with NRA officials in 1934, Armour workers Stella Sontoniski and Patricia Lewis detailed the toll that speedups and gang reductions had exacted in their departments. Martin Murphy explained that the much-heralded wage increase applied only to certain employees, and that the companies financed the raise by replacing males with lower-paid female labor. He emphasized the routine and flagrant violations of section 7(a) occurring almost daily, complaining that "if it hadn't been for the laws and the government backing us up, I'd never have asked the men to join." Others complained of being forced to punch out and labor without pay for several hours a day—a practice Armour and Swift workers termed "working for the church," in reference to their employers' charitable donations.[53]

By mid-1934 packinghouse workers were impatient with the federal government. When set up the previous year, the NRA had promised a code of fair competition for the industry, but the packers had frustrated all efforts to draw up and implement such guidelines.[54] Their brazen subversion of section 7(a) coupled with deteriorating conditions outraged workers who had expected to benefit from the New Deal. Writing to President Roosevelt, John Reilly, a worker at Miller and Hart, demanded to know "What is the meaning of all of this? Are the packers seeking a free hand to throw workers back to starvation wages, long drugery [sic] hours, or are they all going for big money to donate to the Republican whom they like so well." Unbeknownst to workers like Reilly, regional NRA staff members were trying to persuade the agency to impose a code on the recalcitrant industry. Similarly, sympathetic Labor Board officials were working with Amalgamated leaders to force compliance with 7(a). Both these efforts were in vain. By early 1935, the NRA abandoned its attempt to bring the packers to terms. "The Blue Eagle flew over our plant," remarked one worker in disgust.[55]

The situation in the stockyards at the end of 1934 was a stalemate. The three unions found themselves in approximately the same position that they had held a year earlier. Organization was limited to small beach-heads—a few of the independent houses and certain departments in the larger plants. The packers' campaign against them had been demoralizing, but new leaders had come forward to take the places of those discharged and the disdain which the employers showed for the NRA provided an issue to organize around. Les Orear, one of the Communists at work in the Armour plant, explained how activists took advantage of adversity. "There were laws that the packers weren't living up to, we pointed that out. They had been ordered to do this and that by the labor board, yet they willfully ignored those directives, we pointed that out. They were making millions and millions of dollars and yet they still would shortchange people on their paychecks, we harped on that kind of thing, tried to focus all the little re-sentments in one direction." A sense of empowerment, Orear continued, was vital to the union campaign. "You had to break down this belief that the company was God and you did it by revealing all the faults and hy-pocrisy. You did it by convincing people that together they were just as strong, maybe stronger, than the bosses."[56]

Yet, union organizing seemed to have reached its limit in 1934. Small cores of activists, scattered throughout the yards, had responded to the first stirrings. The bulk of packinghouse workers had not. Organizers believed that mass sentiment was behind them. "The idea that there should be a union was generally acceptable," recalled Herbert March. "People at that time had had it up to here, up to their ears. They had gone through a real period of suffering and oppression and they were ready to revolt." How-ever, fear held them back—fear that the old racial divisions would reassert themselves, fear that the packers would play nationalities off one another, fear of losing one's job, fear of the boss.[57]

The Search for Unity

In order to break out of the stalemate, union leaders recognized that they had to find a way to better coordinate their respective organizing efforts. Cooperation between the SLC and the PHWIU had worked smoothly in some areas, but Communist activists in the large plants were isolated and cut off from the SLC's membership in the independent houses. Meanwhile, the Amalgamated continued to remain aloof, resentful of incursions on what it considered its jurisdictional domain. Some kind of unity among the three groups was necessary if the impasse was to be broken. The stirrings of packinghouse workers in Omaha, Kansas City, and across Iowa made attaining this goal even more imperative, as they looked to Chicago for direction and leadership. However provisional it might be, an alliance between the three groups was necessary because independently each one represented only a segment of the labor force. Each drew its strength from a different working-class tradition, and each possessed special resources that were vital for a successful and powerful organization.[58]

Led by skilled butchers, the Stockyards Labor Council represented the latest institutional expression of a militant craft tradition dating back to the 1917 era and beyond. It commanded the largest following in the yards, an estimated five thousand workers, but was limited to the small independent packinghouses. While more radical than the AFL mainstream, the rebel craftsmen who headed the SLC were still hesitant about embracing an inclusive industrial form of organization. Especially problematic was the question of race. The SLC did not enjoy much of a following among black workers—probably no more than 10 percent of its membership were African Americans.[59] While SLC leaders recognized the theoretical need to embrace black workers, they lacked the practical and objective means of reaching them. Yet because of their skill and intimate knowledge of the labor process, SLC activists were uniquely placed to provide leadership and coordination to shop-floor activities in their plants.

The PHWIU was the product of a very different, less indigenous, tradition. Leninist in orientation, it operated as a vanguard organization, implanting committed cadres in the industry. Significantly younger than the veteran butchers who launched the SLC, these radicals lacked real roots in the packing industry. Nevertheless, their years of community organizing had yielded potentially important ties to the Back-of-the-Yards neighborhood, and their connection to the Communist movement supplied contacts and resources extending well beyond the confines of the stockyards. In addition, they possessed skills that were at a premium: as one CP colonizer put it, "we take these things for granted now, but not everyone knew how to make up a leaflet or run a mimeograph machine."[60] While its membership was small, the PHWIU alone had established bases in the large plants. Moreover, of the three unions only the PHWIU employed female organizers; and these women provided the union movement's only bridge to departments like canning, sliced bacon, and sausage manufacture. Most importantly, it was the Communists who held the key to cementing black participation in the union movement. Not only had they begun to solidify alliances with black workers on the Armour and Wilson killing floors, they had earned the respect of younger blacks through the Party's leading role in the unemployed movement in the Black Belt and the National Negro Congress. Attuned to black concerns and grievances, and fiercely committed to interracialism, the Communists held the most valuable piece of a complex puzzle.

Heir to another tradition within the labor movement, the Amalgamated Meat Cutters represented the bureaucratic craft unionism of the AFL. Its association with past failures made it a particularly poor organizational vehicle, and its current practices only accentuated this deficiency. Nonetheless, the AMC possessed invaluable resources which could only benefit the union movement. It was a national organization, with locals in almost every major meatpacking center. Of the three groups, it was the only with the financial reserves necessary to underwrite a serious campaign in the industry. Its legitimacy in the eyes of the AFL gave it ties to Washington and, more importantly, to the Chicago Federation of Labor. Still headed by John Fitzpatrick, who maintained an interest in the stockyards even though he had backed away from his earlier progressivism, the CFL remained a potential ally of any organizing effort. Its treasury, staff, newspaper, and radio station could only benefit the packinghouse unions, as could the active support of the city's building trades that the CFL's sanction would bring.

Indeed, for a brief moment in the summer of 1934 the AMC appeared to be on the offensive as a second strike broke out amongst the restive livestock handlers. Incensed over a reclassification scheme, eight hundred handlers stopped work in late July. With over forty thousand extra head of cattle in the yards—animals shipped in from drought-stricken areas by the government—and a blistering heat wave, the handlers had selected an opportune time for a walkout. However, despite sympathetic intervention by the Federal Mediation and Conciliation Service, the Amalgamated frittered away the opportunity and further tarnished their reputation.[61]

While the case for unity among the three packinghouse unions was logical and attractive in theory, activists found it difficult to achieve in actual practice. Throughout the latter part of 1934, tentative steps were taken toward forming a unified movement. The PHWIU moved closer to the SLC by bringing its members into that group but still retaining its own organizational autonomy. While something less than a formal merger, the new arrangement was solidified when Herbert March joined Kampfert, Martin Murphy, and Frank McCarty, a hog butcher at Roberts and Oake, on the executive committee. Within the SLC, the Communists formed a kind of left opposition, pushing it toward a more inclusive industrial form of organization and calling attention to black concerns. At the insistence of

March and other leftists, the council advanced blacks into leadership positions and began to actively involve its rank and file, holding weekly mass meetings and sponsoring social activities.[62]

Friction accompanied these changes in orientation. Murphy in particular was rankled by the Communists, whose superior organization and discipline allowed them to have a decisive influence in the council. Antifascist resolutions introduced by the Communists and statements about foreign policy probably had little impact outside of the council's meetings. Nevertheless, they annoyed some of the "pure and simple" unionists, and may have embarrassed them in front of more conservative associates. Murphy felt compelled to tell a Settlement House colleague that the Reds were firmly under his control, adding for good measure, "I make them come right up and kiss the flag every once in a while just to make sure of them." For their part, the Communists suspected Murphy's motives and felt that his ties to the 1917–22 era were more a liability than an asset. In March's view Murphy "was purely an opportunist trying to build a union. Sure he had sympathy for the workers but that was only secondary. And he came in with a group of men, so-called organizers, all of whom were petty hoodlums." Other SLC leaders like Kampfert and McCarty, however, supported the general direction in which the Left pushed the council (in fact, McCarty joined the Party soon afterwards). In reality, it was Murphy who was under the control of the Left and militant center. More serious a problem was the social consequences of interracialism. The appearance of a carload of black workers at Columbia Hall, where the council was headquartered, raised white neighbors' eyebrows, and black attendance at dances and picnics certainly stretched prevailing mores, even though both races practiced rigid self-segregation. Nonetheless, given the bitter period of frustration and disillusionment which followed the 1921 strike, this modest progress represented a significant advance.[63]

The question of a larger strategy also was addressed in 1934, when the SLC attended an Iowa conference engineered by the Austin, Minnesota, Hormel union. Factionalism and personal rivalry plagued the meeting— also attended by a delegation from the Cedar Rapids, Iowa, Wilson plant— which failed to produce much in the way of a coherent plan for advancing unionism in the packinghouses. Still, it did represent an attempt to close ranks and significantly took place wholly outside the AFL. By making personal contact with packinghouse activists from other areas, Chicago unionists had taken a first, halting step toward the construction of the regional network that soon would play a pivotal role in bringing the CIO into the meatpacking industry.[64]

Despite these initiatives, the union movement in the Chicago stockyards gained little new ground in 1934. The only notable exception was the incorporation of the United Food Processors—an organization that began as a company union at the High Grade plant, a small hog slaughtering facility. In a classic example of what the Communists termed a "united front from below," SLC organizers forged ties to workers at High Grade and used these to bring the rank and file into the council over the objections of the Processors' leadership.[65] Yet this bright spot notwithstanding, the stalemate that existed a year earlier had not been broken. When the Amalgamated rebuffed SLC appeals for a joint organizing drive, the council took the unexpected step of dissolving itself—over the strenuous objections of Martin Murphy—and directing its members to join the Meat Cutters.[66]

Several factors explain this surprising move. Anxious to tap the Amalgamated's resources, SLC activists felt that they could control the local organization in Chicago. They believed that with Dennis Lane ailing and secretary Patrick Gorman in effective control, the Meat Cutters might be more receptive to industrial unionism. Another factor was involved as well. The dissolution of the Stockyards Labor Council coincided with a change in Communist Party policy from the ultra-left "Third Period" to the "Popular Front." In terms of the Party's trade union practice, this turn meant that TUUL affiliates such as the PHWIU abandoned dual unionism and joined the AFL organizations in their respective industries. Given the leading role played by Herbert March in the SLC's decision to disband and in negotiations with the Amalgamated that produced a free transfer of membership, the change in Party line was more than a merely coincidental event.[67]

Once inside the Amalgamated, SLC activists began agitating anew for a major organizing drive in the stockyards. At first, Gorman seemed to support this idea but he soon backtracked. The first hint of trouble came when the International opposed plans to use volunteer organizers and insisted instead on sending in outside staff members to conduct the campaign. When the SLC presented its plan—which included industrial organization, an emphasis on racial solidarity, and cooperation with community institutions—the Amalgamated balked. Further signs of trouble soon cropped up. Workers at the Hammond plant refused to have anything to do with the Meat Cutters, and two hundred union members in Armour's pork-cutting department lost interest in maintaining their organization. Worse, unorganized workers declined to respond to the Meat Cutters' personnel. Some even refused to speak with them. "These guys represented all that had gone wrong in the past, all the screw ups and missed opportunities," explained

Les Orear. "They didn't forget that it was the Amalgamated who had wrecked things the first time around." By the summer of 1935, the SLC's decision to fall in with the AMC appeared to be a mistake.[68]

One way to salvage the situation emerged. Elected delegates to the Chicago Federation of Labor, Herbert March and Frank McCarty proposed in July 1935 that the CFL oversee the stockyards campaign. This overture did not sit well with Gorman, who turned down Fitzpatrick's request that the Amalgamated send an official representative to discuss the packing-house "problem." The Chicago dissidents had become a thorn in his side, and he had no desire to further their power—even if that meant writing off the Chicago packinghouses. The rebuff probably pushed Fitzpatrick into the arms of the former SLC men, for he opened the CFL session which took up March's proposal with a scathing attack on the Meat Cutters, calling them to task for destruction of the first Stockyards Labor Council in 1919. Although the decision was opposed by some craft union delegates, the CFL moved to take up a drive in the stockyards on an industrial basis.[69]

The Amalgamated now found itself in a curious position. An organiz-ing drive in the heart of the meatpacking industry was underway, direct-ed by a group of rank-and-file dissidents in concert with the powerful CFL. Meanwhile, the international union stood on the sidelines. In August, Gor-man moved to reassert the Amalgamated's strength, sending two represen-tatives to a CFL meeting to present the International's own program for organization. His choice of "Big Bill" Tate, one of the union's few black organizers and a former sparring partner to Jack Dempsey, was a shrewd one. Unlike most of the Amalgamated's Chicago staff, Tate had earned the respect of a number of packinghouse activists and his influence was respon-sible for what little gains the AMC made in the yards. But Tate's speech to the Federation backfired. After a long-winded review of the Amalgamat-ed's activities since the 1921 strike, he concluded with his union's "pro-gram." Stunned activists listened while Tate pleaded for a boycott of non-union retail meat markets. "When you go into a butcher's shop, how many of you look around to see if there is a union shop card? It would help us a lot if you would refuse to patronize a store that does not display the union card. . . . it would give us all the assistance we ask of you." Here was graph-ic proof of the Amalgamated's outmoded thinking. An economic boycott might have some effectiveness in the retail sector of the industry, but it was an inappropriate and misguided strategy for organizing the packinghous-es. Rather than showing the AMC's commitment to the drive in the yards, Tate's oration demonstrated the union's bankruptcy.[70]

Against the International's wishes, the CFL went ahead with its plan to aid the dissidents. The federation planned to kick off the drive during its

annual Labor Day celebration at Soldier Field, but when the city parks commissioner, who also happened to be a vice-president of Armour, denied the
CFL use of the facility, Herbert March devised a dramatic alternative: a parade starting from the Amalgamated's headquarters, progressing around the
stockyards, and winding up at Sherman Park, the site of the mass rallies of
1919. March recalled that AMC officials opposed the plan, but since the CFL
"was honoring them, so to speak, they couldn't very well decline." Despite
harassment from the police department's Red Squad, the parade was a success. Several thousand marched through Back-of-the-Yards, showing residents that the Chicago labor movement was lining up behind them in their
fight against the packers. Reluctantly, officials of the Meat Cutters participated, conveying the impression that they sanctioned the drive as well.[71]

Once out of public view, however, the Amalgamated attempted to scut-
tle the organizing campaign, cutting off funds it had promised the SLC
when the merger took place and discontinuing per capita payments to the
CFL. It also began pressuring Fitzpatrick through the American Federation
of Labor. These machinations dampened but did not stall activity in the
stockyards. An organizing committee headed by Kampfert succeeded in
restoring the gains made by the SLC before its dissolution and extending
organization into a number of other independent plants, including Empire
Packing, Lincoln Meat, C. A. Burnette, and Wimp Packing. By the end of
1935, several of the smaller houses were operating under signed contracts
with the Amalgamated. At Roberts and Oake, where McCarty worked skinning pork bellies, the shattered union was rebuilt—only to be wiped out
for a second time when management again shut the plant. Before this happened, black activists there, led by Jesse Vaughn and Reverend Hurie Lee,
brought workers of the Levi Casing Company into the union fold. Although
employed by Levi, these workers labored in a number of plants gathering
and cleaning hog intestines for use as sausage casings and for sale as chit-
terlings. Their daily tasks brought them in contact with Vaughn's work
group, and organization proceeded from this relationship. Yet no matter
how encouraging the gains made among the independents, the key to the
yards were Armour, Swift, and Wilson. These three large plants remained
elusive prizes, out of the grasp of the movement.[72]

Enter the CIO: The Packinghouse Workers
Organizing Committee

Frustrated in their efforts to work within the Amalgamated Meat Cutters,
Chicago's packinghouse activists looked on with great interest when John
L. Lewis formed the Committee for Industrial Organization following the

tumultuous 1935 AFL convention. They saw in the CIO the possibility of overcoming the tensions that had limited their effectiveness within the Meat Cutters, as well as a means for uniting the region's divided independent movements under a single umbrella. The personal prestige of Lewis coupled with the militant reputation of the miners seemed strong enough to counter the independent unionists' reluctance to surrender their local autonomy—the sticking point that had undermined the 1934 unity conference. Further, packing unionists hoped to receive organizing help as well as funds from the Mine Workers treasury with which to conduct a vigorous drive in their industry.

These ambitious hopes were premature. Lewis at this time was treading carefully, unwilling to break completely with the AFL. Because the Amalgamated had supported the minority report which became the CIO platform, Lewis and his advisers chose not to challenge the AMC's jurisdiction over the packing industry. Even after it was clear that a split with the federation was unavoidable, CIO leaders refrained from antagonizing the Amalgamated, hoping that they could woo the Meat Cutters into joining them. Packinghouse workers, however, immediately sprang into action. Throughout the fall of 1935 and on into the following year, the loose regional network that stretched westward from Chicago coalesced. Led primarily by the Independent Union of All Workers, from Austin, Minnesota, these scattered activists mounted a relentless pressure campaign. Establishing a "Committee for Industrial Organization in the Packing Industry," they barraged Lewis and John Brophy with an endless stream of letters, telegrams, and personal visits all aimed at receiving some kind of CIO backing.[73]

Gorman and other Amalgamated officials tried to fend off these initiatives. They dismissed the Austin and Cedar Rapids organizations as "company unions" comprised of "a group of secessionists headed by a few soldiers of fortune." Inflating their own position in the industry by pointing to the headway made by the Chicago dissidents, they prevailed upon Brophy to recommend that the independents join the Meat Cutters. Perhaps cognizant of the SLC's fate within the AFL, the independents scornfully rejected the suggestion and proposed a joint drive with CIO sanction. Now it was Gorman's turn to decline. This strange waltz continued throughout 1936, with the CIO serving as a mediator between the Meat Cutters and the various rank-and-file movements.[74]

In Chicago, CIO successes in the automobile and steel industries breathed new hope and optimism into the weary union movement in the stockyards. "It just was like everything caught aflame everywhere," remembered Jesse Vaughn. Jim Cole, a black beef butcher, recalled that "when they began organizing out in the steel towns and out in South Chicago, everybody wanted to know when the CIO was coming to the Yards." Many packinghouse workers had friends and relatives involved in the CIO's Steel Workers Organizing Committee, and "watched very closely as things developed, always thinking about whether that kind of thing could work here in packing." For their part, black workers sensed that the new union movement was pursuing a radically egalitarian course, with black organizers playing leading roles rather than backseat ones.[75]

The militants in the Amalgamated sensed this feeling of expectation and decided that the moment had arrived to "get out from under Pat Gorman's thumb." In January of 1937, a committee of eighteen men and women met in the back room of a tavern at Forty-eighth and Paulina and discussed making a direct appeal to CIO regional officials. A delegation was dispatched to visit SWOC's midwestern director, Van A. Bittner. Apparently taken by surprise, Bittner and his assistant, Nick Fontecchio, turned the group away, telling them to return with signed union cards if they wished to receive serious consideration. Several days later, the group returned with two hundred signed cards bearing the simple inscription, "I want a CIO union in the packing industry." Unconvinced, Fontecchio told the delegation that more impressive evidence was needed before the CIO would move. Undeterred, the packinghouse activists printed up new cards and smuggled them into the plants. With the sit-down strikes in Ohio's rubber plants and Detroit's automobile factories filling the headlines, the response was overwhelming. "I knew we were going to make it when those cards began rolling in," one organizer recalled. Within a month, Bittner's office was deluged with thousands of cards from the packinghouses. Lacking the authority to authorize an official campaign, he nonetheless sanctioned use of the CIO's name.[76]

Events came to a head in the spring of 1937. In the stockyards, the first real breakthrough occurred in the large houses. In late March, Armour workers led by the pork trim and hog kill formed a local union and, claiming affiliation with the CIO, began to spread their organization into other parts of the plant. Using squads of four to six workers, they visited other departments during lunch breaks and held dressing room meetings. Out in the open for the first time, the Armour local began holding public meetings at Sikora's Hall, a popular tavern and meeting room at Forty-eighth and Marshfield. "It was like a snowball rolling downhill," March remembered. The packing companies countered with a nine-cent wage increase, and Wilson announced a new vacation plan for its employees. The announcements further fueled the movement, as workers took this move as proof of their growing power and flocked to the union in even greater numbers.[77]

At the same time, the Communist Party mobilized its entire Chicago apparatus behind the drive in the stockyards. Having established a comfortable working relationship with Bittner and the SWOC, the CP added its voice to the chorus demanding a campaign in the stockyards and directed its neighborhood units to make organization of the packing industry their first priority. Jack Johnstone personally oversaw the Party's efforts, and devoted special emphasis to swinging black lodges, churches, and other community institutions behind the drive.[78]

Meanwhile, the Amalgamated's balancing act was coming to a close. In April, CIO officials expressed their dismay that despite the Meat Cutters' promise to undertake an organizing drive in the packinghouses, they had not done so. Gorman responded by complaining about the many communications crossing his desk that indicated the CIO was actively enrolling packinghouse workers. Meeting with Gorman in early May, Lewis bluntly delivered an ultimatum: "You must stand on one side or the other," he told the Meat Cutters' leader. "These men are going to be organized—you have got to stand with the CIO or with the American Federation of Labor." When its executive board met a few days later, the Amalgamated cast its lot with the other craft unions, choosing to remain in the Federation. The day after this decision, the CIO began issuing charters to packinghouse unions. On 24 October 1937, the Packinghouse Workers Organizing Committee was formally established, under the leadership of Van Bittner. Arthur Kampfert, who had been unable to secure work in the packing industry and was laboring as a paper handler at the *Chicago Tribune*, was tapped to serve as Chicago regional director.[79]

Union organizing in the Chicago stockyards began long before the establishment of the PWOC. For four years, groups of rank-and-file activists had attempted to build viable organizations. They had explored a variety of avenues, ranging from independent unionism to working within the AFL's Amalgamated Meat Cutters, and had met with varying degrees of success. In addition, they had forged links with packinghouse activists in other areas and together had tried to develop a strategy for organizing the industry. The formation of the PWOC marked the culmination of these early efforts and the opening of a new stage in the struggle to democratize the autocratic world of the packers.

In the fall of 1937, the interracial alliance that characterized the PWOC and, later, the United Packinghouse Workers of America, was not fully formed. Its outlines could be discerned—and were, in fact, prefigured by the brief merger of the PHWIU and the SLC. Veteran white butchers had joined forces with black militants and left-wing activists. This coalition had withstood the pressure of powerful divisive forces: the opposition of the craft-oriented Amalgamated, the concerted attacks of the packing companies, and the powerful racism of the dominant culture. However, it remained embryonic in form. While the alliance had taken hold at the leadership level, its extension to the mass of packinghouse workers remained a task for the immediate future. Building on the formative experience of the early depression, the PWOC set about accomplishing the unprecedented and difficult task of welding together black and white workers under the banner of the CIO.

5

Organizing the Stockyards, 1937–40

The CIO's 1937 entry into the meatpacking industry was a decisive event. On both the national and local levels, the formation of the Packinghouse Workers Organizing Committee gave direction and coherence to a previously fragmented movement. It not only served as an institutional umbrella under which different political and organizational groupings could coexist but also provided a bureaucratic structure capable of coordinating the movements of union activists in different plants and cities. At the same time, the involvement of the CIO in the packinghouse workers' struggle had an enormous psychological impact on those involved. The sense of participation in a national working-class movement, the feeling of empowerment derived from knowledge of workers' victories elsewhere in the country, and the personal prestige and imposing presence of John L. Lewis, all boosted the union campaign in the stockyards. "Suddenly, we weren't alone anymore," recalled one Chicago packinghouse worker. "It seemed like the auto workers in Detroit and out in steel and over here in the yards that we were all pulling together, fighting for the same thing and it made it seem like anything was possible."[1]

Yet, caution must be exercised when assessing the role played by the CIO in the packinghouses. To lend too much weight to the intervention of Lewis and his lieutenants obscures the actual process by which organization was built in the plants. As detailed earlier, the union movement in the yards began several years before the CIO's establishment and had an ambivalent relationship with "organized labor." Moreover, the founding of the PWOC did not alter the rank-and-file nature of the packinghouse workers' campaign in Chicago. Workers continued to rely on each other to extend union organization, department by department, plant by plant, through the yards.

The persistence of this rank-and-file character resulted from both an accident of timing and the considerable tension that existed between rank-and-file packinghouse unionists and their CIO-appointed leaders. The PWOC was set up at a time when the momentum of the CIO's ongoing campaigns in auto and steel had been arrested or even reversed. In Chicago, the 1937 Memorial Day Massacre and the defeat of the "Little Steel" drive both dampened the sense of insurgency which had developed over the course of the previous eighteen months and caused CIO officials to proceed more cautiously in other areas. Responding to these reverses, the CIO lent only paltry financial assistance to the PWOC's initial efforts. Certainly nothing resembling the one million dollars poured into the steel campaign ever reached the packinghouse workers.[2] Indeed, for its first four months the PWOC was essentially a paper organization, with only two staff members actually in the yards on a daily basis. Unlike the case of steel—where a sizeable central bureaucracy, the Steelworkers Organizing Committee (SWOC), was imposed upon workers—the PWOC did not subsume existing organizations but built upon them. This allowed rank-and-file activists considerable leeway and freedom of maneuver. "We sort of ran an independent show," recalled Jesse Prosten, a self-described "free-lance" organizer in Boston and Chicago who later headed the union's grievance department.[3]

The frequent use of direct action tactics, a reliance on volunteer organizers, and a pronounced receptivity to radical influences characterized the style of unionism practiced by the PWOC in the late 1930s. Effective leadership resided on the shop floor. Stewards and committeemen rather than official staff members directed the union's day-to-day activities. Lewis's handpicked chair of the PWOC, Van Bittner, and his associates struggled to control these rank-and-file energies. They failed to impose a centralized top-down structure on the new union, but their efforts to contain the ferment in the yards produced a chronic and strongly felt tension between themselves and unionists in the packinghouses.

This conflict was apparent from the first, but originally it was a more a matter of personality and style than the product of interunion politics. Van Bittner was a dour, sharp-tongued individual who called forth little loyalty among those who worked with him. He never gave the packinghouse campaign his undivided attention, devoting much time and energy to steel organizing and internal CIO intrigue. Many packinghouse activists resented the fact that Lewis allies without experience in the industry filled the PWOC's top positions. Robert Schultz, a butcher who labored in packing towns across the Midwest, derisively labeled the CIO-appointed officers "a bunch of coal miners," referring to their backgrounds as Lewis underlings in the United Mine Workers.[4]

The PWOC's efforts to limit workers' self-activity and to direct the thrust of the campaign in the stockyards fueled this conflict. The resulting tension ensured the persistence of independent organizing activity and the construction of rank-and-file networks which operated at a remove from the official union apparatus. The activities of these informal bodies rather than the more visible initiatives of the PWOC leadership are the proper focus of an investigation of CIO organizing in the Chicago stockyards.

While the public maneuverings and pronouncements of PWOC officials, company spokesmen, and government mediators deserve attention, developments on the shop floor are more revealing. It was here that organization was extended beyond a committed core of activists and began to encompass the mass of workers. Similarly, on the shop floor, especially in the critical killing departments, the PWOC proved able to exert the most power. The legal protection afforded by the Wagner Act, the union's use of the National Labor Relations Board, and other forms of federal mediation were important, but ultimately it was the union's ability to control the production process that brought the packing companies to terms. Long before the large packers entered into a formal collective bargaining relationship with the PWOC, local activists had won de facto union recognition in many departments. Moreover, the union's first victories resulted not from discussion around the bargaining table but from concerted pressure at the point of production. As one packinghouse worker poignantly stated, "It was a bunch of guys in bloody aprons that got us these things, not some pretty-smelling, sweet-talking lawyer in a hundred dollar suit."[5]

The single most important challenge facing the PWOC in this period was the construction of an interracial and interethnic alliance. The entire project of industrial unionism in the meatpacking industry hinged upon the successful forging of solidarity across the historic divides of color and country. The groundwork for such unity had been laid earlier in the decade, largely through the efforts of the Communist-led unemployed movement, the Packinghouse Workers Industrial Union, and, to a lesser extent, the Stockyards Labor Council. Tendencies toward class fragmentation had not been extinguished, merely contained. They could reassert themselves with startling speed and cruel consequence, especially when prompted by employer resistance or rival unionism.

Before the PWOC could stand up to the packers, functional unity had to be extended beyond the local leadership and instilled at the mass level. The workplace was the primary arena in which solidarity was forged. The union's penchant for direct action actively involved a large proportion of its membership and gave workers of different races and nationalities the experience of common struggle. Many of the PWOC's first successful actions sprang from the grievances of black workers; and in a number of instances union pressure resulted in the remedying of longstanding inequities. Equally important was the visible example set by integrated committees and executive boards. In fact, a disproportionate number of early union officers were black, and the leadership provided by these men and women went a long way toward breaking down white stereotypes of black inferiority.

The PWOC's community activism reinforced efforts made inside the packinghouses to weld workers together into a self-aware unit. In the white community the most important institution resulting from this activism was the Back-of-the-Yards Neighborhood Council. Formed in 1939 as a result of PWOC initiatives, the council included representatives from various community groups and not only ameliorated interethnic tensions but also promoted an attitude of tolerance toward neighboring blacks. Within the Black Belt the PWOC maintained a visible presence and built supportive relationships with the major black churches, sponsored an impressive variety of athletic teams, and launched a youth organization. In addition, the New Deal shift of black voters away from the GOP provided another vehicle for interracial working-class unity in the form of the local Democratic Party. The PWOC's support of Edward Kelly's Democratic machine meant that party politics no longer divided black and white packinghouse workers. It also meant that when trouble flared in the stockyards, the union could look to city hall for assistance.

Hidden History: Initial Gains in the Little Six Plants

When the CIO launched its organizing committee in meatpacking, activists in the small Chicago houses were best positioned to take advantage of the institutional cover now afforded them. While organization in the large plants was uneven, many of the Little Six facilities, with employees numbering in the hundreds rather than thousands, boasted very high—in some cases close to 100 percent—union membership. Beyond their numerical strength, unionists in the small plants derived additional encouragement from the knowledge that their skills were vital to production. Butchers in these houses retained more of the all-around knife skills eliminated elsewhere years earlier. Each worker performed at least two jobs, as the same gangs who dressed chilled meat in the morning killed hogs in the afternoon for the following day's work. The PWOC registered its first real gains in the Little Six plants and then, using them as bases, organized the larger houses.[6]

Within weeks of the PWOC's establishment, the National Labor Relations Board held its first representation election in the stockyards. In early November 1937, the 450 workers at Miller and Hart voted overwhelmingly to have the CIO serve as their bargaining agent. In a move that portended the hard road that lay ahead, the company recognized but adamantly refused to negotiate with the newly certified union. After several abortive attempts to meet with management, the plant's workers swung into action. On 13 November they labored through the morning and began killing hogs in the early afternoon. When two hundred freshly slaughtered carcasses hung from the line, the union steward called the process to a halt while the bargaining committee again sought a meeting with the plant superintendent. Amidst the confusion, a government inspector lent a degree of urgency to the request: unless the hogs entered the cooler within the hour, he would have no choice but to condemn the carcasses, costing the company thousands of dollars. The superintendent capitulated and ushered the union committee into his office for a meeting.[7]

Events developed similarly at the Roberts and Oake plant, where workers had battled the company for a number of years. In the past, whenever the union seemed on the verge of gaining a majority, management closed the killing floor, retained only a skeleton crew, and shipped in split hogs from its facility in Marshalltown, Iowa. After the various union locals in the yards came together in the PWOC and organizing at Roberts and Oake surged forward, management shut the entire plant for a short period, hoping to break the momentum of the drive. When it reopened, the union succeeded in gaining regular hearings with management but made little progress toward securing an agreement with the company. In a carefully coordinated action, black and white butchers worked through their noontime break, filling the "dead rail" with large five-hundred-pound carcasses. With the government inspector watching the clock, local president Jesse Vaughn sought out the superintendent and raised the question of a formal agreement. When the superintendent balked, Vaughn pointed to the sagging dead rail. "That man went this high off the floor," Vaughn recalled.

"Oh my god," he said, "I'm done." Within a few days, the Roberts and Oake local wrested a signed agreement from the company, the first in the yards.[8]

These actions underscore two elements which helped define the next stage in the struggle for collective bargaining in the industry: the intransigence with which the packers responded to the challenge of union certification and the process of negotiation, and the packinghouse workers' reliance on direct action to bring their employers to terms. At Miller and Hart, workers could have appealed to a sympathetic NLRB for support when the company stonewalled them. The Roberts and Oake local had retained Chicago labor lawyer Alfred Kamin to represent them. In both cases, union leaders opted to pressure the company through well-timed job actions rather than pursue their objectives through bureaucratic channels.[9]

Throughout the autumn of 1937 and on into the following year, workers in the Little Six plants provided a sense of dynamism and movement to the PWOC. While union strategists did not consciously opt to focus their energies upon the independent plants, these small packers formed the weakest link in the solid front with which the industry hoped to confront the PWOC. Least able to afford a protracted battle with the union, and most vulnerable to interruptions in production, the Little Six had compelling reasons to seek accommodation with their workers. Initially, this took a number of forms, depending upon the relative strength of the local and the resolve of management. A signed contract, like the one at Roberts and Oake, was unusual. More common was an informal, unwritten agreement covering a number of issues. Significantly, the thrust of these agreements was noneconomistic: the union sought to secure the recognition of its representatives, regulate layoffs, insure the payment of a uniform base wage, reduce speedups, and lighten job loads. In this sense they harkened back to the understandings reached between shop committees and individual foremen during the 1917–21 period, except now they were negotiated on the plant level.

Unionists regarded these agreements not as substitutes for a contract but as stepping-stones along the path to formal recognition. Lowell Washington explained, "you had it take it slow, a step at a time, to make sure that you was bringing everybody along with you." An incremental process unfolded that drew in other workers and built confidence. "First you get them to just talk with . . . your people out on the floor. The other guys see that and they think, 'hey, they got something, this union's gonna get some action and I better get on board so I can get a piece of it.' Then you can start pushing a little harder, asking for a little bit more." Since the agreements were informal at this stage, enforcement was a problem. Washington admitted that a foreman might "try to chip around the edges, you know take a man off the gang here or maybe squeeze a bit more work out of someone." Workers tolerated a certain amount of "give and take," but if management repeatedly violated an important part of the accord they "pushed back."[10]

This pressure could take a number of forms. It might simply be a disguised slowdown reminiscent of the kind of guerrilla warfare practiced by packinghouse workers since the origins of the modern industry. Or it might take the form of a stoppage on the part of a work gang or department. When Agar arbitrarily increased one older worker's quota, the butchers on either side of the man silently picked up the slack. When the foreman noticed this assistance, he moved to stop it by reassigning them to different positions. Gradually, the entire department came to a halt. "We had to protect this oldtimer—not just for his sake but to show those younger guys that we meant what we said and weren't gonna be pushed around. 'Cause if they could do that to that old man, sure as hell they were gonna try something on the rest of us."[11]

At other times, conflict escalated into a walkout. At the P. D. Brennan plant, for example, one of the first understandings reached between union stewards and supervisors limited the weight of loaded hand trucks used to cart trimmed meat from the cutting department. After management exceeded the agreed-upon limit, and negotiations led nowhere, local president Charles Balskus led the entire plant out on strike. Two days later the company gave in, assenting to respect the weight limit and to provide extra help to men pushing the cumbersome trucks up inclines.[12]

Although the independent plants were not clustered in one area of the stockyards, physical isolation did not deter the emergence of solidarity among them. When Illinois Meat locked out its killing- and cutting-floor workers in the summer of 1938, unionists from the other Little Six plants swelled their picket line. Similarly, when the Oppenheimer Casing Company discharged forty-two union activists, the Agar killing floor—which supplied Oppenheimer with hog intestines—shut down in protest. This kind of unity extended to the large plants, where workers closely watched developments elsewhere in the yards. During a prolonged stoppage at Miller and Hart, a rumor swept through the Swift hog kill that the animals coming up the chute came from the struck packer. The union steward, Philip Weightman, stopped the chain and demanded to check the animals. Weightman had no way of determining who owned the hogs since they bore no brands or telltale marks. Nevertheless, he slowly inspected each carcass on the line, pretending to look for revealing signs—a charade which demonstrated solidarity to both the idled workers and the hapless supervisors.[13]

Repeated job actions in the Little Six plants allowed local unions to perfect their shop-floor organization and to accustom their membership to disciplined, carefully orchestrated activity. All this occurred with minimal guidance from PWOC staff. Early in the summer of 1938, though, the district office began to take a more active interest in these locals as the push for a contract covering the Little Six plants began. Such a drive required the coordination and direction that only the district staff could provide. Although intimately attuned to shop-floor dynamics, rank-and-file leaders were still inexperienced negotiators who were ill at ease with the legal jargon and procedures surrounding contracts. Many PWOC officials, especially those hailing from other industries, had only rudimentary knowledge of the workings of a packinghouse and the special problems faced by workers and management. Soon, a symbiotic relationship developed between local unionists and the PWOC staff, with the latter heading the actual negotiations and the former continuing to direct pressure on the companies from within the plants.

The assignment of the PWOC's assistant national director, Henry Johnson, to the Little Six negotiations proved fortuitous. "Hank" Johnson was a charismatic black Communist who had been on the SWOC payroll before his transfer to packing. The son of a Wobbly from West Texas, he was well known in the black community. He had spent a number of years organizing for the International Workers Order, was a founder of the National Negro Congress, and had used his legendary oratorical abilities to bring blacks into the steelworkers union. Described by Les Orear as "the kind of human being that people gravitated to," Johnson rapidly emerged as one of the PWOC's most important leaders. His appointment itself demonstrated that the new union was committed to black advancement; and his smooth, polished manner and educated speech pattern reassured many whites who held stereotypical notions about blacks' abilities. "This was terribly important," Jane March recalled, "because at this time everybody was questioning all these black guys coming into the leadership." Johnson's ability to win the hearts of whites as well as blacks, Orear observed, "did a great deal to cement and make real the sense of trust and unity" within the union.[14]

Even before his formal assignment to the PWOC, Johnson had some contact with packing locals, especially the black-led ones at Roberts and Oake and the Armour Soap Works. When organizing first began at the latter plant, union founders Richard Saunders and Burrette King sought out

Johnson after hearing him speak at a community gathering in the Black Belt. Although he knew little about the inside of a packinghouse, Johnson worked with the two inexperienced men, lending counsel on legal rights under the Wagner Act, tactics, and strategy. Later, his keen negotiating abilities and "golden tongue" gave the PWOC an advantage when facing the packers' lawyers. Referring to the first signed contract, Jesse Vaughn of Roberts and Oake noted, "Johnson took us by the hand, told us how to do it."[15]

Johnson's lawyerlike demeanor not withstanding, several of the small packers balked at the negotiating table. Unionists charged that financial contributions and other assurances from Armour and Swift stiffened their resolve. When contract talks began to drag, job actions swept the plants as the union attempted to move things along toward a successful conclusion. When Roberts and Oake broke off talks, a stoppage in the plant the following day brought them back to the table. Later, when management at Miller and Hart agreed to each point submitted by the union but refused to sign the accord, a sitdown coaxed the needed signatures. The packers tried to show that they too could play industrial hardball, locking out over two thousand workers in late July. However, this seems to have been a gesture borne out of desperation: a week later the dispute ended with a written agreement in place in all but one of the Little Six plants.[16]

This first contract called for paid vacations, a thirty-two-hour week guarantee, checkoff of union dues, and time and a half for overtime. Although the packers refused an outright wage increase, they agreed to an "adjustment" which brought rates in line with those at the large houses. "It wasn't much to brag about," Pat Balskus recalled. "But at the time . . . it was the biggest thing in the world. Especially for the old-timers who had seen the union crushed so many times. They never thought they would live to see the day."[17]

Since workers at the small packinghouses came to terms with their employers well before the PWOC was in a position to negotiate with the large packers, they were able to play important roles in the union drives on Armour, Swift, and Wilson. "It was the Little Six that organized the big plants, not the other way," Lowell Washington insisted. "Without us it would have been years before Armours and Swifts got organized." The teams of volunteer organizers upon whom the PWOC relied to make contact with workers as they left the yards, in the taverns along Ashland Avenue, or at their homes in the evenings contained disproportionate numbers of Little Six activists. In certain parts of the yards complex, workers came in contact with one another during the course of the workday. Women from Roberts and Oake frequently visited with workers on break from the Armour hair house, located less than a hundred yards from their own plant. Over the course of several weeks, they signed up the entire division. Perhaps as important as the actual communication between workers was the model and inspiration provided by the Little Six contracts. "Here was the example, the living proof that it could be done," declared one organizer, who added, "believe me that counted for an awfully lot to people who might be a little bit uncertain and afraid."[18]

Organizing Armour: Autonomy and Dignity on the Shop Floor

Up to this point organization in the large plants had been largely clandestine. At the Armour Soap Works, for example, Richard Saunders, Burrette King, and other pro-union activists used the cover of a "Sportsman's Club" to build support for the PWOC. At the main Armour plant, only workers on the killing floors, previously organized by the PHWIU, openly flaunted their membership in the union, although at least a third of the seventy-five hundred workers were dues-paying members of Local 347. The situation at Swift and Wilson was muddled, with two or three core groups of activists organizing independently of each other. Phil Weightman recalled attending his first Swift union meeting and discovering with a mixture of chagrin and shock that only two others were in the room. "The sentiment was there," Vicky Starr explained somewhat apologetically, "it was just that organization lagged very far behind."[19]

The elevation of Herbert March and Sigmund Wlodarczyk to the PWOC staff in early 1938 gave the Armour effort a needed boost. March was widely respected for his work with the PHWIU, and many activists considered him the "main symbol in our industry of the fighting kind of unionism which drew workers to the CIO." Barred from the plant, March could be found almost every noontime, behind the wheel of the PWOC's soundtruck at the center of the yards at a location dubbed "CIO Corner." Wlodarczyk was an important asset as well, enjoying both a high profile and extensive contacts among white ethnics in the plant and community. At about the same time, Refugio Martinez joined the union's team of full-time organizers. He began working with Swift activists, especially the sizeable contingent of Mexicans who labored on the loading docks and pickling departments. The Wilson plant, however, remained a backwater. While over a thousand Wilson workers had signed CIO cards, none had come forward and volunteered to start the formidable task of organizing within the plant. John Wrublewski remembered that he and his workmates often talked about the progress of the CIO campaign, but they "kept waiting and waiting" to be approached. "I wasn't gonna be the first one," he recalled, "but I sure of hell would have done just about anything they asked me." With its resources stretched thin, and a seemingly lukewarm response from workers in the plant, the PWOC assigned a low priority to Wilson.[20]

The immediate challenge facing March and Wlodarczyk was finding a way to bring Armour Local 347 out into the open. In 1937 the company had responded to the formation of the PWOC by discharging many of the more visible activists; the fear created by these firings now acted as a brake on further organization. Pete Davis, a black beef butcher who had worked at Armour since 1923, was fired for refusing to remove his union button. Known to management as a staunch PWOC supporter, Davis had been caught a few weeks earlier with union literature in his locker. Word of the discharge spread through the plant, prompting other workers to remove their buttons. Punitive actions occurred in other departments. Jesse Perez and twenty-two other workers from the loading dock, a center of union strength, received indefinite layoffs. The few men from the gang who were recalled, including some twenty-year veterans, found themselves placed on the most menial and low-paying jobs.[21]

Compounding the problem of intimidation was Armour's revival of its company union. The packers first dusted off these organizations in early 1937, hoping that employee representation might provide an alternative to the adversarial groups then forming in their plants.[22] After the Supreme Court upheld the Wagner Act, which outlawed such employer-dominated organizations, the packing companies simply withdrew the management representatives and renamed the bodies. In the case of Armour, the Joint Conference Board disbanded itself only to reemerge as the Employees Mutual Association (EMA). At Swift, where the old company union never completely died, the new body was christened the Security League. Because of Swift's paternalism it enjoyed an unusual degree of support. Van Bittner reported to the CIO Executive Board that it was "one of the most effective in the country."[23]

Armour EMA spokesmen later claimed that over 80 percent of the workers in the plant cast ballots in an election for officers in mid-1937. Worker testimony before the NLRB made it clear, however, that this support was coerced. The election was held in the plant during working hours, with loyal employees carrying ballot boxes from department to department, keeping record of how workers voted. Those who declined to participate were warned that their refusal jeopardized the vacations promised them. In the beef-casing department, where an entire gang of PWOC members refused to mark ballots, an EMA official threatened that unless they voted they would find themselves "out on State Street." Anna Novak was told that her pay would be cut to twenty-five cents an hour unless she participated in the election. She stood firm, but the women around her capitulated.[24]

The PWOC rejoined by filing charges with the NLRB, but hearings did not commence until January 1938. In the meantime, the EMA openly competed with the CIO in the plant, making special efforts to recruit butchers and other knife workers. "They tried to buy these skilled guys off by making them employee representatives and fixing it up so that they had soft jobs, or didn't work very much, or could walk around," March recalled. In addition Armour allowed EMA representatives free access to all departments, paid the salaries of its officers, furnished them with an office, and kept the organization's funds in a company bank account.[25]

Despite the illegality of this setup, the EMA's visibility made many workers question the strength and viability of the PWOC. Gertie Kamarczyk, who had seen Armour use the company union to counter the Amalgamated in 1921, recalled that in 1937 "all of us girls were for the CIO. But none of us was too sure that it had much of a chance in those first days, so we just waited to see which way things were gonna go before we got too involved." Armour's tactic of crediting improvements won by the PWOC to the EMA contributed to this hesitancy. On the sheep kill, for example, well-organized CIO supporters forced the company to reduce the speed of the line, upgrade their wage rates to those paid at Swift, and eliminate the onerous practice of extracting unpaid overtime labor from the gang. Several days later, the EMA newsletter heralded the victory as its own.[26]

The EMA also gave Armour a rationale for its refusal to meet with PWOC representatives. When Local 347's bargaining committee requested an appointment with superintendent D. W. King in October 1937, they were told that the company recognized the Mutual Association as the sole bargaining agent representing its employees. Subsequent requests, including a letter from Van Bittner to Armour president Robert Cabell, elicited the same response.[27] Frustrated in their effort to gain an audience with top management, and facing a long delay before the Labor Board opened hearings, the union set about perfecting its in-plant organization. Superintendent King could be adamant in his refusal to recognize or meet with the union, but departmental level foremen and supervisors had little choice in the matter if they intended to meet their production quotas. "It isn't what

you may say in the meeting that worries the boss," PWOC leaders instructed. "It's what happens on the job that he pays attending to."[28]

Under Herbert March's direction, volunteer organizers formed a "Committee of 100," a group built around a core of black militants from the killing floors who had been agitating for a union since the formation of the
PHWIU in 1933. It also included a number of older white unionists such
as William Mooney, a carpenter who had labored at Armour since 1928; Jake
Byra, a twenty-year veteran based in the pork-cutting department; and
George Kovacavich, a Croatian who had migrated to Chicago from the Iowa
coalfields where he had been active in the UMWA. By virtue of their long
service and union backgrounds, these men were able to sway many of the
more reticent whites over to the PWOC. Many of them, journalist DeWitt
Gilpin noted at the time, "still carr[ied] bullets from the strike of '21." Organized into smaller "flying squads," they conducted lunchtime "raids" on
weak departments where they held dressing room meetings, circulated
membership cards, and engaged individuals in conversation. In one two-
month period, the committee brought in over two thousand new recruits.[29]

On occasion, these forays developed into confrontations with EMA representatives. When pork butcher and Local 347 president Al Malachi led a
raid on the canning room, he encountered EMA president James Holmes
lecturing women workers there on the evils of the PWOC. A heated im-
promptu debate ran for several minutes before Holmes decided to call security guards. A member of the assembled crowd recalled the skirmish with
relish: "the CIO boys just made that company man look like a fool. He was
sputtering and all red in the face. Even Miss Mitchell [the forelady] was
smiling . . . finally he just slunked away and we didn't see no more of him
after that." Not all such encounters ended this way. Guards who caught up
with unionists organizing on the job were known to deliver well-placed jabs
to the kidneys, or worse, as they removed the offender. On at least one
occasion a pitched battle erupted between the "company dicks" and workers, with the latter brandishing sharpening steels and knives as weapons.[30]

As new members were brought into the union, the Armour local developed an unusually large corps of shop-floor representatives. By mid-1938,
almost every one of the plant's one hundred departments contained a head
steward with seven to twenty assistants, depending on the size of the department. There was a dual rationale behind these numbers. First, the union
relied upon its stewards to complete the task of extending its presence into
the far corners of the plant. "Speeches at an occasional mass meeting don't
organize a union," Hank Johnson explained. "The real job of organizing has
to be done everyday by the men and women who work right in the plant."

Second, the union shared responsibility as widely as possible in order to protect itself against corruption. "We felt that the employers always bought us out," Jesse Prosten explained. "They bought the officers of the union in the old AFL style. So we had one steward for every ten people. We figured, well, if you're going to buy some you can't buy them all." Each of these stewards carried the authority to represent workers and, if need be, call a halt to production. Such action did not require clearance from the local's executive board or the PWOC staff.[31]

Departmental autonomy meant that stoppages, slowdowns, and other job actions were frequent occurrences. Workers used them to achieve a variety of goals, but most of the time direct action was used to force de facto recognition of union representatives. Local 347 developed a tactic, referred to as "whistle bargaining," which effectively compelled foremen to resolve grievances. Each steward wore a whistle around his or her neck. Whenever a supervisor declined to discuss a grievance, the steward gave a blast on the whistle and the department halted work. When the issue was resolved, the steward whistled twice and production started up again. The shrill reverberations echoing through the plant told workers—even those isolated in anti-union strongholds—that the PWOC was flexing its muscles.[32]

Armour workers, like those in the Little Six plants, used their power over production to improve shop-floor conditions and redress long-standing inequities. Wage issues and other economic matters were a secondary concern. "It wasn't really the money that mattered," Sophie Kosciolowski explained. "I wanted to feel like a human being, that I had some dignity, you know. I didn't want to feel like they owned me."[33] Many of the job actions which swept the Armour plant in the spring and summer of 1938 sought to defend workers against the debasement and humiliation they routinely suffered. Helen Zajac, who worked stuffing and linking sausages, recalled that her boss relished penalizing latecomers and slow workers by taking them off their regular jobs and having them push loaded racks of sausage across the department. "This was a real killer—usually they had a big brawny man doing it—a lot of the girls just couldn't even move that thing," she explained. After an especially frail worker collapsed following a morning of the grueling punishment, a group of women in the department approached the union for relief. Only a few of them were PWOC members and the department was poorly organized. The next day, the men who trucked meat scraps into the sausage room struck, demanding the transfer of the spiteful supervisor. After a tense standoff during which the machinery sat idle, the foreman agreed to apologize to the gang and to stop assigning women to heavy tasks. "We never had a problem with him after that," Zajac noted, "and that department became 100 percent CIO!"[34]

A major concern of Armour union activists was the stabilization of the work year. In 1938, the "Roosevelt Recession" magnified the usual round of spring layoffs—probably the greatest cause of disruption in the lives of packinghouse workers. Almost seven thousand yards workers lost their jobs in February alone, including over fourteen hundred at Armour. By the end of March, many departments were operating with half the usual number of hands as the company adjusted to the shrinking flow of livestock.[35] Since Armour tended to lay off union members before nonunion workers, Local 347's demand for the recognition of seniority assumed great importance. A beef kill stoppage won informal acceptance of the seniority principle in that department, and subsequent actions on the killing floors protested discriminatory layoffs elsewhere in the plant. In addition, the local established a relief committee which helped unemployed workers secure WPA jobs, referred them to other employers, and in a few cases disbursed cash to needy families.[36]

Strategically situated killing-floor workers used their power to defend workers in other departments where the union was weak or where the company could afford to ignore interruptions in production. However, the impulse to rationalize the chaotic vagaries of packinghouse work was nearly universal. In the canning room, for example, the unequal distribution of work meant that some women put in up to forty-eight hours a week, while others suffered layoffs. Under the leadership of Anna Novak, a CP member, workers won an equal distribution of hours, even though this meant that the older women sacrificed their $40 paychecks. This represented an important breakthrough for the PWOC amongst Polish women, for even though the canning room had been a special target of the union drive in the plant, up until this point workers had resisted organizers' entreaties. Moreover, actions that resulted in improved conditions served simultaneously as potent organizing tools. In the department where Todd Tate labored, giant steam cookers generated heat intense enough to cause workers to pass out. A union-led walkout—"virtually unheard of in that department"—led to the installation of ventilation fans and the enlargement of the existing windows. "This was a big boost to the power of the union," Tate recalled. "Don't forget, we didn't even have a contract then. Guys said, 'well, if the union can do that maybe I want to join.'"[37]

Even subtle displays of power helped break down the fear and uncertainty holding workers back from the union. Various forms of slowdowns, communicated silently through body signals, demonstrated workers' strength yet shielded them from management reprisal. For instance, an action which unionists at Armour's Soap Works dubbed "Rizz-ma-tizz" began when a steward walked through a given department with his arms across his chest, or his hat cocked to one side. Workers then appeared to labor at breakneck speed while, in reality, cutting back production. Only when the shift ended and the foreman tallied his production did he realize "the screws would be on him" because the gang had fallen short of its quota. Other forms of pressure were more elaborate, requiring precision timing and coordinated execution. The "stop and go" strike began in one department and attracted the attention of management. Just before the superintendent arrived at the stricken section of the plant, workers resumed production while another, distant department halted. The process was repeated as often as necessary. Such actions involved hundreds of rank-and-file members and, in Herbert March's words, "gave them the experience of being organized before we'd won the [NLRB] election, much less had a contract."[38]

Successful stoppages also pointed up the powerlessness of the company union. When a March 1938 job action against a speedup on the beef kill ended with a return to the old rate, company union supporters in the department marched to the PWOC office to cast their lot with the CIO. A few months later, the EMA suffered a further blow to its standing. William Weatherby, a seventy-one-year-old black sheep kill worker, who for years contributed thirty-five cents a week for company-sponsored unemployment insurance, was denied benefits after being laid off. After the EMA appealed the man's case and lost, CIO activists forced Armour to reconsider by shutting down the three killing floors. Sometimes, job actions could be more pointed—as when the offal and casings departments joined hog kill workers in protesting the actions of an EMA representative who appeared on the floor to pin buttons on new hirees.[39]

Had the company union challenged Armour on specific issues, it might have restored some of its waning credibility. But its officers were so dependent upon the company that they saw no need for confrontation. When the Labor Board finally opened hearings on the Armour case, EMA secretary-treasurer Talley painted a picture of industrial relations that bore no resemblance to the tug-of-war occurring within the plant. "If there are any labor disputes at all I don't know anything about them." As it was, each successful action boosted the PWOC while weakening the company union.[40]

The NLRB's September 1938 ruling was everything that the union's attorneys could have hoped for. Finding that Armour "actively aided and assisted in the formation and administration" of the EMA while impeding the organizational efforts of the PWOC, the board ordered the company union disbanded, called for the reinstatement of Pete Davis and another discharged activist, and directed that a representation election be held within thirty days.[41] While this ruling greatly benefited the PWOC, the lengthy delay of almost eleven months between the initial appeal to the NLRB and its final decision taught union activists to be wary of depending upon state intervention. This distrust of the government was especially pronounced among the Communist organizers close to Herbert March. Vicky Starr recalled that this group took William Z. Foster's 1937 pamphlet "What Means a Strike in Steel" as their bible. In this work, Foster cautioned against a policy which "divert[ed] the whole thrust of the union away from the companies and into a hopeless morass of governmental committees, court actions, and time-killing mediation."[42]

This outlook was made clear during a celebrated incident that occurred in the Armour plant in June 1938. Walter Strabawa, a Polish steward on the pork cut and treasurer of the local, was fired after being caught cooking meat on the steam pipes that ran through the department—a traditional practice that the company frowned upon but never prohibited. When a union committee comprised of stewards from a number of departments threatened a general stoppage unless Strabawa was reinstated, Armour suggested referring the case to the NLRB. "You're looking at the Labor Board in this plant right now," came the reply. After the pork cut halted work and the strike spread through adjacent departments, the company relented. According to Hank Johnson, the action "demonstrated that the workers of Armours have another means of defense equal to the service being given by the NLRB." Local 347 officer Al Malachi elaborated on this statement, explaining, "we have so completely organized the Armour workers that it is no longer necessary to refer these discrimination cases to the NLRB where the company would fight them for months."[43]

The active involvement of rank-and-file union members in shop-floor activity contributed to the project of racial solidarity. In addition to giving workers the experience of common struggle, direct action was employed to redress specific racial grievances. The best known example concerns the Local 347's successful effort to force the removal of stars from the time cards of blacks—a practice adopted by management so that when gang reductions were necessary, department supervisors could readily identify blacks for layoff. After Charles Perry, a black worker and union activist on the hog kill, was laid off despite his high seniority, simultaneous stoppages on the hog, beef, and sheep kills brought the practice of tagging time cards to a halt.[44]

Whites tended to back such actions—not necessarily out of a commitment to black rights but because racial grievances were articulated through the union in the traditional terms of job rights. Reciprocity was a factor in white support as well, since in numerous instances the predominantly black killing floors shut down to support the demands of white workers in other departments. Moreover, many whites deferred to the leadership provided by blacks, who accounted for a disproportionate number of stewards and committee members. In part this was because black packinghouse workers were better educated and more self-assured than their white counterparts. A union official told an inquiring sociologist that "the Negro is the best informed on union procedure and is most articulate. The foreign groups understand, but aren't articulate because of language difficulties."[45]

Armour attempted to prey upon white workers' prejudices. Supervisors took workers aside, pointed to the union's egalitarian policies and integrated committees, and suggested that it was a black organization that self-respecting whites should shun. Capitalizing upon the discriminatory hiring practices it had maintained for years, the company planted rumors in many of the lily-white departments that the PWOC aimed to introduce black workers at the expense of white jobs. The union's willingness to combat discrimination and its outspoken egalitarianism may have cost it the support of some racist whites. But any damage was more than offset by the widespread support it gained among blacks. Even the older African American cohort that experienced the 1919 betrayal by the "white man's union" was solidly loyal to the PWOC. Jim Cole, a beef kill butcher who had entered the yards the year of the race riot, spoke for many blacks when he told a WPA interviewer, "I don't care if the union don't do another lick of work raising our pay or settling our grievances . . . I'll always believe they done the greatest thing in the world getting everybody who works in the yards together, and breaking up the hate and bad feelings that used to be held against the Negro."[46]

By the autumn of 1938 the PWOC had regained much of its early momentum in the Chicago stockyards. The Little Six locals had secured contracts and helped push forward organizing campaigns in the large plants. Although progress was painfully slow at Swift and Wilson, significant gains were made at Armour. Here, in the face of stiff employer resistance, workers fashioned a powerful organization which they used to wrest de facto recognition of the PWOC from the company. Although Armour steadfastly refused to bargain on a plantwide basis, the union was able to represent workers in shop-floor disputes. Despite the company's attempts to sow seeds of discord, the dominant tendency was toward interracial solidarity.

The discharge of leading union activists and the presence of the Employees Mutual Association slowed the drive, but at the same time provided
two conspicuous points around which the union could agitate. The Labor
Board decision eventually led to the removal of these obstacles, and the
drive picked up additional speed. One PWOC leader captured this feeling
in colorful terms: "It was like a pimple on an elephant's ass. They [the com-
pany] couldn't stop that thing from rolling; it was just too far gone."[47]

"Like a Snowball Rolling Downhill": Armour Local 347

Armour did everything in its power to stop the PWOC drive. The period
following the NLRB decision until the union finally secured a contract with
the company in January 1940 was one of unparalleled violence in the stockyards. Four days after the Labor Relations Board handed down its ruling,
the union's headquarters were bombed. Two months later thugs attempted to assassinate Herbert March, and on several occasions Hank Johnson
narrowly escaped armed attacks. In November 1938, assailants burst into
the home of stockyards local president Ben Brown and beat him senseless.
Subsequent investigations uncovered evidence of ties between Armour and
a number of ex-convicts and Chicago gangsters. The company also employed less draconian tactics, most notably persuading the Amalgamated
Meat Cutters to take the place of the discredited EMA as an alternative to
the CIO.[48]

Yet while Armour pursued, in Hank Johnson's words, "the same law-
less, feudalistic path as Tom Girdler and Henry Ford," national and local
developments fueled the union movement and created new possibilities,
the most important of which was the progress made by Armour workers
in other packing centers. In March 1938, the PWOC boasted of having
strong local unions in thirteen of the company's sixteen major slaughtering facilities. In Kansas City and Omaha, organization approached the
strength of the Chicago plant, with the union routinely settling grievances
and building toward formal recognition. Workers in the Chicago plant
learned of these gains through their shop paper, the *Cleaver*, which regularly reported news from the company's far-flung enterprises in an effort
to develop a wider consciousness. "I tried to let people understand their
importance in the Armour empire . . . to let them know the country was
looking to us," stated the paper's editor, Les Orear.[49]

In early September, as Local 347 members were looking forward to hosting a national conference of Armour delegates, workers in Kansas City temporarily upstaged them by occupying the plant there. The incident that sparked the sit-down was relatively simple—the company refused to pay workers for time spent discussing a grievance with management—but it capped months of protracted conflict, and what started as a departmental protest soon enveloped the entire packinghouse. The occupation made national news, and photographs of defiant workers atop the plant circulated widely. The PWOC quickly sanctioned the takeover and threatened to bring out other plants in the Armour chain in support of the Kansas City local. "We believe a grievance of one worker is a grievance of the entire union," announced Assistant National Director Don Harris. In an expression of solidarity, Local 347 refused to work on any products that might be shipped to Kansas City. The strikers held the plant for four days, until sympathetic city officials presided over a compromise settlement. In the first signed agreement between the PWOC and Armour, the company agreed to refer the dispute to arbitration and not discipline the employees who participated in the sit-down.[50]

Two weeks later, reports of another dramatic strike galvanized Chicago's packinghouse workers. This one erupted at the Swift plant in Sioux City, Iowa, where killing-floor workers struck over management's refusal to recognize the authority of the union's grievance committee. Strike leaders anticipated that the stoppage would last only a few minutes before the company acceded to their demand. However, when Swift discharged the gangs and arranged for the arrest of seventeen union leaders under Iowa's conspiracy laws, the strike spread through the entire plant. It soon developed into a drawn-out battle, lasting four months and resulting in sensational national press coverage when, three weeks into the strike, a "riot" erupted as sheriff's deputies escorted strikebreakers into the facility. The presence of 260 national guardsmen, who cordoned off the area surrounding the plant, allowed Swift to resume operations the following day. The strike gradually dwindled as strikebreakers freely entered the plant and forty local union leaders were jailed for riotous behavior and other felonies. In late January 1939, unionists conceded defeat. Despite this outcome, the Sioux City strike, coupled with the success in Kansas City, imparted a sense of insurgency to the CIO's drive in the meat industry.[51]

The overwhelming victory posted by Local 347 in the NLRB representation election the next month fueled this feeling even further. Although the turnout was smaller than expected, the victory was particularly impressive given the company's "boycott" of the election. Armour refused to allow Labor Board officials access to the plant, forcing the hasty construction of an alternative polling place in an abandoned storefront outside of the yards. Then, on the day of the election, the company locked the gate nearest the polling station. They also posted foremen and superintendents near the storefront to give workers the impression they were being watched. Despite the light turnout—slightly over half of the seven thousand workers eligible to vote did so—this triumph at Armour's flagship plant had an enormous impact upon the union movement. "The impetus of winning an election, and the attitude that developed as a result . . . was such as to strengthen the movement for organization immensely," recalled Herbert March. "You'd win an election, and the guys, instead of being afraid of employers, and having to bow down to them, they felt we're equals, we're somebody, and by God, the bosses better listen to us instead of us just listening to them."[52]

In the weeks that followed, thousands who had stood back out of fear or calculation came over to the union. Organization extended into previously aloof departments. In dried beef, for instance, Sophie Kosciolowski had been agitating amongst her workmates for more than a year with little result. The daughter of a veteran unionist, she first entered the industry in 1918 at age thirteen. A housewife in the late 1920s, she returned to Armour in 1931 after her divorce and was one of the first women to become involved in the PWOC. After months of frustration, the election victory suddenly provided her with an opening. When a widely disliked foreman engaged in particularly abusive behavior, Kosciolowski led the two hundred women in the department out of the plant to the union hall where they enrolled en masse. When the foreman arrived the following day, he saw "CIO" pasted over the face of the time clock. "Everybody, the superintendent, the foremen from other floors, everybody came to look at what happened, women with union buttons on." Union leaders accounted for this change in temperament through reference to the NLRB election triumph. In the eyes of many previously uncommitted workers "a new day had dawned," March explained, "they had attained full citizenship in industry as far as they were concerned."[53]

Winning the NLRB certification election did not translate into a collective bargaining relationship with Armour. Indeed, the company was more determined than ever to resist the union. Just prior to the poll, Armour president Robert Cabell flatly rejected another PWOC request for a meeting. "We do not believe that there are any issues of importance between the Company and its employees at the present time. . . . We cannot see at this time that any purpose would be served through a conference with your committee," he bluntly stated. Don Harris responded by outlining a series of demands for Cabell, including the adoption of a formal seniority system, equal pay for equal work, and the checkoff of union dues. Hank Johnson answered by inviting the CEO to join mechanical department workers in trying to eat a meal in their dressing room where swarms of insects made even the simple act of breathing difficult. Cabell did not take the PWOC leader up on his offer. He retorted instead by asking the U.S. Circuit Court of Appeals to overturn the union's election victory, charging that ineligible employees had cast ballots.[54]

While the court considered the appeal, which it eventually rejected, Local 347 continued to consolidate its position inside the plant. "It became a pure situation of how much muscle you had" in a given department, March recalled. Where the union was strong, foremen had little choice but to recognize its representatives. On the powerful beef kill, for example, foremen requested permission from the union's steward before processing additional cattle. Where organization was relatively weak, workers employed stoppages or slowdowns in nearby or adjacent areas to implement some kind of understanding. Thus, the hog-killing department ceased work in order to enforce an informally agreed upon seniority system in hog offal. In departments which were pockets of anti-unionism, the local utilized a variety of tactics to shift the balance of power. "Colonizers" transferred into these areas and agitated, usually by discovering what grievances workers held and organizing action around them. They also sought out the natural leaders of informal work groups and devoted special effort to their recruitment. When necessary, the union used more heavy-handed methods: preventing holdouts from entering the plant, depriving them of tools, or refusing them assistance on heavy jobs. Recalcitrants might discover leaflets branding them as scabs or "suckholes" circulating in their neighborhood. On a number of occasions, stoppages occurred when unionists refused to labor with nonunion workers. "We [didn't] intend to wait for a contract to get a closed shop," chief steward Paddy McNichols stated. "You just didn't work in that plant unless you supported the union. They wouldn't tolerate it," Herbert March explained.[55]

Still, the union was unable to move toward a written contract with Armour. Maintaining the fiction that no important issues stood between the company and the union, Cabell continued to stonewall the PWOC. This stance was made possible only by his isolation from the day-to-day struggle in the plant. By contrast, superintendent King and his assistants could not afford such inflexibility. By the fall of 1938, the ever-present threat of workplace action forced them to concede that the union did represent "individuals" and agree to hold weekly negotiating sessions with Local 347's grievance committee. No doubt under severe pressure from his superiors, King met regularly with the committee and listened to workers' complaints, but initially settled very few grievances. The union responded by applying the same kind of direct action tactics in the conference room that it had perfected on the shop floor. "We decided the stalling had to stop," Herbert March recounted. "We refused to let them out of the place. . . . We kept them there a couple of times until nine o'clock at night settling grievances. Everybody was hungry and mad but we wouldn't turn them loose." Although settling issues on a case-by-case basis taxed the union's resources as well as those of the company, it represented a major accomplishment for the local. It testified not only to the de facto recognition granted it by plant management but to the power wielded by unionists at the point of production itself.[56]

By Thanksgiving of 1938 the stockyards were a beehive of organizing activity. While Armour workers continued to wrest small concessions from the company—an extra man on the chain on the beef kill, the replacement of iron wheels with rubber ones on loading dock trucks, the right of stewards to clock the speed of the line—those at Swift and Wilson began to stir.[57] Mobilization at the Wilson plant followed the same general pattern established in the other packinghouses. Union organizing originated on the heavily black killing floors during the years immediately prior to the establishment of the PWOC, spread to adjacent casing and offal departments, and encompassed the cutting rooms before branching into other areas of the plant. Swift differed from this model. Here, union founders tended to be skilled whites scattered in smaller, often ancillary departments. An elevator mechanic, Ralph Gantt, launched the organization along with Henry Schoenstein, a sausage maker described as the "guiding spirit" of the local. Another key pioneer, Joe Kinch, worked in the glue house; and Lee Hutton, one of the PWOC's great orators, labored in the soap plant. Only after these activists established small footholds did the powerful killing floors slowly begin to come over to the PWOC.[58]

Swift Local 28 used the same kind of workplace activism that had become the union's hallmark both to extend organization and to exact concessions from the company. In addition to securing an informal agreement respecting seniority, Swift workers eliminated the much-despised practice of "working for the church"—the daily hour of unpaid labor that foremen extracted from the killing-floor gangs. Elmer Thomas told a WPA interviewer about the creative means used. "They had those big sheep-fat cups hanging on the chains. We'd see they were working us past supper hour. Man farthest away from the foreman would whistle and all the guys at work would start hollering s-o-u-p and whistling and banging the cups around." The deafening din soon had the desired effect. "They couldn't fire us all and we made so much racket they quit that particular chiseling."[59]

In a move that boosted the standing of the local and immeasurably added to the PWOC's reputation as a defender of black rights, Swift workers used carefully choreographed stoppages to pressure the company into revising its hiring practices. According to the union, Swift had discriminated against black job seekers since the onset of the depression, and had not hired a single black woman since 1929. Now it pledged to employ blacks in proportion to their numbers in the Chicago population.[60]

Local 25 at Wilson did not shrink from militancy either. It used a series of "quickie" strikes in early 1938 to protest the company's prohibition against the distribution of leaflets and its harassment of union activists. "Industrial action" was also used to stop discrimination at Wilson. When the foreman in John Wrublewski's department refused to allow a black to fill a vacant scaler's position, claiming that "coloreds can't count too well," workers purposely miscalculated their cuts and then punched out early, feigning an inability to read the clock. The exasperated foreman called the men back and allowed the black to take the job. Building on the growing feeling of interracial solidarity forged by these kinds of spontaneous displays, the local scored another victory when it extracted an official apology from the company for ordering three long-service black employees out of sight when a visitors' tour approached their work area. Using the incident to mount a general attack on Wilson's Jim Crow policies, the union not only gained a great deal of favorable publicity but began a concerted program to root out such practices throughout the yards. In 1939, referring to the earlier antagonism of ethnic whites and the racist policies of the packers, one black worker stated "with the CIO in, all that's like a bad dream gone."[61]

The insurgent quality that the PWOC's drive assumed in late 1938 was made clear by the stockhandlers strike that occurred in November. The previous year, the handlers had defected to the CIO from the Amalgamated Meat Cutters under the leadership of Ben Brown, a Missouri cattleman, and Frank Monoghan, a crusty veteran who first entered the yards in 1894. After sweeping to an easy victory in an NLRB election in February 1938, the local encountered stiff resistance to its efforts at securing a contract from the packer-controlled Union Stockyards and Transit Company. As the company stalled, the handlers contended not only with a series of violent assaults but with renewed competition from the AMC. The strike began when the company called Chicago police into its offices to eject the local's bargaining committee and then locked out the remaining six hundred members.[62]

The Stockyards Company picked a poor time for confrontation. With extra cattle in the pens for the annual Livestock Exposition, the handlers had an extra degree of leverage. Drawing upon the assistance of thousands of packinghouse workers, they turned the lockout into an efficient strike. A mass picket in front of the Meat Cutters' hall on Halsted Street turned back a small group of workers who volunteered to break the strike on behalf of the AFL union. "We had so many pickets there we didn't know what to do with them," recalled a union official. The strike threatened to spread into the plants themselves when killing-floor workers refused to handle the "scab livestock." Union leaders at Armour, in fact, led their members out on a "holiday" to support the stock handlers. In many other plants, work ceased as a result of the general chaos and excitement in the yards.[63]

The blow that broke the company's resolve came from an unexpected quarter. Chicago mayor Edward Kelly had gained an unsavory antilabor reputation as a result of the 1937 Memorial Day Massacre of steelworkers in South Chicago. Anxious to repair the damage, and to harness working-class votes to his Democratic machine, Kelly now intervened in the dispute. For years, the Union Stockyards had paid the city only a nominal fee for unlimited use of water pumped from the Chicago River. Threatening to raise the price of the water—needed not just for maintenance purposes but to sustain livestock—Kelly convinced the company to bargain with the union and helped arrange a settlement that called for recognition of the PWOC as exclusive bargaining agent, a small wage increase, a weekly guarantee of forty hours, and time and a half for overtime.[64] The victory was a vivid demonstration of the interconnectedness of the yards complex and of packinghouse workers' collective strength. Kelly's support earned him the unqualified backing of the PWOC in municipal elections held the following April. His bold intervention marked the start of a long relationship between the union and the local Democratic Party.[65]

The reappearance of the AFL's Meat Cutters posed a new challenge for the PWOC. In 1937 the Amalgamated had helplessly watched the mass desertion of its packinghouse membership to the CIO. It now moved to recoup the loss by presenting itself as a responsible, "business-like" alternative to the militant, "action-prone" CIO. This stance played well with the packers but only served to alienate packinghouse workers. While the AMC's journal claimed that "the packing plant worker is beginning to realize that there is magic in the word Amalgamated, the old, reliable, and the one alert . . . organization for the employees in the Butchering trade," very few workers responded to the call. Try as it might, the Amalgamated was handicapped by the burden of its past. Responding to the AMC, one packinghouse worker gave voice to the sentiments of thousands when he wrote, "Yes, we can look back over the last 25 years and see with remorse what your organization has done for us poor slaves of Packingtown. We can see what was done for us in 1921, 1922."[66]

The AMC further eroded its credibility in the yards when it eagerly absorbed the remnants of the company unions after the Labor Board ruled these organizations illegitimate. Armour's moribund Employees Mutual Association received a new lease on life when it was chartered as AMC Local 661. This rival union fared poorly and never seems to have had a following in the plant. Its very existence opened up the Amalgamated to charges of "playing company union for the bosses," and allowed the PWOC to emphasize its very different "fighting" character. When the PWOC expelled Armour local president Al Malachi for pocketing members' dues payments, his appearance as an Amalgamated officer allowed the CIO to attack it as a "stool pigeon outfit."[67]

Finally, the Meat Cutters' ambiguous record on the race question meant that it had no real chance of reaching the critical mass of black workers in the yards. Older blacks remembered the Jim Crow policies that led the AMC to ruin in the 1917–21 period; and younger workers needed to look no farther than the Amalgamated's segregated locals in the Chicago retail trade to see that the union had not reformed. Reports of overtly racist practices circulated widely. Amalgamated officials seemed oblivious to the need to recruit blacks to the union. At times, they displayed an astounding ignorance of the racial dynamics powering the resurgence of packinghouse unionism. One International officer told interviewers that he considered blacks poor unionists. "You know as well as I do that they are shiftless, easily intimidated and generally poor calibre," he remarked. Admitting that a few blacks "make good loyal union men," he then added, "the others are for the most part not useful to the labor movement and would be much better off picking cotton in the South." Unthinkable (or at least unmentionable) within the PWOC, such sentiments insured the marginalization of the AMC in an industry so dependent upon black labor.[68]

Unionism beyond the Yards

In contrast to the AMC, the PWOC extended its activities beyond the confines of the workplace and into the social lives of its members. In the Back-of-the-

Yards, one of the more important forces driving the union's community-based activism was the Yards branch of the Communist Party. Especially influential were a group of young women led by Vicky Starr. In 1939 they convinced the PWOC to sponsor a Packingtown Youth Committee comprised of representatives from twenty-six young people's organizations, including the Settlement House, the YWCA, and the various Catholic sodalities. Concerned about teenage unemployment, the Youth Committee proposed employing local teens to convert a vacant lot into a recreational center. The group secured the support of Joseph Meegan, the director of Davis Square Park, and interested social worker Saul Alinsky in the project. Within a short time, the Youth Committee became something much larger and more important—a federation of community organizations known as the Back-of-the-Yards Neighborhood Council.[69]

Involving representatives from nine of the ten Catholic churches, and sanctioned by Chicago's liberal Bishop Bernard Sheil, the council enjoyed almost instant legitimacy. Parish clubs, nationalist lodges, small business groups, athletic organizations, and the union were represented as well. The PWOC put its best foot forward: the Communists who initiated the council remained in the background, while Sigmund Wlodarczyk served as the union's delegate. The council rapidly made its influence felt in the community. Churches, previously opposed to the union, began to accept it. Tentative at first, this support grew stronger and effectively ended the packers' use of the Catholic church as an antilabor organization.[70]

The key to this shift in policy was a group of young priests assigned to the various parishes of the district—Edward Palinski from St. John of God (Polish), Ambrose Ondrak from St. Michael's (Slovak), Roman Berendt from Sacred Heart (Polish), and Joseph Kelly from St. Rose (Irish). Native-born and relatively free from the immigrants' suspicions of other nationalities, these priests were far more progressive than their immediate superiors. Father Kelly often quipped that they all were Democrats and the pastors all Republicans. Many of them had attended seminary together at St. Mary of the Lake and enthusiastically followed the leadership of Bishop Sheil. While anticommunist, they supported organized labor and urged their parishioners to join the PWOC.[71]

The council helped the union gain the support of neighborhood merchants, explaining that improvements in workers' standard of living would translate into an increase in their purchasing power. "There was a double lesson for us all," Herbert March stated. "The community saw the value of unionism, and the union discovered the power of thorough community organization." Most importantly, by promoting an ethos of cooperation and tolerance, the council helped ameliorate some of the ethnic rivalries that had plagued the neighborhood for generations. It actively challenged ethnic boundaries, bringing Poles and Lithuanians together and integrating the previously outcast Mexicans into the community. "We discovered that every parish had the same problems and unity meant effectiveness," remarked Father Ondrak.[72]

Through the council, activists mobilized the community's religious and ethnic organizations in a direction that reinforced and strengthened the PWOC's challenge to the packers' domination of the area. Especially important were the council's efforts to promote racial harmony. It defended the union when it was race-baited, spoke out against incidents of racial violence, and pleaded for an attitude of acceptance. One of the more innovative techniques used to combat discrimination was the council's rumor committee. Individuals found guilty of spreading rumors fomenting hatred were hauled before the council and publicly reprimanded. When a rumor started that blacks were pushing whites around on public conveyances, six priests from the council donned civilian clothes and rode the buses and trolleys for a week. They discovered no such offenses and this finding was read from every pulpit. The council also organized trips through the black community so that clergymen and others could study the conditions with which blacks contended.[73]

Other cultural and social activities brought white and black workers together in unprecedented ways. An ambitious union-sponsored sports program organized on an interracial basis included weekly bowling tournaments and, depending on the season, basketball and baseball games. "It makes us better friends so that we'll stick together in the organization whatever comes" explained Adam "Popeye" Kurzon, a butcher at Illinois Meat known as the "daddy of the bowling competition." The establishment of the "CIO Juniors" in 1939 offered unionists' children recreational and educational facilities well beyond the means of individual families while enabling black and white youngsters to interact with one another in an open setting. Dances and picnics provided similar opportunities.[74]

Utilizing both the PWOC hall and the facilities of the University of Chicago Settlement House, these programs brought black workers and their families into the Back-of-the-Yards for the first time. The union also made considerable headway integrating many of the taverns which made up "Whiskey Row" along Ashland Avenue and the eateries surrounding the stockyards. Boycotts by white union members could bring considerable economic pressure to bear upon establishments refusing to serve blacks. Occasionally friction developed. Richard Saunders humorously recalled one white woman's hysterical reaction when a group of black unionists visited her home to speak with her husband. Herbert March remembered that integrated teams of organizers going door to door sometimes dodged bricks and stones, and white workers usually escorted blacks through those residential sections where threats of violence continued to lurk. Nevertheless, a significant softening of racial attitudes occurred Back-of-the-Yards as a direct result of the PWOC's involvement in the community.[75]

By the close of the decade, the hatreds of the past appeared to be giving way to a new understanding. The *Chicago Defender* noted in 1939 that before the coming of the union, the standard folk wisdom was that "no Negro had better show his face west of Ashland Avenue after dark.... Today because the PWOC planted the seed of unity in the stony soil of Packingtown Negroes walk freely and in safety." While this assessment may have been overly optimistic, the people of Packingtown had come a long way. One need only recall that during the 1919 riot, much of the violence against blacks was perpetrated by street gangs outside the yards. Twenty years later, youth gangs kept protective watch over the PWOC hall. "It got so round there that you had better not mess with that hall, 'cause them kids around there, you mess with that hall, you had them to contend with before you got to us," recalled one black unionist.[76]

Since black packinghouse workers did not reside in a single, concentrated geographic area, the PWOC's ties to the black community were more diffuse than those linking the union with Back-of-the-Yards. Still, the PWOC maintained a high profile in the Black Belt; its presence grew out of the daily social activities of the more than five thousand black packinghouse workers and their families who lived there. The CIO's farm equipment and steel unions might be perceived as outside organizations, Lowell Washington explained, but the PWOC "belonged . . . just as much as the [Pullman] Porters did or the Baptist church."[77]

The church, in fact, formed the PWOC's most important institutional link with the black community. Unlike the 1917–21 period, when the black clergy vigorously opposed unionism, a majority of churchmen now offered their outspoken support. Many of the pastors of the larger congregations, such as the Olivet Baptist Church, invited union representatives to speak or offered the use of their facilities for meetings. Richard Saunders recalled that he and Burrette King first approached Hank Johnson after hearing him speak at a church; and Lowell Washington remembered a meeting that was "packed to the rafters" with union supporters. In addition, the informal gatherings of worshipers that occurred each Sunday after the conclusion of church services provided an opportunity for low-key union organizing.

While not religious himself, Washington occasionally attended church to make contact with other workers. Several of the deacons of Washington's church were active PWOC members and approved of the organizing; and on at least one occasion, the pastor included a union appeal in his sermon.[78]

Just as significant was the relationship between black unionists and the dozens of small storefront churches in the Black Belt. The president of the PWOC local at Levi Casing, Reverend Hurie Lee, looked after the economic needs of his workmates with the same energy and passion that he devoted to the spiritual needs of his congregation. Isaac Ladson, a deeply religious leader of the Armour local, used the same powerful rhetoric and emotional manner when he addressed meetings of Local 347 that he employed when preaching at his Pentecostal church. Jeff Beckley, another Armour leader and one of 347's first presidents, relied upon his stature and reputation as a righteous churchgoer to gain a hearing among colleagues for his views about unionism. The *Chicago Defender* reported that no fewer than twenty Armour stewards dressed in overalls during the week but wore black cloth on Sunday; and this figure probably applied to the other large packing plants as well.[79]

The Democratic Party provided the PWOC with another vehicle through which it exercised influence in Chicago's black community. The presidential election of 1936 completed the swing of black voters away from the GOP that had begun four years earlier. Roosevelt polled an unprecedented 63.7 percent in the 1st Congressional District, whose boundaries encompassed most of the Black Belt. Over the next three years, the remaining vestiges of Republican political strength crumbled. The Democratic ward organizations that arose to fill the vacuum were new and relatively open. As a result, the union was able to involve itself in local politics in the black community in a way that was impossible Back-of-the-Yards where old-line Irish bosses continued to dominate the party.[80]

In 1938, black packinghouse unionists individually involved themselves in Arthur Mitchell's bitter and ultimately successful congressional campaign against black GOP stalwart Oscar DePriest. The following year the PWOC itself entered the political arena, supporting Earl Dickerson's run for an aldermanic post in the city's Second Ward. Hank Johnson served as an adviser to the Dickerson campaign; and packinghouse workers leafleted for him in the community, arranged transportation to the polls, and marshaled support for him in the plants. Dickerson's election administered the coup de grace to what remained of the old alliance between African Americans and the GOP. The defeated incumbent, William Dawson, turned his back on the Republicans and joined the Democratic machine. In office

Dickerson provided a consistent prolabor voice in city hall, and he soon acknowledged his debt to the union. In 1939 he came to its defense in charged testimony before Congressman Martin Dies's inquisitorial Committee to Investigate Un-American Activities. Dickerson also pushed Mayor Kelly closer to the CIO. One indication of the new political constellation was Kelly's appointment of a PWOC lawyer to a vacant judgeship in 1939.[81]

The cause of industrial unionism in general and the PWOC in particular received additional support in the Black Belt through the activities of the organized Left—especially the Communist Party and the National Negro Congress. In early 1939 the CP had recruited close to five hundred packinghouse workers to the Party. Probably half of these members were black. The Party boasted of another eight hundred black cadres in the ten branches that comprised its South Side section, and made its influence felt through a broad range of front organizations. The Chicago branch of the NNC was especially active, listing approximately five hundred persons on its membership rolls in 1938. The PWOC's Hank Johnson was one of the more visible NNC leaders in Chicago and throughout the nation, giving the union a connection with the Congress at the highest level. Many rank-and-file unionists, especially stewards and local officers, participated in the NNC as well.[82]

Over the Top at Armour

In the spring of 1939 the PWOC stepped up its efforts to wrest a contract from Armour. Nationally and locally, the union had strengthened its position. Workers in five additional Armour plants had voted for the CIO, giving the PWOC bargaining rights in seventeen of the packer's twenty-nine houses. Within the Chicago flagship plant, the union consolidated its grip on the production process. Each issue of the *CIO News* trumpeted small victories: the addition of a dozen workers to the sheep kill gang, the reversal of Armour's decision to eliminate the beef-casing department, a reduction of production standards on the pork trim. Grievance sessions, previously held weekly, now occurred on a daily basis. Membership topped the 90 percent mark and reached into formerly unorganized departments.[83]

Armour locals in Kansas City, Sioux City, South St. Paul, and St. Joseph, Missouri, reported similar advances. With the exception of the Omaha plant, where certification was pending, the PWOC had a lock on all of Armour's major packinghouses. Yet a sense of deep frustration was growing. The union was no closer to securing a contract with any of the large packers than it had been a year earlier. Local activists regarded a contract as the logical culmination of their efforts—a legal device which would codify and safeguard their gains. The security provided by a closed shop and dues checkoff would allow them to extend organization to the rest of the industry. PWOC leaders shared these aims but had another objective as well. The reliance of local unions upon direct action, and their success with these tactics, generated an autonomy which made them difficult to control. Without a contract and the grievance machinery that such an agreement would establish, stoppages and job actions would continue indefinitely. The Sioux City Swift strike had been a sobering lesson, one which Bittner and his associates did not want to see repeated. Immediately after the strike, they attempted to restrain local unions by prohibiting unauthorized stoppages but their directive was uniformly ignored. Master agreements with the packers, they hoped, would curb the locals' zeal and allow the national bureaucracy a greater hand in the direction of the union.[84]

Although a rupture soon would occur between packinghouse unionists and their CIO-appointed leaders, in early 1939 their goals still paralleled each other. Armour formed a logical target for the union's resources; and, because organization was most advanced in the Armour chain, a strike threat here carried significant weight. Moreover, a focus on Armour, the largest and most powerful packer, fit nicely into the successful "bellwether" strategy employed by the CIO in steel and auto. Finally, Armour's persistent defiance of the Labor Board meant that the PWOC could rally support by portraying the company as un-American and outside the law—one leaflet linked the intransigent company with Hitler's fascists by referring to the "Packerbund"—while linking its cause to Roosevelt and the New Deal. The belief that the government, both federal and municipal, would protect workers in their struggle was widespread. "If Armour forces us to strike some of you may end up dead in the street," warned Sigmund Wlodarczyk, adding "I don't think that's going to happen. There's a New Deal in Chicago and Mayor Kelly has told us that he won't let the Yards be turned into another battleground."[85]

When PWOC delegates from the Armour plants convened in Chicago in April, they were eager for a showdown. They directed PWOC officers to contact president Cabell again and request a conference at which to negotiate a master agreement, but did not wait for a reply to begin raising strike sentiment. Almost immediately, Don Harris and Hank Johnson set out on speaking tours through Iowa, Nebraska, Missouri, and Minnesota. In Chicago, local Armour activists used the recently established PWOC Joint Council to prepare yards workers for the upcoming conflict. This ef-

fort included mass rallies at CIO corner, drilling of pickets, and the purchase of radio time with which to appeal to workers throughout the city.
"We wanted all the workers in all the plants to feel like they were part of
this thing," recalled Vicky Starr. When Armour replied to the PWOC request in mid-May, flatly refusing to meet, the response was expected and
occasioned little notice and no alteration in strategy.[86]

In addition to steeling the membership for battle, union leaders wanted to catch the attention of the federal government. They succeeded, for
the Department of Labor assigned its "ace conciliator," P. W. Chappell, to
the case and monitored developments closely. Chappell quickly grasped
the nature of the situation. "There is no use kidding ourselves," he stated
in an early report, "the Company is not going to negotiate a general agreement unless pressure of the most severe type is brought to bear." A meeting with Frederick Prince, the chairman of Armour's Board of Directors,
confirmed Chappell's assessment. Prince struck the mediator as "a product of the [18]80's and [18]90's who can be influenced not by reason but by
force alone . . . he is a fine example of an Economic Royalist." Aware of
rank-and-file pressure on PWOC leaders and of the strength of shop-floor
organization in Chicago and elsewhere, Chappell urged his superiors to
intervene.[87]

Packinghouse workers were ready to "hit the bricks" in 1939. The disciplined organization built up in the plants exceeded anything contemplated by the GM strikers and would have sustained a national strike for several weeks. Chappell bore few illusions about the union's strength. The
PWOC "seems to be developing quite a buildup," he reported prior to a
mass meeting of delegates representing every local in the country. Held in
the Chicago Coliseum and addressed by John L. Lewis and Bishop Sheil,
the meeting, Chappell thought, might "develop into just the push needed
to start the real fireworks."[88]

Attended by an estimated fifteen thousand packinghouse workers and
supporters, the mass rally followed a policy conference at the union's
Marshfield Avenue district headquarters. There, the delegates authorized
a national strike against Armour and left open the option of striking other Big Four packers. They also petitioned President Roosevelt to assist
them in getting a contract with Armour by acting as a mediator. According to press reports, the climax of the convocation came when CIO president Lewis rose to address the crowd and promised to place the resources
of the entire organization behind the drive on Armour. Packinghouse
workers "are now serving notice on Armour & Company that their patience is nearing an end," he warned. "If the company continues to refuse

collective bargaining it must accept the consequences of its own actions." The daily papers also gave prominent coverage to Bishop Sheil, who cited both the Declaration of Independence and papal encyclicals in his message of support.[89]

For most of the workers gathered in the Coliseum, however, the high point was the arrival of Herbert March. A few days earlier gunmen—reputedly hired by Armour—had shot and wounded March, and it was not known whether he would appear at the rally. News of the attack quickly spread throughout the union and contributed to the large turnout in Chicago. Jesse Prosten, who drove from Boston to Chicago to attend the conference and rally, remarked that "all they did when they shot him was to speed up the operation." Pat Balskus recalled that the sight of March, swathed in bandages and wearing a sling, in the hall caused a murmur that grew into a roar which distracted the speaker. "Lewis was a hero, a big man," she explained, "but Herb was a real life hero because he was one of us. Herb was the union, and to see him there that night gave me a kind of strength that ten John L.'s couldn't have come close to."[90]

The extravaganza in Chicago generated a flurry of behind-the-scenes activity. Aware of the strike threat and informed that "packers intend to fight until the bitter end," Secretary of Labor Frances Perkins tried to bring the two parties together. At the same time the Chicago City Council, urged on by Dickerson and other South Side aldermen, attempted to persuade Armour to open talks with the union. The company steadfastly refused to budge, persisting in its claim that the PWOC's NLRB election victory was invalid. It asserted that it had engaged in collective bargaining and, in fact, was in compliance with the law. Strike agitation, Armour charged, arose not from its employees but from union leaders, many of whom had no real connection with the packing industry.[91]

Armour also received support for its position from the Amalgamated Meat Cutters. After the PWOC's mass rally, the AMC's Patrick Gorman went on the radio to refute statements made by Lewis. He warned that the Meat Cutters would not sit idle while "communistic elements" within the CIO attempted to steal what his union had spent years building. CFL president Fitzpatrick assisted Gorman, attacking Bishop Sheil for involving the church in the labor dispute and claiming that most of the audience in the Coliseum were steelworkers from South Chicago and Father Divine followers. Fitzpatrick also helped the Amalgamated secure an audience with the city council, where Gorman forwarded the claim that the AMC had enrolled a majority of workers in Armour's Chicago plant. Although PWOC supporters on the council countered Gorman's claim with evidence to the contrary, Bittner felt compelled to respond. The CFL's interference, he charged, "means just two things, insanity or crookedness." The union's journal took a more action-oriented position with regard to their AFL rivals. "The time has come to drive them out of the packinghouses and back to the butcher shops where they came from," it prescribed.[92]

The Amalgamated's interference had a negligible impact in the yards. If anything, it confirmed workers' opinion of the Meat Cutters and eliminated whatever remaining support the AFL enjoyed. A more serious threat to the PWOC was the hearing that the Amalgamated received in Washington. In early September, Secretary Perkins succeeded in bringing Armour's general manager, Harvey Eldred, and a team of lawyers to Washington for talks. Although the Armour officials refused to meet in the same room as PWOC representatives, Perkins managed to open the way for a settlement. After Bittner agreed to drop the union's demand for a national agreement—a unilateral decision that later caused much internal strife—Eldred gave in and empowered plant superintendents to bargain with the PWOC. At this critical juncture Gorman and CFL secretary Joseph Keenan arrived. Able to convince government officials of the validity of their claim despite Chappell's warning that "the Company is actively cooperating with the Amalgamated . . . in an effort to have them organize several of their plants in order to forestall the CIO," the AFL forced the packinghouse workers to agree to hold another representation election.[93]

As plant-by-plant negotiations began, workers in Armour's Chicago facility geared up for the election. The Amalgamated desperately tried to postpone the date of the poll, knowing that it could remain a player only as long as the government was uncertain of its actual strength in the plant. Within the yards, the contest between the two unions grew acrimonious. On one occasion, an AFL sound truck was demolished by angry PWOC members. Another violent incident occurred when the AFL attempted to hold a noontime rally at CIO corner. When the Amalgamated's business agents appeared in limousines, a "reception committee" of four thousand workers attacked the procession. "Here we're finally getting a union and these guys are trying to save the company union. It was like scabbing," recalled a PWOC leader. Unable to campaign within the stockyards, the AMC took to the airwaves and to leafleting in neighborhoods where packinghouse workers lived. Even here they were not immune from attack. Stephan Janko remembered answering a knock on his front door and finding a Meat Cutters representative. "I didn't know who it was at first, but when I found out I went for the ax handle. They didn't come around after that." Sensing that their cause was a losing one, the AMC abandoned its efforts to delay the contest at Armour. Gorman agreed to an election on 21 November "to get the matter over with."[94]

One final, unexpected, hurdle remained for the PWOC to clear. Four days before the scheduled election, Martin Dies's Committee to Investigate Un-American Activities opened hearings in Chicago on Communist influence in the meatpacking industry. Herbert March, Hank Johnson, and Walter Strabawa, the financial secretary of the Packinghouse Workers Chicago Council, received subpoenas. The *Tribune* ran lurid banner headlines decrying the Red plot. The hearings clearly were meant to affect the balloting in the Armour plant—a point made explicit when Amalgamated officials made a last ditch plea from the witness box for workers to "think American" and repudiate the "foreign Red Russian policy of the CIO."[95] The union leaders managed to turn the inquisition into a platform of their own. They easily discredited Dies's star witness, the disgraced Al Malachi. March graphically described living conditions Back-of-the-Yards and disingenuously suggested that improving the standard of living there could aid "in stopping the spread of subversive ideas." He referred to the two occasions on which he had been shot, asked Dies to investigate rumors of Armour's employment of Nazi sympathizers, and described the PWOC's civic activities. Johnson exposed the criminal records of local Amalgamated officers and succeeded in convincing the committee to summon them to the hearings. He concluded his testimony by suggesting that Dies remain in his home state of Texas and look into the un-American activities of the Klan and lynch mobs. In addition to alderman Dickerson, Charlotte Carr of Hull House and Malcom Sharpe of the University of Chicago Law School appeared as voluntary witnesses to testify in support of the PWOC and protest the committee's interference in the election.[96]

When the votes were tallied on 21 November, the PWOC's margin of victory exceeded that of the previous October. Particularly careful Labor Board supervision ensured a large turnout. Over four thousand Armour workers cast ballots for the CIO. Slightly more than a thousand chose the Amalgamated, and about the same number marked the no union box. Armour accepted the union's victory and declined to challenge the results. The path toward a contract was now clear of obstacles. By the time Local 347's bargaining committee sat down with Armour officials in January 1940, the PWOC had an agreement in place in Kansas City and had just concluded a pact covering the Chicago Soap Works. Using these documents as models, the union quickly negotiated a contract recognizing the PWOC as sole bargaining agent and providing for strict adherence to seniority, the adjustment of grievances, a thirty-two-hour weekly guarantee, an improved vacation plan, and equal pay for equal work. Base pay of 62.5 cents an hour for men was left untouched, while the female rate rose by a penny to 52 cents.[97]

Although modest, these first agreements still represented a major breakthrough. They marked the realization of a goal that had eluded packinghouse workers since organizing began in the late nineteenth century. Although the contracts lacked provisions for union security and left wage rates essentially unchanged, the workers covered by them now regarded themselves as collectively equal to their employers. Before the agreement, Sophie Kosciolowski explained, "the only difference between an outright slave and us was that we could go home." Having brought the company to terms, Gertie Kamarczyk felt "like a human being with real rights, a real whole person for the first time in my life."[98]

Yet, in a certain sense, the contract that Armour workers won in 1940 was an anticlimax. It codified in the conference room the series of small victories they had secured during the previous two years of struggle on the shop floor. The involvement of the Department of Labor had hurried events along toward a conclusion; and the deft negotiating on the part of the PWOC leadership had forced the company to compromise. But it was the exertion of workers' power at the point of production that ultimately led to the settlement. The company's formal recognition of the union was important, to be sure. But, as Herbert March realized, "when it came down it was really a reflection of the fact that it was something that was battled through in the plants by the workers." In early 1940, the first of the big packers had been brought to terms. Swift and Wilson were next on the agenda. Over the next three years, internal factional battles would loom as large as the contest with the other packers. The union was just coming into its own.[99]

6

Chicago's Packinghouse Workers during World War II

Like many other packinghouse workers, Lowell Washington entered the military shortly after the Japanese attack on Pearl Harbor. When he left Chicago, the union which he helped build had just begun to establish bargaining relationships with the large packers. After a long struggle, the PWOC had brought Armour to terms. Strong locals existed within the Swift and Wilson plants. These organizations exerted a powerful presence on the shop floor, but were still preparing for Labor Board certification elections and operating without benefit of written contracts. When Washington returned three years later, the situation in the stockyards had been thoroughly transformed. Master agreements imposed by the government covered each of the three large packers; and the PWOC had become an autonomous international union, the United Packinghouse Workers of America (UPWA). "Guess they got on fine without me," Washington drily commented.[1]

The most dramatic change confronting Washington, however, was the recomposition of the workforce that had taken place during his absence. "There were more black faces in there than I ever saw before. Black guys on jobs that whites used to hold down solid, black guys all around, and girls too." he explained. The labor shortage that accompanied defense mobilization allowed hundreds of white packinghouse workers to escape the stockyards. Karl Lundberg, for example, hung up his bloodstained overalls in his locker at Swift for the last time just when Washington boarded a carrier bound for the South Pacific. Having secured a high-paying job at an armaments plant, he looked forward to "putting some money in the bank while doing my bit for Uncle Sam." Despite attempts to open defense employment to African Americans, racist hiring practices in most firms remained intact. Meanwhile, the stockyards continued to play its historical role of providing jobs and the opportunity for advancement to blacks. Thousands of new migrants from the South made their way to Chicago seeking to take advantage of the need for industrial labor. By the end of the war, black employment in meatpacking reached an unprecedented 40 percent.[2]

This demographic shift occurred at a critical juncture in the union's development and had a decisive impact upon its character. The enlarged black membership sustained the shop-floor militancy which distinguished the initial organizing period and provided the additional dynamism necessary to bring the Swift and Wilson plants into the union. These newcomers also expanded the constituency of the overlapping black and Communist networks within the PWOC/UPWA. Based in Chicago, these twin "orbits" extended to packing centers in the west and south. They helped give coherent institutional expression to rank-and-file interests, allowing packinghouse workers to resist the bureaucratizing pressures of the union's CIO-appointed leaders.

These orbits were personified by the two charismatic figures most closely associated with them: Hank Johnson and Herbert March. Johnson presided over the black network. His days with the International Workers Order and the steelworkers provided him with contacts in almost every major industrial center, and his activities on behalf of the National Negro Congress further extended this circle. In addition to using these ties to help build the PWOC into a national organization, he contributed to the creation of a broader racial consciousness within the union by introducing black activists from Chicago to their counterparts elsewhere. While solidly on the left, Johnson's politics were essentially pragmatic. He worked for a time within the Communist Party, rising to a post in the district politburo, but gradually distanced himself from the CP when his affiliation threatened to limit his movement within the labor hierarchy.[3] This black network orchestrated a series of campaigns to influence PWOC staff appointments, determine national bargaining policy, and push for an international union charter. In 1940 Johnson and several of his colleagues followed John L. Lewis and broke with the CIO. His subsequent attempts to pull packing locals into the United Mine Workers' District 50 illustrate both the nature of the loyalties involved and limits of the network's influence.

Herbert March stood at the center of the left-wing network. The most visible Communist in the industry, he never disguised or denied his political affiliation. March worked openly to build Party organizations in the Chicago packinghouses and coordinated his activities with cadres elsewhere in the union. Briefly cast out of meatpacking in 1940 as part of a purge of radicals, March returned the following year at the behest of CIO officials to counter the influence of Johnson's District 50 "disrupters." The CIO's reliance on the Communists to prevent the fragmentation of the union ensured a strong left presence for many years. At its peak in the late 1940s, the CP boasted between four and five hundred members in the stockyards, with probably an equal number of sympathizers.[4] Its greatest source of support came from black workers, and it recruited heavily among younger African Americans who entered the yards in the early 1940s. Like black cadres in other industries and locales, these recruits tended to regard the CP more as a militant civil rights organization than as a Marxist political group.[5]

At the same time, the wartime hirees produced a new stratum of black leadership within the union itself. More race conscious than the generation preceding them, they used their newly acquired power to attack remaining manifestations of in-plant discrimination such as hiring bars, restrictions on promotion, and the existence of lily-white departments. In several cases, blacks allied with the Left and won control of local unions by advancing a program of militancy and action against racial grievances. Simultaneously, young black activists rose to positions of prominence within the union apparatus, where they worked to institutionalize a civil rights program. Generally sympathetic to the Left, these officials and their constituents cemented the Communists' position within the union.

Demographic change coupled with intensified racial militancy placed considerable strain upon the coalition between white and black workers that lay at the heart of the union. Previously, white ethnics had supported action against discrimination because blacks articulated racial grievances in traditional trade union terms of seniority and job rights. Beginning in the 1940s, though, black packinghouse workers increasingly advanced demands that extended beyond the workplace. Union involvement in housing controversies and protests against racial violence in the larger community alienated many white workers, as did the strident rhetoric used by black leaders. Feeling that "the union is for the colored," many whites distanced themselves and withdrew from active participation.[6] Although containable in the 1940s, this strain foreshadowed the more pronounced and damaging black insurgency of the 1950s discussed in the final chapter.

The dynamics prevailing at the union's base during this period of consolidation shaped the emerging bureaucracy. Examined in detail below, the dynamic elements of this process can be briefly enumerated here: the persistence of independent rank-and-file activity, the transmission of a tradition of shop-floor militancy to a new cohort of workers, the operation of autonomous networks of unionists, and the emergence of a new black leadership. The essential context in which all of this unfolded was the world war. The exigencies of defense production imposed a new set of constraints upon shop-floor activity and produced a new political atmosphere to which the labor movement was forced to adapt. The manner in which the Packinghouse Workers responded to these challenges was conditioned, in the final analysis, by the impulses and tendencies animating its mass base.[7]

Wilson Local 25: Race, Gender, and Unionism

By 1940, Chicago's packinghouse workers had accomplished an unprecedented task in forging a coalition which encompassed black and white and enjoyed the support of a majority of the labor force. Of course, there were definite boundaries to this alliance. Many older white workers, especially the foreign born, remained aloof from the union or only lent it passive support. Cautious, fearful of the company, and suspicious of persons outside their ethnic enclave, they clung to a "wait and see" attitude. Perhaps the weakest element within the alliance was the large bloc of white women concentrated in the sausage, bacon, casings, and by-product departments. Isolated by both prevailing gender relations and the competitive work culture generated by the piecework system, these women tended to resist union appeals even after the victory at Armour. The PWOC campaigns at Wilson and Swift highlighted these organizational weaknesses. Although ultimately successful, the difficulties encountered by the union in these plants illustrate the limits of interracial unionism in the early 1940s.

The presence of company unions complicated the Wilson and Swift situations. The Labor Board ruling against Armour's Mutual Association applied only to that company; and although the PWOC brought legal action against the other two packers, the Wilson Employees Representative Committee (ERC) and the Swift Security League operated with impunity, competing with the PWOC for workers' loyalties. In each of these plants, the company union attracted workers who, for a variety of reasons, opposed the CIO.

In the case of Wilson, management revived the moribund company union, the Joint Representation Committee (JRC), in the mid-1930s, soon after organizing began in the stockyards. As in the past, its delegates were drawn from the ranks of long-service employees, with skilled workers and old stock immigrants heavily represented. Irish beef boner John Ryan served as the JRC's chair while another Irishman, Edward Murphy, a cooper who had been with the company for thirteen years, represented the mechanical division. Emil Rogalla, a sausage maker with fifteen years service, served as the Chicago plant's delegate to national JRC convocations; and Terry Lynch represented the beef division. In a period when the workforce was overwhelmingly Slavic, these names indicate the company's search for loyalty amongst an older but rapidly diminishing section of its employees. Indeed, the only Pole on the JRC, Walter Piotrowski, was unusual in that he labored on a number of semiskilled jobs throughout the plant, had a wife and son working for Wilson, and was involved in promoting company-sponsored athletics long before he became active in the organization.[8]

Most workers paid little heed to the reactivated JRC. It maintained a low profile, administering recreational activities, maintaining fire prevention and safety committees, and overseeing a modest charitable fund. It met several times each week with management representatives to handle grievances and attend to routine business, but few of these grievances resulted in meaningful victories: an extra cashier for the company's meat market, the installation of additional drinking fountains, and a commitment to improve the quality of food in the plant cafeteria. Turnouts for the annual election of delegates was low, especially in production departments.[9] Following the Supreme Court's 1936 upholding of the Wagner Act, Wilson modified the structure of the company union, withdrawing management representatives and changing its name to the Employes Representative Committee, so as to appear in compliance with section 8(2) of the law prohibiting company interference. In early 1937, as the CIO campaign gathered momentum, Wilson formally recognized the ERC as the bargaining agent for its employees and raised the profile of the now nominally independent company union in an attempt to use it as a bulwark against the PWOC.[10]

Although many Wilson workers regarded the ERC with the same indifference or suspicion they accorded its predecessor, others came to see it as a bona fide alternative to the CIO. Walter Piotrowski, the secretary of the new body, remembered that when the ERC held its first elections the majority of workers in the plant refused to mark their ballots. "They just laughed at us," he recalled. In the print shop, PWOC militants led by George von Thun bodily ejected the ERC representative when he appeared with ballot box in hand, a reception that was not unusual in well-organized areas of the plant. Yet, the ERC did enjoy some support. George Keim, a compositor in the print shop, preferred the ERC to the CIO because the former organization had more moderate leaders. George Geweke shunned the PWOC because of an unhappy experience with unionism at another employer. To many, the ERC seemed safer precisely because it bore the stamp of company approval. John Quinn, an initial PWOC supporter, turned to the new company union out of a belief that it was better positioned to deliver material benefits. "After all, the C.I.O. had done nothing for me and I thought it was useless." Quinn's pragmatic choice was one made by hundreds of others.[11]

Although the PWOC had a sizeable following in the Wilson plant, it was unable to persuade workers that it was the best vehicle through which to advance their interests. As late as January 1940, the Wilson local was struggling to make the kinds of concrete organizational gains that had allowed Armour 347 to triumph. Appearing that month on an NLRB ballot opposite the ERC, it lost by a narrow margin, attributing defeat to its failure to attract women into its ranks. Perhaps cognizant of this deficiency, the company hired an additional seven hundred female workers in the weeks preceding the contest.[12]

Women packinghouse workers resisted unionism for a number of reasons. John Wrublewski, who spent his evenings prior to the 1940 election campaigning door-to-door for the PWOC, observed that "it wasn't the younger girls, the wives and daughters of the guys in the union that held out on us." Rather, it was an older group of women, "those that was in there from way before we got the thing going. After all those years those old Polish ladies had it pretty good and they didn't want to rock the boat." Especially in departments where piecework allowed women to take home weekly checks as large as those earned by skilled butchers, the union appeal fell flat. One woman who packaged sliced bacon told a WPA interviewer that she feared the loss of her high-paying but relatively easy job. She stated that the women in her department disapproved of the CIO union for "butting in where they weren't wanted." Despite the PWOC's careful explanation that the implementation of seniority would offer greater job security, management effectively played upon these fears. Foremen sometimes exacerbated the situation by inflaming racial prejudices in these traditionally all-white departments. "They'd tell them 'the niggers are gonna get your jobs,' and boy did that set them off," Wrublewski explained.[13]

Even when female workers supported the PWOC a number of obstacles militated against their active involvement in it. Foremost among these was the masculine culture of unionism. As Ruth Milkman points out, "organized labor presented an alien territory for many women. Even more than the factory itself, the union was a traditionally male world." Although the PWOC did make a systematic effort to incorporate women, it could not overcome resilient patriarchal traditions and customs in a few short years. Most women were accustomed to deferring to males. This was especially true of those from ethnic backgrounds. Pat Christie explained that when pushed to increase the level of their participation many of the Polish women with whom she worked said, "Ah, let my husband join. Let my husband go to meetings. Let the men do it, it's not for women to do."[14]

Many black women commented on the inclination of white women to defer to males. This tendency frustrated Marian Simmons, who angrily declared, "those white women, they still seemed to think that the men were looking out for their best interests." Furthermore, active female unionists risked developing unsavory reputations. Simmons recalled one such woman, noting that other workers spread an unfounded rumor that she was sexually involved with the black leaders of the local. "With that going against her, that being circulated, well then she finally became quiet. She wasn't as active." These incidents occurred with enough frequency to give many women pause before they ran for union office or volunteered for committee assignments.[15]

Despite these difficulties, many women did become involved in the PWOC. The union issued special appeals to its female membership and established a women's division which held weekly meetings for women workers. Attuned to the strain placed upon single mothers, the PWOC joined with unionized social workers to offer free counseling for "home front problems." Of greater significance, though, was the increasing attention devoted to securing equal pay for equal work. While female packinghouse workers traditionally earned less than their male counterparts when performing comparable labor, during the early 1940s this became an especially acute problem. The packing companies sought to take advantage of the wartime manpower shortage by placing women on jobs previously held by men and paying them at the lower female rate. The male rate for the semiskilled work of trimming beef bladders had been 75.5 cents an hour; women performing this task earned only 65.5 cents. Even unskilled common labor was subject to the same kind of differential. Male workers who hung pork livers on a rack received 75.5 cents per hour while females earned only 62 cents.[16]

By fighting for equal pay, the union made a direct, material appeal to female packinghouse workers. Women laboring in the unorganized plants learned of the advances made at Armour and the Little Six houses and began to see the union as an important ally. This is not to argue that the union was blind to gender difference or that it pursued a policy of strict equality. Many male activists regarded the struggle for equal pay as a defense of existing wage levels rather than an attempt to improve the condition of female workers. At the same time that it battled to secure equal pay, the union perpetuated traditional distinctions between male and female jobs. However, this often occurred in such a way as to win rather than lose the support of women workers. At Omaha Meat, one of the small plants in the stockyards, supervisors harassed newly hired women by requiring them to lift over their heads the same heavy loads as men. The local union contested the practice and succeeded, through the use of job actions, in having two women placed on the job alongside individual men. Although it preserved the distinction between male and female jobs, workers hailed this outcome as a victory.[17]

In the 1940s, a small group of female leaders gained prominence at the local level. Although it is difficult to explain why these women defied convention, some generalizations can be made. Most female activists had personal lives that differed in significant ways from those of other women workers. Many were free from traditional family ties. Eunetta Pierce, a black steward and officer at Omaha Meat, explained "I was twenty-one. I wasn't married, and I didn't care whether I worked today or tomorrow. . . . For them to tell me 'you're fired,' hell, that was like an everyday word. I didn't care; I'd go find another job." Like many black women, Ercell Allen moved to Chicago from Memphis when the war started. She came alone and welcomed the ready-made social circle offered by the union. Katie Mae Washington migrated from Mississippi and entered the yards at about the same time. Living at a boardinghouse, she was free from supervision and able to "get powerfully involved in the union."[18]

Other women activists came from union families that encouraged their participation in the labor movement. Eunetta Pierce's father, a mechanic at Checker Cab and a founder of the union there, instilled a union orientation in his daughter at an early age. Well before she started work in meatpacking, Pierce was strongly committed to organization and believed that "nobody's going to give you nothing, you got to take it." Other prominent female unionists, like Vicky Starr and Pat Balskus, were Communists whose organizational activity stemmed from their political affiliation. Wives and girlfriends of male union leaders were more likely to assume active roles than other women. Balskus's husband, Charles, was president of the Brennan local. Mary Smith, one of the few women to hold office in the Wilson local, became involved only after she argued with her husband about his devotion to the union. "Many times I was peeved when he said he was going to one of his meetings. I didn't think it possible that one could spend so much time on union problems," she explained. Exasperated, her husband invited her to attend one of his steward meetings. Impressed with what she witnessed, Smith volunteered to serve as an organizer in the plant and later was elected financial secretary of the local.[19]

Female unionists believed their effectiveness was limited by male indifference toward their concerns. Sophie Kosciolowski recalled that whenever she raised the question of women's problems at meetings, some of the men "always had a sort of snicker or a smile. It was always sort of funny you know, as if women couldn't possibly have a serious or important contribution to make." Marian Simmons made the same point and illustrated it by referring to a demand for company-provided child care forwarded by women at a Kansas City conference. The male-dominated gathering accepted a resolution on the issue, but there the matter died. "The union just didn't pick it up," Simmons stated. "The door was open for it, but it was just another speech as far as they were concerned."[20]

At the same time, male attitudes about women's proper roles restricted their participation in local union governance to sex-stereotyped posts such as recording or financial secretary. Even men who "believed in equality and that women should have rights didn't crank the mimeograph, didn't type," Vicky Starr noted. She remembered the constant rebuffs she received from PWOC leaders when she pressed for female organizers on the the district payroll. "When the union came around giving out jobs with pay, the guys got them. I and the other women didn't." Only in rare instances did men accept women as their equals in the union. Their chauvinism not only hindered the activities of women leaders but often warned female workers away from participation in the union. Helen Zajac, for instance, never expressed interest in her local beyond paying her monthly dues. "I just felt there was no use trying to go where I wasn't wanted," she explained.[21]

Women contended with these kinds of problems in all packinghouse locals. In some situations—such as those prevailing in the small processing plants where women made up a majority of the workforce—the problem was not especially severe. In other instances, women's alienation from the union thwarted its organizing drive. This is what occurred at the Wilson plant. Here, the PWOC recognized the source of its initial defeat and responded by making special overtures to the women in the plant. Departmental meetings, the appointment of additional female stewards, and the formation of a women's committee reinvigorated the second Wilson campaign. Especially effective in reaching Wilson women were the overtures made to them by union's recently formed Polish Committee and female unionists from other packinghouses. This attention helped overcome Wilson workers' sense of detachment from the movement in the yards. Located at a remove from the Armour and Swift plants, Wilson was the only major packer west of Ashland Avenue. The plant "was a little bit on the outside," recalled Les Orear. "They were a little isolated over there and in my circles nobody hardly knew much about Wilson."[22]

In the summer of 1940 the Wilson situation changed dramatically. A number of factors were involved in a sudden shift away from the ERC and toward the PWOC. In addition to advances made amongst women workers, Walter Piotrowski and five other officers of the company union broke with management over the continued campaign against the CIO. Clearly something of an opportunist—for he first approached the AFL Meat Cutters—Piotrowski eventually settled in the PWOC camp. Packinghouse activists made the most of this defection, using minutes of ERC meetings and other materials provided by the renegades to highlight the ERC's collusion with the company. Hundreds of workers followed Piotrowski's path away from allegiance to Wilson, marking the defection as a turning point in the struggle. "Well, at that point folks got a feeling that the CIO was here to stay," recalled John Wrublewski.[23]

In September the union cause received a further boost when the NLRB opened hearings to consider whether the ERC was merely the old JRC in disguise. In addition to local press coverage, each week special issues of the *Wilson Sparks* reported on the proceedings. As well as trumpeting evidence of the ERC's relationship with the company and the privileges and perquisites enjoyed by its representatives, *Sparks* commented pointedly on the inability of the company union to prevent speedups, firings, and abuse of workers. Perhaps most damaging to the credibility of the ERC was the testimony, offered by disillusioned company union representatives, that the January election had been marred by the stuffing of ballot boxes and the intimidation of voters.[24]

In early 1941, the Labor Board ruled in favor of the PWOC and ordered Wilson to disband the ERC. Although CIO organizers could now claim with some justification that "We have the national administration behind us" (a refrain repeated over the PWOC sound truck stationed outside the plant), the company appealed the decision through the federal courts and rechristened the tarnished ERC the "Wilson Workers Independent Union." By the time that the courts rejected Wilson's appeal almost a year later, the PWOC was in an almost impregnable position. Having successfully used the Labor Board to force a series of reinstatements, it began to fashion an in-plant organization wielding considerable power. In a second election held in December 1942, the PWOC won handily; the margin of more than two thousand votes testified to the overwhelming support it now enjoyed.[25]

A critical factor in this victory was the support given the union by newly hired black workers. At least half of the two thousand additional employees added to the company's payroll during the war were nonwhite.[26] These workers augmented the local's core of support; a large number of them became departmental stewards or served on various union committees. In doing so they helped revitalize the sagging local and countered the antiunion sentiment of other workers.

The involvement of these black workers, especially the women among them, differed from the patterns prevailing in other industries. During the war, CIO unions in the mass production sector found it difficult to incorporate new hirees into their organizational structures. While maintenance of membership provisions ensured the numerical expansion of their base, the unions' ability to function effectively at the plant level and resolve grievances suffered as a result of legal constraints upon the use of the strike weapon and pressures generated by restive, newly proletarianized workers. The inability of many unions to adequately mollify workers' resentment over the deterioration of working conditions and the freezing of wages led to the alienation of large sections of the rank and file and the decomposition of shop-floor organization. The wartime experience of the CIO's automobile, electrical, and rubber unions exhibited a discernible decline in shop-floor solidarity, militancy, and democratic participation. "The maintenance of labor peace in an era when grievances were rife," one study concluded, "required a permanent weakening of those elements in the union structure upon which trade union power ultimately rested."[27]

Two key features distinguished the PWOC/UPWA from other CIO unions in this regard: the unusually high proportion of black workers in the meatpacking industry and the union's ability to preserve its prewar traditions of workplace militancy and direct action. Black workers regarded their union differently than did their white counterparts. In addition to seeing unionism as a means to gain greater economic security, they looked upon it as a vehicle with which to advance the struggle for racial equality. This was especially true of the new African American cohort that entered the stockyards during and immediately following the war. Distinguished by its willingness to challenge established racial norms which their fathers and mothers had accepted as immutable, this generation found the PWOC's appeal far more salient than did white workers. Again, the case of the Chicago Wilson plant serves as an illustration.

Sam Parks moved to Chicago from Memphis in 1941. Lured north by industrial wages, he commuted to work at a coke plant near Joliet for a short time before securing a job at Wilson where his brother-in-law was employed. Charlie Hayes entered the Wilson plant at about the same time, having arrived in the city a few weeks earlier from Cairo, Illinois. He sought employment in the yards on the advice of an uncle who labored there. Neither man regarded their positions as permanent, nor did they intend to become involved in the union. Parks planned to become an attorney and was attending classes at evening college. Hayes came to meatpacking with some industrial experience under his belt. In addition to laboring as a railroad section hand, he worked at a hardwood flooring plant where he helped found a local of the Brotherhood of Carpenters and Joiners. His experience with the AFL left him highly ambivalent about unionism. "Heck, when I first started in the stockyards, the farthest thought from my mind was to pick up the cudgels of a union again," he recalled. Within a very short period, however, both men had emerged as leaders of Local 25.[28]

It was the PWOC's stand on racial equality that initially attracted Hayes and Parks. Soon after starting work in the freezer department, Parks encountered overt discrimination. He recalled that supervisors "treated people in that Wilson plant just like I happened to see when I was living in the South in Memphis as a kid, the way I saw white people treat workers down there. And I figured, hell, this is Chicago, this is supposed to be the home of freedom, ain't no white man got no business doing no Negroes that way up here." He channeled his anger and frustration into the union, organizing a departmental sit-down strike in protest of the foremen's behavior. Hayes turned to the union after his ambition to become a skilled electrician was crushed. He attempted to enter a local vocational school but was turned away on account of his race. The rebuff led him to embrace the PWOC and work to "change the system."[29]

Many other black workers followed a similar path. Hayes and Parks merit special attention because their involvement in Local 25 extended beyond departmental leadership. After the 1942 election victory, the two men joined forces with white leftists to wrest control of the local union away from its older, more conservative leaders. They did this by advancing a program of militant action around racial grievances which included frequent resort to work stoppages despite the union's formal adherence to the CIO's no-strike pledge. Once in power, this group pioneered the use of the contract and grievance mechanism to integrate previously lily-white departments and open skilled mechanical jobs to blacks.

The group of leaders holding office in the Wilson local at the time of its NLRB certification reflected the divided nature of the workforce. Dock Williams, the president of the local, was a black man in his late forties who had worked for the company since 1913. A combat veteran of World War I, Williams was a loud, assertive leader. His self-assurance and experience won him a sizeable following among the plant's older black workers. He shared power with Mary Smith who, according to Parks, "kept the whites in line" through her relationship with the company. While no evidence exists that supports the contention that Williams and Smith had the ability to discharge or demote workers who challenged them, it is clear that they were able to influence hiring decisions and that they declined to challenge job segregation. A widespread feeling existed among the membership that the two leaders were "a little too cozy" with management. To Hayes, Williams and Mary Smith seemed to operate like "out and out representatives of the company." Sam Parks went a step farther, stating that "they were a company union, although they had a CIO label and everything else."[30]

It was not difficult for militants like Parks and Hayes to challenge this leadership clique. They received assistance from the union's district office, headed at the time by Herbert March, in the form of staff support, funding, and guidance. March also put the black activists in contact with white Communists working in the plants' mechanical gangs. Carl Nelson was a pipe coverer who had been at the forefront of the PWOC drive at Swift before being fired and had put in a short stint at Armour prior to his employment at Wilson. Joe Zabritski, a pipe fitter, had labored at Reliable Packing in the early 1930s. He left the industry after contracting "hog itch," a chronic dermatological condition, but returned at the start of the war hoping to learn a skilled trade. Zabritski's and Nelson's jobs allowed them to roam the entire plant under minimal supervision. Their CP connections gave them additional resources which they put to use in the factional fight within the local. The presence in the strategic beef-cutting department of another Communist, Anton Pasinski, further augmented their strength. Pasinski had labored at Wilson since 1920 and formed an important link between many of the older Poles and the new black militants.[31]

By uniting with white Communists in the plant, Parks and Hayes provided an alternative, interracial pole around which workers could rally. Although their increasing identification with the Left allowed Williams to tag them as Reds and may have caused some workers to hesitate, their program of militant, confrontational unionism won many converts. For example, John Wrublewski thought the upstarts were "a bit too radical, kind of out there." He nevertheless supported them because they "were a hell of a lot better than what we was used to having. . . . These guys were ready and willing to fight."[32]

They were especially ready and willing to fight for black rights. After a slate headed by Parks and Zabritski deposed Dock Williams's administration in an acrimonious election, the Wilson local began an assault on racial discrimination in the plant.[33] Their most notable success came when hog and beef kill workers walked off the job to force the integration of the traditionally lily-white sliced bacon department. The action came after the local had unsuccessfully attempted to use the grievance procedure to allow black women to transfer into the prized jobs. Parks recalled that the workers, wearing their bloody overalls and carrying their knives, marched from the killing floors to the company's front office where they sat themselves on top of desks. The secretaries were understandably terrified. "They thought the revolution had come," Parks chuckled. A phone call from the plant superintendent to a Wilson executive settled the matter and the men returned to work.[34]

The Wilson local did not hesitate to employ stoppages to enforce its demands, even when such actions violated the no-strike pledge. Indeed, it was the company's intransigence that contributed to the union's reliance upon workplace action. Wilson was the last of the large packers to sign an agreement with the PWOC. It began negotiating with the union only when compelled to do so by the NLRB in 1940. Even then it adhered to its traditional anti-union stance until 1943 when the National War Labor Board imposed a contract.[35] In the lengthy interim period, work stoppages and slowdowns were often the only ways in which the local could get management to respond. Once the contract was in place, such action was not always necessary. Local 25 used the contractual grievance machinery to eliminate some of the last vestiges of in-plant discrimination. In the immediate postwar period, it succeeded in placing black apprentices in the skilled white mechanical gangs. In a much celebrated incident, the local utilized the contract's anti-discrimination clause to force the reinstatement of Jake McKinney, a black worker who was fired after punching a foreman who called him "Sunshine." McKinney's left hook subsequently became an enduring piece of union folklore.[36]

The alliance between young black militants and Communist cadres which revitalized the Chicago Wilson local occurred in less dramatic fashion elsewhere in the union. In a number of important ways, this alliance resembled the relationship between black workers and the CP that prevailed in the early 1930s during the heyday of the Unemployed Councils. Above all, this alliance was a pragmatic one. The Party's appeal to blacks like Parks and Hayes had less to do with ideology than a perceived ability to advance the fight for equal rights both at the workplace and in the community. "I was interested in the black masses and I thought these guys had the right answer," Parks explained. The CP's zealous defense of black rights struck an especially responsive chord among the wartime cohort. "We wanted to get free from where we were," Hayes recalled, "I didn't care who helped us. Help us, you know, that was the general attitude." Even black activists who neither shared the Communists' outlook nor even recognized their political affiliation welcomed them as allies. Marian Simmons, who emerged as the leading civil rights activist in Kansas City, explained, "I could have cared less who those people were, I needed some support. I'm trying to put over a program, and these people . . . as long as they were white and they were going along, I wasn't going to question anybody about their personal business."[37]

The Communists themselves were surprisingly nonideological in their overtures to other workers. Vicky Starr noted, "you didn't talk about socialism per se. You talked about issues and saw how people reacted . . . you couldn't talk about socialism and what it meant in an abstract sense. You had to talk about it in terms of what it would mean for that particular person." For many leftists in the industry, their identities as Communists and labor organizers merged together into an inseparable whole. Herbert March, who brought more packinghouse workers into the CP than any other individual, explained that he told potential recruits that Party membership would help them become better unionists. Rather than stress ideology or discuss theoretical issues, March recruited workers through his involvement in the day-to-day struggle with the packers. "By example of the way I conducted myself I was able to attract people," he recalled. "I would offer explanations of some things. I would reason as a Marxist. . . . Just by functioning and playing a role as an effective leader I was able to attract people into the Party."[38]

This overriding concern with the "nuts and bolts" of unionism frequently brought Communists in meatpacking in conflict with the Party. CP officials repeatedly pressed them to be more forward in their political activities. Jack Johnstone, for instance, complained bitterly about the difficulties he encountered "making comrades working in the unions remember they have Party duties to perform." Other functionaries took them to task for not taking up national questions and foreign policy issues in their union work. On several occasions, when recruitment was not proceeding as quickly as Party officials desired, packinghouse leaders suffered severe criticism for refusing to provide the names and addresses of workers.[39]

Communists in the yards valued their autonomy and, at times, were disdainful of the Party hierarchy. "There were a lot of stupid, grandstand quarterbacks in the Communist movement trying to run things," March stated. With little understanding of the situation in the industry, and often comically out of touch with the working class, CP bureaucrats frequently handed down directives that, if carried out, would have produced disastrous results. In 1939, for example, when the PWOC was engaged in a bitter battle with the Amalgamated over representation rights at Armour, the district politburo attacked the CIO as a "decadent organization" and ordered its packinghouse section to cooperate with the AFL! Fortunately for the PWOC, Communists in meatpacking enjoyed a significant degree of independence from the Party apparatus and interpreted CP policy as they saw fit. In addition, March's relationship with top Party leader William Z. Foster furnished him with additional room to maneuver. Respected as the Party's leading authority on trade unionism, Foster shielded union activists from reproach and reprimand on several occasions.[40]

The influx of black packinghouse workers into the CP further enhanced its autonomy. This growth in black membership coincided with the exit of many white cadres. The 1939 Nazi-Soviet pact damaged the Party's standing among eastern European ethnics; and the Soviet invasion of Poland later that year prompted many workers to break completely with the Communists. The Party's decision to dissolve its shop units hastened the demographic shift within its packing organization. When white CP members attached themselves to the Party's neighborhood organizations, they quickly lost interest and drifted away. "They were interested in unionism, most of them were stewards and active union people, and they'd go to meetings and they'd want you to sell the *Daily Worker*," Jane March explained. The void was filled largely by black recruits for whom neighborhood issues and community problems—police brutality, access to services, dilapidated and overpriced housing—carried special resonance.[41]

The Paternalistic Tradition: Swift and Company

The PWOC had difficulty organizing the Chicago Swift plant. Initially concentrated in ancillary departments, union activity progressed slowly in the main area of the plant. Support from the strategic killing floors and cutting departments came only after the 1939 victory at Armour. The Swift campaign then dragged on until January 1942, when Local 28 won representation rights in an NLRB election. In later years, some Swift unionists claimed that this delay was politically motivated. Hank Schoenstein, a founder of the Swift local, charged that the "key reason was the communist boys. They wanted the prestige of signing up the Armour local first." Such an explanation may have served as ammunition against the Left, but it does not withstand historical scrutiny. Swift proved "a hard nut to crack" because the company's long-standing paternalism secured for it the allegiance of large numbers of workers. This was true not just in Chicago but across the country. In fact, the only major packinghouses that the CIO never organized were the Swift's Kansas City and East St. Louis plants.[42]

A half-cent extra pay, a slightly more generous vacation policy, an especially active company union known as the Security League, and an impressive range of recreational activities fostered a sense of devotion absent in the other packinghouses. "They pat you on the back and make out you're just one of the family," remarked Mary Hammond, "I used to think Swifts was the cream." Another worker, Elizabeth Washington, believed that Swift was "more for their employees than any other company. They try to do the right thing for them." Although the company passed out of the control of the Swift family in 1937, Harold Swift, the son of Gustavus, served as chairman of the board and continued to exert an influence over its operations. Even as staunch a unionist as Philip Weightman felt a personal loyalty to the company based on the "family feeling" prevailing in its plants.[43]

Swift's policies were still a long way from those in effect at National Cash Register or Endicott Johnson, where welfare capitalism was carried to an extreme. Nevertheless, Swift was the only large packing company to adopt something other than a bareknuckles approach to labor relations. "Their bonus payments were a little better, their industrial relations policy a little more civilized, the opportunities for advancement were a little more systematized," Les Orear observed. These policies undoubtedly "had an effect on the workers, or at least some of 'em," admitted another PWOC member. "They thought that they were better somehow cause they worked there. . . . You'd talk to Swift people and a lot of them would say, 'we don't need no union, we can go and talk about our problems and get things straightened out.'" Swift employees often pointedly compared their open-door policy with the more adversarial system operating in the other plants. "Armour's hasn't got nothing like that," Elizabeth Washington remarked, "We're privileged to talk to the superintendent. At Armour you got to have a committee." This policy of access remained in effect even after the PWOC gained enough of a foothold in the plant to force management to negotiate over grievances. When the union requested weekly grievance sessions, the company responded that it preferred daily meetings. "That was shocking," Weightman recalled. "I said, 'these guys are all ready for us.'"[44]

Older, foreign-born workers felt the tug of company allegiance most strongly. Swift carried more long-service employees on its payroll than did the other packers. An industrial sociologist who studied the company found that 20 percent of the white men in the Chicago plant had labored there for sixteen years or more, and that another 11 percent had put in between eight and fifteen years of service. By the early 1940s, these largely Polish and Lithuanian workers had accumulated enough time to be protected by the company's seniority plan and to qualify for the pension scheme it offered. Many of them had experienced the union defeats of 1904 and 1921, and were fearful that the CIO would meet the same fate. Unwilling to risk the modicum of security they had gained, these workers believed that loyalty to the company was a more promising strategy than unionism. They tended to be skeptical of the younger, more Americanized workers who supported the PWOC. "Unions come and go, but Swift and Company remains," one aged Pole told a PWOC organizer.[45]

Many older whites also kept their distance from the union because of its willingness to involve blacks and to offer them leadership positions. Charles Sukoff, who had worked at Swift since 1902, wanted little to do with the CIO. "The union is all colored," he opined. "The whites in our department say, 'let the colored run it.'" Skilled workers in the all-white mechanical gangs objected to "being thrown in with colored butchers." Many of these men had craft union experience and periodically contemplated inviting the AFL into the plant to organize tradesmen on a separate basis. The PWOC's outspoken position on equal rights further estranged many whites. William Coyne put it most strongly. "I get disgusted looking at the *Flash* [the local's newsletter]," he complained. "Negro rights is all it is. They worry about the South and the Dixon lines and they put the union stamp at the bottom." Racial attitudes thus reinforced the generational split in the ranks of white workers at Swift.[46]

Older African American workers at Swift were divided in their loyalties as well. Many did go over to the PWOC, especially on the killing floors, but others withheld their support. More than in the other plants, older blacks "felt that they owed their job to the goodwill of Mr. Swift." First hired in an era of limited employment opportunity, many of these workers had climbed up the job ladder and held highly skilled, well-paying positions when the PWOC began challenging the ways in which the company conducted its business. For a number of these workers, the company union offered an alternative to the confrontational unionism of the CIO. One worker explained his backing of the Security League in precisely these terms: "It protects us against any other union because when you are a member of the Security League that shows that you are satisfied with your employer—that you don't want any other union to come in and make trouble for you." While Swift never allowed the league to represent workers on a collective basis, it did handle individual grievances, manage the pension fund, and handle the distribution of insurance benefits. Never a thinly disguised anti-union tool like the Armour EMA, the Security League presented the PWOC with a formidable obstacle.[47]

Union leaders recognized that Swift's sophisticated personnel policies required a different approach than that taken at Armour and Wilson. "Swift has a system and it is pretty neat. But the closer you look, the better you understand it," Hank Johnson explained. "It is to fight the union without fighting the union. They pay a few cents more and always allow workers to discuss their problems. They never fight organization openly." Asked if Swift intimidated union organizers, Owensby Lee, a black leader of Local 28 and its president during this period, replied affirmatively, but added "so cleverly you would never detect it." Rather than appeal to Swift workers by emphasizing economic issues, PWOC activists stressed the union's ability to ensure that the company lived up to its paternalistic promises. One issue of the local paper even termed the union "insurance against any unforeseen detriment to your livelihood, your job." A contract between the PWOC and Swift, organizers explained, would codify the company's haphazard seniority and informal security provisions and thus safeguard workers.[48]

Because of the strong sense of company identification at Swift, the union discovered that the use of organizers from other plants was ineffective. Their presence allowed company loyalists to portray the PWOC as an outside organization bent upon disrupting the company's traditional practices and special relationship with its employees. Phil Weightman recalled telling union officials, "Give us the guidance and we'll organize the plant because you can't." The PWOC supplemented the activities of the in-plant organizers by adding Arthell Shelton to its staff and assigning him to the Swift drive. A protégé of Hank Johnson, Shelton was a black beef butcher who led the ill-fated 1938–39 Sioux City strike. Having spent most of his working career at the Swift plant there, he understood the hold that the company exercised over its employees and was able to communicate with them as an insider. Much of the initial progress made by the union on the killing floors was due to Shelton's influence.[49]

Refugio Martinez, a former Swift worker who had been on the PWOC district staff since 1938, assisted Shelton. The choice of Martinez was a shrewd one, for the Swift plant contained a sizeable number of Mexican workers who responded eagerly when approached. Although Martinez had worked at Swift for only a short time, he was well known to Mexican workers. In addition to his leadership in the Unemployed Council, Martinez was active in the Frente Popular Mexicano and the Vincent Toledano Club, an organization of militant workers loosely affiliated with the Communist Party. According to Herbert March, the Toledano Club independently enrolled most Mexicans in the yards into the PWOC.[50]

Rank-and-file activists within the plant, however, performed the bulk of the organizational work. The local targeted certain departments for "colonization" and contrived to transfer its organizers into them. Vicky Starr, for instance, transferred into the sliced bacon department and began to convince the white women there to support the union. The years she spent cultivating contacts among the Poles now paid off. Within ten months, the department was solidly behind the PWOC. The turning point, Starr recalled, came when a woman who worked near the freezer entrance died of pneumonia. Focusing upon safety issues, she brought the department into the union. In similar fashion, the union broke down resistance in the sausage room, another Polish enclave. Stanley Piontek, a Polish beef boner, transferred into the department and managed to recruit many of the staunchly anti-union women there by referring to his own conversion to the union cause. Initially wary of the PWOC because of the number of blacks involved, Piontek overcame his prejudice after working closely with African Americans on the local's executive committee. "Stanley had a way of convincing people because he could talk about his own experience of initially opposing the union and then changing his attitude," Phil Weightman recalled.[51]

Another reason behind Piontek's success was his focus upon the company's recent modification of the bonus system in the sausage department, an alteration which amounted to a poorly concealed speedup. Since management constantly adjusted the quota and adjusted the calculation of the bonus, workers found themselves in frequent conflict with their employers. Growing discontent with Swift's application of the Bedaux system provided an issue that PWOC organizers used to appeal to even the most diehard company loyalists. In the spring of 1940 unhappiness with the system crystallized in a series of job actions aimed at restoring old rates. "Workers all through the plant are realizing that the 'Bonus' is a slave driving system which must be brought under control," the union's newspaper stated. Led by unionists, many of these actions resulted in substantial victories. On the hog kill, for instance, management agreed to reduce the pace of the line by one hundred animals per hour.[52]

By the summer of 1940 Local 28 succeeded in neutralizing the Security League. Having filed an unfair labor practice charge with the Labor Board late the previous year, it declined to wait for a ruling. Rather than organize a boycott of company union elections, a tactic successfully employed at Armour, the union urged its members to participate in them. Rather than vote for candidates, however, workers scrawled "CIO" across the face of the ballot. When the results were tabulated, the spoiled ballots forced upon Security League officials the realization that their support was waning. The union also successfully ran its own candidates for office in the company's Benefit Association, a body that oversaw employee pensions and insurance payments, and had them raise substantive issues which the company could not address. By the time the Labor Board handed down its ruling on the Security League, Swift had voluntarily agreed to withdraw its recognition. Still the PWOC welcomed the decision. As Art Shelton put it, the ruling buried the league completely and insured that "the body [was not] left around to annoy people with its smell."[53]

The local's newsletter, the *Swift Flash*, proved an especially effective organizing tool. Unionists used it to pinpoint and air grievances, report on successes in the plant, and keep workers abreast of developments elsewhere in the yards and in other packing centers. Ridicule was a potent weapon. Something as simple as publicly revealing the nicknames workers assigned their foremen or poking fun at a particular supervisor's petty rules served the important function of demystifying authority. "Two-face Smith" was lambasted for forcing his gang to pile products in the freezer with the fan running. "Half-wit" Benson, the lard room foreman, was taken to task for insisting that workers ask permission to use the washroom. "You would think that his department was some concentration camp in Europe," the *Flash* editorialized. Because of its feisty tone and irreverent content, the *Flash* was widely read. It often contained appeals directed to union holdouts. One issue, for example, opened with an article entitled "The Church Speaks for Labor" which reported on Bishop Sheil's backing of the PWOC. Another edition tabulated the company's record earnings along with a description of the Swift family's opulent lifestyle. It asked, "Think what you are doing for Swift and Company. Think who is producing the profit. Think about your condition and the condition of the Big Shots."[54]

One testament to the effectiveness of the *Flash* was the length to which management was willing to go to prevent its distribution. First the com-

pany tried to bar the paper from the plant, citing an obscure health regulation prohibiting newsprint from coming in contact with food. When the
union pointed out that such an ordinance undoubtedly would apply to the
various publications that Swift provided its employees, management reverted to more heavy-handed methods. Having determined who was
bringing the *Flash* into the plant, the company assigned special security
details to follow them. One of these workers was Phil Weightman. He characteristically ignored the guards tailing him and continued to deposit the
newsletter in dressing rooms and toilets. "What you're doing when you're
doing that is not bravo for yourself, you're building courage in the workers you represent," he explained. After several weeks of this cat and mouse
game, Swift compromised and provided the union with a box in the plant
cafeteria where it could leave bundles of the paper.[55]

Through the *Flash* and other literature, in speeches and in one-on-one
conversations, and most importantly through its activities on the shop floor,
the PWOC articulated a style of class struggle unionism that produced
solidarity by focusing workers' anger and resentment upon the employer.
"We created an impression that the boss is your enemy. The fellow worker
beside you is not the enemy," Weightman explained. Since the departmental
foreman personified the authority of the company for most workers, it was
he who bore the brunt of the union's attack. "He's the guy that gives you
orders. He's the guy that writes your time out. He's the fellow that recom-
mends your discharge. About the only thing he don't do is hire you, but
he can get rid of you," Weightman continued. The nature of capitalist production ensured that even loyal long-service workers had gripes with their
foremen. The PWOC saw these grievances as openings, using them to chip
away at the company's image of itself as benefactor and to build support
for its own program. Gradually, one department at a time, the local consolidated its position in the plant.[56]

By the autumn of 1941 union leaders felt confident enough to petition
for an election. A recent PWOC victory at Swift's large Omaha plant showed
the company's vulnerability.[57] At the same time, the Chicago campaign
received an enormous boost as a result of a suit brought by the union
against Swift for violating the overtime provisions of the Fair Labor Standards Act. Initiated several years earlier, the case reached a dramatic conclusion just as the local was preparing for the election. In November, a judge
enjoined the company from working its employees more than forty hours
a week without overtime pay. Local 28's leaders had just finished testify-
ing, and the union was able to take credit for the injunction. Then, only a
few weeks before the poll, Swift agreed to compensate hundreds of work-

ers for overtime hours. Again, the PWOC was able to take responsibility for the decision. The back pay announcement electrified the plant and yielded a last-minute burst of enthusiasm for the union. The fervor carried over to election day, when the PWOC won with a comfortable margin of more than fifteen hundred votes.[58]

The wartime cohort of workers that played such a critical role in revitalizing the Wilson local seems not to have exerted a similar effect at Swift. Employment in the plant did rise significantly during the first years of the war—an additional three thousand workers were added to the company's payroll between the start of defense mobilization and the time of the election—but very few of these new hires emerged as union leaders.[59] While they supported the PWOC and undoubtedly were an important factor in the union's election victory, the insular nature of the Swift local and the workers' distrust of outsiders probably mitigated against their immediate rise into positions of responsibility. Almost all the officers of Local 28, from its inception to the time Swift closed the plant in the early 1960s, were long-service employees.

The pronounced insular character of the Swift local also frustrated the Communists' efforts to exert a controlling influence. While leftists occasionally held office in Local 28—Vicky Starr as vice-president and Solomon Hawkins as chief steward and, later, president—they never held the kind of sway over the organization as they did at Armour and Wilson. In the mid-1940s, the Swift local emerged as a leading force in the anticommunist opposition bloc within the union. It resisted CP efforts to dominate the joint council, expelled several of its members for plotting to seize control of the local, and even moved its office out of the district headquarters.[60]

However, the local's opposition to the CP was not motivated by political differences. Swift leaders saw eye to eye with the Communists as far as union strategy and tactics were concerned; they worked with them in negotiations and followed their lead in civil rights activities. Phil Weightman, who became something of a conservative after his 1948 ouster from the union, went out of his way to credit the CP for its contributions toward the building of the union. "I may not have been as aggressive as I was if it hadn't been for them, you see. The fact that they were talking and urging this and that and the other, that I thought was for the wrong reasons, but they were *good* things that they were suggesting. That makes the difference." Instead, the anticommunism of the Swift local was informed by the same parochial guarding of its autonomy and independence that rendered outside organizers useless and prevented newcomers from exercising influence. All outside attempts to influence Local 28, including those flowing first from the CIO-appointed leaders of the PWOC and later from the international union, met fierce and dogged resistance. UPWA president Ralph Helstein, a frequent target of the local's ire for close to two decades, recognized as much. "They wanted to run their own show. Regardless of the issue or the nature of the problem, they had to call the shots," he recalled.[61]

Building a National Organization: Black Workers and the Formation of the United Packinghouse Workers of America

Both the Swift organizing campaign and the transformation of the Wilson local occurred against a backdrop of intense factionalism. The major fault line in this struggle pitted rank-and-file workers against Van Bittner and other CIO-appointed PWOC leaders. As early as 1939, dissatisfaction with Bittner's administration was widespread. However, local unions in this period tended to ignore rather than oppose the national office. As the PWOC consolidated its position in the industry and began to push for master agreements with the packers, regional groupings of packinghouse workers came in close contact with one another. By 1941, these groups had coalesced into a formal opposition movement whose major goal was the formation of an autonomous international union.

The same kind of militancy and flair for dramatic confrontation that characterized the shop-floor struggle informed the opposition movement's fight with the union bureaucracy. Pickets, sit-downs, and mass gatherings were now directed at CIO officers, as the dissidents first organized to remove Bittner and then to oust his successor. By 1942 their push for an international had produced a series of district meetings, many held in defiance of the national office. The following year, they secured CIO approval of a constitutional convention; and in October 1943, the PWOC passed out of existence and the United Packinghouse Workers of America (UPWA) was born.

The movement drew its strength from three sources. Hank Johnson and his network of black unionists centered in Chicago provided the initial catalyst. The Communists, also based in Chicago but with major pockets of influence elsewhere, were another source of leadership, and one that proved more durable in the long term. The third element was comprised of militant workers from outlying locals in Iowa, Nebraska, and Minnesota. This last group was not as cohesive as the first two; its members were not bound together by race or by political persuasion. Fiercely independent, they represented an extreme antibureaucratic tendency within the PWOC, but one that was limited by a parochial worldview.

These "straight trade unionists" lived in small, predominantly agricultural communities, many of which supported only a single packing plant. They did not possess the contacts in other cities and regions that defined the black and Communist orbits. Their union philosophy contained many elements associated with syndicalism: they believed in workers' control over production, felt that an inclusive form of organization was the best means for achieving this end, considered direct action to be the most efficacious tactic in the struggle with capital, and were deeply distrustful of all political parties and appeals.[62] Yet, it was a syndicalism profoundly tempered by localism. Their horizons rarely extended beyond an immediate circle of friends and relatives; work and the union itself provided their most important contacts with different types of individuals and new ideas. While receptive to the notion of transforming the position of wage earners in American society, they were concerned above all with accomplishing immediate objectives. Workers should be able "to make a decent living and enjoy some of the better things in life," stated Casper Winkels, a ham boner from the Hormel plant in Austin, Minnesota. "Why shouldn't a working man have that right as well as anybody else?" Most of these unionists rejected the need for fundamental social change, believing that by restructuring patterns of authority and organization in the realm of work they could achieve economic security and stability.[63]

The fusing of the three layers—blacks, Communists, and straight trade unionists—into a coherent opposition movement within the PWOC represents, on a national level, the same pattern of packinghouse unionism seen in Chicago. There, in the mid-1930s, militant blacks allied with left-wing organizers and more conservative white trade union veterans to launch the organizations that came together under the PWOC umbrella. Now, the same groupings came together to resist the administration imposed by the CIO. The three layers coexisted uneasily. Their differences in outlook generated tensions that occasionally threatened to split the dissident movement apart, but the common goal of organizational autonomy prevented this rupture from occurring.

The roots of the factional conflict that gave rise to this opposition movement lie in the PWOC's 1939 negotiations with Armour. The conference of local union delegates that met in Chicago to authorize a national strike against Armour had strongly opposed plant-by-plant negotiations, feeling that such a concession would allow the company to shunt work from one plant to another and thereby whipsaw the union into oblivion. Johnson and

Don Harris, as well as Communist officials in the Chicago district, supported a national strike. Van Bittner, however, viewed the course with alarm,
fearing that it might undermine his authority and greatly enhance the position of the Left within the union. Meeting with Secretary of Labor Perkins at the height of the crisis, he agreed to withdraw the demand for a
national contract and bargain instead on a plant-by-plant basis. He made
this decision unilaterally, without consultation with other PWOC officials
or rank-and-file delegates.[64]

The response nationally and locally was predictable. Packinghouse activists reacted angrily upon learning of Bittner's subterfuge, charging him
with selling out Armour workers and venting two years of accumulated
frustration with the autocratic PWOC chairman. They began organizing to
replace the "dictator maniac" with an elected packinghouse worker accountable to the membership. Bittner reacted defensively and further aggravated the situation by purging the leading Communists from the organization. Assistant National Director Don Harris was released immediately;
and once the union secured the Chicago Armour plant, Bittner first relieved
Herbert March of his responsibilities and then fired him. These moves enraged workers who recognized the contributions of Harris and March. "The
present setup is a machine. They hire and fire who they please. It is by the
national office and not the packinghouse workers," a unionist from Austin, Minnesota, complained. "Bittner hires organizers that will go out and
persecute organizers and stewards. To Hell with organizing the unorganized and getting national contracts, so far as Bittner is concerned," a circular signed by fifty representatives charged. He "rules without rhyme or
reason" grumbled a local officer from Fort Dodge.[65]

The conflict simmered for most of 1940. Johnson, who had escaped the
purge of leftists by distancing himself from the CP, began to engineer an
opposition movement. Bittner was most likely aware of his activities but
hesitated to discharge such a prominent black leader. In the autumn, however, Johnson forced his hand by following the lead of John L. Lewis and
organizing support for the presidential campaign of Wendell Willkie. This
ill-calculated appeal outraged a number of local leaders who shared the
resentment of the national office but were unwavering in their loyalty to
Roosevelt. Bittner, whose UMW background may have raised questions
about his own allegiances in CIO circles, acted quickly, dismissing Johnson
in November.[66]

Johnson's dismissal brought the simmering conflict into the open. The
black-led Little Six locals with which Johnson had worked closely regarded the firing as not just another manifestation of Bittner's despotic rule but

an outright racial affront. They protested by withholding dues payments from the PWOC and by mounting a campaign to force Johnson's reinstatement. The Chicago PWOC Council, dominated by Johnson supporters, registered its displeasure by breaking off contact with the national office, discontinuing its subscriptions to the *CIO News,* and refusing to pay for thousands of union buttons it had ordered. In late November, several carloads of packinghouse workers traveled to the CIO's Atlantic City convention to appeal personally to John L. Lewis for Johnson's return. Once there, they hooked up with other PWOC representatives from Iowa and Minnesota and merged their request with demands for the removal of Bittner, and the formation of an autonomous international union.[67]

The dismissal of two additional black leaders and Johnson associates, Art Shelton and Frank Alsup, undercut the dissidents' remaining grip on the bureaucracy but prompted additional locals to side with them. Richard Saunders and Burrette King brought the Armour Soap Works over, motivated at least in part by racial solidarity. "How can PWOC officials expect us to explain to our membership that there is no discrimination in our Union when Mr. Van A. Bittner and his officers have fired the three best Negro organizers in our union?" demanded a letter signed by the leaders of four Chicago packing locals. Communist-influenced Armour 347 regarded the movement differently, joining with the dissidents because they saw a wedge with which to open space within the CIO for a reform of the PWOC. Spurred by a variety of reasons, all having to do in some way with distrust of and disaffection from the national office, the movement spread to other areas and a national opposition began to take shape. The St. Paul Council defected from the PWOC; and the Kansas City Council was bitterly divided. Dozens of other locals began withholding dues payments. In May 1941, PWOC officials worried openly about the "disruption" which had spread as far west as Los Angeles and as far south as Fort Worth.[68]

Their apprehension was justified, for the opposition was becoming increasingly well coordinated. Through the spring and summer of 1941, "night riders" headed out of packing towns when the afternoon shift ended, drove hundreds of miles to meet other packinghouse workers at a given location, and then returned in the early morning light to punch in for another day's work. Chicago unionists Jesse Vaughn and Burrette King were particularly active, roaming far afield from Chicago's South Side to build support for the movement. In late May, they appeared in St. Paul. A week later they were in East St. Louis, addressing a special mass meeting about the need for an international union. Days later they were reported in Fort Dodge. A small packing local at Detroit's almost entirely black

Hygrade plant turned out close to 100 percent of its membership for a special meeting on the subject. Voting to provide funding for its own organizers, the local sent them out to join Vaughn and the others on the night-riding circuit.[69]

The dissidents did not confine their travels to the Midwest. Groups of them journeyed as far as Washington to confront CIO leaders; and a large delegation of packinghouse workers led by Vaughn and King set up picket lines outside CIO president Philip Murray's office in Pittsburgh. Murray consented to see the protesters, who had disrupted delicate negotiations between SWOC and Bethlehem Steel, and, in a move that indicated the gravity of the situation in packing, promised them a meeting with his representatives where they could present their case against Bittner and argue for an international union. When Murray's emissaries, Allan Haywood and James Carey, arrived in Chicago in April 1941, they expected to meet with a handful of local union leaders, gather testimony, and then depart. They were little prepared for the sight that greeted them at their hotel: over a hundred workers, representing PWOC locals from Mason City to Fargo, had assembled on a few days' notice to discuss the conflict within the union.[70]

When Carey suggested that the group elect a committee with whom he and Haywood could meet privately, the packinghouse workers objected, demanding that all present be given a chance to speak. The hearings lasted several days, with the CIO representatives meeting for several hours at a time with different groups of delegates. Some opposed Johnson and told of the dissension he had sown in their locals. "Every meeting that you go into, they take these meetings over," explained Pete Brown, who represented one of the small houses in Chicago. Others supported Johnson and gave examples of his negotiating prowess and organizational talents. Others warned of the pernicious influence of Harris and the "comrades." In revealing testimony, several of the the delegates from Omaha, the center of anticommunist sentiment, attacked Harris and other left-wingers for promoting interracial mingling, while the sole black to speak against Johnson prefaced his remarks by affirming his fidelity to his race. All of the delegates, however, strongly favored the establishment of an international, and all were united in their dislike of Bittner. "This does not seem to be a fight between left and rights," an exasperated Carey remarked. "The lines are drawn a lot of different ways."[71]

Less than halfway through the hearings it became evident that Bittner's days as PWOC chair were numbered and that the CIO emissaries favored some kind of move in the direction of an international union. Packinghouse delegates left Chicago without firm assurances but with a sense that momentum was on their side. At this point, the straight trade unionists from Iowa joined with the Austin, Minnesota, local to seize the initiative by drawing up a step-by-step plan for the formation of an international union.

The brainchild of Austin union founders Joe Ollman and Frank Ellis, the plan called for the holding of a series of regional conferences comprised of local representatives and free from CIO interference and control. These conferences would formulate a draft constitution, establish an agenda, and determine a set of governing rules for a founding convention. Cognizant of the considerable organizational resources at the CIO's disposal, Ollman urged packinghouse activists to shift their focus away from the appointment of individuals to positions of power in the PWOC and to concentrate upon the building of an international union from the ground up. "Unless we have an organized group of packinghouse workers to go into a constitutional convention, the same bureaucrats in the PWOC will tell you what to do," he warned. "They will have an organized group and the only way you can defeat an organized group is with another one." In early July, the Austin group presented its plan and a resolution at a conference of midwestern PWOC locals held in Mason City, Iowa. The resolution passed, as did a similar one at a gathering of Michigan and Ohio locals a few months later. Adopting a slogan which referred to past betrayals—"No '21 in '41"— packinghouse workers began to press Murray and other CIO officials to make good on their assurance of an autonomous organization.[72]

In July 1941, with dues receipts off by 30 percent, the CIO responded to packinghouse workers' pressure, replacing Van Bittner with another mineworker, J. C. "Shady" Lewis. This choice was understandable from the CIO's perspective. Lewis's loyalty to Philip Murray was unquestionable. Moreover, he had experience in the packing industry, having served as a director of the PWOC's Iowa and Minnesota district, and was familiar with local leaders in a much wider area. However, the selection of Lewis did not sit well with packinghouse workers. His tenure as district director had been a stormy one, marked by repeated clashes with the independent-minded Austin local and by a relentless campaign against the Left. Packinghouse workers had expected one of their own to be named to the post, and the choice of another "damn coal miner" was especially irritating. The appointment of Lewis J. Clark, the conservative and staunchly anticommunist leader of the Cedar Rapids Wilson local, as vice-chair of the PWOC, did little to mollify the widespread resentment.[73]

The CIO also moved to take the steam out of the opposition movement by offering staff appointments to a number of previously purged activists

and by implementing a new policy that stipulated increased contact between local unions and the national office, frequent district meetings, and
regular wage and policy conferences which would take up, among other
items, the question of a timetable for the establishment of an international. Rather than serving the intended purpose of deflecting criticism, however, the district meetings and policy conferences became forums in which
delegates aired their complaints about PWOC officials and voiced impatient demands for a constitutional convention.[74]

The PWOC's drive to secure master agreements with the large packers
further fueled rank-and-file sentiment for the prompt chartering of an international by bringing together local delegates from each chain. In July of
1941, for instance, hundreds of Armour workers convened at a national
wage conference and, casting aside the cautionary advice of Lewis and
other officials, pressed through a resolution calling for a general strike
against the company if it continued to stonewall in negotiations. The gathering also selected a new bargaining team which, for the first time, contained local representatives in addition to officials from the national office.
Responding to the strike threat, the newly constituted National Defense
Mediation Board intervened in the volatile situation and pressured Armour
to consent to a master agreement covering twenty thousand workers in the
fifteen plants in which the union held bargaining rights. Signed in early
September, the wage provisions of the agreement narrowed the gender
deferential by providing a five-cent increase for men and a six-cent raise
for women. It also provided for exclusive recognition of the union, modest paid vacations, and departmental seniority. These advances strengthened the hand of packinghouse dissidents who now claimed, with some
justification, that the union had reached "maturity" and deserved to be
released from its bondage to the CIO.[75]

As Lewis's reforms were implemented, and while negotiations with
Armour proceeded, a fissure developed within the ranks of the opposition
movement that had important long-term consequences. Recognizing that
a new international would not include them, Johnson and several of his
closest associates, including Art Shelton and Frank Alsup, joined United
Mine Workers' District 50 and began wooing packinghouse locals away
from the CIO. They met with modest success, pulling only a small local at
a Chicago rendering plant and a group of East St. Louis stockyard workers into the Mine Workers. However, they posed a significant threat to the
PWOC. The growing rift between John L. Lewis and the CIO reverberated
through many unions. Throughout the Midwest and in portions of the
South, PWOC field representatives worriedly reported District 50 raids on

packinghouse locals. In Chicago, Johnson's black followers at the Armour Soap Works began organizing ragpickers, glue works, and fertilizer plants into District 50, even though they themselves remained within the PWOC. Black militants in the Wilson plant and on the Armour killing floors also supported the rival organization. Indeed, black workers in a number of midwestern industrial centers came to regard District 50 as an alternative to the CIO, offering an opportunity for staff advancement and an environment in which racial identity could be preserved.[76]

In Chicago the District 50 threat was serious enough to warrant drastic action on the part of the PWOC national office. Lacking ties to and the confidence of rank-and-file workers, the PWOC turned to the Communists for assistance. Herb March, who had left Chicago to organize steelworkers in Maryland, returned to prevent a bolt of packing locals out of the CIO. The greatest danger was Armour 347. While the local's desertion from the PWOC was unlikely, Johnson exerted a powerful influence over many black workers, especially those on the killing floors, and a number of the local's white officers, including chief steward Scotty Mackenzie, were among his most outspoken supporters. A split in this flagship local would have been especially damaging. March had always remained aloof from Johnson, considering him an opportunist even when the two men worked together. Now March and other Communists began organizing against the Johnson group and discrediting his allies. Eventually, they ousted them from all positions of importance in the local. Elsewhere in Chicago, and wherever the Party wielded influence, Communists worked to neutralize the District 50 threat.[77]

In countering the Johnson group, the Communists both assumed leadership of the movement for an international and also cemented their position within the PWOC. In Chicago, the CP reestablished its control of the Armour local and became a major influence on the PWOC Joint Council. As detailed above, it extended its organization into the Wilson plant as well. Henceforth, the Communists were a permanent fixture in the packinghouse union, at both the leadership and mass levels. March's return to the area and the Party's entrenched position in meatpacking affected the fortunes of the left wing of the CIO in the city as well. Within a short period March and Robert Travis, a Communist from the Farm Equipment union (FE), had established the Cook County Industrial Union Council as a rival to the CIO's Chicago Council, a conservative body dominated by the steelworkers. Eventually the two councils merged, but the Left had secured a strong base from which to influence CIO organizing and politics for many years.[78]

The influence of District 50 receded only after Johnson's death in 1944.

In that year he and Shelton suffered a bitter falling-out over an organizing campaign at a utility company in a northern Indiana town. Shelton initially headed the campaign, but Johnson commandeered it and produced a contract without involving Shelton. During a United Mine Workers' inquiry into the matter, Shelton pulled a pistol out of a briefcase, shot once, wounding Frank Alsup, who was in the room, and then emptied the remaining bullets into Johnson. Five hours later he was dead. Thus ended the trade union career of a man whom many workers later likened to Martin Luther King, and who enjoyed a following that was almost religious in its devotion to him. In later years, the Johnson legend assumed a mythic quality among the black workers who came in contact with him at a formative point in their lives.[79]

In the spring of 1942 the struggle for an international picked up momentum. J. C. Lewis incensed packinghouse workers when he reopened the Armour contract without consultation. Hastily backpedaling amidst a storm of protest, he inadvertently fortified local activists by establishing a ten-person National Policy Committee made up of elected rather than appointed representatives. The committee became a forum for the pro-international forces and checked the chairman's hand at every turn.[80] When Lewis abruptly resigned in July, CIO leaders again bypassed union officials with roots in meatpacking and chose another mine worker, Sam Sponseller, to head the organization. Opposition to this appointment dwarfed the outcry that followed that of Lewis. The PWOC's Chicago staff wrote to Murray to urge reconsideration. The Armour local claimed the selection "will only open the door for disruption by District 50." And Detroit locals protested loudly, suggesting the appointment of Art Kampfert "or some other PWOC worker like him." Sponseller, however, had resigned himself to a caretaker's administration and generally supported the creation of an international. He tried to slow the movement down, but never really hindered its development. He seems to have been chosen for his ability as a conciliator. Richard Saunders remembered him as "slick talker who would swell your head." Unlike his predecessors, Sponseller disdained conflict. "He would come in, whatever you said more or less, he would indicate that he was in favor of it, then do nothing," Saunders recalled. Jesse Prosten was more critical. "We didn't like what he stood for," he stated. "Sponseller represented the roots of bureaucracy that was starting to develop within the labor movement of the 1940s." Despite the furor that greeted his appointment, Sponseller was a fitting choice for someone to act as midwife to the birth of the international.[81]

Still, packinghouse workers were impatient and unwilling to abide by the timetable established by the national office. Only days after Sponseller took office, the Sioux City PWOC locals went on record demanding an international. A month later, a larger group of Iowa locals entertained a resolution calling for the immediate formation of an international. In September 1942, Fort Dodge hosted an unsanctioned conference which unanimously resolved to issue a call for a national gathering of PWOC delegates to make arrangements for a constitutional convention. The national office at first tried to halt the meeting, but when Sponseller saw it was going to proceed regardless of his disapproval he backed off and endorsed the call for a conference.[82]

After two preparatory meetings, the constitutional convention was held in Chicago in October of 1943. As Joe Ollman forecast, CIO leaders attempted to control the proceedings. "They finally capitulated and allowed us to have our own union," recalled Herb March, but "they didn't necessarily want us to select our own leadership." Particularly important to Allen Haywood, who brokered the convention for Murray and the CIO, was limiting the power of the Communists in the new organization. Although Haywood succeeded in neutralizing a movement to elect Communist Meyer Stern secretary-treasurer, packinghouse activists exacted a dear price by forcing Haywood to abandon support for the CIO presidential candidate, Sponseller. Because the drafting of the constitution was largely outside the CIO's control, it ultimately produced an executive board that reflected the various component parts of the rank-and-file movement. Lewis J. Clark assumed the presidency of the new union as the result of the compromise with Haywood. His base in the Cedar Rapids Wilson plant was representative of the straight trade unionists who had powered the opposition movement. The first vice-president, Frank Ellis of Austin, represented the more radical element in the coalition. A former Wobbly, he was the founder of Austin's Independent Union of All Workers, and worked easily with Communists, Socialists, and Trotskyists alike. "Everybody who was a radical was a friend of Frank's," Herb March remarked.[83]

Especially significant was the election of Philip Weightman as second vice-president, implicit recognition of the critical role of black workers in the building of the union. The theme of interracial unity graphically expressed itself in the logo adopted by the new union—black and white hands grasping each other. This potent symbol served as an important introduction to new workers. "When you joined this union, the first thing you see is a black hand and a white hand," noted Ercell Allen, who had entered the Chicago stockyards just a few months earlier. "We did things together, black and white." The preamble to the UPWA constitution addressed this crucial dynamic in straightforward prose. Stating that packinghouse workers represented multiple nationalities, races, creeds, and political beliefs, it recognized that in times past "these differences have been used to divide us and one group has been set against another by those who would prevent our unifying." Workers successfully organized only by "overcoming these divisive influences and by recognizing that our movement must be big enough to encompass all groups and all opinions."[84]

The turbulence of the PWOC era also shaped the representative mechanisms built in to the new union. Delegates from each district independently elected directors who not only served as regional overseers but sat on the executive board of the union as well. Workers elected Herbert March director of the Chicago area. With Meyer Stern, the director of the union's northeastern district, he represented the Communist Left within the officialdom. This arrangement allowed for a certain independence from the national office and, in effect, built opposition into the structure of the United Packinghouse Workers. For most of its twenty-five-year existence, factional differences animated the UPWA and prevented the emergence of the kind of one-party machine that came to dominate the Automobile Workers and other unions. The arrangement also made coalition government imperative. Blacks, leftists, and the "broad middle" of straight trade unionists thus depended upon one another on the political plane, just as they did within the packing plants.

The formation of the United Packinghouse Workers of America represented the institutionalization of the alliance between different groups of packinghouse workers. Leftists working with black militants and white trade union veterans formed a coalition in the mid-1930s which organized the plants in the Chicago stockyards. In the early 1940s, this alliance expanded geographically to include "straight trade unionists" from the other midwestern packing centers, and other blacks and Communists. The protracted struggle with the CIO in the early 1940s reinforced this coalition, even as the Johnson episode and District 50 threat introduced lines of stress. The character of the international union that emerged in 1943 reflected these conditions. Local unions remained remarkably autonomous; the power of elected officials was limited; and ultimate power continued to reside with departmental stewards and other shop-floor leaders. The union apparatus in meatpacking was not a structure external to the extended drive for organization—something imposed from above—but rather the formalization of that very drive itself.

7

The Path Not Taken: The Formation of the United Packinghouse Workers of America

The Ford plant where Karl Lundberg labored after leaving Swift turned out armored trucks for the military. Lundberg first worked on the assembly line, riveting steel plate onto vehicle frames, before becoming an inspector, a position in which he earned slightly more than he had as a rumper on the beef kill. Conditions at Ford compared favorably to those in the packinghouse. The work was lighter and cleaner, even if it was more monotonous than at Swift. Lundberg remained with Ford for twenty years, satisfied with the niche he had found for himself. One of the few aspects that bothered him, though, was the union representing the plant's workers. Although the United Auto Workers enjoyed a reputation as one of the CIO's more militant and progressive unions, Lundberg was disappointed in it. He watched as unresolved grievances piled up, as stewards stood by helplessly while workers were disciplined, and as the local officers turned a deaf ear to rank-and-file concerns. "In the packinghouse, if you had a problem with the boss it got taken care of right then and there," he recalled. "Over at Ford, well you filled out a piece of paper and you waited. Sometimes you waited days, sometimes weeks, sometimes you never heard anything more."[1]

Schooled in the packinghouse workers' aggressive, confrontational style, Lundberg considered himself a "one hundred and ten percent union man" when he graduated from the yards. After several years at Ford, his commitment to the labor movement began to waver. He continued to pay his dues and lent support to the union, but the UAW was not an important factor in his life. When he moved to a middle-class west side community in 1952, very few of his neighbors were active unionists. "People were busy with their homes and their families. They worked hard but when that whistle blew, they just wanted to put it all behind them and relax a bit and enjoy the good life," he commented.[2]

Sometime in the mid-1950s, Lundberg turned his back permanently on unionism and the UAW. More than thirty years later, the incident that provoked this break was still sharp and clear in his mind. Having completed a day's work, Lundberg was heading to the time clock with another worker to punch out when the foreman called them back. Ordered to sweep up metal filings left by another worker, the men refused. An altercation ensued and a security squad escorted Lundberg's companion out of the plant. The following day Lundberg learned his friend had been fired. He approached the department steward, who equivocated before finally declining to take the matter up. Lundberg sought out one of the local's officers for assistance. The man also hedged. "That fella began to quote the contract. I knew he wasn't going to do anything and I got so damn disgusted," he recalled. At Swift, "the whole place would have been shut down tighter than a drum, and this guy's quoting the contract. What the hell good's a union that won't stand and fight? Nothing but a dues collecting set up, really. Well that was it for me." Lundberg continued to pay his monthly dues—the checkoff provision of the contract meant that they were taken directly out of his paycheck—but he stopped attending union meetings, declined invitations to union social functions, and ignored the stewards and other officials with whom he came in contact at work.[3]

Karl Lundberg's experience points to one of the more significant features of packinghouse unionism during the war and afterwards. In an era when the United Auto Workers and other CIO unions shed their oppositional character, abandoned the vigorous shop-floor activity that secured the gains of the 1930s, and became increasingly unresponsive to the concerns of their membership, the UPWA retained its militancy, continued to rely on rank-and-file pressure in the packing plants, and resisted the bureaucratization of its governing and decision-making procedures. Moreover, at a time when the mainstream of the industrial union movement allowed itself to become incorporated into the liberal-democratic state, largely through its subordination to the Democratic Party and its acceptance of cold war liberalism, the packinghouse union asserted its independence and affirmed the legitimacy of political dissent within its ranks. The Packinghouse Workers also preserved their commitment to social equality. The union continued to advance the interests of its black membership by supporting the civil rights movement and playing a direct role in numerous local struggles for racial justice. In many ways, the UPWA represented a path not taken by the larger CIO unions.

Examination of this alternative path is valuable for a number of reasons. Delineation of the contours of what might be termed "packinghouse exceptionalism" provides a comparative perspective from which to view the accomplishments and limitations of other, larger, and more influential CIO unions like the UAW. Beyond this it offers insight into the growing debate about the origins of organized labor's decline in the postwar period.

In seeking to explain the erosion of union power and influence, recent scholarship has focused on the system of industrial relations that emerged during World War II and was consolidated in the years that followed. Numerous writers have explored the accord between capital, labor, and the state which redefined the stakes, tools, and terrain of industrial conflict. Concentrating upon the intervention of the federal government in the form of regulatory agencies and the courts, they argue that labor renounced its goals of redistribution, workers' control, and political power in exchange for union security, contractual limitations upon employers' power, and greater distributional gains. In David Milton's reductionist but fitting formulation, the "great bargain" was a classic trade-off: the exchange of power for money. Labor's right to organize and to make material demands upon on the system was purchased at the price of capital's right to control over the work process and business practices of the firm. Spontaneous shop-floor activity, as well as other forms of independent workers' power, were placed beyond the pale of the law and vigorously opposed by both unions and companies.[4]

While these contributions help frame the terms of the debate and impart a welcome degree of theoretical specificity to a usually relentlessly empirical endeavor, they say little about the ways in which the accord was implemented at the plant and shop-floor levels. More helpful in this regard has been the work of another group of scholars who have trained their sights on the precise mechanisms through which rank-and-file activity was subdued. They argue that the war mobilization effort provided the economic and ideological context required to routinize union activity in such a way as to diminish the legitimacy of rank-and-file activity, institutionalize leadership authority, and increase government influence in union affairs. Responding to worker unrest during the war, CIO affiliates appealed to the government to protect "responsible" unionism through the insertion of maintenance of membership and checkoff provisions into their contracts. This enmeshed the unions in the legal apparatus of the state and thrust them into a new role as disciplinarians. Accountable for unsanctioned strikes, union leadership reduced the autonomy of local unions, developed more rigid and formal lines of authority, and harshly penalized union cadres who rejected their new responsibilities. This dynamic led to a permanent weakening of those elements in the union structure upon which trade union power ultimately rested. It widened the gulf between workers and the union bureaucracy, as the unions emerged from the war less as advocates for their members than as buffers mediating between capital and labor.[5]

The history of the United Packinghouse Workers during this critical transition period suggests that the shift from the militant, institutionally fluid unionism of the 1930s to the accommodationist and bureaucratic unionism of the postwar era was not inevitable. The UPWA was subject to the same kinds of pressures as other unions during the war. It contended with increased government regulation, rank-and-file turbulence, and employer hostility. Yet its response to these problems was markedly different from that of most CIO unions. Instead of imposing strong centralized organization over local affiliates, the UPWA developed an impressive array of internal institutions that sustained democratic processes within the union and ensured that the locus of power remained fixed at the union's base.

Rather than clamp down on rank-and-file activity, the UPWA encouraged shop-floor militancy and used it to police its contracts with the packers. This allowed local unions to transmit the tradition of direct action which characterized the initial organizing era to a new generation of workers in the packinghouses. Whereas wartime job actions in automobile, rubber, and other mass production industries tended to be unsanctioned "wildcats" lacking the "overall union-building context" of the previous decade and representing outpourings of frustration on the part of undisciplined workers, stoppages in meatpacking had the opposite character. "It was amazing how quickly [new hires] were able to absorb the whole concept from other workers who were there," a UPWA official recalled. "We had the experience of building our union up through the period of the war which involved constant stoppage, slowdown, fight around issues, constant militancy around issues was at the heart of the union. As a result the rank-and-file was unusually militant and had a strong feeling of the union being their organization." Participation in job actions thus signified the socialization of new workers into the adversarial culture of dynamic local unions rather than their alienation from it. Far from representing a breakdown in discipline or a weakening of leadership's ties with the rank and file, wartime stoppages in the packinghouses were the continuation of an earlier tradition of struggle.[6]

The UPWA was able to pursue this alternative path for two reasons. First, the rank-and-file origins of the union coupled with its unusually high degree of shop-floor organization made it impossible for the international union to tame workers' independent activity in the plants. The packing companies' continued resistance to the union forced the UPWA to rely upon its power at the point of production and to recognize the authority of departmental stewards and informal work-group leaders. Secondly, the UPWA's black membership base continued to expand during the war and throughout the decade that followed. Occupying central positions in the production process and concerned with issues extending beyond benefits and pay, black packinghouse workers formed an activist-oriented source of militancy within the union. They pushed it to continue to oppose the discriminatory practices of the packers and to step up involvement in civil rights activities in the larger community. This social activism kept the UPWA from falling into the narrow "business unionism" which came to characterize other unions in the postwar period. At the same time, the union's black membership proved largely impervious to the appeals of anticommunism and continued to support left-wing leaders.[7] To a lesser but still significant extent, white workers' acceptance of racial diversity translated easily into tolerance of political diversity. The UPWA thus maintained room for the Left to operate, refused to purge Communists from its ranks, and supported independent political action. Although these policies led to the union's isolation from the rest of the labor movement, they did not damage its ability to represent workers or secure "bread and butter" gains for them. On the contrary, responsiveness to its membership's concerns solidified rank-and-file identification with the union and preserved its vitality.

In responding to the wartime context, packinghouse workers negotiated the constraints imposed by a changing system of industrial relations in a manner that diverged from that of other CIO unions. Despite the brake applied by union security measures, packinghouse workers did not hesitate to employ job actions when they felt employers were taking advantage of the no-strike pledge to chisel away at union gains. Ranging from departmental stoppages to occasional plantwide walkouts, these actions were tightly orchestrated maneuvers sanctioned by union leadership. Although the UPWA used the National Labor Relations Board and the National War Labor Board to secure master agreements and improvements in working conditions, it emerged from the war with a pronounced distrust of the state's regulatory machinery. This antistatist tendency received powerful reinforcement from the union's defiance of the government during its 1946 strike, an action which resulted in significant wage and contractual improvements, and its refusal to comply with the requirements of the Taft-Hartley Act prior to its disastrous 1948 strike.

The most distinctive feature of the divergent path followed by the UPWA in the 1940s and 1950s was its vigorous civil rights program. The UPWA recovered from its 1948 strike defeat by rebuilding the union around its black membership. This entailed elevating what had been a general policy into a specific program for rooting out racist practices and attitudes within the union and in the plants. In Chicago, mobilized black workers extended this anti-discrimination program beyond the workplace, involving the union in housing controversies and protests against racial violence. At a time when other unions rapidly backtracked on their commitment to black rights, the Packinghouse Workers pressed forward. Renewed civil rights activity served to retain the active support of the membership and revitalize other union programs. On the verge of collapse in 1948, packinghouse unionism entered the 1950s stronger than ever before.

"Keep the Bastards Toeing the Line": Job Actions and Worker Militancy during World War II

The war was a financial boon for the packing companies. As early as 1939 production levels in the industry showed a dramatic rise. By the fall of 1940, defense mobilization was in full swing. Government contracts for meat and canned goods returned the packers' profits to predepression levels and kept the Chicago plants operating at full capacity. With the entry of the United States into the war, the packinghouses began operating around the clock, increasing their payrolls by as much as 30 percent to keep up with the voracious demand. After a succession of lean depression years, Armour, Swift, and Wilson reported net returns of more than 10 percent in 1941. War had brought the prosperity that the New Deal had been unable to deliver.[8]

While the packers' shareholders benefited from the defense-induced recovery, their employees did not. Packinghouse workers took advantage of the availability of overtime hours, but here their benefits stopped. Wages, standardized by the master agreements, lagged behind those in other industries. Moreover, the National War Labor Board's "Little Steel Formula" froze packinghouse workers' pay at 1941 levels for the duration of the war while inflation crept upwards, producing a decline in real earnings.[9] At the same time, full production resulted in a deterioration of working conditions inside the plants. Line speeds increased and foremen drove their gangs harder in order to meet higher production quotas. Over union objections, management retimed piecework and established new standards which resulted in more arduous work routines and less pay. One telling measure of the worsening situation was the rise in injury rates. During the war, meatpacking was the fifth most dangerous industry in the United States. UPWA president Lewis J. Clark summed up the situation in 1944 when he wrote to Upton Sinclair that despite the union's gains of the previous decade, "the packing industry is still in many respects a 'jungle' with perhaps less luxuriant undergrowth but with just as dangerous and even treacherous forces at play."[10]

Unionists found particularly frustrating the packers' use of new hirees to erode existing standards and wage rates. The vast influx of inexperienced workers, especially women and blacks, enabled the packing companies to replace many highly-paid veteran workers with cheaper labor. In the Armour plant, for instance, management replaced male sausage stuffers and cutters earning 70 and 75.5 cents an hour with recently hired women paid 62 cents. In violation of the seniority provisions of the contract, foremen directed the displaced men to other departments and assigned them jobs at rates lower than their usual positions. Responding to grievances on these matters, Armour flatly refused adjustment, claiming that the stuffing job had been "changed in its entirety," that "the direction of the working force is in the hands of the company." Often this kind of situation placed new workers in uncomfortable positions, pressed from one side by the employer and from the other by fellow workers. In Armour's canning room, one new hiree broke down in tears and fled to the locker room when her placement on a redesigned job prompted a showdown between the steward and foreman.[11]

Local unions responded aggressively to this deterioration in working conditions. The same kinds of direct action tactics that earlier secured recognition, extended union organization, and ultimately brought management to the bargaining table were now utilized to "hold the line" and defend earlier gains. This response placed union officials in a dilemma. Along with other CIO leaders, they had pledged not to strike for the duration of the war, and although the War Labor Board had denied requests for wage increases, it did award the UPWA maintenance of membership and automatic dues checkoff provisions. Under the terms of the agreement, unresolvable shop-floor disputes were to be referred to the board for arbitration. Unaccustomed to the bureaucratic resolution of their grievances, and increasingly impatient with the lengthy delays involved in the process, packinghouse workers took matters into their own hands. "We took the position we didn't have the time to waste to go through no grievance procedure," recalled Todd Tate, a steward in the Armour plant at the time. The wave of stoppages and slowdowns which swept through the packing industry placed the union's national leadership in the uncomfortable position of pressuring local officials to control the restive and independent-minded rank and file.[12]

Most wartime stoppages were limited, departmental actions over specific issues; they usually lasted only a few hours and rarely involved more than a few dozen workers. Significantly, stewards and leaders of informal work groups directed these actions, which generally lacked the spontaneous undisciplined character of "wildcats" in other industries. When the Wilson hog kill foreman declined to follow the agreed-upon procedure of adding extra men to the gang when large sows were being slaughtered, for example, the shackler and his helper refused to handle the animals coming up the chute. After half an hour, during which an assistant superintendent conferred with the department steward and the men involved, a compromise was reached and work resumed. At Armour, eight butchers in the pork cut engaged in a successful fifteen-minute stoppage, protesting the poor quality of the meat given them. However, these strikes sometimes escalated into more serious conflicts—as when the discharge of an Armour worker led to a three-day stoppage involving 360 workers and costing the company more than fifteen hundred lost man-hours.[13]

The National War Labor Board's inability to process the cases brought before it compounded the problem of wartime strikes. Unresolved grievances swamped the board's limited resources. By the end of 1943, it was grappling with between ten and fifteen thousand new cases from all industries each month. Routine delays of up to a year led local union leaders to regard the board as a "sort of box canyon" where disputes sat unprocessed while the problems that gave rise to them continued to cause unrest. Aware of the paralysis gripping the NWLB, they sanctioned stoppages and other job actions. "What could we do?" Vicky Starr asked, "it was so blatant." She explained that while union leaders counseled patience and would have preferred to resolve disputes off the shop floor, they were unwilling to allow bureaucratic delays to erode the union's position. "The companies were pushing, pushing, pushing and we weren't getting anywhere telling workers to wait, just sit tight, and let the board take care of things," Les Orear recalled. "Remember, these were people used to taking care of their own business."[14]

The packing companies' refusal to negotiate over grievances further aggravated the situation. Matters that before the war were settled easily and in routine fashion between stewards and foremen now became major points of contention. By the middle of 1944 supervisory personnel at Armour were referring virtually every grievance to the plant superintendent, effectively disempowering foremen and creating havoc on the shop floor as delays of two and three weeks became commonplace. The "taking up and settling of grievances is prolonged beyond all reason," union lawyers complained in an effort to explain the turmoil in the plants, adding that "this incites further discontent, demonstrating to the workers the futility of collective bargaining." At a War Labor Board hearing Armour workers testified that even when the local managed to settle grievances, management tarried for weeks before implementing the decision, adversely affecting morale and stimulating unrest. "We are sitting on a powder keg, constantly, just ready to explode," explained Local 347's Joe Bezenhoffer.[15]

Throughout the war the UPWA charged that the packing companies were deliberately provoking stoppages by harassing workers and violating established seniority procedures. Union security provisions had been granted over the companies' strenuous objections, and now the packers hoped to secure their revocation by inciting violations of the no-strike pledge. Finally in late 1944, they petitioned the Labor Board for the removal of maintenance of membership and dues checkoff provisions.[16] Although denied, this request forced the UPWA International's officers to step up their efforts to compel local leaders to halt the stoppages. Earlier that year, the board had denied union security measures to the United Auto Workers because of violations of the no-strike pledge in Chrysler plants, and the UPWA did not want to suffer a similar fate. President Clark warned local unions that failure to discipline their members would result in harsher sanctions, including the replacement of local executive boards with International administrators. At the same time, the national office began asking local officers for detailed explanations of each stoppage and, for the first time, holding them accountable for shop-floor actions.[17]

These attempts to curtail job actions were ineffectual. Local union officers gave lip service to the no-strike policy, but looked the other way when they felt conditions warranted direct action. In response to government pressure, the UPWA national office methodically investigated hundreds of stoppages and slowdowns, sending strongly worded inquiries to local unions and patiently explaining the Labor Board situation. For their part, local officials played a game of responding to these missives but continuing to sanction shop-floor action. Richard Saunders explained that "we'd send a nice letter back to them telling them we'd investigate right away and we did," adding with a smirk, "we never did come up with anything but we'd investigate."[18] The UPWA executive board, newly elected and cognizant of its limited powers, rarely made good on its threats. Only twice did

President Clark demand that locals impose disciplinary measures against their members. In one case, the local fined each striker a single dollar; in the other case, local officers limited disciplinary measures to the pay lost during the stoppage, calling this "penalty enough."[19]

Growing rank-and-file sentiment in favor of rescinding the no-strike pledge caused the union's executive board to proceed cautiously. At the UPWA's 1944 convention, a resolution reiterating support for the pledge encountered serious opposition, and early the following year President Clark reported that most of the large locals were demanding its repeal. Aware of how resentment toward Van Bittner, J. C. Lewis, and Sam Sponseller had boiled over in full-scale rebellion, the UPWA International's officers wisely decided to ride rather than attempt to tame the wave of turbulence below them.[20]

District directors found the balancing act most difficult to maintain. Caught between workers' unhappiness over conditions and the government's demand for uninterrupted production, they led a schizophrenic existence, perpetually wavering between their twin roles as executive board disciplinarians and as advocates for constituents whose support kept them in office. In Chicago Herbert March's situation was made doubly difficult by the Communist Party's wholehearted support of the no-strike pledge. While never adopting the rigid stance assumed by CP functionaries in the automobile or electrical unions (where wildcats were terminated and local officers removed), March nonetheless used the power of his office in the union and his influence within the Party to try to contain shop-floor disturbances within acceptable limits. "We managed to hold things down," he recalled. "You have no idea what the situation during the war could have produced in terms of stoppages had leadership attempted to push for them."[21]

March and other officials were resourceful in their efforts to "hold things down." Fending off impatient Party bureaucrats who wanted more zealous enforcement of the no-strike pledge, March realized that workers' actions were largely beyond his control and that heavy-handed attempts to clamp down would alienate them. "The development of the stoppage among these workers grew out of the industry; it wasn't anything that we invented," he explained. Publicly, he spoke out in favor of the no-strike pledge. Virtually every issue of the *District One Champion* contained a strong editorial penned by March on the necessity of uninterrupted production; and at the union's 1944 convention he rose in the midst of heated debate to declare his support for the pledge and to question the motives "of those who on the slightest provocation seek to raise the issue that we must through one subterfuge or another destroy the no-strike pledge." He and other officials also appealed to workers' pragmatic side, arguing that continued stoppages might jeopardize the UPWA's request that the Labor Board adjust wage differentials and institute such benefits as portal-to-portal pay and knife-sharpening time.[22]

Yet, when it came down to actually policing the shop floor, union leaders—Communist and non-Communist—displayed considerable tolerance of rank-and-file self-activity. Representatives of the international office often handled stoppages by placing blame squarely upon the company, even while attempting to cajole workers back to their jobs. Jesse Prosten, a Communist and chief troubleshooter for the International, explained that plant-wide walkouts loomed behind every stoppage, "We were very much worried about touching a match to a tinder box and having the whole thing go off." Union officials thus turned job actions to their advantage, using them to pressure management to concede to workers' demands as a way of resolving the problem and resuming production. "We'll get them back to work if you agree to settle this thing," March recalled telling management. Local union officers and departmental stewards soon learned how to protect themselves and their director by carefully covering their involvement in job actions. Ercell Allen recalled how her local's president, Peewee Redmond, planned a plantwide stoppage over repeated seniority violations. Redmond told workers that once they left their posts and assembled in the plant cafeteria, he would appear and urge them to return to their jobs. They should ignore his pleadings, he instructed, as this would provide him with extra leverage in dealing with management. James Samuel proudly recalled that even when pressed, Armour workers never disclosed who ordered a stoppage. Unable to pinpoint stewards or other officials as ringleaders, management reluctantly solicited their assistance in working out compromises.[23]

For their part, rank-and-file packinghouse workers regarded wartime job actions as a justifiable means of resolving shop-floor disputes. Many workers made a crucial distinction between strikes and job actions, with the former understood as plantwide walkouts designed to force union recognition or contract gains, and the latter signifying internal pressure brought to bear on individual supervisors to defend hard-won gains and to ensure compliance with existing agreements.[24] Moreover, the notion of "equality of sacrifice" promulgated by CIO leadership in order to make palatable the steady erosion of labor's power during the war took on a different meaning for rank-and-file workers. They regarded the wartime no-strike agreement as a pact with capital that carried mutual responsibilities—

if the employer violated the agreement then unionists had the right to use their power at the point of production to remind him of his obligations. "It wasn't just a one way street," one leader explained, "if they're able to violate their commitment, what would be wrong with us violating ours, too?"[25]

Workers frequently justified their actions in patriotic language, accusing the packers of aiding the Axis and subverting the war effort by breaking their accord with labor. Referring to Armour's repeated provocations, including actions "that in normal times" would lead to the shutting of the entire plant, one paper sketched "Armour's blueprint for Hitlerism" for its readers. A shop-floor mimeograph sheet, the *Fresh Sausage News*, ran an article on foreman Louis Rumf, "the Little Hitler" who played favorites and harassed female workers. Similarly "Big Fat Mama Miller," forelady in sweet pickle, was linked with the war effort, for in her "the Gestapo is losing a valuable stooge." Even a new security fence erected around Armour's general office became grist for the mill since it "could have given the Axis gang lots of trouble had the metal been used to put in guns and bullets instead."[26]

Many rank-and-file leaders—departmental stewards and local officers working in the plants—viewed wartime job actions as a necessary means of introducing new workers to the union and of maintaining a disciplined membership. Shop-floor militancy, Todd Tate explained, was the most effective way of training new hirees in the UPWA's method of resolving grievances. It "made an impression on them and they got to know quicker what the union movement meant." At a time when the union was losing many experienced cadres to the military, Tate added, concerted shop-floor action helped train the recruits and prepare them to assume leadership positions. Many new hirees' first contact with the union came not when a representative approached them for a chat but when they suddenly discovered themselves in the midst of a job action. In this way, the union's tradition of militancy and shop-floor control was transmitted from one group of workers to another. The continuation of shop-floor activity in the packinghouses thus reinforced the UPWA's rank-and-file orientation and countered the potentially debilitating effects of the no-strike pledge.[27]

The predominance of black workers in the industry contributed to the frequency of wartime work stoppages. They were less influenced by patriotic appeals—and, in fact, tended to recast mobilization rhetoric into an attack on discrimination. Many wartime stoppages occurred over racial grievances, and black packinghouse workers regarded these as neither unpatriotic nor narrowly economic actions. Rather, they saw them as part of a larger civil rights mobilization that occurred within northern black communities in the 1940s. The 1941 March on Washington Movement had given birth to an aggressive new phase in the struggle for black equality, one in which industrial workers took center stage. Adopting the slogan of the "Double V," for victory over fascism abroad and Jim Crow at home, black workers began to press for access to better jobs and the elimination of hiring and promotion barriers. Roosevelt's Executive Order 8802 banning discrimination in plants with defense contracts was the most visible product of this struggle. By no means did it end the battle; skirmishes continued to be fought on the plant and departmental level for the duration of the war.[28]

This wartime civil rights mobilization had a strong impact in meatpacking, where the union had not only established a precedent for attacks on racism but had cultivated broad, interracial support for such measures. Thus while black assertiveness in the automobile industry gave rise to Detroit's renowned "hate strikes" and compelled the UAW to slow the pace of its fair practices campaign, the same dynamic in the packing industry pushed forward the UPWA's civil rights program and helped sustain the membership's active involvement in the union. It also contributed in a major way to the wave of work stoppages which regularly afflicted the packinghouses.[29]

During the war, black workers in Chicago's packinghouses fought to integrate departments that continued to operate on an all-white basis. High turnover rates and the departure of many whites from the industry created numerous skilled openings. By the middle of the war, many black men had accumulated enough seniority to make the transition smoothly. A decade of interracial union organizing softened white resistance to black upgrading, even if it did not entirely eliminate it. The large influx of black women, however, created a problem that was not easily resolved. As new hirees, most black women lacked the seniority needed to advance into more desirable jobs. Moreover, the existence of departmental rather than plant-wide seniority in many plants effectively deprived many longer-service black women of a contractual mechanism with which to break out of traditional slots.[30]

The more militant locals employed stoppages to force the entry of black women into white job preserves. The successful efforts of the Wilson local to integrate the sliced bacon department has been noted earlier. Other job actions around similar problems occurred frequently, though they tended to be less flamboyant than the walkout led by Sam Parks at Wilson. Although black men usually initiated these job actions, they did so less out of an awareness of gender discrimination than a more generalized commitment to racial equality. Black women, of course, were acutely aware of the interplay between racial and gender dynamics which held them in subordinate positions. Later, in the 1950s, they would more forcefully articulate their own concerns within the union. For now, their economic needs and the agenda of the men fit comfortably together.[31]

In this way, the union's racial activism helped sustain its shop-floor militancy. The shooting war against fascism sanctioned home-front workers' fight against racism. Sam Parks explained that in his mind both Hitler and Senator Bilbo were common enemies and that to combat one was to combat the other. Writing to his brother-in-law from a foxhole, Lowell Washington expressed a similar belief, hoping that when he returned home, blacks would have "given the crackers the same kind of licking" he was giving the Japanese. As for the ongoing struggle with the packers, Washington directed his brother-in-law, a laborer at Armour, to "keep the bastards toeing the line." By 1945, when black veterans like Washington began returning to their jobs, they were among the most vigorous supporters of union action against Jim Crow. "Guys came out of the military and they didn't give a damn about the Ku Klux Klan," Richard Saunders observed. "You had a breed of people who said, hell, I'm entitled to this—I want it." Eddie Humphrey, who had served in a black regiment, emotionally explained that after returning home "I couldn't see myself being discriminated against . . . we died, our blood had been shed for this country, and I felt . . . that we should get a better deal out of it. Instead of crumbs we wanted us a slice of the pie." The involvement of these veterans legitimized job actions and further blunted the appeal of the no-strike pledge.[32]

This kind of racial activism, asserting itself within the context of wartime curbs on shop-floor activity, contributed to the autonomy and independence of local unions. Although the UPWA executive board equivocated about the no-strike pledge, it solidly supported the union's stand on black rights. Racial friction in other industries, especially auto, worried International officers who were well aware of the tragedy of 1919. A 1944 board meeting devoted extensive discussion to racial polarization in Detroit in the wake of the previous year's violence. Meyer Stern sounded a note of alarm, stating "there is race antagonism and we are not doing anything about it and it will explode in our face." Anticipating the problems of peacetime demobilization and economic contraction, Philip Weightman added that "the whole race issue is coming to the front more and more in Chicago, in street cars, busses, and everywhere."[33]

Accordingly, as action around racial grievances at the union's base reached an unprecedented level, the UPWA leadership simultaneously moved to strengthen its commitment to equality in order to prepare for the postwar situation. The convergence of these two developments produced an aggressive and dynamic civil rights policy which operated at multiple levels of the union.

The Chicago district was the driving force behind the institutional elaboration of this egalitarian orientation. District director Herbert March had been responsible for the insertion of anti-discrimination clauses in the new national agreements negotiated in 1943, a device first utilized in local contracts. Later, he pushed to have this clause strengthened by extending it beyond employees to job applicants. Vice President Philip Weightman had been outspoken in his pressure on wartime government agencies to eliminate discrimination; he also began to exert a forcible influence within the CIO after his appointment to the Congress's Civil Rights Committee at the end of the war.[34]

These two leaders retained exceptionally close ties to their constituents in the plants—March with the Armour and Wilson locals and Weightman with the Swift local out of which he had emerged. Armour 347 was especially involved in civil rights activities during the war years because of both the growing left-wing presence in the plant and the dramatic increase in black workers laboring there. The local involved itself in virtually every civil rights campaign in the city and initiated several of its own, including a 1943 petition drive protesting police brutality after the shooting of an unarmed sixteen-year-old youth, a mass rally called in response to four lynchings in Georgia, and a premature but concerted effort to desegregate the city's major league baseball teams. In addition, March's role as president of the Chicago Industrial Union Council placed him in a position to coordinate packinghouse activities with those of other progressive unions, especially the Farm Equipment Workers. It was under March's direction that, following the 1943 Detroit riots, the Industrial Union Council pressured the mayor's office to establish a race relations committee to monitor the local scene and defuse potentially explosive situations.[35]

Philip Weightman was exceptionally vocal on the need for a permanent Fair Employment Practices Committee. Locally, within the UPWA, and inside the CIO he was a leading figure in the campaign to extend the life of the wartime agency. The UPWA, in fact, pioneered use of the FEPC to compel employers to alter their hiring practices, utilizing shop-floor power to prompt committee investigations and then again to insure that the packing companies actually implemented the agency's recommendations.[36] The packinghouse workers' mobilization behind the FEPC was so important that the union dispatched a delegation to Congress in 1945 to testify in favor of a permanent body before a Senate subcommittee. UPWA assistant general counsel Tilford Dudley made clear the way in which the FEPC augmented the power of local activists inside their plants. "Not infrequently merely the hint from a steward or other local officer that the issue of discrimination will be presented by the union to the Fair Employment Practice Committee is sufficient to bring about a satisfactory adjustment with the management directly," he explained.[37]

Despite their political differences, March and Weightman worked well together. Indeed, their common interest in the struggle for black equality contributed to the relatively harmonious wartime relationship between the Communists in the district and the more conservative union activists in the orbit of the Swift local. In 1945, the two leaders moved even closer together when they cochaired the newly established International Anti-Discrimination Committee, a body set up to mobilize local unions behind an ambitious campaign to root out racist practices within the UPWA, fight against discrimination in employment and housing, lobby against black disfranchisement in southern states, and agitate for the creation of a permanent Fair Employment Practices Commission. While many other districts in the UPWA remained lukewarm or indifferent about the work of the "A-D" Committee, the Chicago district used the new bureaucratic departure to launch a program of action on the local level and to legitimize even more aggressive and far-reaching activity.[38]

The most vivid example of this expanded civil rights militancy was the district's involvement in the Airport Homes controversy. Immediately after the war, the Chicago Housing Authority opened a westside project for military veterans and their families. Two of the veterans assigned homes in the new development were black, and one of them, Theodore Turner, worked at one of the small packinghouses in the stockyards. When the black veterans attempted to move into their bungalows, they encountered an angry mob of two thousand whites. Police, called to the scene by the besieged families, sided with the crowd and told the black men to leave the area. The incident raised an outcry in the black community, and leadership groups such as the NAACP protested firmly but politely through established channels. The UPWA response was more direct. Eighteen local unions mobilized their resources and, in addition to pressuring the mayor to ensure adequate police protection, sent teams of packinghouse workers to the Airport project each night to guard the homes of the black families. By day, packinghouse delegations called upon white residents and attempted to win their support. Although tensions initially rose—as indicated by a cross burning and the formation of a supremacist organization apparently in league with the ward's Democratic political machine—the black families secured their rights and city police eventually extended protection.[39]

These kinds of activities represented an extension into the community of policies operative within the union since organizing first began in the 1930s. The UPWA's willingness to combat racial inequality had enormous appeal to the new black workers entering the industry in the late 1940s. "Guys who might not be interested in attending meetings, being a steward or something might look at these kinds of things and say, 'hey, there's something here for me,'" Lowell Washington explained, adding that "once they got involved, it don't matter how, it made us stronger all across the board." Moreover, the Packinghouse Workers' civil rights initiatives involved whites as well as blacks and thus reinforced the interracial solidarity initially born out of the need to counter the employers' economic power. Actions like the defense of the families at the Airport Homes tended to involve white unionists already sensitized to injustice and committed to redress, but affected other white workers as well. While a minority chafed at the increasing attention devoted to black concerns, most white packinghouse workers in this period accepted the union's anti-discrimination activities.[40]

The UPWA's second convention, held in Omaha, sent an unmistakably clear message to the membership about the commitment to equality and interracial unity. When the hotel hosting the convention refused to house black delegates arriving from across the country, packinghouse leaders moved the entire convention out of hotel's salon and into the cramped union hall despite stifling 102-degree heat. When it became clear that alternative accommodations could not be arranged because of omnipresent segregation, out-of-town delegates lodged with Omaha unionists. Those present for the four-day conclave never forgot this inspired protest. For many whites, especially those from areas with small black populations, this was their first encounter with racial discrimination. "I think they would have preferred being in the Hotel Continental where we were supposed to be," one participant recalled, "but they did it and there's a learning process in there." Even Omaha packinghouse workers had their eyes opened by the incident. District director A. T. Stephens admitted as much when he rose from the floor to accept blame, apologize, and confess that Omaha's Jim Crow policy was "something we never knew existed here before."[41]

The evolving wartime relationship between the union bureaucracy and the rank and file in the UPWA was strikingly different than that in most other CIO unions. Rather than indicating the existence of a gulf between leadership and workers, wartime job actions in packing represented a continuation of the confrontational style of unionism developed in the 1930s. The paralysis of the Labor Board, the packing companies' continued resistance to the union, and the racial militancy of the union's black membership combined to preserve the power and autonomy of local unions. Because of its regular use of direct action and its special relevance to black workers as a civil rights vehicle, the UPWA emerged from the war with an active membership and a strong, disciplined organization. These features had a major impact on its postwar trajectory.

From Reconversion to Taft-Hartley: Worker Militancy and State Power

As the war wound to a close, industrial workers in the United States grew increasingly restless. Four years of austerity, frozen wages, and constraints upon union activity had produced a widespread sense of grievance that went beyond any single issue. While the cessation of hostilities and a return to normalcy was welcome, reconversion to peacetime production caused considerable anxiety. The elimination of overtime hours meant a sharp reduction in take-home pay—in meatpacking, where there had not been a wage increase since before Pearl Harbor, this cut was as deep as 30 percent—and postwar inflation was expected to make this problem more acute. Moreover, many new hirees feared that the return of eight million veterans would flood the labor market and, coupled with layoffs, squeeze them out of their jobs.[42]

In the fall of 1945, this restlessness expressed itself in the form of the greatest strike wave in United States history. By the end of 1946, government statisticians had counted more than six thousand strikes involving well over seven million workers. Many of the strikes, perhaps even most of them, lacked official union sanction and resembled the kinds of wildcats that had plagued industry since the start of the war. The most severe and protracted conflicts, however, were those planned and directed by international unions. These included nationwide strikes in the oil, coal, rubber, automobile, and meatpacking industries. For the most part, historical study has centered either on the wildcat phenomenon or the UAW's action against General Motors, which catapulted Walter Reuther to the head of the auto workers union. The UPWA's 1946 strike, which affected Big Four plants across the country and several independent houses, merits examination. It illustrates the next stage in the development of the union's alternative style, as well as providing the background for both its response to the passage of the Taft-Hartley Act the following year and its conduct of a second nationwide strike in 1948.[43]

Wages formed the key issue in the packinghouse strike. In a 1945 decision, the National War Labor Board had acceded to union demands for the adjustment of piece rates but had denied its request for an across-the-board ten cents per hour increase. It also established a Meat Packing Commission empowered to standardize wage rates and adjudicate grievances pertaining to them, but this was no substitute for a straightforward raise.

Now, with the end of defense prosperity in sight, packinghouse workers decided to push for what they regarded as a long overdue pay hike. While this was the major issue, another concern lurked just below the surface. Many leaders remembered the assault on unionism that followed the relaxation of government controls after World War I and urged strong action to prevent a repetition of the attack. Vice President Frank Ellis, who had been working in an Omaha packinghouse during the 1919–21 period, warned other UPWA officers not to depend on the Labor Board or federal intervention. "We can't afford to mess around much longer," the old Wobbly asserted, "that is the thing that defeated the meat cutters after the last war." These sentiments were widely shared. A display of strength, many packinghouse leaders felt, was necessary in order to forestall a backlash against the union. Accordingly, after a wage and policy conference settled on a demand for a raise of twenty-five cents, the union petitioned the government in October of 1945 for a strike vote in accordance with the War Labor Disputes Act.[44]

With the strike deadline fixed for 16 January 1946, the UPWA had an interim period of over two months to prepare for the conflict during which it took steps to ensure a maximum of rank-and-file participation. It initiated a drive to enroll remaining nonunion workers and moved to appoint additional stewards in plants which might prove weak spots. It established a National Strike Strategy Committee of over two hundred local delegates who, along with the International officers, would oversee all aspects of the strike from negotiations to picket-line instructions. In addition, committees within each local union and from each metropolitan council were set up to organize mass pickets around the plants, food commissaries, and community support. The national committee instructed the locals to incorporate all elements of the workforce in the strike in order to maintain unity and to guard against racial or ethnic divisions. Above all else, the union stressed the importance of broad participation. "Never should the idea be developed that you have enough people for your activities," the union's strike manual admonished. "When people are idle and not involved in any specific thing to help win the strike, demoralization sets in."[45]

In all the major packing centers the strong community support given to the union was reminiscent of the labor conflicts of the late nineteenth century. In Chicago, the union's ties with the Back-of-the-Yards Neighborhood Council proved especially beneficial. The council raised more than $8,000 for the union's strike fund, helped convince area priests to support the union's demands publicly, and began making arrangements for food donations and emergency relief. Local businesses agreed to extend credit during the strike and to suspend installment payments. Father Edward Plawinski, the council's president, took to the airwaves in a radio broadcast and defended the union's right to strike, reiterating the church's support for unionism. Later, he appeared with three other prelates on the UPWA picket line ringing the Swift plant. Leo Rose, a furniture store owner and president of the Back-of-the-Yards Businessmen's Association, spoke for many merchants when he explained his partisan stand, "I do my business with working people not with Armours or Swifts." Joseph Meegan was more dramatic. "It is our people. It is our cause. It is our fight," he declared. In the black community, churches and civic leaders lined up behind the UPWA as well—a profound change from its stance in 1921. A support committee which included the president of the local NAACP branch, the editor of the *Chicago Bee*, and several ministers coordinated South Side assistance. In an indication of how attitudes had changed, the once anti-union Urban League offered support and the Wabash Avenue YMCA volunteered its facilities.[46]

The Amalgamated Meat Cutters reluctantly agreed to go along with the UPWA's demands. Initially, AMC secretary Gorman had attacked the "trigger tactics" of the CIO union and, after the UPWA fixed its deadline, announced that his membership would remain at work in the event of a strike. However, when the packing companies appeared no more willing to compromise with the Amalgamated than the UPWA, Gorman threw in his lot with the CIO. Yet, this unity was not seamless; there were significant differences in the approach of the two unions. While the AMC explicitly hoped for federal intervention, the UPWA made clear that such interference would be unwelcome and could only aid the packers. "We have no doubt that these packing companies, relying on the hope of government seizure, will use every effort possible to break the strike," Clark warned. Government seizure of the packinghouses, he stated, would prove "the complete bankruptcy to which the responsible officials of the government have sunk."[47]

Efforts to reach a settlement before the deadline went nowhere. After several frustrating rounds of talks, the UPWA lowered its demand to seventeen and a half percent—the figure proposed by Truman's fact-finding board in the General Motors dispute—but the packers offered no more than a seven-and-a-half-cent increase. With the two sides so far apart, negotiations broke off. On 16 January, the meatpacking industry was shut down as both AFL and CIO unionists came out solidly. Although some of the independent plants continued operations, the strike effectively curtailed production across the country. In Chicago and in other packing centers, packinghouses sat idle, ringed by mass pickets as workers waited for either the companies or the government to make the next move.[48]

With auto and steel workers also out on strike, the government decided to act. After receiving assurances from AMC leaders that they would order their members back to work, President Truman seized the packinghouses on 24 January. Invoking the War Labor Disputes Act, he directed the unions to abandon their strike. The Amalgamated dutifully responded, calling off the action and accepting a settlement of fifteen cents. The UPWA responded in a contrasting manner. Gathering in special session the day after Truman's order went into effect, local union representatives condemned the seizure as a "strikebreaking action" and voted overwhelmingly to defy the order to return to work. Recognition that government "seizure" allowed existing management to remain in control while a fact-finding commission investigated the dispute influenced this decision, as did awareness that both General Motors and U.S. Steel had recently rejected the findings of commissions in their industries. Moreover, wartime experience with the delays and deferments of government boards made packinghouse workers hesitant to call off the most successful strike in their history without some concrete gain. When Secretary of Agriculture Clinton Anderson informed the group that the law provided criminal penalties for impeding the return of strikers to seized plants, the UPWA reaffirmed its decision to hold out until the government guaranteed that the packers be bound by the recommendations of the commission investigating the issues in the dispute.[49]

This tenacity paid off. The UPWA's willingness to resist the government resulted in a binding settlement of sixteen cents an hour retroactive to the previous August—not quite the amount for which the union had asked, but better than that secured by the Amalgamated. Building upon this victory, the union again threatened to strike when the master agreements expired in the fall of 1946. This time, the packers chose not to fight. They granted a further increase of seven and a half cents an hour, and also agreed to narrow both the male-female and North-South geographic wage differential.[50]

More important than material gains, though, was the effect of the strike on both the UPWA's membership and officers. The shared experience of participation in the strike and successfully defying the government was an empowering one for the rank and file. It confirmed their wartime militancy and their distrust of the state, corroborating union leadership's wariness of the federal government. It also marked the end of the International's attempts to tame the independent activity of the locals, for it graphically demonstrated the power to be had through reliance on the rank and file.

The 1946 strike also led to an important change in the UPWA Executive Board. Delegates to the union's convention, held in June in Montreal, replaced Lewis J. Clark with Ralph Helstein, formerly the UPWA's general counsel. During the strike, Clark had alienated the members of the strategy committee. Behaving erratically, he disappeared suddenly for hours at a time, showed himself unable to follow discussions, and provided a minimum of leadership. "Clark was a nonentity," UPWA staff member Norman Dolnick recalled. "He didn't know what was going on. He couldn't negotiate; he didn't know how to negotiate; he didn't want to negotiate. He just wanted all the honors and all the perks that go with being president." Apparently, during the showdown with the government, Clark suffered some kind of breakdown in front of the entire strategy committee. In contrast, Helstein emerged as an unparalleled strategist during the strike. He handled all negotiations with the packers and, after Clark's collapse, served as the union's spokesman. His dynamic performance convinced those present of his talents.[51]

On the surface the selection of Helstein is a puzzling one given the packinghouse workers' bitter resentment of Van Bittner, J. C. Lewis, and all the outsiders who staffed the PWOC. An educated lawyer, Helstein stood at an even greater remove from the average worker than did the ex-miners appointed to oversee the union in its formative years. Yet, during the strike he had demonstrated his knowledge of packinghouse conditions, developed an easy rapport with workers, and stood with them as they defied the government. Politically, his selection as UPWA president was a brilliant stroke. Since he had not come out of the plants, Helstein was not tied to any particular local or regional power center. He was neither associated with the CIO—in fact, CIO representatives at the convention worked frantically to block his election—nor identified with any political faction. Precisely because of his origins and independence, Helstein was able to mediate between the various factions within the union. Acceptable to all parties, he immeasurably strengthened the political coalition that lay at the heart of the UPWA.

Although they had no way of knowing it at the time, the delegates who elected Ralph Helstein in 1946 chose a leader whose philosophy was well suited to the UPWA's style of unionism. His experience as a labor lawyer for the left-wing Minneapolis Teamsters and the syndicalist-influenced Austin Hormel local left him with a reluctance to rely on the power of the state. After the 1946 strike, for example, when the union's executive board contemplated bringing the many company violations of the contract into the courts, Helstein registered his opposition. "I think unions should stay as far away from the courts as they can get," he told the board. "When it comes to playing around with our contracts, the further we stay away from the courts, the better we are."[52]

Moreover, he was a civil libertarian who believed that the union should contain room for all political persuasions, a creed that helped the UPWA survive the McCarthyite storm of the early 1950s with its democratic traditions intact. Helstein valued rather than feared the political diversity inside the union. "If people always agree you never have progress, you get stultified and frozen," he later explained to an Omaha audience. "It is only as the a result of disagreement . . . of clashes of opinion that you go on, and out of these opinions you try to find the best answer and you move onward."[53] This outlook was especially appealing to the UPWA's left wing, whose wartime detente with the right had given way in late 1945 to increasingly acrimonious infighting. Throughout the period leading up to the 1946 strike, Clark and Weightman wielded the crudest sort of anticommunism in a futile effort to chisel away at Herbert March's influence in the Chicago district. For the most part their attacks remained internal to the union and did not attract wider publicity; nor did they attempt to appeal to rank-and-file packinghouse workers. Nevertheless, the left feared that the 1946 convention would see a formal move to exclude Communists from full participation in the union and moved to support Helstein when the time came. His political independence made him an attractive choice, but initially this was less important to the left than the fact that he could viably oppose Lewis J. Clark. "Who the hell would have thought of a lawyer," Jesse Prosten remembered, "but he was trusted, and he was an honest guy, and he was a liberal guy."[54]

The support given by Prosten and others further illustrates the autonomy of UPWA Communists from the Party bureaucracy. Fearing that CIO envoy Alan Haywood would make good on his threat to remove Lee Pressman as the congress's general counsel if the CP did not abandon the Helstein candidacy, Party Trade Union Commission chair George Morris ordered March and his comrades to drop their support. Morris traveled to the convention to personally deliver this edict, and March remembered angrily rejecting it. "George, go scratch. I'm a member of the National

Committee and I'm directing you to keep your nose out of our goddamn business. We're going to go through with this." A compromise with Haywood, whereby Clark saved face by running unopposed for secretary-treasurer, stayed the heavy hand of the CIO. Helstein's election preserved the center-left alliance in the union and created vital breathing space for the Communists at a time when many other CIO unions were moving to isolate them. "I knew we had to make a turn," March commented. "It made for an unusual union. The Packinghouse Workers became a union under Helstein—for a time at least—in which there was tolerance of all sorts of viewpoints, a democracy in a true sense."[55]

Helstein assumed command of the UPWA just when the labor movement was entering a period of profound crisis. Truman's attack on the United Mine Workers in November of 1946 and the launching of a campaign to revise the Wagner Act mark the start of an economic and legislative backlash against organized labor which culminated with the passage of the Taft-Hartley Act in June 1947. At the same time, the wartime alliance between the United States and the Soviet Union gave way to cold war, allowing anticommunism to emerge as a powerful divisive force within labor's ranks. Again, the UPWA responded to these twin obstacles in a way that distinguished it from other unions. It neither capitulated to the onerous requirements of the Taft-Hartley Act nor succumbed to the considerable pressure brought to bear upon it to purge the Left and lend support to the Democratic Party.[56]

Passed over President Truman's veto, the Taft-Hartley Act placed a number of legal restrictions upon the labor movement. It circumscribed union activity by outlawing the closed shop, secondary boycott, and jurisdictional strike. The legislation allowed the federal government to influence the timing of strikes by instituting a mandatory sixty-day "cooling off" period. It also permitted employers to sue unions for breach of contract and prohibited union financial support of federal candidates. Especially onerous to the many left-wing unions in the CIO was a provision forcing unions to register with the secretary of labor and requiring officers to file non-Communist affidavits. Access to the certification machinery of the NLRB was contingent upon the meeting of these requirements. This last measure not only encouraged anticommunist sentiment within the labor movement but meant that duly elected leaders who happened to be Communists faced an unsavory choice of resigning, concealing their political affiliation, or exposing their union to an employer offensive without the protection of the federal government.[57]

Immediately after passage of the act, both the AFL and CIO condemned it and promised to work for repeal while resisting complying with its provisions. John L. Lewis emerged as the most outspoken foe of compliance, denouncing the act as "the first, ugly, savage thrust of fascism in America." This tough stand was short-lived. Unwilling to forego the protection of the NLRB and return to an essentially pre-Wagner style of unionism, the labor movement rapidly backtracked. In October 1947, the AFL voted to comply with the act, prompting Lewis to again withdraw the UMW from the federation. A few weeks later, the CIO adopted a neutral position, leaving the issue of compliance up to affiliate unions. The door was effectively shut on mass resistance in late November when the UAW executive board decided to file affidavits with the federal government. Still, a number of smaller CIO unions, including the left-wing United Electrical Workers, the Farm Equipment Workers, and the UPWA continued to resist and remained in a state of noncompliance.[58]

Taft-Hartley's restrictions on union tactics threatened the kind of militant, action-oriented unionism developed by the packinghouse workers. The provision requiring non-Communist affidavits affected two executive board members—Herbert March, then publicly identified as a member of the CP's Central Committee, and Meyer Stern—and potentially dozens of other Communist union officials. Most of the other International executive board members favored a program of resistance. Again sounding a syndicalist note, Frank Ellis warned against "becoming tied to the apron strings of government agencies which are, in fact, hostile to us." Joe Ollman, the Trotskyist director of the union's Minnesota district, was even more forceful. Taft-Hartley is the "slaughter pen for labor," he asserted, and the "filing of the affidavits is the electric prod that is being used by the N.A.M. [National Association of Manufacturers] and every anti-labor force in the country to drive us into that slaughtering pen." Helstein, too, adamantly urged opposition to the new law.[59]

In July 1947, a special conference of local union delegates formalized the UPWA's opposition to the Taft-Hartley Act. Acting upon a resolution submitted by the executive board, the delegates affirmed the officers' decision to refuse to register with the state and to file non-Communist affidavits. They further resolved to "deliberately and purposely violate" the act's restrictions on political activity and to "shun any use of the law" in dealing with the employers. The conference declared its intentions to respect its collective bargaining commitments and urged the packers to do likewise, warning that "we will see to it that our contracts are enforced." The delegates announced their intention of defending their gains through the now-traditional use of direct action by instructing union leaders not to sign any contract including a no-strike provision. The conference went on record as calling for a strengthening of the steward system and the development of secondary leadership in the plants. A memorandum distributed after the gathering reiterated the need for shoring up shop-floor organization and reminded local unions that "the success with which the steward system functions will largely measure our ability to withstand the union-smashing pressure that is here in the form of the Taft-Hartley law."[60]

This stand isolated the Packinghouse Workers from the mainstream of the labor movement. After the CIO capitulated and adopted its neutral position on Taft-Hartley compliance, the outlines of the split within its ranks that culminated two years later with the purge of ten "Communist dominated" unions became discernible. By adopting a program of resistance, the UPWA found itself in the company of a number of other left-wing affiliates, and this situation worried some of the union's more conservative leaders. Equally troubling were reports of attempted raids on UPWA plants by the Amalgamated Meat Cutters. Since the UPWA could not appear on NLRB ballots if the AMC forced representation elections, several of the more cautious union leaders began to reconsider the wisdom of continued noncompliance. "Unless we are able to use that [NLRB] machinery, in my opinion the union will be destroyed," Vice President Phil Weightman declared at a November 1947 executive board meeting. The two southern directors, G. R. Hathaway and A. J. Pittman, echoed his concern and referred ominously to the Labor Board's refusal to certify the UPWA after a successful representation contest in a Jacksonville, Florida, plant.[61]

A vigorous debate ensued among the union's top leadership. Those opposed to compliance recognized the problems accompanying their position. "How are you going to go to the workers in the plant, the guys who want to keep their union; the guys who are worried about the possible raids, the election that is coming up and explain to them and make them understand why they cannot be on the ballot," they asked while at the same time urging continued resistance. Ever forceful, Joe Ollman warned that far from offering protection, compliance would weaken the union and render it defenseless against future attacks. Helstein supported him, arguing that the delays and restrictions incorporated in the NLRB process made the use of government machinery an impediment to organization. The better course—albeit the more difficult one—was to resist. "Those unions that do not comply, that take this thing the hard way," Helstein concluded, "are the unions that are going to be in a better position to survive than the ones that comply and operate under any illusions that they have any protection from this nefarious piece of legislation."[62]

Still, the more conservative board members held out in favor of conforming with Taft-Hartley's requirements. Eventually, a compromise was
reached in the interest of unity: the union's four nationally elected officers
would sign the affidavits, allowing the Communist district directors to
remain on the executive board. Vice President Weightman and Secretary-
Treasurer Clark had no problem submitting the documents. Helstein and
Frank Ellis, though, harbored grave personal doubts. The former, in fact,
was so disturbed that he contemplated resigning. Grasping the larger issues, he wrote to a confidant that "I don't think that fundamentally the
problem has to do with affidavits at all." Rather, the Taft-Hartley law "is
designed for the purpose of forcing conformity on the American people and
making it difficult for anyone who dissents to express his views." After
several weeks of reflection, Helstein opted to go along with the board's
decision and submitted an affidavit.[63]

This halfway measure failed to satisfy the government, which notified
the UPWA that it was necessary for all officers to file the non-Communist
documents. When the union's leaders met again in late January 1948, southern officials pressed the case for conforming with the law. Asserting that
southern organization would collapse without access to the NLRB, Pittman
called for the resignations of March and Stern. Presenting a "sign or resign"
motion, Hathaway implored the Communists to place the needs of the
membership ahead of their personal ethics and principles. March, who had
been silent throughout the debate, now spoke up. Refusing to either resign
or sign the affidavit, he proposed referring the issue to the next convention. "Labor has been sucking at the tit of the government in order to get
nourishment, and in order to get strength, and the thing that we have to
realize is that at this time the tit has gone dry," he declared. The substitute
motion passed by a narrow margin, leaving the UPWA in noncompliance
and without access to the NLRB.[64]

The 1948 Strike and Aftermath

The UPWA's defiance of the federal government in 1946 and its resistance
to the Taft-Hartley Act shaped the way in which the union responded to
its next challenge—the reopening of contract negotiations in 1948. When
talks broke down, the UPWA again decided to wage a national strike
against the large packing companies. Again, the key issue was a wage increase. The union demanded a twenty-nine-cent increase; the packers offered a hike of only nine. Summarizing widely held opinion, Helstein urged

a strike, even if it resulted in acceptance of the companies' offer. "The people will still feel better because we fought about it and didn't take it right away," he explained. In February 1948 close to 90 percent of the union's membership voted in favor of the action. The National Strike Strategy Committee reconvened and established 16 March as its deadline. In characteristic fashion, the UPWA rejected Truman's last-minute request that it delay the strike until the completion of a presidential inquiry. On the morning of the deadline, one hundred thousand packinghouse workers "hit the bricks" for the second time in as many years.[65]

This time, though, the context surrounding the conflict was far different from that prevailing two years earlier. The UPWA did not enjoy the support of the Amalgamated, which had secretly settled with the packers at seven and a half cents and remained at work. This made it impossible to shut down the entire meatpacking industry and greatly reduced the effectiveness of the strike. Furthermore, Taft-Hartley's mandatory sixty-day strike notice prevented the union from taking action during the peak livestock rush and allowed the packing companies precious preparation time. Taft-Hartley injunctions and court-issued restraining orders further hampered the union's ability to curtail production and saddled the UPWA with staggering legal costs. "We learned the hard way about Taft-Hartley," a poststrike assessment soberly noted, "the worst fears that we had through studying the law have been substantiated in practice." By May, the union had been served with over fifty court orders restricting mass picketing and other activities. "If there were any cities where such injunctions were not issued, I don't at the moment know where they were," Helstein stated after the strike. In some packing centers, the courts effectively opened the plants by barring virtually all picketing. In Fort Worth, for instance, a judge allowed local unions only two pickets for the entire yards complex. Defiance of these injunctions resulted in the arrests of more than two thousand strikers and National Guard intervention in Minnesota and Iowa.[66]

The changed political atmosphere ruled out a quick settlement and encouraged the packers to actively resist the union. Talks broke off on the second day of the conflict and did not resume until the final week. In contrast to 1946, the strike dragged on for thirteen weeks, with the packers recruiting strikebreakers and attempting to foment back-to-work movements. Violence was widespread; and three strikers lost their lives, including Chicago unionist Santo Cicardo, a member of the Armour local killed when a truck crashed through a picket line. Rather than encountering the kind of neutral state intervention which led to the conclusion of the 1946 strike, the UPWA faced armed troops in many packing centers and was called upon, in the critical final week, to answer subpoenas from a hostile congressional committee chaired by Michigan's archconservative Clare Hoffman.[67]

In Chicago, community support coupled with the union's strong organization and assistance provided by other CIO unions ensured a solid showing. As in 1946 the Catholic church and the Back-of-the-Yards Council assisted the strikers. Soup kitchens at the University of Chicago Settlement House and the union hall fed over three thousand workers each day. In the Black Belt, the newly hired director of the Urban League, Sidney Williams, chaired the South Side Committee to Support Packinghouse Strikers and coordinated assistance from black churches and fraternal organizations. Around-the-clock picketing of the stockyards insured the active involvement of thousands of striking workers, and the union tapped the energy and interest of others by holding daily classes and discussion groups. The strike built upon a cultural and organizational foundation laid over the course of the previous decade and reinforced during the 1946 conflict. The strike also facilitated cultural exchanges and fusions, as black and white workers spent time together outside of the work setting. The black spiritual and civil rights anthem, "I Shall Not Be Moved," was adapted for use on the picket line. And Armour worker and bluesman Floyd Jones immortalized the packinghouse workers' struggle in a song entitled "I Need Another Dollar":

I left home this mornin' boys about half past nine,
I passed the stockyards and knows them boys is still on the picket line.
You know I need another dollar,
You know I need to make a dollar,
The cost of living has gone so high I don't know what to do.

Drawing upon these considerable resources, Chicago's packinghouse workers were able to mount a protracted struggle against their employers.[68]

Chicago's police openly sided with the packing companies, harassing pickets and facilitating the entry of strikebreakers into the plants. Mayor Kennelly, who sat on Wilson's board of directors, convened a special detail of police under the direction of "red squad" leader Captain George Barnes that attacked UPWA picket lines with batons and brass knuckles on several occasions. Barnes's men also illegally seized and detained packinghouse workers leafleting at the elevated stations near the yards until pressure from the Chicago Industrial Union Council secured their right to assembly and freedom of speech. After a series of particularly flagrant police assaults and the arrest of pickets for weapons violations, a union delegation to the mayor and Police Commissioner Prendergast exacted a promise that strikebreakers as well as union pickets would be disarmed. Violence between police and strikers flared again several days later when, in defiance of a restraining order, ten thousand pickets assembled at the stockyards.[69]

Much of the violence in Chicago resulted from company attempts to employ strikebreakers and dispatch them through the picket lines. At first the packers relied upon foremen and supervisory personnel, but this tactic was ineffective due to the merciless harassment these men received as they passed to and from work and the ostracism they encountered in their communities. UPWA strike bulletins reported that several foremen had walked out of the Swift and Armour plants and joined the picket lines. Armour also attempted to use foremen to cajole wavering workers into returning to their jobs, sending them to workers' homes in the evenings. By the end of March, the packers had reverted to more brazen tactics, securing replacement workers at employment agencies located away from the stockyards, hauling them by truck into the plants, and lodging them inside. When strikers discovered such agencies, special teams were dispatched to "turn over a few tables and close the place up."[70]

In early May, Chicago reported only 150 scabs in each of the three large plants. Nevertheless, the larger picture was quite grim, with signs of collapse in many of the outlying packing centers. In South St. Paul, National Guardsmen broke through UPWA picket lines and, despite what can only be described as hand-to-hand combat, escorted strikebreakers into the plants. A similar situation occurred in both Sioux City and Waterloo, Iowa. Severe legal repression in the West limited pickets; and in Omaha a back-to-work movement was taking shape. To make matters worse, the Amalgamated had petitioned for NLRB elections in a number of plants. "It was some rough times," Todd Tate recalled.[71]

Within a fortnight, Chicago itself showed signs of cracking. The stockhandlers, pulled in the middle of the strike, returned to their jobs to respect the Union Stockyards and Transit Company's back-to-work order. Demoralization began to set in in the wake of this defection which, in Herb March's view, "had the same effect as dropping a sledgehammer between the eyes as far as a strike is concerned in Chicago." The Swift local weakened first; within a few days of the handlers' defection reports indicated that over fifteen hundred workers crossed the picket lines circling the plant. When the company announced the resumption of slaughtering operations in its beef and sheep departments, hundreds more entered to secure their jobs. At Armour the situation was marginally better, but even here several hundred unionists joined strikebreakers inside after receiving telegrams from the company setting a deadline of 10 May, after which point they would forfeit all senior-ity rights. On 15 May, Helstein noted worriedly that delegations were report-ing "that their lines were beginning to break, and the morale was shattered, and that good union people, stewards in many cases, were prepared to go back to work and scab." Three days later the National Strike Strategy Com-mittee voted to accept the packers' offer of nine cents and to call off the strike providing the companies agreed to rehire all workers. In the days that fol-lowed packinghouse workers returned to the plants, unsure whether their union would survive. In the Wilson chain, the conflict lasted an additional two weeks; when it ended, work resumed without a contract. "The compa-ny just outlasted us," Charles Hayes noted, "there's no question about it." It was an unconditional defeat.[72]

More important than the conduct of the strike itself was its aftermath. With close to six hundred local leaders discharged, unable to pay salaries or settle grievances, the UPWA all but ceased functioning as a union in the months following the defeat.[73] Furthermore, the question of Taft-Hartley compliance returned with pressing urgency. Facing more than two dozen representation elections, the UPWA desperately required access to the NLRB machinery if it hoped to survive. The issue of compliance coupled with criticism of the International over the strike gave rise to intense fac-tional infighting. In the summer of 1948 an anticommunist opposition movement took shape. Fueled by these internal issues and further stimu-lated by the left wing's support for the presidential campaign of Henry Wallace (who had supported the strike), this movement both mounted a political challenge to the Helstein administration and agitated for a purge of Communists from the UPWA.[74]

This crisis was the most formidable challenge the UPWA faced. In a recovery that later assumed a legendary character, the Packinghouse Work-ers repaired its shattered organization, secured the reinstatement of all but a handful of the discharged activists, and emerged victorious in every NLRB representation election. Although it made concessions to the opposi-tion movement—most notably the resignation of Herbert March as district director—it weathered the factional storm without capitulating to the forces of anticommunist reaction. In large measure, this recovery was made pos-sible by the conscious decision, taken in the period immediately following the strike defeat, to rebuild the union around its black membership—a decision that had momentous consequences for both the social character of the union and the course followed by the UPWA in the 1950s.

The pending NLRB elections made Taft-Hartley compliance the most pressing issue for the UPWA after the return to work. In early June, Herbert March agreed to resign. In a statement published in the *Packinghouse Worker* he declared "I have always disdained to conceal the fact that I am a Communist. I have always felt that my Communist views strengthened my ability to serve this union." His decision to resign, he explained, was a reluctant one resulting from the need to avoid a bitter internal conflict at a time when unity was vital. But he also noted pointedly that other unions that "took the compliance road also stopped fighting for higher wages and better working conditions." Meyer Stern left the Party and filed an affidavit with the government. These changes allowed the union to appear on election ballots but hardly solved the problem of fending off AMC raids and decertification efforts.[75]

The Amalgamated attempted to capitalize upon worker dissatisfaction with the protracted strike and portrayed itself as a more responsible union that avoided foolhardy confrontation. Criticizing the UPWA for leading workers on a suicide mission, an Amalgamated circular presented the Meat Cutters as a sober alternative to "Big Chief Windbags" of the CIO. "For fifty years we have shied away from strikes," the leaflet began. "We have used our ears to LISTEN TO REASON. We have used our legs to trod to many conferences with our employers so that a problem could be SETTLED AMICABLY," it continued. Most packinghouse workers did not respond to these appeals. The Amalgamated, long a discredited force in most packing centers, now bore the additional burden of having remained at work while the UPWA waged a lone struggle. So too the fact remained that the UPWA eventually settled for a penny more than the AFL had accepted without a fight—a gain more symbolic than material but quite powerful nonetheless. In addition, as Ralph Helstein noted, "we were able to call them pariahs for coming along and trying to feed off a corpse—well some corpse it turned out to be!" As the UPWA's string of NLRB election victories grew longer, the AFL's interest in the packinghouses receded. A year after the strike, the UPWA had been recertified in two dozen packinghouses, often by margins of four to one.[76]

A crucial factor in the UPWA's ability to retain the support of its members was its successful reinstatement of discharged activists. Jesse Prosten, the union's chief negotiator in this process, secured the jobs of almost all the workers fired during the strike. The Chicago Armour plant suffered the heaviest loss, with seventy-one unionists let go. Within nine months, Prosten arranged for sixty-five of these to return to work while the remaining six opted to quit. Praised for this performance, Prosten shared credit with the discharged local leaders, explaining that most of them relinquished their rights to back pay in exchange for the rehiring of their members. These small victories stood in marked contrast to the way in which the Meat Cutters conducted itself after the 1921–22 defeat.[77]

Although unsuccessful, the 1948 strike strengthened members' attachment to the UPWA. Looking back forty years later, Wilson leader Charles Hayes deemed the strike a victory of sorts. "We won," he explained, because "the people realized that they couldn't work for Wilson without a union." Other participants agreed with this assessment. Noting that at the time he "thought it was all over as far as the union was concerned," Lowell Washington recognized that in the long run the strike marked a turning point for the UPWA. "After we took that kind of licking the people said, hell, let's never *ever* be in a position where we risk losing it again. It was a defeat, sure, but it made us more militant 'cause we knew just what we were up against." Charles Fischer, a Kansas City union leader, agreed as well, adding that although the packers savored their victory, the intensity of the conflict sobered them. "It taught the company a lesson," he explained. "They lost millions of dollars out of that deal, and they knew we could do it again." The UPWA's one-year contracts signed with Swift and Armour at the end of 1948 bear out these views. An additional increase of four cents demonstrated that the struggle had not been in vain; and the 1949 agreements provided important additional gains.[78]

In the month between the end of the strike and the UPWA's special convention in June, an opposition movement coalesced inside the UPWA. Calling itself the "CIO Policy Caucus," this group organized around the goal of ousting the Helstein administration, breaking the center-left alliance, and bringing the Packinghouse Workers in line with CIO domestic and foreign policy. Bringing together genuine anticommunists and dissidents critical of the strike's conduct, the CIO Policy Caucus had its strongest support in the Chicago Swift plant and in the Omaha packinghouse locals. Anticommunists were particularly incensed by the visible position maintained by Herbert March in the union. After his resignation, the International hired him as a field representative, a position he used to continue to run the Chicago district. This move rankled Weightman and other leaders of the Swift local, who had crossed swords with the outspoken Communist for several years, and also raised hackles farther afield. Similarly, the continued presence of open Communists Les Orear and Jesse Prosten in the International office disturbed right-wingers. Many of these unionists had been stung by the sensationalized press reports of "red domination" of the UPWA that accompanied the strike; others, aware of the movement in other CIO affiliates to isolate the Left, wondered why their union seemed to move in an opposite direction.[79]

The support given the third-party campaign of Henry Wallace by the UPWA's leadership and by the union's left wing exacerbated the factionalism. As early as February 1948, Helstein had declared his intention to vote for the Progressive Party candidate despite the decision of the CIO Executive Board to enforce loyalty to the Democrats. Stating that Truman's drafting of rail strikers, threatened use of the military in coal and maritime disputes, and tacit support for the Taft-Hartley Act marked him an enemy of labor, the UPWA president urged packinghouse workers to cast their ballots according to their conscience regardless of CIO policy. In Chicago, pro-Wallace sentiment ran high. "Practically all our pickets were wearing Wallace buttons," Herb March noted; and the district's strike bulletin, the "Packinghouse Picket," regularly ran articles favorable to the former vice president. A "Packinghouse Workers Committee for Wallace" included Local 347 president Leon Beverly, chief steward Joe Bezenhoffer, and union founders George Kovacavich and Mike Santina. Wilson local leaders Sam Parks, Charles Hayes, and Joe Zabritski were members as well. Moreover, Oscar Wilson, Jr., a member of the district staff, stood as a candidate for the Illinois General Assembly on the Progressive ticket. A year earlier these activities would not have caused much of a stir in the union. Indeed, the UPWA's 1946 convention endorsed a number of third party candidacies and declared its general support for independent political action. By in mid-1948, with CIO leaders joining liberals in attacking the Wallace campaign as Communist-inspired, the UPWA's right wing found additional material for its brief against the Helstein administration.[80]

The Policy Caucus adherents finding fault with the Helstein administration's direction of the strike were a loose and disparate grouping. They initially included representatives from some of the extremely militant western locals that had wanted to carry on the struggle after the National Committee called it off, as well as interested but uncommitted delegates from local unions critical of the tactics and strategy employed during the conflict. These criticisms included the timing of the strike, the decision to take on all of the big packers instead of concentrating on a single company, and the Chicago stockyards debacle. The point that carried the most force, though, was that of Taft-Hartley compliance; and in this issue the trade union militants and anticommunists in the Policy Caucus found a unifying theme. Indeed, the first speaker from the floor at the June convention, Ben Taylor from the South St. Paul Swift local, attacked the International officers for their tardiness in complying with the law. Opposition leader Glenn Chinander, also from South St. Paul, connected the disastrous outcome of the strike with the UPWA's opposition to full compliance, accusing board members of yielding to the "personal interests of one or two members" at the expense of the union. Several Policy Caucus leaders called for a "house-cleaning"; and Phil Weightman went so far as to suggest the resignation of the entire executive board. Before the convention had reached full swing it was apparent that the CIO Policy Caucus was a substantial force with which UPWA leaders had to reckon.[81]

The climax of Policy Caucus efforts came with the election of officers. Uniting behind a slate topped by Svend Godfredson, editor of the *Packinghouse Worker*, and including Weightman and Art Kampfert as vice presidential candidates, the opposition appealed to a wide audience. Godfredson was anything but a conservative. A founder of the Austin Hormel local and lifelong socialist, he tempered the political character of the opposition roster. Weightman attracted significant support amongst black workers, for he had been one of the union's most visible civil rights champions for several years. He had worked assiduously to cultivate contacts within the CIO, based upon a shared anticommunism, and at the convention benefited from the support of CIO envoys. Kampfert's candidacy was calculated to appeal to veteran white unionists and anticommunists in the Chicago district where he had allied with Weightman against Herbert March. The opposition candidate for secretary-treasurer, A. J. Pittman, assured the votes of the UPWA's more conservative southern districts.

The opposition slate was uneven and riddled with inconsistencies, reflecting the contradictions and instability of the CIO Policy Caucus. Godfredson shared neither Weightman and Kampfert's anticommunism nor the resentment over the strike's conduct that motivated other members of the opposition. Queried about the impulse behind his campaign, he replied that "I felt that any group had a right to have a candidate run in his own union. And I, as a person having come from the shop, had a right to be a candidate. . . . I didn't want a union established where the president didn't need an opposition, where everything was decided beforehand." His claim that he would not have purged Communists from the union's staff put him at odds with right-wing leaders of the Policy Caucus, who had pledged to do so. While Weightman's appeal was considerable, Kampfert was widely perceived to be too old for the demands of the post. Indeed, he died within the year. Pittman's carping personality made him unpopular amongst those workers who had extended contact with him, but more significantly his timidity on civil rights issues was a distinct liability inside the UPWA.[82]

The weaknesses of the opposition's candidates notwithstanding, the slate garnered an impressive number of votes. But not enough. Although it lost every race, the administration's margin of victory was never larger than 6.4 percent. Almost all of the Chicago locals supported the Helstein bloc, as did the left-leaning ones in Meyer Stern's eastern district. Especially significant was the overwhelming support given the administration by the "straight trade unionists" in Iowa. The results demonstrated that anticommunism, so potent a force in other CIO unions, had marginal appeal in the UPWA. Communists in the union were open about their political affiliations and many leftists, such as Jesse Prosten and Herbert March, played visible public roles. The ability of these leaders to "deliver the goods" meant far more to most workers than their politics. The opposition's efforts to blame the outcome of the 1948 strike on the left and to portray Communists as outsiders with external allegiances failed. "We were part of the people we worked with," Jesse Prosten observed. "I was some fucking nut who was a Red as far as they were concerned, but I was the guy who produced for them." The Communists in the UPWA had deep roots amongst packinghouse workers who understood and acknowledged their role in launching the union in the 1930s and appreciated their militant leadership.[83]

The 1948 convention provided the center-left coalition with the support and authority it required to continue to steer the UPWA along its alternative path. The reelection of the Helstein bloc allowed the administration to execute some housecleaning of its own. "Now we feel we have sufficient strength on the Board to dispose of the services of many who have constantly carried on factional activities," Helstein wrote recently retired Joe Ollman. However, mindful of the direction in which the rest of the labor movement was heading, packinghouse leaders made a number of significant concessions. Most important among these was the decision to downplay support for the Wallace campaign. Responding to CIO influence, they replaced a resolution declaring neutrality on the volatile third party issue with an unexceptional one affirming support for CIO policy. Seemingly trivial, this move, coupled with the collapse of a viable right-wing, helped the UPWA avoid the fate of the other left-wing union purged by the CIO the following year. Even here, the UPWA found a middle ground, declining to interfere with the pro-Wallace activities of local bodies.[84]

Later in the year, CIO pressure prompted other concessions to the winds of anticommunism swirling through the labor movement. Some of these were minor, as when Helstein responded to Alan Haywood's urging and publicly refuted legitimate claims made in the *Daily Worker* that the CIO had maneuvered to swing support behind the opposition slate at the June convention. Other concessions were of a graver and more ominous nature. Furious with the way in which Herb March continued to dominate district affairs from his post as field representative, dissidents in the Swift local sought the assistance of CIO officials. Again responding to CIO pressure, the UPWA fired March in January 1949. A. T. Stephens, once a close colleague of March's, apologetically told him, "Herb, you're too heavy for us to carry." Undaunted, March continued his active involvement with the Chicago locals as an "organizer" on the payroll of Armour Local 347.[85]

By early 1949, the factional controversy inside the UPWA had died down, although it never extinguished entirely. The CIO Policy Caucus enjoyed a final hurrah with a convention in Cedar Rapids, Iowa, attended by more than fifty local officials, at which complaints about staff dismissals and Wallace support received an airing. The meeting produced an ill-advised dues-withholding movement which lasted only a few months and involved a mere handful of local unions. The Helstein administration easily isolated the rebels, and the movement collapsed when the International placed the Chicago Swift local under its direct control. While Local 28 remained a hotbed of anti-administration sentiment, the Policy Caucus was defunct. The final blow came at the union's 1949 convention when delegates, including some of the more outspoken western opposition leaders, voted not to seat representatives from the Chicago Swift local, effectively repudiating the movement.[86]

As they moved to put their house in order, UPWA leaders simultaneously confronted the more pressing task of rebuilding the union. The discharge of local leaders and stewards in the wake of the 1948 strike left the union's shop-floor organization in a weak and uncertain state. Especially alarming were reports and rumors of racial antagonism in many plants. Much of this friction stemmed from conflicts between the returning strikers and scabs who now enjoyed "super-seniority" and refused to relinquish jobs secured by crossing the picket lines. Although both races furnished strikebreakers in roughly equal numbers, white support for the union following the defeat was lower and more muted than that given by black workers. Commenting on this general pattern, one union official ominously observed, "historically, we are paralleling in some areas the 1921 situation with the races reversed."[87]

In response to this situation, the union bureaucracy moved to demonstrate positive activity to its demoralized rank and file. While working to secure reinstatements and to reach agreements with the packers, it stepped up its civil rights activities. Within weeks of the strike defeat, the executive board arranged for Fisk University's Race Relations Institute to conduct a series of "self-surveys" of racial attitudes and practices among packinghouse workers. Designed to involve the union's members and prevent the fragmentation of hard-earned interracial unity, the surveys also helped

keep workers' interest alive. Queried about the rationale behind this program, Helstein explained, "I felt there had to be something affirmative
going on outside of an area in which the companies could screw us. . . . [We]
started that program and our people suddenly had something that the
union was able to do."[88]

Directed by sociologist John Hope II, the surveys quantified the high
level of black activity in the UPWA and also identified the continued existence of discriminatory practices in the industry.[89] More important than
specific findings was the survey process itself, which not only involved
workers in union activity at a time when the UPWA was unable to operate
in its traditional manner but also served as a springboard for the development of a formal civil rights program. Starting in 1949, the UPWA began
systematically integrating anti-discrimination activities into its organizational and educational departments. The following year, its convention
established an Anti-Discrimination Department, run by black vice president
Russell Lasley. The "A-D" Department directed local unions to establish
anti-discrimination committees to oversee the elimination of discriminatory
practices in the plants and encouraged them to extend the struggle into the
communities. In this manner, what previously had been a general policy
now became a specific program operating at various levels of the union
apparatus.[90]

The impact of the new program varied greatly according to locale. In
areas where there had been little preexisting civil rights activity, it encouraged black workers to assert themselves and insist that contractual prohi-
bitions against discrimination be respected and that local unions eliminate
their own prejudicial practices. Even in areas where black workers were a
minority of the workforce, the backing they received from the International enabled them to exert disproportionate power.[91] By successfully mobi-
lizing black UPWA members, the new program served as a catalyst which
helped rehabilitate steward systems and local committee structures. Indeed,
during the recovery period, anti-discrimination programs provided the
"only vehicles through which stewards could be consistently active." Thus,
what originated as an accelerated civil rights campaign evolved into a
broad-ranging effort to strengthen and sustain local unions.[92]

In Chicago, the district which had always led the union in activism
around racial issues, the new anti-discrimination program buttressed preexisting local initiatives and pushed forward the union's civil rights activities. Compared to many other areas, the Chicago locals of the UPWA
emerged from the 1948 strike relatively unscathed. In a short time, they
repaired their in-plant organizations and began to register further gains

eliminating job barriers within the packinghouses. At the Wilson plant, for example, the local's A-D committee organized training classes so that black aspirants to traditionally white skilled positions could qualify for apprenticeships in the mechanical gangs. Elsewhere, local activists utilized the established grievance machinery and seniority provisions of the contract to chip away at racist practices. "Where the company wasn't pressed to implement the contract, they didn't bother," Todd Tate recalled. But when the union brought pressure to bear, the contract became a powerful empowering device.[93]

The most significant advance in this area was Local 28's victory over Swift and Company. Local union members policing the company's hiring office discovered and documented the practice of turning away black women while continuing to employ whites. The union filed a grievance under the no-discrimination provision of the contract, and while this moved through institutional channels, workers constantly pressured the company through a series of mass rallies and workplace action. Eventually, an arbitrator ruled in favor of the union and ordered Swift to employ the women named in the complaint with back pay. The victory had important repercussions, as the A-D Department successfully encouraged locals elsewhere to follow the Swift precedent.[94]

Armour workers succeeded in integrating the last remaining lily-white departments in the plant and then began pressuring the company to promote blacks into supervisory positions. Later, they pushed the civil rights struggle beyond the limits of the union contract when they extended the scope of the no-discrimination clause to employees not under the UPWA's formal jurisdiction. Coordinated by Herbert March in his capacity as an "organizer" for Local 347, the resources of the entire district were massed against Armour in an attempt to have the company employ blacks in clerical and sales capacities. Mass noontime rallies involving workers from all plants, letter-writing campaigns, and newspaper publicity drives brought pressure on the company's front office. When Armour stubbornly refused to modify its practices, the union characteristically raised the level of militancy with a series of two-hour stoppages. These actions, joined with threatened legal action based on an executive order prohibiting discrimination in firms with government contracts, led to Armour's capitulation. As with the Swift case, this victory spurred other locals into action. Within a year, the Wilson and Cudahy companies, as well as a number of smaller packers, began employing blacks in their front offices.[95]

Building upon the precedents established at the end of the war years, Chicago's packinghouse workers in the late 1940s and early 1950s pushed the civil rights struggle beyond the plants and into the larger community where it joined forces with other activist organizations. Especially notable was the UPWA's involvement in protests over racial violence during the city's Peoria Street Riot in 1949 and, later, during the Trumbull Park housing controversy. The first of these incidents occurred when a white mob surrounded a house at Fifty-sixth and Peoria Street, where an interracial union meeting was in session. Aaron Bindman, a member of the CIO's Longshoremen's union had invited shop stewards from his local to his home to meet a Hawaiian unionist and discuss the maritime strike there. Neighbors insisted that eight black stewards leave the area, and when Bindman refused this request two days of rioting began. Although one hundred policemen were on the scene, the crowd destroyed Bindman's house. Even though packinghouse workers were not involved, several lived in the general area and the UPWA quickly emerged in the forefront of a community-wide mobilization. Allying with the Chicago Urban League, now under the directorship of the progressive-minded Sidney Williams, the UPWA helped launch the Chicago Committee to End Mob Violence (CEMV), comprised of representatives from 125 civic organizations. The CEMV brought considerable pressure to bear upon Mayor Kennelly, who had flatly refused to make any statement about the disturbance, demanding that he ensure adequate police protection. A well-publicized move to research mayoral impeachment prompted Kennelly to issue a statement and resulted in a meeting with the commissioner of police. The committee also exposed the exploitative practices of banks and real estate companies that were provoking "white flight" from areas adjacent to the expanding black community. In addition, Chicago's press and media came under attack for its "hush-hush" policy and "conspiracy of silence" regarding the reporting of racial violence.[96]

Significantly, the Chicago Industrial Union Council, now controlled by conservative forces, declined to assist or even lend token financial support. Its president, Michael Mann, attacked the CEMV as a left-wing cabal, and attempted to pressure area unions to avoid cooperating with it. Russell Lasley, who served as the CEMV's vice president, reported to the UPWA executive board that "the regional office of the CIO has given us no help . . . they have attempted to do everything they could do to resist our efforts to organize the negro community." In the period that followed, the CEMV maintained a visible profile in Chicago and helped prevent later disturbances from escalating into full-scale race wars by ensuring publicity, police presence, and political pressure. Unfortunately, Sidney Williams's militancy and willingness to work with the UPWA placed him in a vulnerable position within the Urban League. Conservative opponents red-baited him and complained to national officials that his labor connections stigmatized the branch. Armour and Swift severed their financial ties with the league; and the Chicago Community Fund threatened to withdraw its support unless a retreat from activism was forthcoming. Williams soldiered on until the local branch was reorganized in 1954.[97]

A few years later, when a black family was attacked after moving into a federally subsidized housing project in Trumbull Park, the union again led protest actions aimed at gaining police protection for the besieged family. The union's mass picketing of City Hall was instrumental in forcing the Chicago Housing Authority to uphold the rights of African Americans to purchase homes in the Trumbull Park development. Through this kind of coordinated activity, the union mobilized thousands of packinghouse workers and, through the application of militant union tactics in the public sphere, decisively influenced city politics while pushing older, established black leadership institutions to adopt a more aggressive style.[98]

While UPWA officials inaugurated and sanctioned most of these activities, many union initiatives were launched independently of the International. In late 1948, for example, Sam Parks and other left-wing Chicago trade unionists seized control of the local NAACP branch. Employing stewards to enroll hundreds of packinghouse and automobile workers in the association, they succeeded in electing to office a slate headed by Parks and UAW militant Willoughby Abner. This campaign complemented the International's program of solidifying its contacts with the NAACP, but in its mass mobilization of workers went well beyond anything contemplated by the UPWA's officers.[99]

Chicago UPWA activists also campaigned against discrimination on the part of Black Belt businesses which refused to hire African Americans. Occasionally these skirmishes placed black militants in conflict with the union. When Sam Parks and three other packinghouse workers sat-in at Goldblatt's Ashland Avenue lunch counter in protest over the store's policy of allowing Mexicans and blacks to purchase merchandise but not food, the International and the Back-of-the-Yards Council attempted to persuade him to abandon the action. Parks refused. "Sam raised so much hell in that store I think the walls were vibrating," Charlie Hayes recalled with a mixture of pride and humor.[100]

Parks, in fact, was a center of controversy in this period. Fired by Wilson during the 1948 strike, he was one of a handful of workers whom the company refused to rehire. Using his chairmanship of the district's Anti-Discrimination Committee as a power base, he was a constant thorn in the side of more moderate International officers. Allying with the Illinois Civil Rights Congress, chaired by Communist William Patterson, and with the Negro Labor Council, Parks recruited packinghouse workers for a variety of actions. These included pressuring the Chicago White Sox to bring up players from the Negro leagues, picketing State Street banks and department stores over their refusal to employ black clerks, and protesting the whites-only admission policy of Woodlawn Hospital.[101]

These campaigns formed an important bridge between black industrial workers and the civil rights movement that was emerging in the city. Because of their independent nature and the racial rhetoric they employed, they caused concern and a certain degree of alarm among union leaders. This discomfort can be attributed to three related sources. First, the growing black insurgency in the Chicago UPWA posed a threat to white officials. As early as World War II, militant blacks had grumbled about the fact that whites continued to fill top local and district positions even though blacks held a majority of all elected posts. In the Armour plant, for instance, blacks attempted to oust Local 347 president Joe Bezenhoffer and expressed dissatisfaction with Herbert March's rule over the district. In the period after 1948, when black activists in the Chicago houses grew increasingly well organized and self-aware, they managed to secure additional staff appointments and successfully maneuvered to replace March's successor, Harold Nielsen, with black Wilson leader Charles Hayes.[102]

Moderate UPWA leaders also expressed unease over the way in which the union's aggressive racial militancy isolated them from the rest of the labor movement. Especially after the CIO's 1949 purge of left-wing unions, the UPWA's civil rights activities opened it to charges of fellow-traveling, if not outright Communist domination. In Chicago, where black packinghouse activists often worked closely with representatives from the outcast Farm Equipment and Electrical unions, attacks on the UPWA were endemic. When the Packinghouse Workers hosted a 1950 National Trade Union Conference for Human Rights, which involved representatives from the purged unions and several "front" organizations, the national CIO and the local Industrial Union Council condemned it and ordered affiliate organizations to boycott the proceedings. Even a social event like a UPWA-sponsored Paul Robeson concert called forth howls of protest.[103]

Finally, and most importantly, black insurgency in Chicago raised fears that the interracial solidarity that characterized the union from the onset of organizing in the 1930s was being replaced with fragmentary tendencies. This concern was a legitimate one. The rebuilding of the union around black workers after the 1948 strike exacted a cost of white participation.

Increased civil rights activity, especially the union's involvement in community-based struggles, clashed with the sensibilities of many white packinghouse workers.

Francis Connell, a mechanic at Swift, voiced the sentiments of many whites, stating "as far as discrimination is concerned, the union should do all it can *within* the plant. They should confine it to that. When they talk about discrimination outside, housing, etc., that has nothing to do with the union." A black steward from Connell's local tried to explain that the "union is trying to have as much democracy as possible. . . . For Negroes the union is the only protection we have," but white participation dropped precipitously. Even as staunch a unionist as Gertie Kamarczyk, at this point a thirty-five-year veteran of the industry, stopped attending union meetings. "It was too much of the colored's concern. I didn't really understand it all, and I didn't think they really wanted me there so I just didn't go after a while," she recalled. Coupled with the continued flight of whites out of the industry in the early 1950s, this alienation produced a situation in which local union offices, committees, and even steward systems were dominated by African Americans.[104]

Many, but by no means all, white workers who continued to play an active part in union affairs were either CP members or sympathetic to the Left. Joe Zabritski recalled that "black rights was something that the Party just hammered into you, so we didn't have any problem giving support to a fight for fair housing or for jobs. Besides, it made the union stronger." But even within the CP's packinghouse section, black insurgency had a divisive impact. In the early 1950s, some blacks in the Party struck at white leaders by employing charges of "white chauvinism." Herbert March fell victim to these tactics. From his position as an organizer within Armour Local 347, March continued to wield considerable power in the Chicago district. His adamant insistence on running interracial slates for district offices—a tradition dating back to the union's origins—angered black Party officials outside of packing who felt that African Americans should control the district machinery in its entirety. When March refused to respond to pressure, white chauvinism charges were made against him. Facing an internal trial that threatened to tear apart the Armour local, March opted to depart from the Party and the union. Beleaguered and forced to operate in an unhospitable cold war environment, the CP cannibalized itself. Further weakened by 1952 HUAC subpoenas, the Party ceased being an effective force for interracialism in the union after March's departure.[105]

The new racial balance within the Chicago UPWA received symbolic expression in 1949 when the district headquarters moved from Back-of-the-

Yards to a new location on Wabash Avenue, an area in the heart of a black neighborhood. This relocation undoubtedly contributed to the drop-off in white involvement in the union. Ford Bartlett, a Swift worker, explained "the reason I don't go is that all the meetings are at 48th and Wabash and its all colored there. They say its a bigger place there. But the niggers drink like fish. The neighborhood is too dangerous. I don't even like to *drive* through there." Mary Weidenmann, another white worker, echoed his concerns, "49th and Wabash—I'd never go there! I'd be scared."[106]

By the early 1950s, then, the Chicago UPWA had been transformed from an interracial alliance to an organization headed and directed by blacks. It enjoyed and benefited from white support in the plants, but this support was increasingly passive. Although the Chicago district was part of a larger organization still characterized by a formal biracialism and supporting white regional and International officials, its own features had changed markedly since its inception two decades earlier.

Of course shared workplace grievances and common concerns tempered this tendency toward racial polarization. The interests of white and black workers continued to converge around the material benefits afforded by union membership. Constantly improving contracts and a widening array of benefits allowed the UPWA to retain the allegiance of white packinghouse workers, even as it lost their active support. Only because the union "delivered the goods" was it able to embark upon its crusade for equal rights. Lowell Washington, who never fully shared the extreme racial militancy of many of his fellow black unionists, explained that very few white workers "were going to turn their back on a union that was providing them with the bread and butter." He added that, "it was funny, they might bellyache a whole lot about how things were being run, but right around contract time you could be sure that they'd be right up there asking about what all they was gonna get this time around." Black workers, by contrast, were not satisfied with "bread and butter." They had other pressing needs that were as much social as economic, and they readily turned their union into a vehicle for addressing these concerns.[107]

The Packinghouse Workers' mobilized black membership base enabled the union to recover from the 1948 strike and to resume a trajectory that was quite different from that followed by the mainstream of the labor movement. In the late 1940s and early 1950s, the union bent but did not yield to the forces of reaction which held sway throughout most of the United States. Anticommunism failed to take hold in the UPWA because its appeal had little resonance among black workers. In many instances, left-wing union leaders were able to blunt attacks made upon them and the union by appealing to black workers' sense of justice. "I was invited to a lynching," Armour Local 347 President Leon Beverly charged when summoned before HUAC. "The 'rope' was woven from lies and smears . . . and the mob was howling for blood," he explained to his constituents, who lent him their overwhelming support.[108] Although plant closings decimated the UPWA before the emergence of the southern-based, church-oriented civil rights movement in the late 1950s, the union contributed in significant ways toward the progress made by black people in Chicago. As an institution, it fulfilled the aspirations of a generation of packinghouse workers, both black and white, and brought a measure of democracy to a previously autocratic sector of industrial society. More than just an unlikely tale of bold progressivism, though, the history of the United Packinghouse Workers suggests that an alternative existed to the degeneration and decline of the U.S. labor movement in the postwar period.

Epilogue

In the late 1950s, the structure of the American meatpacking industry was transformed. Due in large part to the rise of an integrated highway transportation system and the development of the refrigerated truck, slaughtering and packing operations shifted away from urban rail centers like Chicago and relocated closer to the point of livestock production in the rural hinterlands. The rapid expansion of grocery chain stores with their own warehouse and supply systems further weakened the old-line packing companies. Simultaneously, the industry became more competitive. The growth of independent meatpackers in the Midwest and parts of the South undermined the dominant position of the Big Four packers. These giants responded to the challenge by embarking upon a comprehensive program of modernization and technological improvement, closing down their older, low-profit urban facilities and replacing them with a decentralized network of new, highly mechanized rural plants.[1]

These plant closings decimated the UPWA. Packinghouses in Chicago, Omaha, Sioux City, Kansas City, Fort Worth, and Oklahoma City closed and operations in the East were gradually phased out. Between 1956 and 1964, over thirty-eight thousand packinghouse workers lost their jobs as employment dropped by 22.3 percent. Restructuring hit black workers especially hard, as African Americans were concentrated in the urban centers slated for closure. The Chicago plant closings exacted a disproportionately heavy toll, depriving the union of its most dynamic black activist base and effectively undermining the most durable source of left-wing support.[2]

The UPWA was forced to grapple with the problems of deindustrialization twenty years before it became a widespread phenomenon, and it did so in an innovative manner. It won clauses in its contracts providing for severance pay, "technological adjustment" stipends, and prior notification of plant closings. In 1959 the union succeeded in convincing Armour to accept a retraining program and to agree to companywide seniority which allowed workers affected by closings to transfer to other Armour plants in accordance with their seniority rights. The same contract established a union-management committee, the Armour Automation Committee, to oversee these programs.[3]

While these pioneering innovations protected thousands of workers and softened the impact of economic dislocation for many others, they were an inadequate response to the large-scale changes occurring in the industry. Since the early 1940s, the UPWA had relied upon the strategy of using its solid base in the plants of the major packing companies to secure contracts which established wage patterns for the entire industry, organized or not. The plant closings destroyed this base. In the Armour chain, for instance, union membership fell from 21,410 in 1956 to 9,149 seven years later. Moreover, the company sabotaged the newly agreed upon security measures by maintaining that many of its new packinghouses were not replacement plants but entirely new facilities with functions independent of their old operations. Management at the new plants allowed grievances to accumulate and routinely laid off active unionists who had recently exercised their transfer rights. The much-vaunted retraining program produced disappointing results. Skills perfected during a career in meatpacking did not readily lend themselves to other vocations; new skills in refrigeration or small appliance repair rarely parlayed into steady jobs. "What you were doing was training people so they could be unemployed at a higher level of skill," Ralph Helstein commented.[4]

In 1963 the UPWA withdrew from the Automation Committee, declaring that it had degenerated into a "facade of humaneness and decency" concealing "a ruthless program of mass termination of employees of long service and cynical manipulation." Later that year, the union struck what remained of the Armour chain in an attempt to force the company to respect the transfer agreements and resolve grievances. After two weeks Armour conceded. This action was the UPWA's last concerted campaign. In 1968, despite considerable internal opposition, the union—a shell of its former self—merged with its archrival, the Amalgamated Meat Cutters and Butcher Workmen in an attempt to sustain industrial unionism in the packing industry. Although a number of UPWA officials assumed positions in the AMC's newly created Packinghouse Division, the style of the Meat Cutters remained unchanged. This was a bitter pill for many former UPWA members to swallow. Thomas Krasick, a forty-year veteran of the industry and a local union founder, expressed the sentiments of many workers when he complained of the AMC leadership, "no one could prove to me that they had gone out and fought sincerely for labor, organized labor or anything. Pork-choppers! Everyone got nice easy jobs with a big salary."[5]

Meanwhile the nonunion sector of the meatpacking continued to grow as the new companies marginalized the Big Four. In 1979, the Amalgamated merged with the Retail Clerks to form the United Food and Commercial Workers (UFCW), the AFL-CIO union which currently enjoys jurisdiction over the country's packinghouses. However, the UFCW's retail membership dominate the organization; at the time of the merger with the Meat Cutters, packinghouse workers accounted for less than 10 percent of the union. By the mid-1980s their overall proportion had shrunk further as an employer offensive effectively deunionized the bulk of the meat industry. Max Graham, a veteran Omaha packinghouse worker, was an active member of the three organizations. He explained their different characters by likening the UPWA to a shot of whiskey: "we was little but powerful. Then we joined the Amalgamated and we got like a mixed drink. Now it looks to me like we're a shot in a quart of Squirt."[6]

In Chicago, Wilson and Company led the exodus from the stockyards, phasing out its killing operations beginning in 1955 and shutting its facility entirely two years later. Armour followed in 1959, and Swift exited in the early 1960s. Today, the Chicago stockyards are an eerie open space filled with the crumbling remains of packing plants and home to packs of wild dogs. Weeds, rubbish, and enormous potholes litter the abandoned cityscape. The Back-of-the-Yards neighborhood has reverted to the slumlike conditions that characterized it prior to the coming of the CIO. Mexicans, Puerto Ricans, and Dominicans now constitute the area's major ethnic groups.

The accomplishments of the UPWA were not erased entirely with the closing of the yards and absorption by the Amalgamated. Thousands of former UPWA members never again were organizationally active, but out of their union experience carried with them a commitment to equality and racial justice that shaped their subsequent behavior and personal lives. Many packinghouse workers, schooled in the UPWA's confrontational style, went on to play activist roles in other unions. Others involved themselves in the civil rights struggles of the late 1950s and 1960s. In 1966, when Martin Luther King brought the freedom struggle to Chicago, the UPWA was a major participant in the Open Housing Movement and the Coordinating Council of Community Organizations. Yet the union's mass base was incontrovertibly eroded—involvement in this phase of the fight for civil rights was limited to International union officials such as Charles Hayes and Addie Wyatt and a few remaining activists still working in area replacement plants. Indeed, well before the mid-1960s, the UPWA's local anti-discrimination programs had ground to a halt as workers left the fading industry. "There was no one to carry them on," Todd Tate recalled.[7]

The history of Chicago's packinghouse workers in the twentieth century was, in many significant ways, out of step with the experience of workers in other industries, locales, and unions. After a long period of fragmentation, Chicago's packinghouse workers came together in the 1930s to form a powerful interracial alliance. The coalition that lay at the heart of this partnership was that forged between black activists and white leftists. Although the broader alliance weakened considerably in the postwar period, especially as white rank-and-file workers withdrew from active union affairs, the coalition at the center never ruptured.

Several factors explain this remarkable durability. Foremost among them is the historical concentration of black workers in the meatpacking industry. In the 1930s when pre-CIO organizing began in Chicago, blacks were not newcomers but seasoned industrial workers who shared workplace experiences and grievances with whites. The structural position of black butchers on the strategic killing floors provided them with additional leverage as a group and, at the same time, helped establish independent black leadership in advance of white-led union organization. Finally, the institutional expression of this alliance—the UPWA—succeeded in transmitting to successive generations of workers the traditions of shop-floor militancy and racial egalitarianism that marked the organizing era. The union's ability to secure contracts with the major packers and to raise its members' standards of living provided a solid "bread and butter" base upon which a crusading "social unionism" could be built.

Notes

Introduction

1. W. E. B. Du Bois, *The Souls of Black Folk* (1903; New York: Fawcett, 1961), 23.

2. Nell Irvin Painter, "The New Labor History and the Historical Moment," *International Review of Politics, Culture and Society* 2 (Spring 1989); David Roediger, "'Labor in White Skin': Race and Working-Class History," in *Reshaping the U.S. Left*, ed. Mike Davis and Michael Sprinker (London: Verso, 1987), 288–89; see also Roediger's "The Crisis in Labor History: Race, Gender and the Replotting of the Working Class Past in the United States" in *Toward the Abolition of Whiteness: Essays on Race, Politics, and Working Class History* (London: Verso, 1994). It must be noted that there are signs of change. In recent years, labor historians have been aggressively addressing many of these issues. Some of the more important recent book-length studies include Eric Arnesen, *Waterfront Workers of New Orleans: Race, Class, and Politics, 1863–1923* (New York: Oxford University Press, 1990); Joe William Trotter, Jr., *Coal, Class, and Color: Blacks in Southern West Virginia, 1915–32* (Urbana: University of Illinois Press, 1990); David R. Roediger, *The Wages of Whiteness: Race and the Making of American Working Class Consciousness* (London: Verso, 1991); Michael K. Honey, *Southern Labor and Black Civil Rights: Organizing Memphis Workers* (Urbana: University of Illinois Press, 1993); and Henry M. McKiven, Jr., *Iron and Steel: Class, Race, and Community in Birmingham, Alabama, 1875–1920* (Chapel Hill: University of North Carolina Press, 1995). In addition, several recent articles demonstrate the continuation of this trend. See, for instance, Bruce Nelson, "Class and Race in the Crescent City: The ILWU from San Francisco to New Orleans," in *The CIO's Left-Led Unions*, ed. Steven Rosswurm (New Brunswick: Rutgers University

Press, 1992); Eric Arnesen, "'Like Banquo's Ghost It Will Not Down': The Race Question and the American Railroad Brotherhoods, 1880–1920," *American Historical Review* 99 (Dec. 1994); Kevin Boyle, "'There Are No Sorrows That the Union Can't Heal': The Struggle for Racial Equality in the United Automobile Workers, 1940–1960," *Labor History* 36 (Winter 1995); and Daniel Letwin, "Interracial Unionism, Gender, and 'Social Equality' in the Alabama Coalfields, 1878–1908," *Journal of Southern History* 61 (Aug. 1995).

3. See, for example, Dennis Dickerson, *Out of the Crucible: Black Steelworkers in Western Pennsylvania, 1875–1980* (Albany: State University of New York Press, 1986); and the otherwise excellent study by Ronald Lewis, *Black Coal Miners in America: Race, Class, and Community Conflict* (Lexington: University Press of Kentucky, 1987). It should be noted that many of the best studies in African American history exemplify this same tendency; see Earl Lewis, *In Their Own Interests: Race, Class and Power in Twentieth-Century Norfolk, Virginia* (Berkeley: University of California Press, 1991).

4. John W. Cell, *The Highest Stage of White Supremacy: The Origins of Segregation in South Africa and the American South* (New York: Cambridge University Press, 1982), 17. For treatment of these theoretical issues, see Robert Miles, *Racism* (London: Routledge, 1989), esp. 41–90; and the articles by John Solomos ("Varieties of Marxist Conceptions of 'Race,' Class and the State: A Critical Analysis") and Harold Wolpe ("Class Concepts, Class Strength and Racism") in *Theories of Race and Ethnic Relations*, ed. John Rex and David Mason (Cambridge: Cambridge University Press, 1986). For extended discussion of the way in which U.S. labor historians have handled these problems, see my "Organized Labor, Black Workers and the Twentieth Century South: The Emerging Revision," *Social History* 19 (Oct. 1994).

5. For an overview of this project, its methodology, and its findings with regard to African Americans, see Rick Halpern and Roger Horowitz, *Meatpackers: An Oral History of Black Packinghouse Workers and Their Struggle for Racial and Economic Equality* (New York: Twayne, 1996); see also James Cavanaugh, "From the Bottom Up: Oral History and the United Packinghouse Workers of America," *International Journal of Oral History* 9 (Feb. 1988).

6. Interview with Joe Zabritski, 4 Dec. 1987, in author's possession.

Chapter 1: "Hog Butcher for the World"

1. Upton Sinclair, *The Jungle* (1906; reprint, New York: Signet, 1960), 40. See also Noelie Vialles, *Animal to Edible* (Cambridge: Cambridge University Press, 1994).

2. See, for instance, "A Visit to the States: The Metropolis of the Lakes," *Times* (London), 21, 24 Oct. 1887; G. W. S. Patterson, *The World's Fair and My Trip Round the World* (Auckland: H. Brett, 1894); and Rudyard Kipling, *From Sea to Sea: Letters of Travel* (New York: Doubleday, 1899).

3. Mary Yeager, *Competition and Regulation: The Development of Oligopoly in the Meat Packing Industry* (Greenwich, Conn.: JAI, 1981); Margaret Walsh, *The*

Rise of the Midwestern Meat Packing Industry (Lexington: University of Kentucky Press, 1982); Louise Carroll Wade, *Chicago's Pride: The Stockyards, Packingtown, and Environs in the Nineteenth Century* (Urbana: University of Illinois Press, 1987); and Jimmy Skaggs, *Prime Cut: Livestock Raising and Meatpacking in the United States 1607–1983* (College Station: Texas A&M University Press, 1986). With the exception of James Barrett's *Work and Community in the Jungle: Chicago's Packinghouse Workers, 1894–1922* (Urbana: University of Illinois Press, 1987), mass production has received only partial treatment; see Siegfried Giedion, *Mechanization Takes Command: A Contribution to Anonymous History* (New York: Oxford University Press, 1948); David Hounshell, *From the American System to Mass Production 1800–1932: The Development of Manufacturing Technology in the United States* (Baltimore: Johns Hopkins University Press, 1984); Alfred D. Chandler, *The Visible Hand: The Managerial Revolution in American Business* (Cambridge, Mass.: Harvard University Press, 1977); and William Cronon, *Nature's Metropolis: Chicago and the Great West* (New York: Norton, 1991).

4. Ford's inspiration owed a great deal to the precedent of Chicago's "disassembly lines." See Hounshell, *From the American System,* 241; and Ford's comments in *My Life and Work* (Garden City: Doubleday, 1922), 81.

5. Walsh, *Rise,* 15–37.

6. Skaggs, *Prime Cut,* 36–37. Percentage calculated from the data provided by Walsh on primary and secondary midwestern packing centers; see Walsh, *Rise,* 20–22. Wade, *Chicago's Pride,* 10; Yeager, *Competition and Regulation,* 12.

7. Wade, *Chicago's Pride,* 8; Skaggs, *Prime Cut,* 36–37.

8. Yeager, *Competition and Regulation,* 9; Rudolph Clemen, *The American Livestock and Meat Industry* (New York: Ronald Press, 1923), 121.

9. Walsh, *Rise,* 36. For fuller discussion of the pre-industrial labor process in meatpacking, see Eric Brian Halpern, "'Black and White Unite and Fight': Race and Labor in Meatpacking, 1904–1948" (Ph.D. dissertation, University of Pennsylvania, 1989), 10–29.

10. Wade, *Chicago's Pride,* 11–13, 25–28, 32–33; Walsh, *Rise,* 20–21, 59–60. For general growth of a midwestern transport system with Chicago at its hub, see Cronon, *Nature's Metropolis,* 63–81.

11. Wade, *Chicago's Pride,* 47–55; Yeager, *Competition and Regulation,* 14. For intra-urban transport see Clemen, *American Livestock and Meat Industry,* 85–86. For varying accounts of the yards complex see Thomas Jablonsky, *Pride in the Jungle: Community and Everyday Life in Back of the Yards Chicago* (Baltimore: Johns Hopkins University Press, 1993), 1–11; Skaggs, *Prime Cut,* 46; and Paul G. Smith, "The Chicago Union Stockyards and the Packing Industry," 12–14, in U.S. Works Projects Administration, Federal Writers Project, box A784, Library of Congress, Washington, D.C.

12. Wade, *Chicago's Pride,* 61–62, 144, 154–57.

13. Robert Slayton, *Back of the Yards: The Making of a Local Democracy* (Chicago: University of Chicago Press, 1986), 21; Wade, *Chicago's Pride,* 66.

14. Slayton, *Back of the Yards,* 21–22; *Historic City: The Settlement of Chicago* (Chicago: Department of Development and Planning, 1976), 10, 45–50. See also

"The Foreign Born: Immigrants in the Packing Industry," in Mary McDowell Papers, box 2, folder 12, Chicago Historical Society, Chicago, Ill.

15. Wade, *Chicago's Pride*, 34, 100, 202; Walsh, *Rise*, 81.

16. Arthur Cushman, "The Packing Plant and Its Equipment," in *American Meat Institute, The Packing Industry* (Chicago: University of Chicago Press, 1924), 107–14. Wade, *Chicago's Pride*, 62–63, 101–2; Gore Marshall, *Through America: Nine Months in the United States* (London, 1882), 91.

17. Wade, *Chicago's Pride*, 227.

18. Giedion, *Mechanization Takes Command*, 93–94, 238–39; for beef-killing operations, see Cushman, "Packing Plant and Its Equipment," 122.

19. Clemen, *American Livestock and Meat Industry*, 215; Wade, *Chicago's Pride*, 64.

20. Mary Yeager Kujovich, "The Refrigerator Car and the Growth of the American Dressed Beef Industry," *Business History Review* 44 (Winter 1970), 460–82. See also Cronon, *Nature's Metropolis*, 233–38; Chandler, *Visible Hand*, 299–300; and Wade, *Chicago's Pride*, 58–63.

21. Ibid. *Tribune*, Nov. 19, 1881; see Wade, *Chicago's Pride*, 107.

22. Chandler, *Visible Hand*, 301; Skaggs, *Prime Cut*, 97–98; Yeager, *Competition and Regulation*, 72. Swift and Armour were the largest of these firms, with Morris and Hammond trailing behind. In the early 1890s, a fifth firm, Schwarzchild and Sulzberger completed a comparable integrated national enterprise and joined the oligopoly (Yeager, 112).

23. Yeager, *Competition and Regulation*, 112–13; David Brody, *The Butcher Workmen: A Study of Unionization* (Cambridge, Mass.: Harvard University Press, 1964), 3.

24. For utilization of byproducts and the establishment of research departments see Harper Leech and John C. Carroll, *Armour and His Times* (New York: Appleton-Century, 1938), 8–9; William Richardson, "Science in the Packing Industry," in *American Meat Institute, The Packing Industry*, 257; and Clemen, *American Livestock and Meat Industry*, chap. 16. Brody, *Butcher Workmen*, 3.

25. Wade, *Chicago's Pride*, 100–104; Armour and Co., *Souvenir* (Chicago, 1893), quoted in Barrett, *Work and Community*, 18.

26. Yeager, *Competition and Regulation*, 114–28. Skaggs, *Prime Cut*, 99; "Meat for the Multitudes," vol. 1 (special issue of the *National Provisioner*, 4 July 1981), 66; Gabriel Kolko, *The Triumph of Conservatism* (New York: Free Press, 1963), 51–53.

27. Barrett, *Work and Community*, 16–17; Federal Trade Commission, *Summary of Report on the Meat Packing Industry* (Washington: GPO, 1919), 16–18; Charles Edward Russell, *The Greatest Trust in the World* (New York: Ridgeway-Thayer, 1905), 5.

28. Barrett, *Work and Community*, 16–17; Yeager, *Competition and Regulation*, 151; Chandler, *Visible Hand*, 400–401; Federal Trade Commission, *Summary of Report*, 40–42, 121–29, 142–44.

29. Alma Herbst, *The Negro in the Slaughtering and Meat-Packing Industry in Chicago* (New York: Houghton Mifflin, 1932), 151. Wade, *Chicago's Pride*, 220.

30. Wade, *Chicago's Pride*, 200, 220.

31. Dominic Pacyga, "Villages of Packinghouses and Steel Mills: The Polish Workers on Chicago's South Side, 1880–1921" (Ph.D. dissertation, University of Illinois–Chicago Circle, 1981), 59, 62; Edith Abbott and Sophonisba Breckinridge, "Women in Industry: The Chicago Stockyards," *Journal of Political Economy* 19 (Oct. 1911), 632–54. For child labor in the yards see also Ernest L. Talbert, *Opportunities in School and Industry for Children of the Stockyards District* (Chicago: University of Chicago Press, 1912), 14–15, 32–33.

32. For persistence of competition see Kolko, *Triumph of Conservatism*, 51–53; and Lewis Corey, *Meat and Man: A Study of Monopoly, Unionism, and Food Policy* (New York: Viking, 1950).

33. Barrett, *Work and Community*, 25; John R. Commons, "Labor Conditions in Meat Packing and the Recent Strike," *Quarterly Journal of Economics* 19 (Nov. 1904), 3–4. Paul Aldrich, ed., *The Packers' Encyclopedia* (Chicago, 1922), 20.

34. Interview with Karl and Helene Lundberg, 23 Oct. 1987, in author's possession.

35. Giedion, *Mechanization Takes Command*, 94, 228; see the graphic description of the hog-killing process in Sinclair, *Jungle*, 40–42.

36. Sinclair, *Jungle*, 42–44; see also Barrett, *Work and Community*, 24–25; Commons, "Labor Conditions," 4–5.

37. Brody, *Butcher Workmen*, 4; Cushman, "Packing Plant and Its Equipment," 126; A. M. Simons, *Packingtown* (Chicago, 1899), 24, quoted in Brody, 5.

38. Barrett, *Work and Community*, 27; A. M. Simons, "What Packingtown Is Striking Against," *Chicago Socialist*, 30 July 1904, 2.

39. *National Provisioner*, 28 Jan. 1905, quoted in Brody, *Butcher Workmen*, 4.

40. *National Provisioner*, 12 Dec. 1908, quoted in Barrett, *Work and Community*, 26–27. *National Provisioner* 17 Oct. 1908, quoted in Brody, *Butcher Workmen*, 4–5. Swift superintendent quoted in Brody, *Butcher Workmen*, 5.

41. Vernon W. Ruttan, "Technological Progress in the Meat Packing Industry," USDA Marketing Research Report no. 59 (Washington: GPO, 1954), 2–3. U.S. Department of Labor, "The Employment of Women in Slaughtering and Meat Packing," Women's Bureau, Bulletin no. 88 (Washington: GPO, 1932), 30–31. Interview with Gertie Kamarczyk, 7 Dec. 1987, in author's possession.

42. *Monthly Labor Review* 33 (Nov. 1936), 31.

43. Pacyga, "Villages," 8–10; Slayton, *Back of the Yards*, 21–26.

44. Slayton, *Back of the Yards*, 25.

45. Interview with Gertie Kamarczyk, 5 Dec. 1987, in author's possession; Slayton, *Back of the Yards*, 112; Jablonsky, *Pride in the Jungle*, 32–40.

46. U.S. Immigration Commission, *Reports*, vol. 13: *Immigrants in Industry: Slaughtering and Meatpacking* (Washington: GPO, 1911).

47. A. M. Simons, "The Packingtown Strike," *Chicago Socialist*, 6 Aug. 1904; interview with Tommy Megan, 27 Apr. 1988, in author's possession.

48. Herbst, *Negro*, 17–20; Halpern, "Black and White," 105–10.

49. See Richard Edwards, *Contested Terrain: The Transformation of the Workplace in the Twentieth Century* (New York: Basic Books, 1979), chap. 9; David M. Gordon, Richard Edwards, and Michael Reich, *Segmented Work, Divided Work-*

ers: The Historical Transformation of Labor in the United States (New York: Cambridge University Press, 1982), chaps. 1 and 5.

50. John R. Commons, "Introduction" in Elizabeth Brandeis and Don D. Lescohier, *History of Labor in the United States 1896–1932,* vol. 3 (New York: Macmillan, 1935), 35.

51. Leech and Carroll, *Armour and His Times,* 232.

52. Pacyga, "Villages," 8–10; "Foreign Born: Immigrants in the Packing Industry."

53. Barrett, *Work and Community,* 40.

54. Slayton, *Back of the Yards,* 88. Wage rates reported in Commons, "Labor Conditions,"3–5. For a summary of jobs in the cattle-killing department, see U.S. Department of Labor, "Wages and Hours of Labor in the Slaughtering and Meat-Packing Industry, 1927," Bureau of Labor Statistics, Bulletin no. 472 (Washington: GPO, 1929), 131–36.

55. Commons, "Labor Conditions," 4–5; for description of hog kill jobs see U.S. Department of Labor, "Wages and Hours, 1927," 136–38.

56. In addition to the 1929 study cited above, see U.S. Department of Labor, "Wages and Hours of Labor in the Slaughtering and Meat-packing Industry, 1931," *Monthly Labor Review* 34 (June 1932), 1405–7, for comparative wage rates.

57. C. W. Thompson, "Labor in the Packing Industry," *Journal of Political Economy* 15 (Feb. 1906), 91–92; interview with Stephan Janko, 15 Mar. 1988, in author's possession.

58. Wade, *Chicago's Pride,* 228–29; Samuel Naylor, "The History of Labor Organization in the Slaughtering and Meat Packing Industry" (M.A. thesis, University of Chicago, 1935), 80.

59. Brody, *Butcher Workmen,* 61.

60. Ibid.; interview with Stephan Janko, 15 Mar. 1988, in author's possession.

61. For tasks and wage brackets see "Rate List Index," United Packinghouse Workers of America Papers, 1973 additions, box M-73-282, folder 36, State Historical Society of Wisconsin, Madison (hereafter cited as UPWA Papers). Slayton, *Back of the Yards,* 88.

62. For Polish immigration see John M. Bukowczyk, *And My Children Did Not Know Me: A History of Polish-Americans* (Bloomington: University of Indiana Press, 1987); for immigrant waves see Barrett, *Work and Community,* 45; Pacyga, "Villages," 27–28; and Slayton, *Back of the Yards,* 18–19, 22–23.

63. Interview with Stephan Janko, 15 Mar. 1988, in author's possession.

64. Barrett, *Work and Community,* 44.

65. Interview with Gertie Kamarczyk, 7 Dec. 1987.

66. Ostrowski quoted in Slayton, *Back of the Yards,* 90; interview with Pat Balskus, 18 Nov. 1987, in author's possession.

67. Barrett, *Work and Community,* 28–29.

68. Interview with Pat Balskus; for the household economy see Barrett, *Work and Community,* 91–91, 95–101.

69. See Barrett, *Work and Community,* 30; and his "Work and Community

in 'The Jungle': Chicago's Packinghouse Workers, 1894–1922" (Ph.D. dissertation, University of Pittsburgh, 1981), 62.

70. Grace Abbott, "The Chicago Employment Agency and the Immigrant Worker," *American Journal of Sociology* 14 (1908); see also Barrett, *Work and Community*, 92–93.

71. Interview with Joseph Zabritski, 26 July 1987, in author's possession; Arthur Kampfert, "History of Meatpacking, Slaughtering, and Unionism," unpublished manuscript, State Historical Society of Wisconsin, vol. 2, 93; Antanas Kaztauskis, "From Lithuania to the Chicago Stockyards," *Independent* 57 (4 Aug. 1904); U.S. Commission on Industrial Relations, Final Report and Testimony, Senate Doc. no. 415, 64th Cong., 1st sess. (Washington: GPO, 1916), 3463–64.

72. Quotation from U.S. Commission on Industrial Relations, Final Report and Testimony, 3513–14.

73. Interview with Stephan Janko, 15 Mar. 1988, in author's possession.

74. Herbst, *Negro*, 3–19.

75. Ibid., 16–17; Horace Cayton and George Mitchell, *Black Workers and the New Unions* (Chapel Hill: University of North Carolina Press, 1939), 228.

76. Henry Pelling, *American Labor* (Chicago: University of Chicago Press, 1968), 63–66, 71.

77. Herbst, *Negro*, 17–19; Cayton and Mitchell, *Black Workers*, 228–29; Barrett, *Work and Community*, 127–31.

78. Herbst, *Negro*, 17–19; Barrett, *Work and Community*, 128–31.

79. Brody, *Butcher Workmen*, 15–16; Barrett, *Work and Community*, 126–27.

80. See Brody, *Butcher Workmen*, 25–33, for the origins and early history of the Amalgamated.

81. Ibid., 34, 38–39; Barrett, *Work and Community*, 132–33.

82. Brody, *Butcher Workmen*, 40–41; see Barrett's discussion of "Americanization from the bottom up" in *Work and Community*, 138–47 and "Americanization from the Bottom Up: Immigration and the Remaking of the Working Class in the United States," *Journal of American History* 79 (Dec. 1992).

83. Brody, *Butcher Workmen*, 42; Barrett, *Work and Community*, 134–36.

84. See the discussion of the "segmented group" and the "nationalist enclave" in Slayton, *Back of the Yards*, chaps. 5 and 6. For interethnic rivalry see Victor Greene, *For God and Country: The Rise of Polish and Lithuanian Ethnic Consciousness in America, 1860–1910* (Madison: State Historical Society of Wisconsin, 1975).

85. For workings of the house committees, see Barrett, *Work and Community*, 155–60.

86. For strategic sites in the labor process, see the interviews with Philip Weightman, Herbert March, and Frank Wallace, United Packinghouse Workers of America Oral History Project, State Historical Society of Wisconsin, Madison (hereafter cited as UPWAOHP).

87. Brody, *Butcher Workmen*, 48–49; Barrett, *Work and Community*, 155, 161–63.

88. Commons, "Labor Conditions," 27; Barrett, *Work and Community*, 155–58; Brody, *Butcher Workmen*, 46–48.

89. Barrett, *Work and Community*, 160; Brody, *Butcher Workmen*, 56; *National Provisioner*, 28 Nov. 1903, 14, quoted in Brody, 48; Harry Rosenberg, "Labor—The Great Strike," in Mary McDowell Papers, box 3, folder 15.

90. Brody, *Butcher Workmen*, 50–51; quotation from "Meat for the Multitudes," vol. 1, 95.

91. *Chicago Tribune* 2 Aug. 1904, quoted in Barrett, *Work and Community*, 165; *National Provisioner*, quoted in "Meat for the Multitudes," vol. 1, 95.

92. Brody, *Butcher Workmen*, 51–58; Barrett, *Work and Community*, 165–82.

93. Brody, *Butcher Workmen*, 55–58; Barrett, *Work and Community*, 179–80.

94. Eric Hardy, "The Relation of the Negro to Trade Unionism" (M.A. thesis, University of Chicago, 1911), 35. Rosenberg, "Labor—The Great Strike," 7. Black workers and the 1904 strike are discussed in William Tuttle, Jr., *Race Riot: Chicago in the Red Summer of 1919* (New York: Atheneum, 1970; reprint, Urbana: University of Illinois Press, 1996), 117–19; and Herbst, *Negro*, 23–27.

95. Sterling Spero and Abram Harris, *The Black Worker: The Negro and the Labor Movement* (New York: Columbia University Press, 1931), 266; Herbst, *Negro*, 22, 24, 27; William Tuttle, "Some Strikebreakers' Observations of Industrial Warfare," *Labor History* 2 (Spring 1966), 193. Quotation from the *Chicago Daily Tribune*, 24 Aug. 1904, quoted in Herbst, *Negro*, 26.

96. Brody, *Butcher Workmen*, 58; Barrett, *Work and Community*, 180.

97. Barrett, *Work and Community*, 168–79.

98. Slayton, *Back of the Yards*, 93; Brody, *Butcher Workmen*, 57–58; Barrett, *Work and Community*, 179.

99. Cayton and Mitchell, *Black Workers*, 230, quotation 241. Estelle Hill Scott, *Occupational Changes among Negroes in Chicago*, report of project 665–54–3–336, U.S. Works Projects Administration, District 3, 1939 (Chicago: WPA, 1939), 78.

100. Tuttle, *Race Riot*, 119. Tillman quoted in Alan H. Spear, *Black Chicago: The Making of a Negro Ghetto, 1890–1920* (Chicago: University of Chicago Press, 1967), 39. For discussion of the 1905 Teamsters strike see Spear, 39–40; and Tuttle, 120–23.

101. John Roach, "Packingtown Conditions," *American Federationist* 13 (Aug. 1906), 534; White statement from *Crisis* 18 (Oct. 1919), 294–95, quoted in Brody, *Butcher Workmen*, 86.

102. Herbst, *Negro*, 19–20; Leech and Carroll, *Armour and His Times*, 219.

103. Interview with Tommy Megan, 27 Apr. 1988, notes in author's possession. Information on taverns drawn from an interview with Robert Ford conducted by James Barrett in the late 1970s and lent to the author.

104. For the emergence of the physical ghetto, see Spear, *Black Chicago*, 11–27. Interview with Gertie Kamarczyk, 5 Dec. 1987.

105. Brody, *Butcher Workmen*, 60; Barrett, "Work and Community," 289.

106. Brody, *Butcher Workmen*, 60–61; *AMC Journal*, Jan. 1905, quoted in Brody, 60.

107. Brody, *Butcher Workmen*, 61; Barrett, *Work and Community*, 180.

108. Brody, *Butcher Workmen*, 72–74.

109. Barrett, *Work and Community*, 180; "Evils of Low Wages in the Stock Yards," *Baltimore Trades-Unionist*, 15 May 1915.

110. For the drive system see Sanford M. Jacoby, *Employing Bureaucracy: Managers, Unions, and the Transformation of Work in American Industry, 1900–1945* (New York: Columbia University Press, 1985), 20–23, 190, 218–19.

111. Ernest Poole, "The Beef Strike," *Independent*, 28 July 1904, 2904, quoted in Barrett, "Work and Community," 59.

112. Kampfert, "History of Meatpacking," vol. 2, 95–96.

113. Barrett, *Work and Community*, 70; Slayton, *Back of the Yards*, 91.

114. Slayton, *Back of the Yards*, 92.

115. Interview with Tommy Megan, 27 Apr. 1988, notes in author's possession; interview with John Wrublewski, 16 Mar. 1988, in author's possession.

116. William Z. Foster, *Pages from a Worker's Life* (New York: International Publishers, 1939), 153.

Chapter 2: The Stockyards Labor Council

1. U.S. Department of the Census, *Historical Statistics of the United States* (Washington: GPO, 1975), 119.

2. Barrett, "Work and Community," 298.

3. "Meat for the Multitudes," vol. 1, 138, 147.

4. Spear, *Black Chicago*, 132, 140; James R. Grossman, *Land of Hope: Chicago, Black Southerners, and the Great Migration* (Chicago: University of Chicago Press, 1989), 4, 71; Chicago Commission on Race Relations, *The Negro in Chicago* (Chicago· University of Chicago Press, 1921), 59–61.

5. Emmett J. Scott, "Letters of Negro Migrants of 1916–1918," *Journal of Negro History* 4 (Oct. 1919), 464, 457.

6. Quoted in Grossman, *Land of Hope*, 4.

7. On the contrast between northern and southern wages see, for example, David Montgomery, *The Fall of the House of Labor: The Workplace, the State, and American Labor Activism* (New York: Cambridge, 1987), 383–84; testimony of Joe Hodges, in Hearings of Judge Samuel Alschuler, 20–23 June 1919, Records of the Federal Mediation and Conciliation Service, National Archives Record Center, Suitland, Md., RG 280, 33/864 (hereafter cited as Alschuler).

8. "Meat for the Multitudes," vol. 1, 138, 147. Figures on wartime profits from *Pioneer* 37 (Jan. 1918), 65–66, quoted in Philip S. Foner and Reinhard Schultz, *Das Andere Amerika: Geschichte, Kunst, und Kultur der Amerikanischen Arbeiterbewegung* (Berlin: Elefanten Press, 1983), 224.

9. Herbst, *Negro*, 151; Spero and Harris, *Black Worker*, 151; George Haynes, *The Negro at Work during the World War and Reconstruction* (Washington: U.S. Department of Labor, 1921), 52–56. For the claim that one out of two black men in Chicago had work experience in meatpacking, see Walter Fogel, *The Negro in the Meat Industry*, Racial Policies of American Industry, Report no. 12 (Philadelphia: Wharton School of Commerce and Finance, 1970), 29; and David Montgomery, *Fall of the House of Labor*, 381.

10. "In the Stockyards District 1917," Mary McDowell Papers, box 3, folder 15; Brody, *Butcher Workmen*, 73.

11. Kampfert, "History of Meatpacking," vol. 2, 97–100.

12. Brody, *Butcher Workmen*, 73; *National Provisioner*, 14 Oct. 1917, 107, quoted in Brody.

13. William Z. Foster, *American Trade Unionism: Principles and Organization, Strategy and Tactics* (New York: International Publishers, 1947), 22; Edward Johanningsmeier, *Forging American Communism: The Life of William Z. Foster* (Princeton: Princeton University Press, 1994), 93–94. See also William Z. Foster, "How Life Has Been Brought into the Stockyards," *Life and Labor* 7 (Apr. 1918).

14. Johanningsmeier, *Forging*, 73–87, 94–95.

15. Foster, *American Trade Unionism*, 22.

16. David Montgomery, *Fall of the House of Labor*, 269.

17. Barrett, *Work and Community*, 191–92; Foster, *American Trade Unionism*, 20–21. For the career and trade union philosophy of Fitzpatrick see John Keiser, "John Fitzpatrick and Progressive Unionism" (Ph.D. dissertation, Northwestern University, 1965).

18. Johanningsmeier, *Forging*, 95; Brody, *Butcher Workmen*, 76; Barrett, *Work and Community*, 195.

19. Barrett, *Work and Community*, 195; Brody, *Butcher Workmen*, 76–78; Foster, *American Trade Unionism*, 25.

20. Herbst, *Negro*, 29.

21. Constitutions quoted in Herbert Hill, "Race and Ethnicity in Organized Labor: The Historical Sources of Resistance to Affirmative Action," *Journal of Intergroup Relations* 12 (Winter 1984), 22; Herbst, *Negro*, 31; Tuttle, *Race Riot*, 125.

22. Herbst, *Negro*, 32; Barrett, *Work and Community*, 194; Foster, *American Trade Unionism*, 22–23.

23. Herbst, *Negro*, 32–33.

24. For SLC efforts to include black workers see Earl Browder, "Some Experiences Organizing Negro Workers," *Communist* 9 (1930), 35–41. Foote is identified in Carl Sandburg, *The Chicago Race Riot: July 1919* (New York: Harcourt, Brace and Howe, 1919), 54. For response of northern blacks see Grossman, *Land of Hope*, 212–13; and Edna Louise Clark, "A History of the Controversy between Labor and Capital in the Slaughtering and Meat Packing Industries in Chicago" (M.A. thesis, University of Chicago, 1922), 106. Fitzpatrick quoted in Herbst, *Negro*, 36–37.

25. Goins quoted in Tuttle, *Race Riot*, 127; McDowell quoted in Spero and Harris, *Black Worker*, 130.

26. Chicago Commission on Race Relations, *Negro in Chicago*, 424. Interview with Lowell Washington, Jr., 28 Apr. 1988, in author's possession.

27. Grossman, *Land of Hope*, 230–31; Sandburg, *Chicago Race Riot*, 57; Barrett, *Work and Community*, 205, 213. On efforts to obtain church cooperation see Labor's Conference Committee, "Meetings Held with Ministers in an Attempt to Secure Their Cooperation in the Interest of Community Welfare," Aug. 1920, Fitzpatrick Papers, box 9, folder 64, Chicago Historical Society, Chicago, Ill.

28. Grossman, *Land of Hope*, 231–33; *Chicago Defender*, 6 July 1918, quoted in Tuttle, *Race Riot*, 153; Barrett, *Work and Community*, 205.

29. Grossman, *Land of Hope*, 231, 234–35.

30. Tuttle, *Race Riot*, 128–29.

31. For Swift see Clark, "History," 102; and Herbst, *Negro*, 33–44. Interview with Gertie Kamarczyk, 5 Dec. 1987, in author's possession. See also Kampfert, "History of Meatpacking," vol. 2, 105–6.

32. Foster, *American Trade Unionism*, 26; Brody, *Butcher Workmen*, 78–79; Johanningsmeier, *Forging*, 100.

33. Dennis Lane, "A Brief History of Organization in Chicago Stock Yards," *Butcher Workman* 5 (Nov. 1919); William Z. Foster, *From Bryan to Stalin* (New York: International Publishers, 1936), 90–93; see also Foster, *American Trade Unionism*, 25–27.

34. Brody, *Butcher Workmen*, 79–80.

35. Foster, *From Bryan to Stalin*, 97.

36. Foster, "How Life," 68; Brody, *Butcher Workmen*, 81–82; Barrett, *Work and Community*, 198–200.

37. Kampfert, "History of Meatpacking," vol. 2, 132; Brody, *Butcher Workmen*, 82; Barrett, *Work and Community*, 200. For full text of Alschuler's decision see Bureau of Labor Statistics, *Monthly Review* 6 (May 1918), 115–27.

38. Mary McDowell, "Easter Day after the Decision," *Survey* 40 (13 Apr. 1918), 38. Fitzpatrick quoted in Tuttle, *Race Riot*, 126–27.

39. Glatt quoted in Tuttle, *Race Riot*, 127; Brody, *Butcher Workmen*, 83; Foster quoted in Edward Johanningsmeier, "William Z. Foster: Labor Organizer and Communist" (Ph.D. dissertation, University of Pennsylvania, 1988), chap. 5.

40. Herbst, *Negro*, 39–40; Brody, *Butcher Workmen*, 84; Barrett, *Work and Community*, 200. "Arbitration of Demands of Employees Filed with the Administrator November 12, 1918," in UPWA Papers, box 1, folder 3.

41. Chicago Commission on Race Relations, *Negro in Chicago*, 428–29; Spero and Harris, *Black Worker*, 274; Barrett, *Work and Community*, 205. For interracial activity see Sandburg, *Chicago Race Riot*, 55; and Browder, "Some Experiences."

42. Barrett, *Work and Community*, 209; Grossman, *Land of Hope*, 220.

43. Testimony of Robert Bedford, Frank Custei, Walter Gorniak, in Alschuler; Gorniak quoted, 525.

44. Testimony of Robert Bedford and Gus Grabe, in Alschuler; Bedford quoted, 221.

45. For a theoretical discussion of the intermingling of racial and class consciousness, see Joe William Trotter, Jr., *Black Milwaukee: The Making of an Industrial Proletariat, 1915–1945* (Urbana: University of Illinois Press, 1984), xiv, 276–77; see also the parallel argument in Barrett, *Work and Community*, 208.

46. Trotter, *Black Milwaukee*, 277; Dave Roediger, "Movin' On Up to the Midwest's Promised Land," *In These Times*, 9–15 May 1990, 18.

47. For the league's early history see Arvah Strickland, *History of the Chicago Urban League* (Urbana: University of Illinois Press, 1966); a more critical

perspective is offered in Preston Smith, "The Chicago Urban League" (Ph.D. dissertation, University of Massachusetts–Amherst, 1988). Tuttle, *Race Riot*, 99; Grossman, *Land of Hope*, 202–3.

48. Grossman, *Land of Hope*, 203; Preston Smith, "Chicago Urban League," 26–31; Strickland, *History of the Chicago Urban League*, 48–49.

49. Grossman, *Land of Hope*, 238; Tuttle, *Race Riot*, 148; Barrett, *Work and Community*, 212. See also Evans's article, "The Negro in Chicago Industries," *Opportunity* 1 (Feb. 1923).

50. Grossman, *Land of Hope*, 228–29, 240; Tuttle, *Race Riot*, 101.

51. Grossman, *Land of Hope*, 201; Tuttle, *Race Riot*, 101; Kate J. Adams, *Humanizing a Great Industry* (Chicago: Armour, 1919), 21.

52. Barrett, *Work and Community*, 213; Grossman, *Land of Hope*, 201; Adams, *Humanizing a Great Industry*, 21; Spero and Harris, *Black Worker*, 268; testimony of Frank Custer and J. W. Johnstone, in Alschuler, 267–69, 277, 508–9, 545. See also George Arthur, "The Young Men's Christian Association Movement among Negroes," *Opportunity* 1 (Mar. 1923), 16–18.

53. Herbst, *Negro*, 35; advertisement quoted in Chicago Commission on Race Relations, *Negro in Chicago*, 423; Tuttle, *Race Riot*, 152; handbill quoted in Spero and Harris, *Black Worker*, 272.

54. Tuttle, *Race Riot*, 131–32.

55. Forrester Washington to John Fitzpatrick, 25 Jan. 1919, Fitzpatrick Papers, box 25, "Negroes" folder.

56. Testimony of Walter Gorniak, in Alschuler, 512; Tuttle, *Race Riot*, 23–30.

57. Herbst, *Negro*, 41; Brody, *Butcher Workmen*, 89–90; Barrett, *Work and Community*, 226; Foster, *American Trade Unionism*, 30. See also "Dennis Lane and the Kiss of Death," *CIO News* (Packinghouse Workers Edition [hereafter cited as *CIO News* (PE)]), 30 Oct. 1939.

58. Testimony of Jacob Wurmle and S. C. Caleb, in Alschuler, 6–21; Wilson information drawn from testimony of George Williams, in Alschuler, 39–51.

59. Testimony of John Maldek, in Alschuler, 75–79; testimony of Joseph Sobyro, in Alschuler, 110–11; testimony of Louis Michora, in Alschuler, 96–100.

60. Testimony of Robert Bedford, in Alschuler, 182–83; testimony of Frank Custer, in Alschuler, 230.

61. Testimony of Robert Bedford, in Alschuler, 150–52, 177; testimony of Frank Custer, in Alschuler, 261–63; see also testimony of Austin, "Heavy" Williams, in Alschuler, 426–54.

62. Testimony of William Bremmer, in Alschuler, 194; Barrett, *Work and Community*, 216; Tuttle, *Race Riot*, 154.

63. Herbst, *Negro*, 42.

64. All quotations from *New Majority*, 12 July 1919.

65. *New Majority*, 12 July 1919, 26 July 1919; Herbst, *Negro*, 43; Kampfert, "History of Meatpacking," vol. 2, 166.

66. The phrase is borrowed from Czeslaw Milosz, quoted in Todd Gitlin, *The Sixties: Years of Hope, Days of Rage* (New York: Bantam, 1987), 3.

67. Descriptions of the riot can be found in Tuttle, *Race Riot*, 4–10, 32–64; and Chicago Commission on Race Relations, *Negro in Chicago*, 1–52.

68. Chicago Commission on Race Relations, *Negro in Chicago*, 11; Barrett, *Work and Community*, 220.

69. Barrett, *Work and Community*, 222–23; Herbst, *Negro*, 46.

70. *Dziennik Zwiazkowy*, 29 July 1919, quoted in Pacyga, "Villages," 294; see also Pacyga, 293.

71. *New Majority*, 2 Aug. 1919; Herbst, *Negro*, 46–49; Cayton and Mitchell, *Black Workers*, 249.

72. Barrett, *Work and Community*, 223; Tuttle, *Race Riot*, 60–61.

73. *Narod Polski* quoted in Pacyga, "Villages," 299. Fitzpatrick quoted in Brody, *Butcher Workmen*, 87.

74. Herbst, *Negro*, 47; Spero and Harris, *Black Worker*, 277; Cayton and Mitchell, *Black Workers*, 248; *New Majority*, 9 Aug. 1919.

75. Brody, *Butcher Workmen*, 88; *New Majority*, 16 Aug. 1919; Fitzpatrick quoted in Spero and Harris, *Black Worker*, 277; Herbst, *Negro*, 47–48.

76. Herbst, *Negro*, 51–52; Grossman, *Land of Hope*, 224.

77. For the Amalgamated's position see Lane, "Brief History." Herbst, *Negro*, 43–44; Kampfert, "History of Meatpacking," vol. 2, 159, 166–67.

78. See the passages in Herbst and Kampfert cited above and Barrett, *Work and Community*, 224–27. Lane quoted in Brody, *Butcher Workmen*, 89; see also Lane, "Brief History." For AMC racial practices, see Cayton and Mitchell, *Black Workers*, 264–68.

79. Brody, *Butcher Workmen*, 90–91; Barrett, *Work and Community*, 228–29; *New Majority*, 24 Jan. 1920.

80. Barrett, *Work and Community*, 229–30; Kampfert, "History of Meatpacking," vol. 2, 208; Herbst, *Negro*, 56–57, 63.

81. The packers' offensive is detailed in Barrett, *Work and Community*, 240–54, quotation p. 245. For Armour's welfare capitalism see Adams, *Humanizing a Great Industry*; Swift's programs are treated in Arthur Carver, *Personnel and Labor Problems in the Packing Industry* (Chicago: University of Chicago, 1928). See also Clemen, *American Livestock and Meat Industry*, 723–35.

82. Brody, *Butcher Workmen*, 102–4; Lane quoted in *New York Times*, 6 Dec. 1921; Kampfert, "History of Meatpacking," vol. 2, 199.

83. Barrett, *Work and Community*, 258–60; Kampfert, "History of Meatpacking," vol. 2, 200–211; *New York Times*, 8 and 9 Dec. 1921.

84. *New York Times*, 29 Dec. 1921; Herbst, *Negro*, 63–65; Cayton and Mitchell, *Black Workers*, 255–56.

85. *Defender* quoted in Spero and Harris, *Black Worker*, 281; for the Urban League's recruitment of strikebreakers see Evans, "Negro in Chicago Industries"; and Strickland, "History of the Chicago Urban League," 73. Herbst, *Negro*, 64–65.

86. Brody, *Butcher Workmen*, 105; *New York Times*, 25 Dec. 1921, 1 Jan., 1 Feb. 1922.

Chapter 3: Chicago's Packinghouse Workers in the 1920s

1. Interview with Stephan Janko, 15 Mar. 1988, in author's possession.

2. Interviews with Gertie Kamarczyk, 5 and 7 Dec. 1987, in author's possession.

3. Interview with Philip Weightman, 7–8 Oct. 1986, UPWAOHP.

4. There is little consensus among historians on the question of working-class affluence and income in the 1920s. Many scholars argue that as a whole workers experienced real gains in income between 1922 and 1929. See, for instance, James R. Green, *The World of the Worker: Labor in Twentieth Century America* (New York: Hill and Wang, 1980), 111; and David Brody, *Workers in Industrial America: Essays on the Twentieth Century Struggle* (New York: Oxford University Press, 1980), 62. Works that argue against a genuine upward trend in workers' earnings include Irving Bernstein, *The Lean Years: A History of the American Worker, 1920–1933* (Boston: Houghton Mifflin, 1972); and Robert Ozanne, *Wages in Practice and Theory: McCormick and International Harvester* (Madison: University of Wisconsin Press, 1968). This latter view receives additional support from Frank Stricker, "Affluence for Whom?—Another Look at Prosperity and the Working Class in the 1920s," *Labor History* 24 (Winter 1983).

5. Kampfert, "History of Meatpacking," vol. 3, 3. For wage rates, see U.S. Department of Labor, "Employment of Women in Slaughtering and Meat Packing"; and U.S. Department of Labor, "Wages and Hours in the Slaughtering and Meat-Packing Industry, 1931." For increased seasonality see Lizabeth Cohen, *Making a New Deal: Industrial Workers in Chicago, 1919–1939* (New York: Cambridge University Press, 1990), 184–86. See also U.S. Department of Labor, "Employment of Women in Slaughtering and Meat Packing," 86–87, 102–3; and Herbst, *Negro*, 99.

6. Richard J. Oestreicher, *Solidarity and Fragmentation: Working People and Class Consciousness in Detroit, 1865–1900* (Urbana: University of Illinois Press, 1986), 67. For attempts to revive the SLC see "Organize All Stockyards Workers Is Aim," *Daily Worker*, 30 Apr. 1924; and the testimony of Arthur Kampfert in Official Report of Proceedings before the National Labor Relations Board, Case no. XIII-R-164, 460, 467, and 473, NLRB Administrative Division, Files and Dockets Section, Transcripts and Exhibits, RG 25, box 817, National Archives and Records Service, Suitland, Md. (hereafter cited as NLRB XIII-R-164).

7. The phrase is taken from Hy Lefkowitz to Rick Halpern, 4 July 1986, in UPWAOHP files, State Historical Society of Wisconsin, Madison.

8. Interview with Philip Weightman, 7–8 Oct. 1986, UPWAOHP. The button incident is also recounted in Kampfert, "History of Meatpacking," vol. 3.

9. Interview with Bruce Nolan, 2 July 1986, UPWAOHP. For similar reactions see the interviews with George and Frances Fletemeyer, 6 June 1986; William Nolan, 12 Feb. 1986; and John Condellone, 17 July 1986, all UPWAOHP. Theodore Purcell, *The Worker Speaks His Mind on Company and Union* (Cambridge, Mass.: Harvard University Press, 1953), 52.

10. Interview with Jane and Herbert March, 25 Nov. 1988; interview with Stephan Janko, 15 Mar. 1988, both in author's possession.

11. Interview with Jane and Herbert March, 25 Nov. 1988; for Armour's police force see also NLRB XIII-R-164, 2 and passim. For Wilson, Interview with Johnny Wrublewski, 16 Mar. 1988, in author's possession. Interview with Pat Balskus, 18 Nov. 1987, in author's possession.

12. For decline in employment see Estelle Hill Scott, *Occupational Changes,* 191–200, 221–41.

13. Horace R. Cayton and St. Clair Drake, *Black Metropolis: A Study of Negro Life in a Northern City* (1945; New York: Harper and Row, 1966), 8–9; and Otis D. Duncan and Beverly Duncan, *The Negro Population of Chicago* (Chicago: University of Chicago Press, 1957), 24, 34, 300.

14. Interview with Lowell Washington, Jr., 28 Apr. 1988, in author's possession. On college-educated blacks see the interview with Herbert March, 21 Oct. 1986, UPWAOHP.

15. Estelle Hill Scott, *Occupational Changes,* 198–200, 223.

16. Herbst, *Negro,* xxii, 77.

17. Interviews with Jesse Vaughn, 4 Oct. 1985 and 23 Oct. 1986, UPWAOHP; Elmer Thomas quoted in Ann Banks, *First-Person America* (New York: Vintage, 1980), 68; Crawford Love quoted in *District 1 Champion,* Feb. 1952 (copy in UPWA Papers, box 346, folder 7).

18. Interview with Tommy Megan, 27 Apr. 1988; interview with Johnny Wrublewski, 16 Mar. 1988, both in author's possession.

19. Hammond quoted in Banks, *First-Person,* 54. Herbst, *Negro,* 75–78.

20. Interview with Herbert March, 15 July 1985; interview with Richard Saunders, 13 Sept. 1985; interview with Milton Norman, 1 Oct. 1985, all UPWAOHP.

21. Mark Reisler, *By the Sweat of Their Brow: Mexican Immigrant Labor in the United States, 1900–1940* (Westport: Greenwood Press, 1976), 102–3; Louise Kerr, "The Chicano Experience in Chicago, 1920–1970" (Ph.D. dissertation, University of Illinois–Chicago Circle, 1976), 24–25; Frank X. Paz, "Mexican-Americans in Chicago—A General Survey" in UPWA Papers, box 342, folder 5.

22. Kerr, "Chicano Experience," 22, 25–26; Paul Taylor, *Mexican Labor in the United States: Chicago and the Calumet Region* (Berkeley: University of California Press, 1930), 87–88; Slayton, *Back of the Yards,* 179–80. Perez quoted in Banks, *First-Person,* 66.

23. Slayton, *Back of the Yards,* 180–82, quotation 182; Kerr, "Chicano Experience," 57; Paz, "Mexican-Americans in Chicago."

24. Slayton, *Back of the Yards,* 182–83, quotations 182; Reisler, *Sweat of Their Brow,* 106, 109–10, 141–42; Kerr, "Chicano Experience," 38; Florence Lyon Gaddis, "Conflict between Mexicans and Poles Living near Ashland Avenue and 45th Street," Ernest Burgess Papers, box 142, folder 3, University of Chicago Special Collections, Joseph Regenstein Library, Chicago, Ill.

25. Slayton, *Back of the Yards,* 181; Taylor, *Mexican Labor,* 93, 123.

26. Slayton, *Back of the Yards,* 183; Kerr, "Chicano Experience," 44–51; interview with Jane and Herbert March, 25 Nov. 1988, in author's possession.

27. For the collapse of boarding, see Barrett, *Work and Community*, 95–96, 101; Louise Montgomery, *The American Girl in the Chicago Stock Yards District* (Chicago: University of Chicago Press, 1918). Interview with Gertie Kamarczyk, 7 Dec. 1987.

28. Interviews with Estelle Zabritski and Mary Hammond in Banks, *First-Person*, 54–57.

29. U.S. Department of Labor, "Employment of Women in Slaughtering and Meat Packing," 18–29, 36–37.

30. Ibid., 14, 75–78, 81; Anna Novak quoted in Banks, *First-Person*, 64.

31. U.S. Department of Labor, "Employment of Women in Slaughtering and Meat Packing," 11–13, 96–99, 102; interview with Gertie Kamarczyk, 7 Dec. 1987. See also the interview with Betty Piontowski in Banks, *First-Person*, 59–60; and Cohen, *Making a New Deal*, 195–96.

32. See Stuart Brandes, *American Welfare Capitalism, 1880–1940* (Chicago: University of Chicago Press, 1976).

33. John Calder, *Capital's Duty to the Wage Earner: A Manual of Principles and Practice on Handling the Human Factors in Industry* (New York: Longmans, Green and Co., 1923), 165–72; Swift and Company Yearbook 1922, 50–51.

34. Swift and Company Yearbook 1923, 48–49; Swift and Company Yearbook 1924, 50–52; Swift and Company Yearbook 1925, 51.

35. The cases handled by company unions at Armour and Swift are analyzed in Barrett, *Work and Community*, 252–54.

36. Interview with Philip Weightman, 7–8 Oct. 1986, UPWAOHP. James R. Holcomb, "The Union Policies of Meat Packers, 1929–1943" (Ph.D. dissertation, University of Illinois, 1957), 28. Interview with Johnny Wrublewski, 16 Mar. 1988, in author's possession. See also testimony of Walter Piotrowski in Official Report of Proceedings before the National Labor Relations Board, Case no. XIII-C-1324, 148–49, 155–57, NLRB Administrative Division, Files and Dockets Section, Transcripts and Exhibits, RG 25, box 2471, National Archives and Records Service, Suitland, Md. (hereafter cited as NLRB XIII-C-1324).

37. Barrett, *Work and Community*, 250–51; testimony of Alphonso Malachi in Official Report of Proceedings before the National Labor Relations Board, Case nos. XIII-C-600 and XIII-R-584, 659–60, NLRB Administrative Division, Files and Dockets Section, Transcripts and Exhibits, RG 25, box 1141, National Archives and Records Service, Suitland, Md. (hereafter cited as NLRB XIII-C-600/XIII-R-584); interview with Kenneth Neidholt, 20 Mar. 1986, UPWAOHP. Final quotation from Calder, *Capital's Duty*, 308.

38. Interview with Milt Norman, 1 Oct. 1985, UPWAOHP; interview with Lowell Washington, Jr., 28 Apr. 1988, in author's possession; Cohen, *Making a New Deal*, 205–6; Holcomb, "Union Policies of Meat Packers," 30.

39. Swift and Company Yearbook, 1931, 55. Edna Louis Clark, "History," 196; NLRB XIII-C-600/XIII-R-584, 77; interview with Les Orear by Lizabeth Cohen, 27 July 1983, copy in author's possession; interview with Milt Norman, 1 Oct. 1985, UPWAOHP.

40. Phrases drawn from the following editorials: "The New Representation

in Industry," *New York Times*, 5 Dec. 1921; "Enter the Public," *New York Times*, 16 Dec. 1921.

41. Carver, *Personnel and Labor Problems*, 35–39; Calder, *Capital's Duty*, 116–22 and chap. 11; and interview with Kenneth Neidholt, 20 Mar. 1986, UPWAOHP. See also Cohen, *Making a New Deal*, 167–69.

42. Interview with William Nolan, 12 Feb. 1986, UPWAOHP; interview with Tommy Megan, 27 Apr. 1988, in author's possession; interview with Kenneth Neidholt, 20 Mar. 1986 and 17 May 1986, UPWAOHP; Neidholt to Rick Halpern, 15 July 1986, in UPWAOHP Project files; and interview with Don Blumenshine, 16 Apr. 1985, UPWAOHP.

43. See Carver, *Personnel and Labor Problems*, 35–39; and Adams, *Humanizing a Great Industry*, 8–9, for the claim that hiring was conducted systematically; interview with Herbert March, 21 Oct. 1986, UPWAOHP.

44. Interview with Tommy Megan, 27 Apr. 1988, in author's possession; interview with Jesse Vaughn, 4 Oct. 1985, UPWAOHP.

45. Interview with Milt Norman, 1 Oct. 1985; interview with Anna Novak in Banks, *First-Person*, 63.

46. Anna Novak quoted in Banks, *First-Person*, 63; interview with Gertie Kamarczyk, 5 Dec. 1987, in author's possession; see also the detailed account of harassment in the interview with Velma Otterman Schrader, 7 May 1986, UPWAOHP.

47. Each of these plans is explained in Carver, *Personnel and Labor Problems*, 124–30.

48. Herbst, *Negro*, 114–16; Purcell, *Worker Speaks*, 236–37.

49. Quotation from Cohen, *Making a New Deal*, 170.

50. Herbst, *Negro*, 118–19; U.S. Department of Labor, "Employment of Women in Slaughtering and Meat Packing," 68.

51. Jackson quoted in Purcell, *Worker Speaks*, 141; Voorhis quoted in Cohen, *Making a New Deal*, 192; U.S. Department of Labor, "Employment of Women in Slaughtering and Meat Packing," 71.

52. Interview with Marian Simmons, 21 and 25 Aug. 1986, UPWAOHP (and field notes from Simmons interview, in author's possession); interview with Philip Weightman, 7–8 Oct. 1986, UPWAOHP.

53. Vicky Starr (Stella Nowicki) quoted in Alice Lynd and Staughton Lynd, *Rank and File: Personal Histories of Working-Class Organizers* (Boston: Beacon Press, 1973), 79; interview with Vicky Starr, 4 Aug. 1986, UPWAOHP; Dalton quoted in U.S. Department of Labor, "Employment of Women in Slaughtering and Meat Packing."

54. Interview with Vicky Starr, 4 Aug. 1986, UPWAOHP; Lynd and Lynd, *Rank and File*, 79; interview with Stephan Janko, 15 Mar. 1988.

55. See Cohen, *Making a New Deal*, 192–96, for discussion of workers' pragmatic response to welfare benefits.

56. For injury rates relative to other industries, see Corey, *Meat and Man*, 248. Adams, *Humanizing a Great Industry*, 13–18; Calder, *Capital's Duty*, 136; Armour and Company Yearbook 1917, 31–32; Swift and Company Yearbook 1926, 53–55.

57. Interview with Jean Solter by Betty Burke, 20 June 1939, U.S. Works Projects Administration, Federal Writers Project, box A707, Library of Congress, Washington D.C. Floyd Bernard, "A Study of the Industrial Diseases of the Stockyards" (M.A. thesis, University of Chicago, 1910); see also Slayton, *Back of the Yards*, 91–92. Interview with Laura Rutkowski, 6 Dec. 1987, in author's possession.

58. Interview with Joe Zabritski, 22 Sept. 1987; interview with Tommy Megan, 27 Apr. 1988, both in author's possession. For blacks and baseball, see Grossman, *Land of Hope*, 201, 228.

59. This phenomenon is discussed in Brody, *Workers in Industrial America*, 71–76.

60. Cohen, *Making a New Deal*, 204–5.

61. Interview with Gertie Kamarczyk, 5 Dec. 1987; interview with Joe Zabritski, 4 Dec. 1987, both in author's possession.

Chapter 4: "Negro and White, Unite and Fight!"

1. *Chicago Defender*, 10 June 1939.

2. The phrase is Lizabeth Cohen's, who explains that this strategy involved meeting "workers on their ethnic, or racial, ground and pull[ing] them into a self-consciously common culture that transcended those distinctions, so as to avoid what happened in 1919 when workers remained politicized within isolated ethnic communities" (*Making a New Deal*, 339).

3. In this sense, the case of Chicago's packinghouse workers supports the interpretation advanced in Mike Davis, "The Barren Marriage of American Labour and the Democratic Party," *New Left Review* 124 (Nov.–Dec. 1980) and reprinted in his *Prisoners of the American Dream* (London: Verso, 1986).

4. Bernstein, *Lean Years*, 297; Harold Mayer and Richard C. Wade, *Chicago: Growth of a Metropolis* (Chicago: University of Chicago Press, 1969), 360.

5. Bernstein, *Lean Years*, 296–98; Cohen, *Making a New Deal*, 222–23; Arthur M. Schlesinger, Jr., *The Crisis of the Old Order, 1919–1933* (Boston: Houghton Mifflin, 1957), 250.

6. See Cohen, *Making a New Deal*, chap. 5, for the collapse of community institutions; Connelly quoted in Bernstein, *Lean Years*, 333.

7. *National Provisioner*, 15 Feb. and 19 Apr. 1930, 25 Mar. 1933; Willard F. Williams and Thomas T. Stout, *Economics of the Livestock-Meat Industry* (New York: Macmillan, 1964), 367; "Annual Employment and Payroll in Meatpacking and Slaughtering, 1929–1938," *Monthly Labor Review* (Mar. 1939).

8. "Annual Employment and Payroll in Meatpacking and Slaughtering, 1929–1938"; *National Provisioner*, 2 May and 15 Oct. 1931, 10 Dec. 1932; Dempsey J. Travis, *An Autobiography of Black Chicago* (Chicago: Urban Research Institute, 1981), 41. Statement of Patricia Lewis in "Conference Held September 25, 1934 with Representatives of the Stock Yards Labor Council Regarding Drawing Up a Code for the Meat Packing Industry," file 34, Labor Advisory Board of the National Recovery Administration, Region 9, box 6380, National Ar-

chives, Washington D.C. (hereafter cited as NRA); interview with Sophie Kosciolowski, 15 Jan. 1971, Oral History Project in Labor and Immigration History, Roosevelt University, Chicago, Ill. (hereafter cited as Roosevelt Project); interview with Sophie Kosciolowski, 1971, Illinois Labor History Society, Chicago, Ill. (hereafter cited as ILHS); interview with Tommy Megan, 27 Apr. 1988, in author's possession.

9. Slayton, *Back of the Yards*, 190. Interview with Jane March (Jacinta Grbac before her marriage to Herbert March), 25 Nov. 1988, in author's possession; interview with Johnny Wrublewski, 16 Mar. 1988, in author's possession; interview with Vicky Starr, 4 Aug. 1986, UPWAOHP.

10. Slayton, *Back of the Yards*, 191; interview with Sophie Kosciolowski, 1971, ILHS; interview with Philip Weightman, 7–8 Oct. 1986, UPWAOHP. For the inadequacy of private charity see Clorinne Brandenburg, "Chicago Relief and Services Statistics, 1928–1931" (M.A. thesis, University of Chicago, 1932).

11. For the unemployed movement see Daniel J. Leab, "'United We Eat': The Creation and Organization of the Unemployed Councils in 1930," *Labor History* 8 (Fall 1967); and Roy Rosenzweig, "Organizing the Unemployed: The Early Years of the Great Depression," *Radical America* 10 (July–Aug. 1976). For Chicago see Helen Seymour, "The Organized Unemployed" (M.A. thesis, University of Chicago, 1937); Steve Nelson, James Barrett, and Rob Ruck, *Steve Nelson: American Radical* (Pittsburgh: University of Pittsburgh Press, 1981), 70–87; and Harold Laswell and Dorothy Blumenstock, *World Revolutionary Propaganda* (New York: Knopf, 1939), 72–73. Interview with Jane and Herbert March, 25 Nov. 1988; interview with Pat Balskus, 18 Nov. 1987, both in author's possession.

12. Interview with Joe Zabritski, 4 Dec. 1987; interview with Pat Balskus, 18 Nov. 1987, both in author's possession. See also the 1970 interview with Katherine Hyndman, Roosevelt Project.

13. *New York Times*, 7 Mar. 1930; Christopher R. Reed, "A Study of Black Politics and Protest in Depression-Decade Chicago: 1930–1939" (Ph.D. dissertation, Kent State University, 1982), 136–38; Frances Piven and Richard Cloward, *Poor People's Movements: How They Succeed, Why They Fail* (New York: Pantheon, 1977), 59; *Chicago Defender*, 23 Apr. 1932.

14. Interview with Joe Zabritski, 4 Dec. 1987; interview with Jane and Herbert March, 25 Nov. 1988, both in author's possession. Cayton and Drake, *Black Metropolis*, 87.

15. Interview with Jane and Herbert March, 25 Nov. 1988; interview with Pat Balskus, 18 Nov. 1987, both in author's possession.

16. Steve Nelson, Barrett, and Ruck, *Steve Nelson*, 76. For elaboration on the "grievance approach" see Clarence Hathaway, "An Examination of Our Failure to Organize the Unemployed," *Communist* 9 (Sept. 1930); and Dorothy Healey and Maurice Isserman, *California Red: A Life in the American Communist Party* (Urbana: University of Illinois Press, 1993; published as *Dorothy Healey Remembers: A Life in the American Communist Party* by Oxford University Press, 1990), 31.

17. Interview with Jane and Hebert March, 25 Nov. 1988; interview with Vicky Starr, 4 Aug. 1986, UPWAOHP; interview with Vicky Starr, 12 Nov. 1987, in author's possession. For the University of Chicago Settlement House see Slayton, *Back of the Yards*, 173–87; and Kerr, "Chicano Experience," 52–53.

18. Interview with Pat Balskus, 18 Nov. 1987, in author's possession. Prior to 1933, four members of the Yards CP/YCL worked in the yards: Balskus, her husband Charles at P. D. Brennan, Joe Bezenhoffer at Armour, and Joe Zabritski at Reliable.

19. Interview with Vicky Starr, 4 Aug. 1986, UPWAOHP; interview with Jane and Herbert March, 25 Nov. 1988, in author's possession; interview with Starr (Nowicki) in Lynd and Lynd, *Rank and File*, 76.

20. Interview with Vicky Starr, 4 Aug. 1986, UPWAOHP. Interview with Vicky Starr, 1 Dec. 1987; interview with Joe Zabritski, 4 Dec. 1987; interview with Pat Balskus, 18 Nov. 1987; interview with Jane and Herbert March, 28 Nov. 1988, all in author's possession.

21. The Coughlinite presence Back-of-the-Yards is difficult to gauge. Evidence is vague and impressionistic. See, for example, the suggestive comments made by Saul Alinsky in Studs Terkel, *Hard Times: An Oral History of the Great Depression* (New York: Pantheon, 1970).

22. On the Binga bank collapse, see Cayton and Drake, *Black Metropolis*, 434–48, 466–67, 721–22; and Cohen, *Making a New Deal*, 231–32. Harold F. Gosnell, *Negro Politicians: The Rise of Negro Politics in Chicago* (1935; reprint, Chicago: University of Chicago Press, Phoenix Editions, 1967), 321; Christopher Reed, "Black Politics and Protest," 57, 73; Monroe N. Work, *Negro Year Book 1937–38* (Tuskeegee: Tuskeegee Institute, 1937), 21.

23. Urban League quoted in Cohen, *Making a New Deal*, 242; Fogel, *Negro in the Meat Industry*, 50–51; Thomas quoted in Banks, *First-Person*, 69; Kampfert, "History of Meatpacking," vol. 3, 6–8.

24. Christopher Reed, "Black Politics and Protest," 102–6, 113–14; Judith Stein, "Blacks and the Steel Workers Organizing Committee," paper delivered at the North American Labor History Conference, Oct. 1985, Detroit, Mich., 13–16.

25. Interview with Todd Tate, 1 Oct. 1985, UPWAOHP; Christopher Reed, "Black Politics and Protest," 49, 98, 115–19, 124–25, 300–302; *Chicago Defender*, 30 Dec. 1939. The *Defender* devoted increasing space to strong criticism of the association as the decade wore on; see, for example, "Is the NAACP Retreating?" *Defender*, 30 June 1934, and "Lawyer and Communist Debate Race Question," *Defender*, 8 Dec. 1934.

26. For Thompson see Gosnell, *Negro Politicians*, 37–62; and Edward R. Kantowicz, *Polish-American Politics in Chicago, 1888–1940* (Chicago: University of Chicago Press, 1975), 137–55. For shifting black voting behavior see Christopher Reed, "Black Politics and Protest," 62–65, 81–95, 194–95, 221–50. Quotation from Cayton and Drake, *Black Metropolis*, 88. For Dawson and the new Democratic machine, see William J. Grimshaw, *Bitter Fruit: Black Politics and the Chicago Machine, 1931–1991* (Chicago: University of Chicago Press, 1992), 74–

79; and Dianne Pinderhughes, *Race and Ethnicity in Chicago Politics* (Urbana: University of Illinois Press, 1987), 63–65.

27. See Gosnell, *Negro Politicians,* 322, 338–39; interview with Paul Rasmussen, 5 Sept. 1986, UPWAOHP.

28. Oliver Cox, "The Origins of Direct Action Protest among Negroes," microfiche copy, Kent State University Library, Kent, Ohio. Christopher Reed, "Black Politics and Protest," 146–57; Cayton and Drake, *Black Metropolis,* 84.

29. Christopher Reed, "Black Politics and Protest," 161; interview with Lowell Washington, Jr., 28 Apr. 1988, in author's possession.

30. Gosnell, *Negro Politicians,* 322–27, 350; *Daily Worker,* 29–31 Jan. 1924, 6–9 Feb. 1924, and 19 Apr. 1924; Christopher Reed, "Black Politics and Protest," 50–53.

31. For general treatment see Dan T. Carter, *Scottsboro: A Tragedy of the American South* (Baton Rouge: LSU Press, 1979); and James Goodman, *Stories of Scottsboro* (New York: Vintage, 1994). For Scottsboro and the black community see Mark Naison, *Communists in Harlem during the Depression* (Urbana: University of Illinois Press, 1983), 57–89. For Chicago, see Gosnell, *Negro Politicians,* 322; and Christopher Reed, "Black Politics and Protest," 135. Harry Haywood, *Black Bolshevik: An Autobiography of an Afro-American Communist* (Chicago: Liberator Press, 1978), 443–44.

32. *Chicago Bee,* 8 Feb. 1931; *Chicago Defender,* 14 Jan. 1933, 1 July 1933. See also Abbott's defense of the CP after the 1935 Harlem riots (*Defender,* 30 Apr. 1935) and his piece on Angelo Herndon (*Defender,* 10 Apr. 1937). For an example of the hysterical reaction of the white press, see the *Chicago Tribune,* 4 Aug. 1931.

33. Christopher Reed, "Black Politics and Protest," 134, 174–77; Gosnell, *Negro Politicians,* 329–31; *Chicago Whip,* 25 July 1931; Horace Cayton, "Black Bugs," *Nation,* 9 Sept. 1931; *Chicago Tribune,* 4 and 6 Aug. 1931; Haywood, *Black Bolshevik,* 443; Cayton and Drake, *Black Metropolis,* 87.

34. *Daily Worker,* 5–13 Aug. 1931; *Chicago Daily News,* 8 Aug. 1931; Christopher Reed, "Black Politics and Protest," 177, 182; Laswell and Blumenstock, *World Revolutionary Propaganda,* 203; Haywood, *Black Bolshevik,* 443; Cayton and Drake, *Black Metropolis,* 86.

35. Otis Hyde, untitled autobiography, in possession of Komozi Woodard, Department of History, University of Pennsylvania, Philadelphia, Pa. Interview with Lowell Washington, Jr., 28 Apr. 1988, in author's possession; Christopher Reed, "Black Politics and Protest," 134. Lizabeth Cohen notes that blacks were disproportionately represented in Chicago's unemployed movement, making up 21 percent of the leadership and 25 percent of the membership (*Making a New Deal,* 266).

36. Haywood, *Black Bolshevik,* 101, 115, 129; Cayton and Drake, *Black Metropolis,* 603; Hyde autobiography; Christopher Reed, "Black Politics and Protest," 133–34, 166. See also Roger A. Bruns, *The Damndest Radical: The Life and Times of Ben Reitmann* (Urbana: University of Illinois Press, 1987), 246–48; and Studs Terkel, *Talking to Myself: A Memoir of My Times* (London: Harap, 1986), 49–51. For DeLemos, see the *Chicago Tribune,* 6 Aug. 1931.

37. Christopher Reed, "Black Politics and Protest," 133–34, 166–68; Cayton and Drake, *Black Metropolis*, 85; Cox, "Origins of Direct Action Protest," 86–92; *Chicago Defender*, 20 Sept. 1931.

38. Interviews with Todd Tate, 1 and 2 Oct. 1985; interview with Richard Saunders, 13 Sept. 1985, all UPWAOHP. Interview with Richard Saunders by Herbert Hill, 1 Apr. 1967, transcript in author's possession.

39. Interview with Herbert March, 16 Nov. 1970, Roosevelt Project; interview with Karl and Helene Lundberg, 23 Oct. 1987; interview with Gertie Kamarczyk, 7 Dec. 1987; and interview with John Wrublewski, 16 Mar. 1988, all in author's possession.

40. Interview with Herbert March, 15 July 1985, UPWAOHP; Brody, *Butcher Workmen*, 153; *New York Times*, 6 Aug. 1933.

41. Kampfert, "History of Meatpacking," vol. 3, 22–23. "Stock Yards Labor Council (1)," 28 Mar. 1934; and "Stock Yards Labor Council (2)," 10 May 1934, both in Mary McDowell Papers, box 3, folder 15. For work relations in the small plants see the interview with Jesse Vaughn, 23 Oct. 1986, UPWAOHP.

42. Interviews with Herbert March, 15 July 1985 and 21 Oct. 1986, both UPWAOHP. For March's background and activities in Kansas City see Roger Horowitz, "The Path Not Taken: A Social History of Industrial Unionism in Meatpacking, 1930–1960" (Ph.D. dissertation, University of Wisconsin–Madison, 1990), 234–35. Horowitz's book, *"Negro and White, Unite and Fight!": A Social History of Industrial Unionism in Meatpacking, 1930–90*, is forthcoming from the University of Illinois Press.

43. H. A. Mills to Fitzpatrick, 20 June 1934, John Fitzpatrick Papers, box 18, folder 131; interviews with Herbert March, 15 July 1985 and 21 Oct. 1986; interview with Vicky Starr, 4 Aug. 1986, all UPWAOHP. Interviews with Joe Zabritski, 21 July and 22 Sept. 1987, both in author's possession; and interview with Starr in Lynd and Lynd, *Rank and File*, 72. Bill Gebert, "The Party in the Chicago Stockyards," *Party Organizer*, Apr. 1934.

44. Kampfert, "History of Meatpacking," vol. 3, 22ff.; Harvey Klehr, *The Heyday of American Communism: The Depression Decade* (New York: Basic Books, 1984), 11–14, discusses CP trade union policy during the so-called Third Period; Brody, *Butcher Workmen*, 153, quotation 160–61.

45. Interview with Tommy Megan, 27 Apr. 1988, in author's possession; quotation from Cayton and Drake, *Black Metropolis*, 315; Report on Conference with Representatives from SLC, 25 Sept. 1934, NRA, box 6380; Martin Murphy to John Shott, 17 Oct. 1934, NRA, box 6379; Report on Livestock Handlers Union Local 517, 5 Feb. 1934, Mary McDowell Papers, box 3, folder 15.

46. Kampfert, "History of Meatpacking," vol. 3, 29; *New York Times*, 27–29 Nov. 1933; Brody, *Butcher Workmen*, 153–57.

47. Interview with Herbert March, July 15, 1985, UPWAOHP; Kampfert, "History of Meatpacking," vol. 3, 27; for the PHWIU's strike in St. Paul, see *National Provisioner*, 18 and 25 Nov. 1933; "Lessons of the Packing Strike," *Party Organizer*, Jan. 1934; and *Packinghouse Workers Voice* (Jan. 1934), in Svend Godfredson Papers, State Historical Society of Wisconsin, Madison.

48. Interview with Stephan Janko, 15 Mar. 1988, in author's possession. For Hammond, see Kampfert, "History of Meatpacking," vol. 3, 24–27; testimony of Arthur Kampfert in NLRB XIII-R-164.

49. For Illinois Meat, see *National Provisioner,* 18 Nov. 1933. Material on Reliable drawn from Interviews with Joe Zabritski, 22 Sept. and 4 Dec. 1987, both in author's possession; interview with Herbert March, 21 Oct. 1986, UPWAOHP; and interview with Herbert and Jane March, 25 Nov. 1988, in author's possession.

50. Kampfert, "History of Meatpacking," vol. 3, 29–33; Report of Chicago Regional Labor Board, 2 Mar. 1934, NRA, box 6379; undated memorandum, "John G. Shott conversation with Martin Murphy," NRA, box 6380.

51. Interview with Lowell Washington, Jr., 28 Apr. 1988, in author's possession; interview with Jesse Vaughn, 4 Oct. 1985, UPWAOHP.

52. Race-baiting is discussed in Kampfert, "History of Meatpacking," vol. 3, 23. For revival of company unionism see Brody, *Butcher Workmen,* 155–56, quotation 155; see also Nicholas Handale to Hugh Johnson, 11 July 1933, NRA, box 6379. NLRB XIII-R-164 reveals privileges accorded company union delegates at Armour; and NLRB XIII-C-1324 details company union activity at Wilson. For the 1934 wage increase see *National Provisioner,* 29 Sept. 1934; and Holcomb, "Union Policies of Meat Packers," 49.

53. Report on Conference with Representatives from SLC, 25 Sept. 1934, NRA, box 6380; Martin Murphy to John Shott, 17 Oct. 1934, NRA, box 6379; office memorandum, John Shott, Labor Advisor, 23 Nov. 1934, NRA box 6380. Quotation in "Stock Yards Labor Council (1)."

54. George Carlson to Frank Ingalls, 30 Apr. 1934, NRA, box 6380; William W. Wood (Institute of American Meat Packers) to George Carlson, 7 Aug. 1934, NRA, box 6379; and "Memorandum—Code for the Meat Packing Industry" [John Shott], 17 July 1935, NRA, box 6379.

55. John Reilly to Franklin Roosevelt, Mar. 1935, NRA, box 6379; see also C. L. Cook to Franklin Roosevelt, 16 Oct. 1934, NRA, box 6379; "Memorandum—Code for the Meat Packing Industry" [John Shott], 17 July 1935, NRA, box 6379; Barbara W. Newell, *Chicago and the Labor Movement: Metropolitan Unionism in the 1930's* (Urbana: University of Illinois Press, 1961), 159.

56. Interview with Les Orear, 19 July 1983, in author's possession.

57. Interviews with Herbert March, 21 Oct. 1986 and 15 July 1985, UPWAOHP.

58. For discussion of early union activity in Kansas City and Sioux City, Iowa, see Horowitz, "Path Not Taken," chaps. 3 and 4.

59. Kampfert, "History of Meatpacking," vol. 3, 23ff.

60. Interview with Vicky Starr, 1 Dec. 1987, in author's possession.

61. W. White to H. W. Kerwin, 24 July 1934, Federal Mediation and Conciliation Service Case Files, RG 280, 170-9872, National Archives and Records Service, Suitland, Md.; *New York Times* 25 July 1934.

62. "Stockyards Labor Council (2)"; Kampfert, "History of Meatpacking," vol. 3, 23, 34–35; interview with Herbert March, 21 Oct. 1986, UPWAOHP; interview with Herbert and Jane March, 25 Nov. 1988, in author's possession.

63. "Stockyards Labor Council (2)"; *Packinghouse Worker*, 21 Nov. 1938; interview with Herbert and Jane March, 25 Nov. 1988, in author's possession; interview with Pat Balskus, 18 Nov. 1987, in author's possession.

64. Kampfert, "History of Meatpacking," vol. 3, 33–35. The Cedar Rapids delegation represented the Midwest Union of All Packing House Workers; see Lewis J. Clark to P. Kreuger, 8 Aug. 1934, NRA, box 6380; interview with Don Blumenshine, 16 Apr. 1986, UPWAOHP; interview with Lloyd Achenbach, 19 Apr. 1986, UPWAOHP.

65. Kampfert, "History of Meatpacking," vol. 3, 34; interview with Herbert March, 16 Nov. 1970, Roosevelt Project; interview with Herbert and Jane March, 25 Nov. 1988, in author's possession; Newell, *Chicago and the Labor Movement*, 160.

66. Kampfert, "History of Meatpacking," vol. 3, 35; Herbert March interviews; and March's testimony in NLRB XIII-C-600/XIII-R-584.

67. For the transition to the Popular Front and its impact on TUUL unions, see Klehr, *Heyday of American Communism*, 118–34, 167–72; and Bert Cochran, *Labor and Communism: The Conflict That Shaped American Unions* (Princeton: Princeton University Press, 1977), 74–77.

68. Kampfert, "History of Meatpacking," vol. 3, 35–39; interview with Les Orear, 19 July 1983, in author's possession.

69. Kampfert, "History of Meatpacking," vol. 3, 35–37; E. Nockels to W. Green, 7 Mar. 1935; Green to Nockels, 9 Mar. 1935, both in Fitzpatrick Papers, box 18, folder 132; and Gorman to Fitzpatrick, 31 July 1935, Fitzpatrick Papers, box 19, folder 134. See also the "Proposal for Action" which the CP addressed to the CFL Executive Committee in box 18 of the Fitzpatrick Papers.

70. Tate quoted in Newell, *Chicago and the Labor Movement*, 161; interviews with Jesse Vaughn, 4 Oct. 1985 and 23 Oct. 1986, UPWAOHP; interview with Herbert March, 15 July 1985, UPWAOHP; interview with Herbert and Jane March, 25 Nov. 1988, in author's possession.

71. For the Labor Day parade, see Herbert March's testimony in NLRB XIII-C-600/XIII-R-584, 30–50; interview with Herbert March by Elizabeth Balanoff, 16 Nov. 1970, Roosevelt Project; and interview with Herbert and Jane March, 25 Nov. 1988, in author's possession.

72. Newell, *Chicago and the Labor Movement*, 159, 162–63; Kampfert, "History of Meatpacking," vol. 3, 37; Vaughn UPWAOHP interviews.

73. Jos. V. Vorhees to John L. Lewis, 29 Nov. 1935; John Brophy to Vorhees, 2 Dec. 1935; Provisional Committee for the Mid-West Conference of All Packinghouse Workers, "A Call to All Packinghouse Organizations and Unorganized Packinghouse Workers"; William Brown to John L. Lewis, 22 Feb. 1936; Jos. V. Vorhees to Sam Twedell, 22 Feb. 1936; John Brophy to Patrick Gorman, 6 Mar. 1936; Lewis Clark to John L. Lewis, 3 Nov. 1936, all in CIO Secretary Treasurer Papers, box 65, Archives of Labor and Urban Affairs, Wayne State University, Detroit, Mich. (hereafter cited as CIO S-T). For description of the extended network among packinghouse workers, see Joe Ollman to Les Orear, 5 Mar. 1957; and "Agreement" dated 16 Dec. 1936, both in UPWAOHP Accessions.

74. Dennis Lane to John Brophy, telegram, 3 Mar. 1936; Lane to Brophy, 18

Mar. 1936; Patrick Gorman to Brophy, 28 Jan. 1936; Lane to John L. Lewis, 3 Mar. 1936; Brophy to Gorman, 6 Mar. 1936; Lewis Clark to Brophy, 1 Aug. 1936; Brophy to Clark, 7 Aug. 1936; Clark to Brophy, 12 Oct. 1936, all in CIO S-T, box 65.

75. Interview with Jesse Vaughn, 4 Oct. 1985, UPWAOHP; Cole quoted in Banks, *First-Person*, 67; interview with John Wrublewski, 16 Mar. 1988, in author's possession. For black response to the steel drive see George Schuyler, "Negro Workers Lead in Great Lakes Steel Drive," *Pittsburgh Courier*, 31 July 1937; see also the articles on racial unity in the CIO in the *Chicago Defender*, 9 Jan. 1937 (maritime), 20 Aug. 1938 (tobacco), and 26 Nov. 1938.

76. Kampfert, "History of Meatpacking," vol. 4, 18–22; Newell, *Chicago and the Labor Movement*, 163; interview with Herbert March, 15 July 1985, UPWAOHP.

77. Kampfert, "History of Meatpacking," vol. 4, 20–24; *Chicago American*, 9 Mar. 1937.

78. Major H. E. MacGuire to Assistant Chief of Staff, G-2, War Department, 23 Mar. 1937, U.S. Military Intelligence Reports—Surveillance of Radicals in the United States, reel 30, frames 381–383 (hereafter cited as USMI-SRUS); Major H. E. MacGuire to Assistant Chief of Staff, G-2, War Department, 15 Apr. 1937, USMI-SRUS, reel 30, frames 409–411; Major H. E. MacGuire to Assistant Chief of Staff, G-2, War Department, 14 Nov. 1936, USMI-SRUS, reel 30, frames 247–251.

79. Brody, *Butcher Workmen*, 164–65; "Minutes of Executive Board Meeting, Chicago, Illinois, May 10, 1937," 2–3, Amalgamated Meat Cutters and Butcher Workmen Papers, reel 98, State Historical Society of Wisconsin, Madison; Dennis Lane to John Brophy, 12 May 1937; Lewis J. Clark to John Brophy 1 June 1937; "CIO Report on Unions in Meatpacking," 17 Aug. 1937, all CIO S-T box 65; Kampfert, "History of Meatpacking," vol. 4, 25.

Chapter 5: Organizing the Stockyards, 1937–40

1. Interview with Lowell Washington, Jr., 28 Apr. 1988, in author's possession; see also interviews with George Fletemeyer and Charlie McCafferty, UPWAOHP.

2. For PWOC finances see Brody, *Butcher Workmen*, 173–74; and the material in UPWA Papers, box 1, folder 7. For the financial assistance given by the CIO to national affiliates see Walter Galenson, *The CIO Challenge to the AFL: A History of the American Labor Movement, 1935–1941* (Cambridge, Mass.: Harvard University Press, 1960), 600.

3. Interview with Jesse Prosten, 18 Dec. 1985, UPWAOHP. See also the comments about local autonomy in the interview with Richard Saunders, 13 Sept. 1985, UPWAOHP.

4. Interviews with Robert Schultz, 6 and 23 Sept. 1985, UPWAOHP.

5. Interview with Lowell Washington, Jr., 28 Apr. 1988, in author's possession.

6. For union density see "Meat Packing Groups Chartered by the CIO," CIO S-T, box 65, folder 2. For work relations in the smaller plants see the interviews with Jesse Vaughn, 4 Oct. 1985 and 25 Oct. 1986, UPWAOHP.

7. Kampfert, "History of Meatpacking."

8. Interview with Jesse Vaughn, 4 Oct. 1985, UPWAOHP; Kampfert, "History of Meatpacking."

9. Interview with Jesse Vaughn, 4 Oct. 1985, UPWAOHP.

10. Interview with Lowell Washington, Jr., 28 Apr. 1988, in author's possession. On incremental accomplishments see also the interview with Herbert March, 21 Oct. 1986; and the interview with Milt Norman, 1 Oct. 1985, both UPWAOHP.

11. Interview with Lowell Washington, Jr., 28 Apr. 1988, in author's possession.

12. *Midwest Daily Record*, 18 May 1938 (hereafter cited as *MDR*).

13. *MDR*, 14 July 1938; *CIO News* (PE), 19 Dec. 1938; Kampfert, "History of Meatpacking."

14. Interview with Johnson by Robert Davis, U.S. Works Projects Administration, Federal Writers Project, box A874, Library of Congress, Washington, D.C.; see also the edited version of this interview, Stephen Brier, "Labor Politics and Race: A Black Worker's Life," *Labor History* 23 (Summer 1982). Interview with Les Orear by Lizabeth Cohen, 27 July 1983; interview with Herbert and Jane March, 25 Nov. 1988, both in author's possession.

15. Interview with Richard Saunders, 13 Sept. 1985; interview with Jesse Vaughn, 23 Oct. 1986, both UPWAOHP.

16. Kampfert, "History of Meatpacking"; *MDR*, 18 May 1938, 30 June 1938, 14 July 1938, 15 July 1938, and 30 July 1938; *CIO News* (PE), 1 Oct. 1938, 19 Dec. 1938.

17. Kampfert, "History of Meatpacking"; interview with Pat Balskus, 20 Nov. 1987, in author's possession.

18. Interview with Lowell Washington, Jr., 28 Apr. 1988, in author's possession; interview with Jesse Vaughn, 4 Oct. 1985, UPWAOHP; interview with Pat Balskus, 20 Nov. 1987, in author's possession.

19. Interview with Richard Saunders, 13 Sept. 1985, UPWAOHP; "Meat Packing Groups Chartered by the CIO," CIO S-T, box 65, folder 2; Kampfert, "History of Meatpacking"; interview with Philip Weightman, 7–8 Oct. 1986, UPWAOHP; interview with Vicky Starr, 1 Dec. 1987, in author's possession.

20. Kampfert, "History of Meatpacking"; reference to March quoted in Paul Street, "Breaking Up Old Hatreds and Breaking through the Fear: The Emergence of the Packinghouse Workers Organizing Committee in Chicago, 1933–1940," *Studies in History and Politics* 5 (1986), 66; for Wlodarczyk and the Polish community see Slayton, *Back of the Yards*, 208, 210–11. For information on Martinez see Frank McCarty to J. C. Lewis, 24 June 1941, UPWA Papers, box 4, folder 5; see also his obituary in the June 1953 issue of the *Packinghouse Worker*. Interview with John Wrublewski, 16 Mar. 1988, in author's possession.

21. See Peter Davis's testimony in NLRB XIII-C-600/XIII-R-584; for impact of Davis's discharge see the testimony of Joe Bezenhoffer, 609–10; also see the account of the firing provided in the UPWAOHP interviews with Todd Tate, 13 Sept. and 1 Oct. 1985. For loading dock see the testimony of Jesse Perez,

Martin Vannek, and Thomas Goodlow, NLRB XII-C-600/XIII-R-584, 509–42, 554–61, and 585–605.

22. *National Provisioner,* 15 May 1937; Holcomb, "Union Policies of Meat Packers," 99–100.

23. Brody, *Butcher Workmen,* 169–73; Testimony of D. W. King in NLRB XII-R-164. See also the testimony of C. H. Talley, 521–22, and Harvey Ellerd, 619–22. Van Bittner quoted in Brody, *Butcher Workmen,* 173.

24. Testimony of C. H. Talley, NLRB XIII-R-164, 528–32; testimony of Arthur Kampfert, NLRB XIII-R-164, 480–81; and testimony of George Irving, NLRB XIII-C-600/XIII-R-584, 244–45. For threats of recrimination against workers, see the testimony of Peter Shields, NLRB XIII-C-600/XIII-R-584, 286–90; testimony of James Wright, NLRB XIII-C-600/XIII-R-584, 332–33; and that of Anna Novak, NLRB XIII-C-600/XIII-R-584, 630–32.

25. Interview with Herbert March, 16 Nov. 1970, Roosevelt Project. Testimony of C.H. Talley, NLRB XIII-R-164, 539–41, 556–59.

26. Interview with Gertie Kamarczyk, 5 Dec. 1987, in author's possession; testimony of Peter Shields, NLRB XIII-C-600/XIII-R-584, 286–311.

27. Testimony of Henry Johnson (incorrectly identified as "Edward"), NLRB XIII-R-164, 55–59.

28. Johnson quoted in *CIO News* (PE), 14 Nov. 1938.

29. Kampfert, "History of Meatpacking"; testimony of Alphonso Malachi, NLRB XIII-C-600/XIII-R-584, 662–65; and Newell, *Chicago and the Labor Movement,* 164. Gilpin quotation from *MDR,* 1 Mar. 1938.

30. Testimony of Alphonso Malachi, NLRB XIII-C-600/XIII-R-584, 662–65; interview with Gertie Kamarczyk, 5 Dec. 1987, in author's possession.

31. For the steward system see Herbert March's article in *CIO News* (PE), 8 Oct. 1938; and Kampfert, "History of Meatpacking." Johnson quoted in *CIO News* (PE), 14 Nov. 1938. Prosten quotation from the interview with Jesse Prosten, 18 Dec. 1985, UPWAOHP; see also the interview with Prosten by James Cavanaugh, 17 Nov. 1980, United Food and Commercial Workers, Retired Leadership Oral History Project, State Historical Society of Wisconsin, Madison.

32. Galenson, *CIO Challenge,* 364; Brody, *Butcher Workmen,* 178; and Newell, *Chicago and the Labor Movement,* 167. Whistle bargaining was maintained in many Chicago plants through the early 1960s; see the interview with Eunetta Pierce, 18 Sept. 1985, UPWAOHP.

33. Interview with Sophie Kosciolowski by Elizabeth Butters, 15 Jan. 1971, Roosevelt Project; interview with Sophie Kosciolowski by Les Orear, 1971, Chicago Stock Yards History Interview Series, ILHS.

34. Interview with Helen Zajac, 3 Dec. 1987, in author's possession.

35. See *Monthly Labor Review,* Mar. 1939, 726–40, for statistical information on the 1937–38 recession in a number of industries; layoffs in Chicago's packinghouses are discussed in Newell, *Chicago and the Labor Movement,* 164; and in the *MDR,* 2 and 9 Mar. 1938.

36. *MDR,* 2 and 9 Mar., 9 and 11 June, and 2 July 1938.

37. Testimony of Ann Novak, NLRB XIII-C-600/XIII-R-584, 634–35; see *CIO*

News (PE), 14 Oct. 1938, for additional examples of worker's rationalization. Interview with Todd Tate, 1 Oct. 1985, UPWAOHP.

38. Interview with Richard Saunders, 13 Sept. 1985; interview with James Samuel and Todd Tate, 1 Oct. 1985, both UPWAOHP. Interview with Herbert March, 25 Nov. 1988, in author's possession.

39. *MDR*, 9 Mar., 16 July, 20 Oct., and 1 Nov. 1938; *CIO News* (PE), 8 Oct. 1938.

40. Testimony of C. H. Talley, XIII-R-164, 534.

41. *Decisions and Orders of the National Labor Relations Board*, vol. 3 (Washington: GPO, 1939), 106; see also Holcomb, "Union Policies of Meat Packers," 96–98, 101.

42. Interview with Vicky Starr, 4 Aug. 1986, UPWAOHP; interview with Starr (Stella Nowicki) in Lynd and Lynd, *Rank and File*, 75. Foster's pamphlet is reprinted as "Steel Strike Strategy" in his *American Trade Unionism* (New York: International Publishers, 1947), quotation 222–23.

43. For the Strabawa incident see the interview with Herbert March, 16 Nov. 1970, Roosevelt Project. Quotations from *MDR*, 11 June 1938.

44. *CIO News* (PE), 2 Jan. 1939; interview with Richard Saunders, 13 Sept. 1985, UPWAOHP; interview with Herbert March, 15 July 1985, UPWAOHP.

45. Quotation from Cayton and Drake, *Black Metropolis*, 309. Statistical data culled from Charles S. Newcombe and Richard O. Lang, *Census Data of the City of Chicago, 1934* (Chicago: University of Chicago Press, 1934), clearly reveals the superior educational levels achieved by black workers. In Back-of-the-Yards, 22 percent of those born abroad received no schooling at all, while only 4 percent attended the equivalent of high school. Of the first-generation Americans residing in the neighborhood, 22 percent reported attending high school. In two select Black Belt neighborhoods, by contrast, 66 percent of all residents completed elementary school, and 26 percent attended high school. A surprising number of black packinghouse workers were college educated but worked in the yards because racist hiring practices gave them few alternatives; see the interview with Herbert March, 21 Oct. 1986, UPWAOHP.

46. Cole quoted in Banks, *First-Person*, 67–68.

47. Interview with Jesse Prosten, 18 Dec. 1985, UPWAOHP.

48. For the bombing of PWOC headquarters see *MDR*, 21 Sept. 1938; and the *Chicago Daily News*, 20 Sept. 1938. A second assault occurred the following April; see *MDR*, 15 Apr. 1939. For the attack on March, see *MDR*, 2 Dec. 1938; *CIO News* (PE), 12 Dec. 1938; "Statement of Herbert March" and Citizens' Emergency Committee on Industrial Relations to James P. Allen, 17 Nov. 1938, both in Mary McDowell Papers, box 3, folder 15; UPWAOHP interviews with March. For Johnson see the interview with Jesse Vaughn, 4 Oct. 1985, UPWAOHP. Brown's beating is covered in the *CIO News* (PE), 21 Nov. 1938; and in the interview with Vicky Starr, 4 Aug. 1986, UPWAOHP. For investigation of stockyards violence, see *MDR*, 19 Nov. 1938; *CIO News* (PE), 5 Dec. 1938, 24 July and 27 Nov. 1939.

49. Johnson quoted in *MDR*, 2 June 1939. For PWOC strength in the Ar-

mour chain see *MDR*, 2 Mar. 1938; and *CIO News* (PE), 1 Oct. 1938. For Kansas City see Horowitz, "Path Not Taken," chap. 4. For Omaha see the interview with Nels Peterson, 3 June 1986; and the interview with Fred Romano, 6 June 1986, both UPWAOHP. Quotation from interview with Les Orear by Sue Davenport, Mar. 1983, Illinois Labor History Society, Chicago, Ill.

50. For extended treatment of the Kansas City plant occupation, see Horowitz, "Path Not Taken," chap. 4. See also the interview with Charles R. Fischer, 22 Aug. 1986; and the interview with Finis Block, 21 Aug. 1986, both UPWAOHP. Harris quoted in the *Kansas City Star*, 11 Sept. 1938. Kampfert, "History of Meatpacking"; *MDR*, 10 and 14 Sept. 1938.

51. Horowitz, "Path Not Taken," chap. 3; see also Roger Horowitz, "'It Wasn't a Time to Compromise': The Unionization of Sioux City's Packinghouses, 1937–1942," *Annals of Iowa* 50 (Fall 1989); and Kampfert, "History of Meatpacking." *CIO News* (PE), 5, 14, and 21 Nov. 1938; *MDR*, 3, 10, 19, and 25 Oct. 1938.

52. The PWOC polled 2,840 out of the 3,418 votes cast; Van Bittner to Carl Shadler, 16 May 1939, UPWA Papers, box 1, folder 5. Kampfert, "History of Meatpacking"; *MDR*, 10 Oct. 1938; *CIO News* (PE), 5 Nov. 1938. Armour interference summarized in "Report on Packinghouse Workers Organizing Committee Threatened Strike in Chicago," 17 July 1939, General Records of the Department of Labor, Records of Secretary Frances Perkins, RG 174, box 35, National Archives and Records Service, Washington, D.C. (hereafter cited as Perkins Records); see also Newell, *Chicago and the Labor Movement*, 166; and the interview with Herbert March, 16 Nov. 1970, Roosevelt Project. March quotation from interview with Herbert March, 15 July 1985, UPWAOHP; for the immediate aftermath, see *MDR*, 16 Oct. 1938.

53. Interview with Sophie Kosciolowski, 15 Jan. 1971, Roosevelt Project; interview with Sophie Kosciolowski, ILHS; interview with Herbert March, 15 July 1985, UPWAOHP.

54. Armour delegates to Robert Cabell, 25 Sept. 1938, UPWA Papers, box 1, folder 5; Cabell's response is reprinted in the *National Provisioner*, 8 Oct. 1938; *CIO News* (PE), 1 and 8 Oct. 1938; Newell, *Chicago and the Labor Movement*, 166.

55. Interview with Herbert March, 16 Nov. 1970, Roosevelt Project. Interview with Todd Tate, 2 Oct. 1985; interview with Richard Saunders, 13 Sept. 1985, both UPWAOHP. *MDR*, 30 Oct. 1938; McNichols quoted in *CIO News* (PE), 5 Nov. 1938; interview with Herbert March, 15 July 1985, UPWAOHP.

56. Interview with Herbert March, 16 Nov. 1970, Roosevelt Project; see also testimony of Frank McCarty, NLRB XIII-C-600/XIII-R-584, 714.

57. *CIO News* (PE), 14 Oct. 1938; *MDR*, 16 and 30 Oct. 1938.

58. Kampfert, "History of Meatpacking"; interview with Philip Weightman, 7 and 8 Oct. 1986, UPWAOHP.

59. For gains at Swift see Kampfert, "History of Meatpacking," vol. 4; Purcell, *Worker Speaks*, 53–58; and Holcomb, "Union Policies of Meat Packers," 143. Thomas quoted in Banks, *First-Person*, 68–69, 70.

60. Kampfert, "History of Meatpacking," vol. 4; and Holcomb, "Union Policies of Meat Packers," 143.

61. Interview with John Wrublewski, 16 Mar. 1988, in author's possession; Kampfert, "History of Meatpacking"; Brody, *Butcher Workmen*, 176; quotation from Banks, *First-Person*, 68–69.

62. Kampfert, "History of Meatpacking"; and *CIO News* (PE), 19 Dec. 1938; Newell, *Chicago and the Labor Movement*, 176–79; *MDR*, 22 Nov. 1938; *New York Times*, 2 Dec. 1938.

63. Interview with Herbert March, 16 Nov. 1970, Roosevelt University Project; Kampfert, "History of Meatpacking"; *MDR*, 22, 23, 26, and 29 Nov. 1938; see also *CIO News* (PE), 28 Nov. 1938. For AFL strikebreaking see *New York Times*, 27, 28, and 29 Nov. 1938; and *Chicago Tribune*, 27 Nov. 1938.

64. *MDR*, 3, 14, and 15 Dec. 1938; *CIO News* (PE), 12 and 19 Dec. 1938, 20 Mar. 1939; *Chicago Sunday Times*, 4 Dec. 1938; and *New York Times*, 5 Dec. 1938. Interview with Herbert March, 16 Nov. 1970, Roosevelt Project.

65. For PWOC support for Kelly in the 1939 municipal elections see *CIO News* (PE), 6 and 20 Mar. 1939, 17 Apr. 1939; and *MDR*, 16 Feb. 1939, 15 Mar. 1939, and 3 Apr. 1939. See also A. L. Hamblen to Assistant Chief of Staff, G-2, 2 and 25 Mar. 1939, USMI-SRUS, reel 30, frames 774–76 and 779, University Publications, Frederick, Md.

66. *Butcher Workman*, July 1937; *CIO News* (PE), 18 Sept. 1939.

67. For the Amalgamated's incorporation of company unions see Brody, *Butcher Workmen*, 181; *CIO News* (PE), 30 Oct. 1939. For Malachi's expulsion and defection to the AFL, see *MDR*, 15 June 1939; and *Armour CIO Weekly*, 16 June 1939, in UPWA Papers, box 9, folder 4.

68. For segregation in the retail trade, see Brody, *Butcher Workmen*, 176. For persistence of AMC Jim Crow practices, see Cayton and Mitchell, *Black Workers*, 265; Cayton and Drake, *Black Metropolis*, 315. Quotation from Cayton and Mitchell, 270.

69. Interview with Vicky Starr, 4 Aug. 1986, UPWAOHP; interview with Vicky Starr, 12 Nov. 1987, in author's possession; interviews with Herbert March, 15 July 1985 and 21 Oct. 1986, UPWAOHP; *CIO News* (PE), 26 June 1939; Sanford D. Horwitt, *Let Them Call Me Rebel: Saul Alinsky—His Life and Legacy* (New York: Knopf, 1989), 62–63. For a complementary account of the origins of the council, but one that omits reference to the role of the Communists, see Slayton, *Back of the Yards*, 195–205.

70. Slayton, *Back of the Yards*, 201, 210–11; Horwitt, *Let Them Call Me Rebel*, 69–71; interview with Herbert March, 15 July 1985, UPWAOHP; interview with Herbert and Jane March, 25 Nov. 1988, in author's possession. On the relation between the union movement and the council, see also *Chicago Daily News*, 14 July 1939.

71. Slayton, *Back of the Yards*, 200–203; see also the article on Ambrose Ondrak by Charles Leavelle, "Abott from Back o' the Yards," *St. Louis Post-Dispatch*, 20 Apr. 1947, photocopy in Herbert March Papers, State Historical Society of Wisconsin, Madison. For St. Mary's see *MDR*, 30 July 1938.

72. Slayton, *Back of the Yards*, 210–11; Agnes Meyer, "Orderly Revolution," reprint from the *Washington Post*, 4–9 June 1945, photocopy in March Papers;

for improved relations with the Mexican community, see Frank Paz, "Mexican-Americans in Chicago," UPWA Papers, box 342, folder 5.

73. Interview with Herbert March, 15 July 1985, UPWAOHP. For council efforts to halt violence, see *CIO News* (PE), 13 May 1940; Horwitt, *Let Them Call Me Rebel,* 123; Meyer, "Orderly Revolution."

74. Kurzon quoted in Kampfert, "History of Meatpacking"; *CIO News* (PE), 28 Nov. 1938, 9 Jan. and 3 Apr. 1939.

75. Interview with Herbert and Jane March, 25 Nov. 1988; interview with Les Orear, 19 July 1983, both in author's possession. Interview with Vicky Starr, 4 Aug. 1986; interview with Richard Saunders, 13 Sept. 1985, both UPWAOHP.

76. *Chicago Defender,* 23 Sept. 1939; interview with Richard Saunders, 13 Sept. 1985, UPWAOHP.

77. Interview with Lowell Washington, Jr., 28 Apr. 1988, in author's possession.

78. Interview with Herbert March, 15 July 1985; interview with Richard Saunders, 13 Sept. 1985, both UPWAOHP. Interview with Lowell Washington, Jr., 28 Apr. 1988, in author's possession; see also Henry Johnson's comments in the *Pittsburgh Courier,* 31 July 1937.

79. Interview with Jesse Vaughn, 4 Oct. 1985, UPWAOHP; author's notes on conversation with Reverend Hurie Lee, July 1986; *Chicago Defender,* 23 Sept. 1939.

80. Christopher Reed, "Black Politics and Protest," 241–44; for Irish political bosses in Packingtown's 14th ward, see Slayton, *Back of the Yards,* 152–71.

81. Christopher Reed, "Black Politics and Protest," 227–28, 250–59; *CIO News* (PE), 6 Mar. 1939; interview with Jesse Vaughn, 4 Oct. 1985, UPWAOHP. On Dickerson see Pinderhughes, *Race and Ethnicity in Chicago Politics,* 63–65; and Grimshaw, *Bitter Fruit,* 65–66. Dickerson's testimony is in U.S. Congress, House, "Investigation of Un-American Propaganda Activities in the United States," Executive Session, Hearings before the House of Representatives, Subcommittee of the Special Committee to Investigate Un-American Activities, 76th Cong., 3d sess., vol. 1, Sept.–Nov. 1939. For judgeship see interview with Herbert March, 16 Nov. 1970, Roosevelt Project.

82. For the growing strength of the CP on Chicago's South Side see Bill Carter's articles in the *Party Organizer,* Feb. and Mar. 1938; A. L. Hamblen to Assistant Chief of Staff, G-2, 16 May 1939, USMI-SRUS, reel 30, frames 821–822. For the NNC see Christopher Reed, "Black Politics and Protest," 289, 310–11; *Daily Worker,* 11 Jan. 1937; *CIO News* (PE), 29 Apr. and 13 May 1940.

83. *CIO News* (PE), 9, 16, 23, and 30 Jan. 1939, 14 Nov. 1938; membership statistics from UPWA Papers, box 4, folder 9.

84. For local activists' attitude toward contracts see the interview with Herbert March, 15 July 1985, UPWAOHP. For the PWOC's attempt to rein in local unions after Sioux City see *CIO News* (PE), 23 Jan. 1939.

85. Johnson quoted in *MDR,* 2 June 1939; "Is There Going to Be a Strike in Meatpacking?" UPWA Papers, box 9, folder 4; Wlodarczyk quoted in Street, "Breaking Up," 68.

86. *CIO News* (PE), 17 Apr., 1, 15, and 22 May 1939; "The Threatened Strike at Armour," *Christian Century,* 9 Aug. 1939; interview with Vicky Starr, 1 Dec. 1987, in author's possession.

87. Brody, *Butcher Workmen,* 200; "Brief to the Members of the Chicago City Council," Perkins Records, box 35. P. W. Chappell to Dr. Steelman, 31 Mar. 1939; Chappell to "My Dear Doctor," 18 May 1939, both in Federal Mediation and Conciliation Service, case files 195-909, RG 280, National Archives and Records Service, Suitland, Md. (hereafter cited as FMCS).

88. P. W. Chappell to J. R. Steelman, 30 June 1939, FMCS.

89. *MDR,* 17 July 1939; *Chicago Daily Times,* 16 and 17 July 1939; *CIO News* (PE), 24 July 1939; "Meat and the Bishop," *Time* 24 July 1939. See also Benjamin Appel, *The People Talk* (New York: E. P. Dutton, 1940), 176–80.

90. For March shooting and reaction, see *MDR,* 17 July 1939; *CIO News* (PE), 24 July 1939; interview with Herbert March, 16 Nov. 1970, Roosevelt Project; interview with Jesse Prosten, 18 Dec. 1985, UPWAOHP; interview with Pat Balskus, 20 Nov. 1987, in author's possession.

91. Steelman to Perkins, 13 July 1939; "Report on PWOC Threatened Strike in Chicago," 17 July 1939; Conciliation Service to the Sec. of Labor, 19 July 1939, all in Perkins Records, box 35; *CIO News* (PE), 7 Aug. 1939. Armour's position is spelled out in the *National Provisioner,* 22 July 1939.

92. For AMC interference, see Newell, *Chicago and the Labor Movement,* 167; Brody, *Butcher Workmen,* 201; Galenson, *CIO Challenge,* 365. For Fitzpatrick's attack, see the CFL's *Federation News,* 5 Aug. 1939. Conciliation Service to Sec. of Labor, 21 July 1939; and Steelman to McLaughlin, 28 July 1939, both in Perkins Records, box 35. *CIO News* (PE), 30 Oct. 1939.

93. Perkins to Eldred, 16 Aug. 1939; Eldred to Perkins, 22 Aug. 1939; Perkins to Cabell, 8 Sept. 1939; Perkins to Bittner, 8 Sept. 1939; Gorman and Keenan to Perkins, 15 Sept. 1939 [telegrams], all in Perkins Records, box 35. Chappell to Steelman, 11 Apr. 1939, FMCS. Brody, *Butcher Workmen,* 202–3; *CIO News* (PE), 28 Aug. and 18 Sept. 1939; "Armour Bargains with Union," *Business Week,* 29 Aug. 1939.

94. *CIO News* (PE), 16 and 30 Oct. 1939; Kampfert, "History of Meatpacking"; interview with Herbert March, 16 Nov. 1970, Roosevelt Project; interview with Stephan Janko, 15 Mar. 1988; Brody, *Butcher Workmen,* 202–3.

95. *CIO News* (PE), 27 Nov. 1939; "Dies Committee Calls Three CIO Leaders in Quiz—Studies Red Activities in Meat Packing Industry," *Chicago Tribune,* 17 Nov. 1939.

96. Interview with Herbert March, 15 July 1985, UPWAOHP; U.S. Congress, "Investigation of Un-American Propaganda," 215–348.

97. Election figures in UPWA Papers, box 1, folder 5. *CIO News* (PE), 5 and 19 Feb. 1940. For Kansas City and Chicago Soap Works settlements see *CIO News* (PE), 5 Feb. 1940; and Galenson, *CIO Challenge,* 366. For Armour contract, Van Bittner to Haywood, 15 Feb. 1940, CIO S-T, box 65, folder 3; Holcomb, "Union Policies of Meat Packers," 113–14.

98. Interview with Sophie Kosciolowski, 15 Jan. 1971, Roosevelt Project; interview with Gertie Kamarczyk, 7 Dec. 1987, in author's possession.

99. Interview with Herbert March, 15 July 1985, UPWAOHP.

Chapter 6: Chicago's Packinghouse Workers during World War II

1. Interview with Lowell Washington, Jr., 28 Apr. 1988, in author's possession.

2. Ibid.; interview with Karl Lundberg, 23 Oct. 1987, both in author's possession. For renewed migration, see Nicholas Lemann, *The Promised Land: The Great Black Migration and How It Changed America* (New York: Knopf, 1991); for rise in black employment see Labor Market Survey Reports in the Records of the Bureau of Employment Security, RG 183, box 103, National Archives and Records Service, Washington, D.C.

3. For Johnson's break with the CP see G. R. Carpenter to Assistant Chief of Staff, G-2, War Department, 9 Nov. 1939, USMI-SRUS, reel 31, frames 18–22; Carpenter to Assistant Chief of Staff, 1 July 1940, USMI-SRUS, reel 31, frames 186–88; and Carpenter to Assistant Chief of Staff, 17 Sept. 1940, USMI-SRUS, reel 31, frames 269–73.

4. Herbert March, "Building a Mass Party in the Packing Industry," *Daily Worker*, 25 Mar. 1946. For CP strength in Chicago's packinghouses see the interview with Vicky Starr, 4 Aug. 1986; the interview with Herbert March, 21 Oct. 1986, both in UPWAOHP. Somewhat suspect but still useful is the testimony contained in U.S. Congress, House, "Communist Activities in the Chicago Area, Part 2," Hearings before the Committee on Un-American Activities, House of Representatives, 82d Cong., 2d sess., 4, 5 Sept. 1952, 3754–72; and U.S. Congress, House, "Communist Infiltration of Vital Industries and Current Communist Techniques in the Chicago, Ill., Area," Hearings before the Committee on Un-American Activities, House of Representatives, 86th Cong., 1st sess., 5, 6, 7 May 1959.

5. See the parallel argument in Robert Korstad and Nelson Lichtenstein, "Opportunities Found and Lost: Labor, Radicals, and the Early Civil Rights Movement," *Journal of American History* 75 (Dec. 1988). For blacks and the Communist Party see Honey, *Southern Labor and Black Civil Rights;* Robin D. G. Kelley, *Hammer and Hoe: Alabama Communists During the Great Depression* (Chapel Hill: University of North Carolina Press, 1990); and Naison, *Communists in Harlem.* Still useful is the older Wilson Record, *The Negro and the Communist Party* (1951; New York: Atheneum, 1971); and the cynical treatment in Klehr, *Heyday of American Communism.*

6. Quotation from Purcell, *Worker Speaks*, 71.

7. For the linking of the problems of class and bureaucracy, see Peter Friedlander, *The Emergence of a UAW Local, 1936–1939: A Study in Class and Culture* (Pittsburgh: University of Pittsburgh Press, 1975), 95–96, 119–20.

8. Testimony of Ryan, Murphy, Rogalla, and Piotrowski in NLRB XIII-C-1324.

9. Testimony of Piotrowski and Lynch, NLRB XIII-C-1324, 148–57, 167–69, 476.

10. These developments are summarized in G. L. Patterson to Nathan Witt, 24 June 1940, "Investigation and Report" in Administrative files for NLRB XIII-C-1324.

11. Testimony of Piotrowski, NLRB XIII-C-1324, 198, 189–91; testimony of von Thun, Raymond Moore, and Homer Irby in "Official Report of Proceedings before the National Labor Relations Board, Case No. XIII-C-1571, In the Matter of Wilson & Co., Inc. and Packinghouse Workers Organizing Committee affiliated with the C.I.O., Chicago, Ill., Jan. 15, 1942," 30–33, 56–58, 343–45 532–33, National Labor Relations Board, Administrative Division, Files and Dockets Section, Transcripts and Exhibits, RG 25, box 3089, National Archives and Records Service, Suitland, Md.; testimony of Keim, Geweke, and Quinn in the same.

12. *CIO News* (PE), 5 Feb. 1940; Kampfert, "History of Meatpacking."

13. Interview with John Wrublewski, 16 Mar. 1988, in author's possession; interview with Gertrude D. by Betty Burke, 15 May 1939, U.S. Works Projects Administration, Federal Writers Project, box A707, Library of Congress, Washington, D.C.

14. Ruth Milkman, *Gender at Work: The Dynamics of Job Segregation by Sex during World War II* (Urbana: University of Illinois Press, 1987), 94; also see Bruce Fehn, "Striking Women: Gender, Race, and Class in the United Packinghouse Workers of America" (Ph.D. dissertation, University of Wisconsin, 1991), 109–16. Interview with Pat Christie by Betty Burke, 14 June 1939, Federal Writers Project, box A707.

15. Interview with Marian Simmons, 21 and 25 Aug. 1986, UPWAOHP.

16. For social work, see the *District One Champion*, 24 Feb. and 12 Dec. 1944. For pay differential see FMCS, Case Files 302–1302, "Armour & Co, Chicago, Ill." For grievances pertaining to equal pay see Callowick to Rasky, 4 Mar. 1944, UPWA Papers, box 189, folder 6; Stephens to Sponseller, 12 May 1942, UPWA Papers, box 5, folder 2; and material in box 193, folder 7.

17. Horowitz, "Path Not Taken," 484–85; interview with Eunetta Pierce, 18 Sept. 1985, UPWAOHP.

18. Interview with Eunetta Pierce, 18 Sept. 1985, UPWAOHP; interview with Ercell Allen, 18 Sept. 1985, UPWAOHP; interview with Lowell Washington, Jr., 28 Apr. 1988, in author's possession.

19. Interview with Eunetta Pierce, 18 Sept. 1985, UPWAOHP; Mary Smith quoted in *CIO News* (PE), 1 Dec. 1941.

20. Interview with Sophie Kosciolowski, 15 Jan. 1971, Roosevelt Project; interview with Marian Simmons, 21 and 25 Aug. 1986, UPWAOHP.

21. Starr quoted in Fehn, "Striking Women," 114; interview with Helen Zajac, 3 Dec. 1987, in author's possession.

22. *CIO News* (PE), 1 and 29 Sept. 1941. Interview with Les Orear by Lizabeth Cohen, 27 July 1983.

23. Kampfert, "History of Meatpacking"; Galenson, *CIO Challenge*, 370; interview with John Wrublewski, 16 Mar. 1988, in author's possession.

24. See testimony of Piotrowski, Lynch, et al. and copies of Wilson Sparks in NLRB XIII-C-1324; *CIO News* (PE), 6 Jan. 1941.

25. Charles Graham to Howard LeBaron, 11 Sept. 1942, in "Wilson & Co, Chicago IL, R-4456"; administrative materials for cases XIII-C-1324 (C-1763), XIII-C-1352, XIII-C-1571 (C-2120) all in National Labor Relations Board, Administrative Division, Files and Dockets Section, Transcripts and Exhibits, RG 25, National Archives and Records Service, Suitland, Md. The second organizing drive can be followed in *CIO News* (PE), 10 Apr., 22 May, 26 June, 3 July, and 11 Sept. 1942. For the election victory see *CIO News* (PE), 25 Dec. 1942; and McCarty to Haywood, 23 Dec. 1942, CIO S-T, box 66, folder 11.

26. See the tables on the employment of nonwhites in the Chicago labor market in both the Records of the Bureau of Employment Security (RG 183, box 103) and the Records of the War Manpower Commission (RG 211, box 90), National Archives and Records Service, Washington, D.C.

27. Nelson Lichtenstein, *Labor's War at Home: The CIO in World War II* (New York: Cambridge University Press, 1982); Martin Glaberman, *Wartime Strikes: The Struggle against the No-Strike Pledge* (Detroit: Berwick, 1980); and Joshua Freeman, "Delivering the Goods: Industrial Unionism during World War II," *Labor History* 19 (Fall 1978). Quotation from Lichtenstein, 202.

28. Interview with Sam Parks, 3 Oct. 1985, UPWAOHP; interview with Sam Parks by Les Orear, 8 Dec. 1980, Illinois Labor History Society, Chicago, Ill.; interview with Charles Hayes, 27 May 1986, UPWAOHP.

29. Interview with Sam Parks, 3 Oct. 1985, UPWAOHP; interview with Charles Hayes, 27 May 1986, UPWAOHP.

30. Williams's testimony before U.S. Congress, House, Subcommittee of the Special Committee to Investigate Un-American Activities, Hearings, vol. 17, Sept. 29, 1944 (Washington: GPO, 1944), 10263–62; interview with Sam Parks, 3 Oct. 1985, UPWAOHP; unpublished manuscript (1986) by Joe Zabritski, copy in author's possession; interview with Charles Hayes, 27 May 1986, UPWAOHP. See also the articles on Williams and Smith in the *Sunday Chicago Bee*, 1 June and 2 July 1944

31. Interview with Joe Zabritski by Les Orear, May 1982, Illinois Labor History Society; interview with Joe Zabritski, 22 Sept. 1987, in author's possession; Zabritski manuscript. For Pasinski see NLRB XIII-C-1324, 578–656, 955–73.

32. Interview with John Wrublewski, 16 Mar. 1988, in author's possession.

33. For the contested election see Dock Williams to Haywood, 26 Oct. 1943, CIO S-T, box 67, folder 2; Lewis J. Clark to Haywood, 21 Mar. 1943, CIO S-T, box 67, folder 4; Dock Williams to Haywood, 27 Apr. 1944, CIO S-T, box 67, folder 5. See also *District One Champion*, 21 June 1944; *Packinghouse Worker*, 1 Sept. 1944; and *Chicago Bee*, 28 May 1944.

34. Interview with Sam Parks, 3 Oct. 1985, UPWAOHP.

35. Holcomb, "Union Policies of Meat Packers," 160–73; see also Brody, *Butcher Workmen*, 206.

36. Zabritski manuscript; interview with Joe Zabritski, 21 July 1987, in author's possession. For McKinney incident, see materials in "Action against

Jim Crow," UPWA Papers, box 347, folder 13. For the anti-discrimination clause see Ralph Helstein to Doug Hall, 12 May 1943, Ralph Helstein Papers, State Historical Society of Wisconsin, Madison.

37. Interview with Sam Parks, 3 Oct. 1985, UPWAOHP; interview with Charles Hayes, 27 May 1986, UPWAOHP; interview with Marian Simmons, 21 and 25 Aug. 1986, UPWAOHP.

38. Starr (Nowicki) quoted in Lynd and Lynd, *Rank and File*, 85; interview with Herbert March, 21 Oct. 1986, UPWAOHP.

39. On Johnstone, see Maguire to Assistant Chief of Staff, War Dept, 11 May 1937, USMI-SRUS, reel 30, frames 436–42; and his article in the Aug. 1937 issue of the *Party Organizer*. For pressure to discuss politics, see for example the article by Jack Martin in the *Party Organizer*, Feb. 1938.

40. Interview with Herbert March, 21 Oct. 1986, UPWAOHP; interview with Herbert and Jane March, 25 Nov. 1988, in author's possession; Hamblen to Assistant Chief of Staff, War Dept, 31 Mar. 1939, USMI-SRUS, reel 30, frame 775. For Foster and CP trade union activists, see Johanningsmeier, *Forging*, 276–82, 301–3.

41. Hamblen to Assistant Chief of Staff, War Dept, 14 Apr. 1939, USMI-SRUS, reel 30, frames 807–12; Hamblen to Assistant Chief of Staff, War Dept., 16 May 1939, USMI-SRUS, reel 30, frames 821–22; Carpenter to Assistant Chief of Staff, War Dept, 4 Oct. 1939, USMI-SRUS, reel 30, frames 931–34; for further information on the disaffection of Poles and Lithuanians from the CP, see the spies' reports in the Union Stockyards and Transit Company Records, box 4, University of Illinois at Chicago, Chicago, Ill. Interview with Herbert March, 21 Oct. 1986, UPWAOHP; interview with Herbert and Jane March, 25 Nov. 1988, in author's possession.

42. Schoenstein quoted in Purcell, *Worker Speaks*, 59–60; for the union's failure at Kansas City Swift, see the interview with Lyman Halligan, 4 Dec. 1985, UPWAOHP.

43. Hammond quoted in Banks, *First-Person*, 55; Washington quoted in Purcell, *Worker Speaks*, 81; interview with Philip Weightman, 7–8 Oct. 1986, UPWAOHP.

44. Interview with Les Orear by Lizabeth Cohen, 27 July 1983; interview with John Wrublewski, 16 Mar. 1988, both in author's possession; Washington quoted in Purcell, *Worker Speaks*, 82. Interview with Philip Weightman, 7–8 Oct. 1986, UPWAOHP.

45. Purcell, *Worker Speaks*, 31, 34.

46. Quotations from Purcell, *Worker Speaks*, 165–66, 174; for white alienation, also see the interview with Philip Weightman, 7–8 Oct. 1986, UPWAOHP.

47. Quotation from Cayton and Drake, *Black Metropolis*, 315–16.

48. Johnson and Lee quoted in Purcell, *Worker Speaks*, 54; Swift Flash quoted in Horowitz, "Path Not Taken," 262; interview with Philip Weightman, 7–8 Oct. 1986, UPWAOHP.

49. Interview with Philip Weightman, 7–8 Oct. 1986, UPWAOHP; *CIO News* (PE), 30 Oct. 1939, 13 May 1940; for Shelton's background, see Horowitz, "Path Not Taken," chap. 3.

50. For the Toledano Club and Mexican radicalism, see Kerr, "Chicano Experience," 86; and interview with Herbert March, 15 July 1985, UPWAOHP.

51. Interview with Vicky Starr, 4 Aug. 1986, UPWAOHP; *CIO News* (PE), 10 July 1939, 27 May 1940; interview with Philip Weightman, 7–8 Oct. 1986, UPWAOHP.

52. Interview with Vicky Starr, 4 Aug. 1986, UPWAOHP; *CIO News* (PE), 10 July 1939, 27 May 1940; interview with Philip Weightman, 7–8 Oct. 1986, UPWAOHP; *CIO News* (PE), 10 June 1940.

53. *CIO News* (PE), 30 Oct. 1939, 29 Apr. 1940; Catherine E. Lewis, "Trade Union Policies with Regard to the Negro Worker in the Slaughtering and Meatpacking Industry of Chicago" (M.A. thesis, University of Chicago, 1945), 68; interview with Vicky Starr, 4 Aug. 1986, UPWAOHP; *CIO News* (PE), 1 Sept. 1941.

54. *Swift Flash,* 26 June 1939 and 25 Feb. 1941, UPWA Papers, box 9, folder 4; *Swift Flash,* 9 Apr. and 19 Mar. 1940, copy attached to "Meeting of Delegates Packinghouse Workers Organizing Committee with Alan S. Haywood and James B. Carey, Special Representatives From National CIO Headquarters," Transcripts, vol. 8, CIO S-T, box 66, folder 3.

55. Holcomb, "Union Policies of Meat Packers," 143; interview with Philip Weightman, 7–8 Oct. 1986, UPWAOHP.

56. Interview with Philip Weightman, 7–8 Oct. 1986, UPWAOHP.

57. "Swift & Company Election Results," UPWA Papers, box 11, folder 10.

58. For the wage-hour suit, see *CIO News* (PE), 4 Mar. 1940, 10 Jan., 17 Mar., and 10 Nov. 1941, and 1 Dec. 1941. For the PWOC victory, see *CIO News* (PE), 16 Jan. 1942.

59. Swift employment figures are found in both the Records of the Bureau of Employment Security (RG 183, box 103) and the Records of the War Manpower Commission (RG 211, box 90), National Archives and Records Service, Washington, D.C.

60. Purcell, *Worker Speaks,* 63–72.

61. Interview with Philip Weightman, 7–8 Oct. 1986, UPWAOHP; interview with Ralph Helstein, Nov. 1983, UPWAOHP Accessions.

62. See the discussion of the syndicalist mood within the workers' movement of the 1930s in Bruce Nelson, *Workers on the Waterfront: Seamen, Longshoremen, and Unionism in the 1930s* (Urbana: University of Illinois Press, 1988), 6–10, 183–85.

63. Interview with Casper Winkels, 5 Dec. 1985, UPWAOHP. For extended discussion of these "straight trade unionists," see Horowitz, "Path Not Taken," chaps. 1 and 3.

64. For delegates' position see Newell, *Chicago and the Labor Movement,* 169–70; and G. R. Carpenter to Assistant Chief of Staff, War Dept, 7 Aug. 1939, "Resume of Labor Situation in Packinghouse Industry," USMI-SRUS, reel 30, frame 888.

65. Weidenheimer to Cunningham, 5 Dec. 1939, UPWA Papers, box 306 folder 11; interview with Don Harris by Paul Kelso, 8 June 1978, Iowa Federa-

tion of Labor Oral History Project, Iowa State Historical Society, Iowa City; McCarty to officers and members of local unions, 20 Mar. 1940, and McCarty to March, 1 Oct. 1940, both in UPWA Papers, box 9, folder 4; Galenson, *CIO Challenge*, 375; J. C. Lewis to Bittner, 23 Feb. 1940, UPWA Papers, box 306, folder 12.

66. Johnson to "Dear Sir and Brother," 1 Nov. 1940; Petersen to Kampfert, 6 Nov. 1940; Kampfert to all officers and members of local unions, 8 Nov. 1940, all in UPWA Papers, box 9, folder 4.

67. Bittner to Jesse Vaughn, 29 Nov. 1940; Taylor to Kampfert, 18 Nov. 1940, both in UPWA Papers, box 9, folder 4. For Chicago Council see Johnson to Earl Young, 25 Feb. 1941; Kampfert to A. T. Stephens, 2 Mar. 1941, both in UPWA Papers, box 9, folder 5; and Strabawa to J. C. Lewis, 26 June 1941, UPWA Papers, box 9, folder 10. For the Atlantic City convention see Report of Roy Franklin in "Minutes of the Seventh Conference of District #2, PWOC," 12 Jan. 1941, UPWA Papers, box 3, folder 3; interview with Jesse Vaughn, 4 Oct. 1985, UPWAOHP; interview with Richard Saunders, 13 Sept. 1985, UPWAOHP.

68. Interview with Richard Saunders, 13 Sept. 1985, UPWAOHP; Vaughn to Bittner, 29 Nov. 1940, UPWA Papers, box 9, folder 4; Franklin to Dougherty, 7 Jan. 1941, UPWA Papers, box 306, folder 4; Kampfert to A. T. Stephens, 2 Mar. 1941, UPWA Papers, box 9, folder 5; Schowalter to Nolan, 23 May 1941, UPWA Papers, box 9, folder 11; Sponseller to J. C. Lewis, 18 July 1941, UPWA Papers, box 5, folder 2. For dues witholding see "List of Locals Witholding Dues," Apr. 1941, CIO S-T, box 65, folder 9; Franklin to J. C. Lewis, 19 June 1941, UPWA Papers, box 4, folder 8; see also correspondence from local unions in CIO S-T, box 65, folder 10. Kampfert to A. J. Shippey, 8 May 1941, UPWA Papers, box 9, folder 5.

69. Schowalter to Nolan, 23 May 1941, UPWA Papers, box 4, folder 11; "Minutes of Meeting of Local 42," 6 June 1941, UPWA Papers, box 5, folder 7; Sponseller to J. C. Lewis, 17 Nov. 1941, UPWA Papers, box 11, folder 8; see also McDonald to J. C. Lewis, 12 Mar. 1942, UPWA Papers, box 7, folder 1.

70. Interview with Jesse Vaughn, 4 Oct. 1985, UPWAOHP; interview with Richard Saunders, 13 Sept. 1985, UPWAOHP; Kampfert to Stern, 14 Apr. 1941, UPWA Papers, box 9, folder 5; PWOC delegates to Philip Murray, 29 Apr. 1940, CIO S-T, box 65, folder 10; "Meeting of Delegates Packinghouse Workers Organizing Committee with Alan S. Haywood and James B. Carey, Special Representatives from National CIO Headquarters," 14–16 Apr. 1941, 8 vols., Transcripts, CIO S-T, boxes 65 and 66, passim.

71. "Meeting of Delegates Packinghouse Workers Organizing Committee," Brown quotation in vol. 5, 199. For comments about race, see the testimony of Bess Gebhardt, vol. 5, 2–5; and the testimony of Sam Sponseller, vol. 5, 36–38. Carey quotation in vol. 2.

72. Locals 1, 9, and 31 to all PWOC locals, Districts 2 and 3, 22 June 1941, UPWA Papers, box 4, folder 10; Sponseller and Franklin to Murray, 7 July 1941, UPWA Papers, box 4, folder 8; Sponseller to J. C. Lewis, 17 Nov. 1941, box 7, folder 1. For Austin's role in the struggle for an international, see Horowitz, "Path Not Taken," 435, 449–51.

73. Horowitz, "Path Not Taken," 453. Murray to officers and members PWOC locals, 7 May 1941, CIO S-T, box 65, folder 8; *CIO News* (PE), 21 July 1941. For early dissatisfaction with Lewis, see Lankford and Johnson to Van Bittner, 11 May 1940, UPWA Papers; Lewis to Kampfert, 17 May 1940, both in UPWA Papers, box 306, folder 12. For Clark's appointment, see J. C. Lewis to all local unions, 7 July 1941, UPWA Papers, box 9, folder 5.

74. *CIO News* (PE), 28 July 1941; Franklin to Ellis, 25 July 1942, UPWA Papers, box 4, folder 10.

75. *CIO News* (PE), 21 July, 4 and 18 Aug., and 15 Sept. 1941. For NDMB intervention see Lewis to Perkins, 11 July 1941; Seward to Lewis, 26 July 1941; Lewis to all Armour PWOC locals, 11 Aug. 1941, all in UPWA Papers, box 1, folder 5; Lewis to Perkins, 26 July 1941; Seward to Lewis, 29 July 1941, UPWA Papers, box 2, folder 9. "Memorandum of Agreement with Armour," CIO S-T, box 65, folder 11; Armour Master Agreement, UPWA Papers, box 1, folder 5.

76. "Report on District 50 and Darling and Co.," UPWA Papers, box 12, folder 3; Hayward to J. C. Lewis, 4 Feb. 1942, UPWA Papers, box 5, folder 5; "Jurisdictional Complaint Against District 50, UMW," UPWA Papers, box 12, folder 3. For Kansas City, see Pinchon to Haywood, 12 July 1942; and Haywood to Pinchon, 16 July 1942, both in CIO S-T, box 66, folder 9. For Chicago, see Williams and Peters to Murray and Sponseller, 4 Oct. 1943, CIO S-T, box 67, folder 3; interview with Richard Saunders, 13 Sept. 1985, UPWAOHP; and Brody, *Butcher Workmen*, 222.

77. Fontecchio to Kampfert, 30 Jan. 1941, UPWA Papers, box 9, folder 5; Kampfert to Stern, 3 Mar. 1941; Stern to Kampfert, 14 Apr. 1941, Bull to Local 31, 4 Apr. 1941, all in UPWA Papers, box 9, folder 5. For Armour 347 see Mackenzie to Haywood, 26 Feb. 1941, and Kosciolowski to Haywood, 30 Apr. 1941, both in CIO S-T, box 65, folder 10; interview with Herbert March, 21 Oct. 1986, UPWAOHP; and interview with Herbert March, 25 Nov. 1988, in author's possession.

78. Interview with Herbert March, 21 Oct. 1986, UPWAOHP; interview with Herbert March, 25 Nov. 1988, in author's possession.

79. Interview with Ed Heckelbeck by Sanford Horwitt, 11 Nov. 1983, transcript in author's possession; Horwitt, *Let Them Call Me Rebel*, 124–25. Interview with Richard Saunders, 13 Sept. 1985, UPWAOHP; interview with Herbert March, 21 Oct. 1986, UPWAOHP.

80. *CIO News* (PE), 8 May 1942; for Policy Committee see materials in UPWA Papers, box 11, folder 4.

81. For opposition to Sponseller, see McCarty, Wlodarczyk et al. to Murray, 16 July 1942; Beckley and March to Haywood, 15 July 1942; McDonald to Murray, 15 July 1942, all in CIO S-T, box 66, folder 9. Interview with Richard Saunders, 13 Sept. 1985, UPWAOHP; interview with Jesse Prosten, 18 Dec. 1985, UPWAOHP.

82. Davidchik to Ballard, 18 and 31 July 1942, UPWA Papers, box 4, folder 2; "Minutes of District Conference of District 3," 2 Aug. 1942, UPWA Papers, box 5, folder 1; Sponseller to Qualley, 2 Sept. 1942, UPWA Papers, box 2, folder 10; Sponseller to Peterson, 12 Oct. 1942, UPWA Papers, box 5, folder 1.

83. Interview with Herbert March, 15 July 1985, UPWAOHP; convention machinations are discussed in Horowitz, "Path Not Taken," 460–65. Interview with Frank Ellis, 2 July 1972, Minnesota Historical Society, St. Paul; interview with Herbert March, 25 Nov. 1988, in author's possession.

84. Interview with Ercell Allen, 18 Sept. 1985, UPWAOHP.

Chapter 7: The Path Not Taken

1. Interview with Karl Lundberg, 23 Oct. 1987, in author's possession.

2. Ibid.

3. Ibid.

4. Karl Klare, "Judicial Deradicalization of the Wagner Act and the Origins of Modern Legal Consciousness," *Minnesota Law Review* 62 (1978); and his "Labor Law and the Liberal Political Imagination," *Socialist Review* 62 (Mar.–Apr. 1982). David Milton, *The Politics of U.S. Labor: From the Great Depression to the New Deal* (New York: Monthly Review Press, 1982), 9–16, 139–67. See also David Montgomery, "American Workers and the New Deal Formula," in *Workers' Control in America* (New York: Cambridge University Press, 1976), 153–81; and Steve Fraser, "The Labor Question," in Fraser and Gerstle, eds., *The Rise and Fall of the New Deal Order* (Princeton: Princeton University Press, 1989), 55–84.

5. Lichtenstein, *Labor's War at Home,* esp. 178–203; James Green, "Fighting on Two Fronts: Working-Class Militancy in the 1940s," *Radical America* 9 (July–Aug. 1975); Freeman, "Delivering the Goods"; Glaberman, *Wartime Strikes.* See also Christopher Tomlins, *The State and the Unions: Labor Relations, Law and the Organized Labor Movement in America* (New York: Cambridge University Press, 1985), esp. 247–81.

6. For wartime strikes in other industries, see Lichtenstein, *Labor's War at Home,* esp. 110–35; interview with Herbert March, 15 July 1985, UPWAOHP.

7. For the impact of anticommunism see Frank Emspak, "The Break-Up of the CIO, 1945–1950" (Ph.D. dissertation, University of Wisconsin, 1972); and Mike Davis, "Barren Marriage of American Labour and the Democratic Party," 69–82.

8. For profits see Brody, *Butcher Workmen,* 203; and Williams and Stout, *Economics of the Livestock-Meat Industry.* For wartime demand, see "Chicago Area Defense Contracts," Records of the Bureau of Employment Security, RG 183, box 99, National Archives, Washington, D.C.

9. Bureau of Labor Statistics Table on pay, Oct. 1945, UPWA Papers, box 196, folder 7. For the "Little Steel Formula," see Lichtenstein, *Labor's War at Home,* 70–72.

10. Table on "Working Conditions and Safety," UPWA Papers, box 9, folder 4; and "The Armour Formula" (1944) in Helstein Papers. Lewis J. Clark to Upton Sinclair, 10 Oct. 1944, Helstein Papers.

11. "Armour Formula" (1944), Helstein Papers.

12. "Supplemental Brief of the PWOC before the National War Labor Board, 1942," UPWA Papers, box 190, folder 1; see materials in UPWA Papers, box 11,

folder 12 and box 5, folder 1 for the union security measures; interview with Todd Tate, 1 Oct. 1985, UPWAOHP.

13. Interview with John Wrublewski, 16 Mar. 1988, in author's possession; "Armour and Co.—Chicago, Chicago Soap Works, Slow-downs, Work Stoppages, and Strikes since August 11, 1944," UPWA Papers box 196, folder 1. Saunders to Helstein, 11 Sept. 1946, UPWA Papers box 196, folder 1; Helstein to Schoenstein, 19 Nov. 1943, UPWA Papers, box 11, folder 10; and "Memoranda on Stoppages," in Helstein Papers.

14. Lichtenstein, *Labor's War at Home,* 120; for the board's internal workings and delays see the interview with Eugene Cotton, 3 Oct. 1985, UPWAOHP; interview with Vicky Starr, 4 Aug. 1986, UPWAOHP; interview with Les Orear, 14 Nov. 1983, in author's possession.

15. "Armour Formula" (1944), Helstein Papers; testimony of King and Bezenhoffer, Official Report of Proceedings National War Labor Board Case No. 111-5760-D, 2300–2311, National War Labor Board, Meat Packing Commission, Dispute Case Files 111-5760 and 111-5762, box 7453, National Archives and Records Service, Suitland, Md.

16. "Armour Formula" and Helstein to Mannheimer, 30 Nov. 1944, both in Helstein Papers. For requests for the revocation of security measures, see "Demands of Armour & Co. for changes in the Master Agreement," UPWA Papers, box 188, folder 12; "Petition for Modification or Cancellation of Union Maintenance of Membership and Check-off Provisions," UPWA Papers, box 12, folder 8; and Winkler to Kott, 7 July 1945, UPWA Papers, box 12, folder 8.

17. For UAW decision, see Lichtenstein, *Labor's War at Home,* 180–93. Clark to Finch, 18 Feb. 1944, UPWA Papers, box 1, folder 6; see also letters of Ralph Helstein to Armour, Swift, and Wilson locals in UPWA Papers, box 1, folder 6, and box 11, folder 10.

18. Interview with Richard Saunders, 13 Sept. 1985, UPWAOHP.

19. Horowitz, "Path Not Taken," 503–4. See also Finch and Barnhart to Clark, 7 Mar. 1944, UPWA Papers, box 1, folder 6.

20. Keenan to Davis, 13 June 1944, UPWA Papers, box 189, folder 6. For Clark's report see Recommendations to UPWA Executive Board Meeting, 2 Feb. 1945, UPWA Papers, box 26, folder 1; transcript of UPWA Executive Board Meeting, 20 Mar. 1945, UPWA Papers, box 27, folder 2; and transcript of UPWA Executive Board Meeting, 28 and 31 May 1945, UPWA Papers, box 27, folder 2.

21. Interview with Herbert March, 21 Oct. 1986, UPWAOHP.

22. Ibid.; *District One Champion,* 27 Jan., 11 May 1944; Proceedings, *Second Convention of the UPWA,* 85.

23. Prosten quoted in Horowitz, "Path Not Taken," 501; interview with Herbert March, 21 Oct. 1986, UPWAOHP; interview with Ercell Allen, 18 Sept. 1985, UPWAOHP; interview with James Samuel, 1 Oct. 1985, UPWAOHP.

24. Interview with Sam Parks, 3 Oct. 1985; and the interview with Henry Giannini, 13 Feb. 1986, both UPWAOHP.

25. Lichtenstein, *Labor's War at Home,* 83ff.; interview with Mary Salinas, 18 Mar. 1986, UPWAOHP.

26. Quoted materials in "Armour and Company Exhibits" in National War Labor Board, Meat Packing Commission, Dispute Case Files 111-5760 and 111-5762, RG 202, box 7453, National Archives and Records Service, Suitland, Md.

27. Interview with Todd Tate, 1 Oct. 1985, UPWAOHP.

28. For civil rights mobilization, see Lichtenstein, *Labor's War at Home*, 124–25; August Meier and Elliot Rudwick, *Black Detroit and the Rise of the UAW* (New York: Oxford, 1979), 108–74; and Herbert Garfinkle, *When Negroes March: The March on Washington and the Organizational Politics for FEPC* (New York: Atheneum, 1969).

29. For hate strikes, see Meier and Rudwick, *Black Detroit*, 162–74.

30. Robert Weaver, "Seniority and the Negro Worker," in the Records of the Fair Employment Practices Committee, RG 228, box 406, National Archives, Washington D.C.

31. See the interview with Ada Treadwell, 29 July 1986, UPWAOHP for discussion of this point; see also Fehn, "Striking Women," 161–83.

32. Interview with Sam Parks, 3 Oct. 1985, UPWAOHP; interview with Lowell Washington, Jr., 28 Apr. 1988, in author's possession; interview with Richard Saunders et al., 1 Oct. 1985, UPWAOHP; interview with Eddie Humphrey, 18 Mar. 1986, UPWAOHP; interview with L. C. Williams, 18 Mar. 1986, UPWAOHP. A parallel argument about black veterans is pursued in Korstad and Lichtenstein, "Opportunities Found and Lost."

33. Transcripts of the International Executuive Board Meeting, 11 Oct. 1944, 115ff., UPWA Papers, box 26, folder 6. For more on the Packinghouse Workers' response to the 1943 riots see *CIO News* (PE), 25 June 1943.

34. Helstein to Hall, 12 May 1943, Helstein Papers. On Weightman's activities see *Packinghouse Worker*, 4 Feb. 1944, 14 Sept. 1944, 2 Mar. 1945, and 22 Mar. 1946; see also interview with Philip Weightman, UPWAOHP.

35. For Local 347, *Packinghouse Worker*, 27 May 1943, 21 Feb. 1944; for Chicago IUC, *Packinghouse Worker*, 2 July 1943; *District One Champion*, 8 Mar. 1944; and material in Records of the Committee on Fair Employment Practice, RG 228, Regional Files Region VI, boxes 709 and 710, National Archives and Records Service, Washington, D.C.

36. These cases occurred at the Wilson plant in Cedar Rapids and the Rath facility in Waterloo, Iowa. See the UPWAOHP interviews with Magnolia Fields, Charles Pearson, and Jimmy Porter. March to Henderson, 14 June 1944; Weightman to Henderson, 14 June 1944, both in Records of the Committee on Fair Employment Practice, RG 228, Regional Files Region VI, box 710, National Archives, Washington, D.C. For the wider campaign on behalf of a permanent FEPC, see Merl E. Reed, *Seedtime for the Modern Civil Rights Movement: The President's Committee on Fair Employment Practice, 1941–1946* (Baton Rouge: LSU Press, 1991).

37. U.S. Congress, Senate, "Hearings before a Subcommittee of the Committee on Education and Labor on S.101 A Bill to Prohibit Discrimination in Employment Because of Race, Creed, Color, or National Origin, or Ancestry and S.459 A Bill to Establish a Fair Employment Practice Commission," 69th Cong., 1st sess., 12, 13, 14 Mar. 1945, p. 59.

38. For establishment of the Anti-Discrimination Committee, see "UPWA Anti-Discrimination Committee," 1 May 1945, CIO S-T, box 113, folder 2; memorandum, 4 Mar. 1945, UPWA Papers, box 345, folder 23. See also materials in UPWA Papers, box 27, folder 5; box 52, folder 10; and box 492, folder 20. For District One implementation, see *Packinghouse Worker*, 6 July 1945.

39. *Packinghouse Worker*, 13 and 29 Dec. 1946; *District One Champion;* see also material in Leon Beverly Papers, State Historical Society of Wisconsin, Madison; and general treatment in Arnold Hirsch, "The Black Struggle for Integrated Housing in Chicago," in *Ethnic Chicago,* ed. Melvin Holli and Peter d'A. Jones (Grand Rapids: Erdman's Publishing, 1984).

40. Interview with Lowell Washington, Jr., 28 Apr. 1988.

41. Interview with Ralph Helstein, 13 July 1983, UPWAOHP Accessions; *Proceedings, Second Convention of the UPWA,* 148–57.

42. For reduced pay see "Real Weekly Earnings in Meatpacking," UPWA Papers, box 196, folder 3; and "Issues of the Meat Strike," 21 Jan. 1946, in UPWA Papers, box 452, folder 11.

43. For the 1945–46 strike wave see Art Preis, *Labor's Giant Step* (New York: Pathfinder, 1964), chap. 23; Lichtenstein, *Labor's War at Home,* 221–30; and George Lipsitz, *A Rainbow at Midnight: Class and Culture in Cold War America,* rev. ed. (Urbana: University of Illinois Press, 1994).

44. For Labor Board's 1945 ruling see "In re Swift & Company, Wilson & Company, Armour & Company, and Cudahy Packing Company and United Packinghouse Workers of America (CIO), Cases No. 111-5544-D, 111-5760-D, 111-6000-D, and 111-5763-D, 20 February 1945," in *Decisions of the War Labor Board; Packinghouse Worker,* 2 Mar. 1945; and "Directive Establishing the Meat Packing Commission," 30 Mar. 1945, UPWA Papers, box 189, folder 6. For the planning and development of the 1946 strike see Brody, *Butcher Workmen,* 228; and the interview with Harold Nielsen, 21 Aug. 1985, UPWAOHP. Ellis quoted in Transcript of UPWA Executive Board Meeting, 28 May 1945, 21, UPWA Papers, box 27, folder 2.

45. "Program for a General Wage Increase," UPWA Papers, box 26, folder 10; National Strike Strategy to all District Directors, 28 Dec. 1945, UPWA Papers, box 198, folder 5; "Manual on Strike Organization," UPWA Papers, box 198, folder 5.

46. For community support, see Slayton, *Back of the Yards,* 221–22; *Packinghouse Worker,* 11 Jan. 1946; Rose and Meegan quoted in Transcript of CBS broadcast, UPWA Papers, box 452, folder 11. For black community see "Community Groups All Out in Support of U.P.W. of A.," *Chicago Sunday Bee,* 13 Jan. 1946, copy in March Papers; and *Packinghouse Worker,* 11 Jan. and 2 Feb. 1946.

47. Brody, *Butcher Workmen,* 228; statement issued by Lewis J. Clark, 11 Jan. 1946, UPWA Papers, box 198, folder 5.

48. *Packinghouse Worker,* 14 Dec. 1945, 11 and 25 Jan. 1946. For the recommendation of seventeen and a half percent, see Nelson Lichtenstein, *Walter Reuther: The Most Dangerous Man in Detroit,* pbk. ed. (Urbana: University of Illinois Press, 1997), 240. Brody, *Butcher Workmen,* 229.

49. "Executive Order 9685 by President Harry S. Truman, January 24, 1946," UPWA Papers, box 198, folder 10; "Notice of Plant Seizure by the Government," UPWA Papers, box 196, folder 10; statement by UPWA, 25 Jan. 1946, UPWA Papers, box 502, folder 15; statement by UPWA, 26 Jan. 1946, UPWA Papers, box 198, folder 5; interview with Ralph Helstein, 13 July 1983, UPWAOHP Accessions.

50. "Report and Recommendations of the Fact-Finding Board in the Meat Packing Industry Case," 7 Feb. 1946, UPWA Papers, box 452, folder 11; Brody, *Butcher Workmen*, 230. For second settlement, see UPWA Statements, 9 and 15 Dec. 1946; Frank Ellis to all local unions, n.d., all in UPWA Papers, box 196, folder 3.

51. Interview with Norman Dolnick, 1 Oct. 1985, UPWAOHP; interview with Herbert March, 21 Oct. 1986, UPWAOHP; interview with Philip Weightman, 7–8 Oct. 1986; interview with Ralph Helstein, 12 May 1983, Iowa Federation of Labor Oral History Project, Iowa State Historical Society, Iowa City.

52. Interview with Ralph Helstein, 12 May 1983, Iowa Federation of Labor Oral History Project; interview with Ralph Helstein, 13 July 1983, UPWAOHP Accessions; interview with Douglas Hall, UPWAOHP; Helstein quoted in Transcript of UPWA Executive Board Meeting, 4 Mar. 1946, 16–17, UPWA Papers, box 27, folder 3.

53. "Address to Dist. No. 3 Conference at Omaha," n.d. [late 1948], UPWA Papers, box 50, folder 14.

54. For the anticommunist campaign see Roche to March, 11 Sept. 1945; Clark to March, 7 Nov. 1945; Weightman to March, 10 Apr. 1946; Clark to March, 29 Apr. 1946, all UPWA Papers, box 308, folder 1. See also Weightman's attack at the meeting of the International Executive Board on 28 May 1946, UPWA Papers, box 27, folder 4. For March's response see March to Weightman, 18 Apr. 1946; March to Clark, 8 May 1946; March to Clark, 17 Oct. 1946, all UPWA Papers, box 308, folder 1.

55. Interview with Herbert March, 21 Oct. 1986, UPWAOHP

56. For antilabor legislation see Joel Seidman, *American Labor from Defense to Reconversion* (Chicago: University of Chicago Press, 1953), 262–69; and Preis, *Labor's Giant Step*, chaps. 24–26.

57. For Taft-Hartley's provisions, see Preis, *Labor's Giant Step*, 314–15; see also Christopher Tomlins, *The State and the Unions* (New York: Cambridge University Press, 1985), 252–316.

58. Lewis quoted in Preis, *Labor's Giant Step*, 319; for CIO capitulation see Emspak, "The Break-Up of the CIO."

59. Ellis to all District Directors, International representatives, and field staff, 26 Nov. 1947, UPWA Papers, box 445, folder 15; Ollman quoted in Transcript of UPWA Executive Board Meeting, 24 Nov. 1947, 102, UPWA Papers, box 28, folder 6.

60. Transcript of the Policy Conference of the UPWA, 15 July 1947, UPWA Papers, box 524; statement on Taft-Hartley, 15 July 1947, UPWA Papers, box 28, folder 5; "Memorandum—Strengthening the Steward System," UPWA Papers,

box 436, folder 3; see also Helstein to all District Directors, 20 May 1947, UPWA Papers, box 477, folder 5.

61. Weightman quoted in Transcript of UPWA Executive Board Meeting, 24 Nov. 1947, 116, UPWA Papers, box 28, folder 6.

62. Transcript of UPWA Executive Board Meeting, 24 Nov. 1947, 98–102, 144–64, UPWA Papers, box 28, folder 6.

63. Helstein to Schultz, 9 Feb. 1948, Helstein Papers; Schultz to Helstein, 10 Dec. 1947.

64. Smith to Clark, 29 Dec. 1947, UPWA Papers, box 44, folder 10; Transcript of UPWA Executive Board Meeting, 30 Jan. 1948, UPWA Papers, box 29, folder 2.

65. Helstein quoted in Transcript of UPWA Executive Board Meeting, 30 Jan. 1948, UPWA Papers, box 29, folder 2. For strike vote, see communications in UPWA Papers, box 202, folder 3. National Strike Strategy Committee Minutes, 13–14 Mar. 1948, UPWA Papers, box 524. Truman to Helstein, 15 Mar. 1948, UPWA Papers, box 29, folder 2; UPWA Strike Bulletin, 16 Mar. 1948, UPWA Papers, box 459, folder 2.

66. "Assessing the Strike—With Special Emphasis on Economic Factors," 9 June 1948, UPWA Papers, box 452, folder 14; *Proceedings, Fifth Convention of the UPWA*, 46. For restriction of picketing see strike reports in UPWA Papers, box 201, folder 7. For financial strain see Transcript of International Executive Board Meeting, 20 Dec. 1948, UPWA Papers, box 30, folder 3; and Helstein to Haywood, 18 Sept. 1948, UPWA Papers, box 45, folder 10.

67. *New York Times*, 17 Mar. and 4 May 1948; U.S. Congress, House, Subcommittee of the Committee on Expenditures in the Executive Departments, "Investigation as to the Administration of the Law Affecting Labor Disputes, Interstate and Foreign Commerce and the Antiracketeering Statute, the Interstate Transportation of Pickets, and the Activities of the Department of Justice, in Connection with Strikes in the Meat-Packing Industry in Twenty States," 80th Cong., 2d sess., 20 and 21 May 1948.

68. For community support and strike activities see material in UPWA Papers, box 201, folder 7; and issues of the "Packinghouse Picket" in Beverly Papers. Floyd Jones performs "I Need Another Dollar" in the Illinois Labor History Society's film, "Stockyards: End of an Era."

69. "Packinghouse Picket," 18, 19, 20, and 22 Mar. 1948; and daily field reports all in UPWA Papers, box 201, folder 7; see also Barnes's testimony in "Investigation as to the Administration of the Law Affecting Labor Disputes," 83–85.

70. Mader to Helstein, 5 Aug. 1948, "Activities of Companies during Strike," UPWA Papers, box 45, folder 5; daily field reports, UPWA Papers, box 201, folder 7; issues of "Packinghouse Picket" in Beverly Papers and in UPWA Papers, box 201, folder 7. Interview with Todd Tate, 2 Oct. 1985, UPWAOHP.

71. "UPWA-CIO Packinghouse Picket," 19 Mar. and 11 May 1948, in Beverly Papers; National Strike Strategy Committee Meeting, 2 May 1948, UPWA Papers, box 524; *St. Louis Post-Dispatch*, 1 May 1948; *Packinghouse Worker*, 30 Apr.

1948; Special Strike Statement by the Minnesota UPWA, n.d., UPWA Papers, box 447, folder 15. Interview with Todd Tate, 2 Oct. 1985, UPWAOHP.

72. March quoted in Horowitz, "Path Not Taken," 573; transcript of UPWA Executive Board Meeting, 15 May 1948, UPWA Papers, box 29, folder 1; Helstein quote from *Proceedings, Fifth Convention of the UPWA*, 48; minutes of the National Strike Strategy Committee Meeting, 18 May 1948, UPWA Papers, box 201, folder 3; interview with Charles Hayes, 27 May 1986, UPWAOHP.

73. For paralysis of the union see Ellis to all Officers, 25 May 1948, UPWA Papers, box 50, folder 3; and "Report of Grievance Department," 16 Mar. 1949, UPWA Papers, box 58, folder 8. See also the interview with Jesse Prosten, 18 Dec., 1985, UPWAOHP.

74. For Wallace's support of the strike, see *New York Times*, 19 Mar. 1948.

75. Transcript of UPWA Executive Board Meeting, 3 June 1948, UPWA Papers, box 29, folder 3; Statement of Resignation Submitted by Herbert March, UPWA Papers, box 308, folder 2; *Packinghouse Worker*, 11 June 1948.

76. For AMC raids, see Jimmerson and Gorman to "Dear Sirs and Brothers," 29 Mar. 1948, UPWA Papers, box 201, folder 7; and "List of All Plants in which the Amalgamated Meat Cutters Attempted Raids since January 1, 1948," UPWA Papers, box 70, folder 4. For election victories see Organization Dept Reports to the International Executive Board: 5 Oct. 1948, UPWA Papers, box 50, folder 4; 20 Dec. 1948, UPWA Papers, box 50, folder 3; 17 Mar. 1949, UPWA Papers, box 56, folder 10; 29 Sept. 1949, UPWA Papers, box 56, folder 12. See also *Packinghouse Worker*, 15 Oct., 12 Nov., 24 Dec. 1948; and 28 Jan., 25 Mar., 9 Sept. 1949. Interview with Helstein, 13 July 1983, UPWAOHP Accessions.

77. See material on discharges in "Jesse Prosten Personal File," United Food and Commercial Workers Accession M80–115, box 35 [unprocessed], State Historical Society of Wisconsin, Madison; interview with Jesse Prosten, 18 Dec. 1985, UPWAOHP.

78. Interview with Charles Hayes, 27 May 1986, UPWAOHP; interview with Lowell Washington, Jr., 28 Apr. 1988, in author's possession; interview with Charles R. Fischer, 22 Aug. 1986, UPWAOHP. 1949 Armour contract in UPWA Papers, box 269, folder 2; *The Union Makes Us Strong*, 11, in March Papers.

79. See material on CIO Policy Caucus in United Packinghouse Workers of America Collection, 51–29–2, University of Texas at Arlington Archives, Arlington, Tex. For March's employment as field representative, see material in UPWA Papers, box 401, folder 1; Schultz to Helstein, 4 Aug. 1948, Helstein Papers. For unease over employment of Orear and Prosten see Minutes of UPWA Executive Board Meeting, 20 Dec. 1948, UPWA Papers, box 30, folder 2. Especially insightful on Policy Caucus motivations are the UPWAOHP interviews with its leaders: Philip Weightman, Svend Godfredson, A. J. Pittman, William Nolan, and Charles R. Fischer.

80. Helstein speech to Second Annual Convention of District 3, 14 Feb. 1948, CIO S-T, box 176, folder 2; Nielsen to Helstein, Mar. 1948, UPWA Papers, box 47, folder 4; interview with Herbert March; issues of the "Packinghouse Picket" in UPWA Papers, box 201, folder 7; "Packinghouse Workers Committee for Wallace

and Taylor," n.d., Beverly Papers. For Brown's campaign and UPWA prior support of independent politics, see Horowitz, "Path Not Taken," 598–99.

81. *Proceedings, Fifth Convention of the UPWA*, 43–79ff.

82. Interview with Svend Godfredson, 18–20 May 1986, UPWAOHP; for Pittman, see Rick Halpern, "Interracial Unionism in the Southwest: Fort Worth's Packinghouse Workers, 1937–1954," in *Organized Labor in the Twentieth Century South*, ed. Robert H. Zieger (Knoxville: University of Tennessee Press, 1991), 168–69.

83. *Proceedings, Fifth Convention of the UPWA*, 157, 178; see also Horowitz, "Path Not Taken," 605; interview with Jesse Prosten, 18 Dec. 1985, UPWAOHP.

84. Helstein to Ollman, 14 July 1948; Ollman to Helstein, 2 July 1948, both in Helstein Papers; *Proceedings, Fifth Convention of the UPWA*, 289–97; Horowitz, "Path Not Taken," 605–6.

85. Tilford Dudley to Helstein, 6 Aug. 1948; Helstein to Haywood, 9 Aug. 1948; and Helstein to John Gates, 13 Aug. 1948, all in Helstein Papers. For outrage over March's employment see, for example, McGann to Philip Murray, 3 Jan. 1949, Charles Owen Rice Papers, FF524, AIS 76:11, Hillman Library, University of Pittsburgh, Pittsburgh, Pa. For demands for March's dismissal see Transcript Executive Board Meeting, 20 Dec. 1948, UPWA Papers, box 30, folder 3. Interview with Herbert March, 21 Oct. 1986, UPWAOHP. March to Executive Officers, 27 Jan. 1949, Stephens to March, 2 Feb. 1949; Helstein to March, 15 Feb. 1949, all in March Papers.

86. For Cedar Rapids meeting see material in United Packinghouse Workers of America Collection, 51–29–2, University of Texas at Arlington Archives. For Swift situation, see the correspondence between Peter McGann and Father Rice and copies of the *Swift Flash* in Rice Papers, FF524, AIS 76:11. Proceedings, Sixth Convention of the UPWA.

87. Transcript of UPWA Executive Board Meeting, 28 Sept. 1950, UPWA Papers, box 32, folder 5.

88. Helstein to Hope, 21 June 1948; Hope to Helstein, 25 June 1948, both in UPWA Papers, box 45, folder 9; Hope to Helstein, Lasley, Long, n.d., UPWA Papers, box 52, folder 10; interview with Ralph Helstein, 13 July 1983, UPWAOHP Accessions.

89. Black workers were executive board members in 73 percent of the UPWA's locals, and held steward positions in 83 percent. Yet white packinghouse workers occupied 96 percent of the industry's job categories; and blacks were wholly absent in 46 percent of these (John Hope II, *Equality of Opportunity: A Union Approach to Fair Employment* [Washington: Public Affairs Press, 1956]).

90. Hope to Lasley, 19 Dec. 1949, UPWA Papers, box 52, folder 10. Program Proposal for AD Department, 26 June 1950; and "Suggestions for Local Anti-Discrimination Committees," both in UPWA Papers, box 342, folder 15. Hope, *Equality of Opportunity*, 110–17; see also Hope's "The Self-Survey of the Packinghouse Union," *Journal of Social Issues* 9 (1953).

91. For examination of this dynamic in Fort Worth, see Halpern, "Interracial Unionism in the Southwest."

92. "Report on District 4 Staff Conference," 15 Aug. 1950, UPWA Papers, box 345, folder 1.

93. Zabritski manuscript; interview with Todd Tate, 1 Oct. 1985, UPWAOHP.

94. For the Swift hiring victory see Kelley to Lasley and Hayes, 22 June 1950, UPWA Papers, box 343, folder 7; *Swift Flash*, 5 July 1950, in UPWA Papers, box 342, folder 7; UPWA Press Release, 21 Dec. 1950, UPWA Papers, box 345, folder 12; UPWA Press Release, 29 Nov. 1951, UPWA Papers, box 342, folder 10; and *Packinghouse Worker*, Dec. 1951. For success elsewhere, "Officers Report—Anti-Discrimination Department," Mar. 1952, UPWA Papers, box 346, folder 24; and Report by Lewis Roach, 20 June 1953, UPWA Papers, box 347, folder 3.

95. "Local 347 Hog Department Bulletin," 6 Apr. 1950, in Beverly Papers; interview with Leon Beverly, 16 Dec. 1970, Roosevelt Project; interview with Ralph Helstein, 12 May 1983, Iowa Federation of Labor Oral History Project; Report on District One AD Conference, 17 Feb. 1952, UPWA Papers, box 384, folder 14; Local 347 Press Release, 11 Dec. 1952, UPWA Papers, box 98, folder 3; *Packinghouse Worker*, Sept. and Dec. 1952, Mar. 1953, and Mar. 1955.

96. For the Peoria Street riot see the description in UPWA Papers, box 343, folder 3. For UPWA involvement see Nielsen to all Chicago locals, 22 Nov. 1949; Lasley to Nielsen, 29 Nov. 1949; circular letter from Williams, Lasley et al., 22 Nov. 1949; circular letter from Hammond, Robinson, Lasley et al., 26 Dec. 1949, all in UPWA Papers, box 52, folder 1. See also discussion of the union's involvement in the CEMV, Transcript of Executive Board Meeting, 19 Dec. 1949, UPWA Papers, box 31, folder 3. CEMV activities also covered in Arnold Hirsch, *Making the Second Ghetto: Race and Housing in Chicago, 1940–1960* (New York: Cambridge University Press, 1983), 61, 246–47; and Strickland, *History of the Chicago Urban League*, 172–75.

97. For CIO resistance to involvement, see Transcript of the UPWA Executive Board Meeting, 19 Dec. 1949, UPWA Papers, box 31, folder 3; and Mann to Haywood and Carey, n.d., CIO S-T, box 197, folder 30. For Williams see Catherine Sardo Weidner, "Debating the Future of Chicago's Black Youth: Black Professionals, Black Labor, and Educational Politics during the Civil Rights Era, 1950–1965" (Ph.D. dissertation, Northwestern University, 1989), 84–106; and Strickland, *History of the Chicago Urban League*, 173–74.

98. For Trumbull Park housing controversy, see the materials in UPWA Papers, box 353, folders 11 and 12; and general treatment in Hirsch, "Black Struggle."

99. Interview with Sam Parks, 3 Oct. 1985, UPWAOHP; National Association for the Advancement of Colored People, Records, series II, boxes 317–18, Library of Congress, Washington D.C.; Weidner, "Debating the Future," 157–71. For the International's overtures toward the NAACP, see Lasley to McGee, 30 Nov. 1948, UPWA Papers, box 342, folder 5.

100. Interview with Charles Hayes, 27 May 1986, UPWAOHP.

101. Interview with Sam Parks, 3 Oct. 1985, UPWAOHP; copies of District One AD Committee *Action* [c.1953] in UPWA Papers, box 349, folder 16.

102. For conflict at Armour and dissatisfaction with March, see the Mem-

orandums dated 4 Dec. 1944, 15 Jan. 1945, 13 Oct. and 26 Nov. 1946, Union Stockyard and Transit Company Records, box 4, University of Illinois–Chicago Circle, Chicago, Ill. For post-1948 insurgency, see interview with Charles Hayes, 27 May 1986, UPWAOHP; interview with Harold Nielsen, 21 Aug. and 4 Sept. 1985, UPWAOHP; Nielsen to Souther, 27 Apr. 1954, UPWA Papers, box 103, folder 6.

103. Mann to all Chicago Industrial Union Council affiliates, 24 May 1950, CIO S-T, box 176, folder 13; Mann to Weaver, 2 June 1950, CIO S-T, box 176, folder 13; Carey to Helstein, 6 June 1950, CIO S-T, box 58, folder 5. See also the copies of *Counter-Action* [1951] in the Philip Weightman Papers, box 1, folder 22, Tamiment Institute, New York University, New York, N.Y.

104. Connell quoted in Purcell, *Worker Speaks*, 176, steward quoted 166; interview with Gertie Kamarczyk, 7 Dec. 1987, in author's possession.

105. Interview with Joe Zabritski, 21 July 1987, in author's possession; interview with Joe Zabritski by Les Orear, May 1982, Illinois Labor History Society, Chicago, Ill. For March's trial and departure see the interview with Herbert March, 21 Oct. 1986, UPWAOHP.

106. Bartlett and Weidenmann quoted in Purcell, *Worker Speaks*, 178, 201. See also the interview with Harold Nielsen, 4 Sept. 1985, UPWAOHP.

107. Interview with Lowell Washington, Jr., 28 Apr. 1988, in author's possession.

108. Untitled leaflet in Beverly Papers.

Epilogue

1. Dale E. Butz and George L. Baker, *The Changing Structure of the Meat Economy* (Boston: Harvard Graduate School of Business, 1960); see also Williams and Stout, *Economics of the Livestock-Meat Industry.*

2. "Summary Fact Sheets Documenting Job Crisis in Meatpacking Industry," UPWA Papers, box 175, folder 5.

3. These programs are discussed in George P. Schultz and Arnold Weber, *Strategies for the Displaced Worker* (New York: Harper and Row, 1966); see also Rick Halpern, "Technological Change and Industrial Relations in Meatpacking: The Armour Automation Committee, 1959–1964," unpublished paper on deposit at the State Historical Society of Wisconsin.

4. Roger Horowitz, "Unions and Companies in Meatpacking, 1943–1983," unpublished manuscript in author's possession; Halpern, "Technological Change," 40–43; interview with Ralph Helstein, 18 July 1983, UPWAOHP Accessions.

5. "UPWA Rejects the Armour Program for Employee Obsolescence," Press Release, UPWA Papers, box 175, folder 5; Halpern, "Technological Change"; interview with Thomas Krasick, 25 Aug. 1986, UPWAOHP.

6. Horowitz, "Unions and Companies"; interview with Max Graham, 6 June 1986, UPWAOHP.

7. Mary Lou Finley, "The Open Housing Marches Chicago Summer '66,"

42; "Alvin Fletcher, "The Chicago Freedom Movement: What Is It?" 156, 166, both in *Chicago 1966: Open Housing Marches, Summit Negotiations, and Operation Breadbasket*, ed. David J. Garrow (Brooklyn: Carlson, 1989); James R. Ralph, Jr., *Northern Protest: Martin Luther King, Jr., Chicago, and the Civil Rights Movement* (Cambridge, Mass.: Harvard University Press, 1993), 66, 71, 157, 207. Interview with Todd Tate, 2 Oct. 1985, UPWAOHP.

INDEX

RICK HALPERN worked as one of the principal interviewers on the State Historical Society of Wisconsin's UPWA Oral History Project. He received his Ph.D. from the University of Pennsylvania in 1989 and now lives in Great Britain, where he is Lecturer in American History at University College London. He is co-author, with Roger Horowitz, of *Meatpackers: An Oral History of Black Packinghouse Workers and Their Struggle for Racial and Economic Equality* (1996).